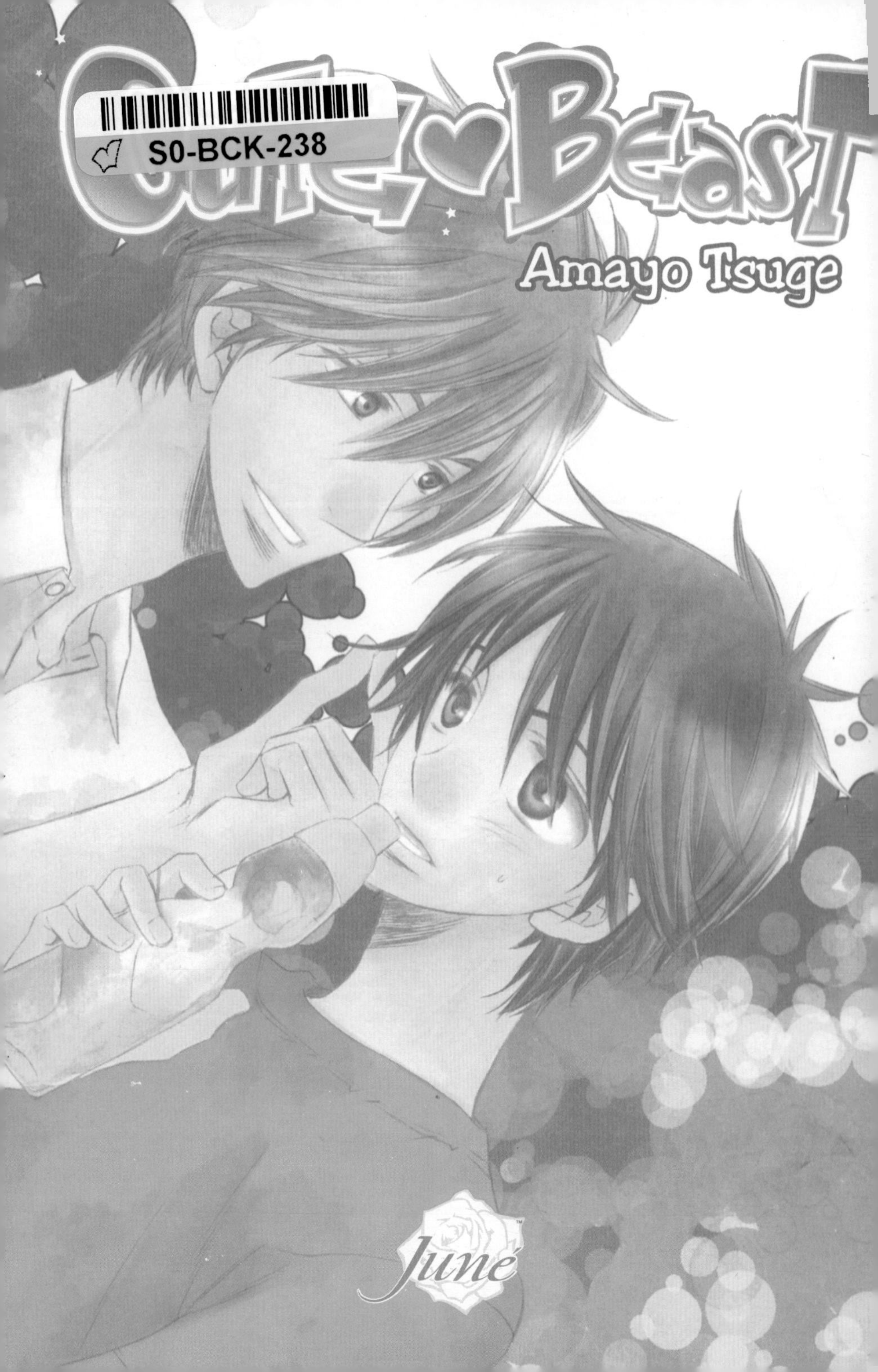
Beast
Amayo Tsuge
Juné

Translation ....Issei Shimizu
Lettering..Wendy Lee
Graphic Design...........................Wendy Lee / Eric Rosenberger
Editing...Wendy Lee
Editor in Chief...Fred Lui
Publisher...Hikaru Sasahara

English Edition Published by
DIGITAL MANGA PUBLISHING
A division of DIGITAL MANGA, Inc.
1487 W 178th Street, Suite 300
Gardena, CA 90248

www.dmpbooks.com

First Edition: December 2007
ISBN-10: 1-56970-773-1
ISBN-13: 978-1-56970-773-9

1 3 5 7 9 10 8 6 4 2

Printed in China

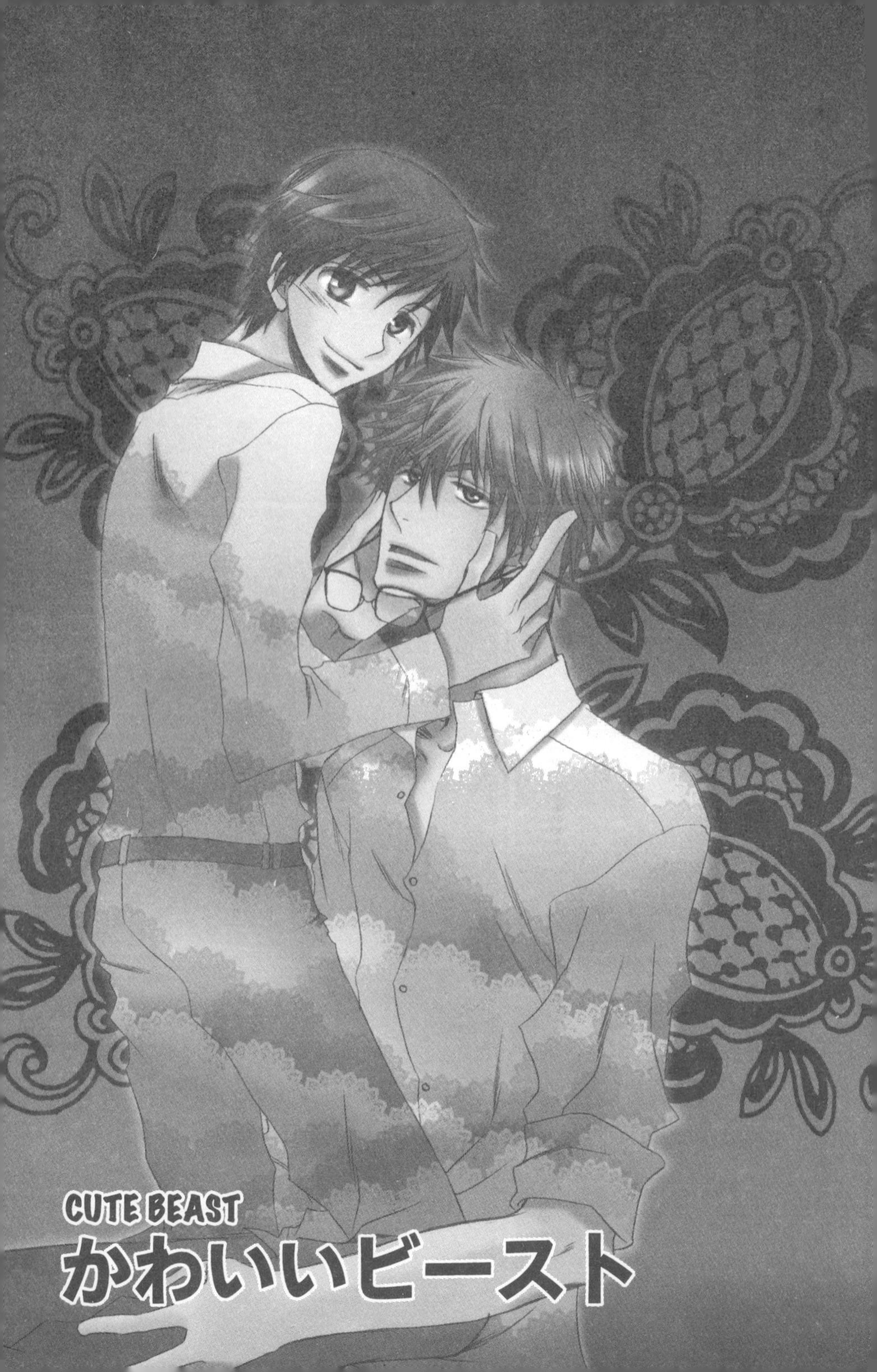

CUTE BEAST
かわいいビースト

かわいいビースト

CUTE BEAST

SECRET ♡ OF HIS FACE ♡

WHAT DO YOU LOOK LIKE WITHOUT YOUR GLASSES?
WHAT ...?
M... MY PARENTS TOLD ME THAT I CAN'T TAKE THEM OFF...
HUH? WHY? ARE YOU GOING TO DIE IF SOMEONE SEES YOUR FACE OR SOMETHING?
DOES YOUR FACE TURN LIGHT INTO DARKNESS OR SOMETHING?
© KINNIKUMAN
A- ARE YOU OKAY?
I'M SORRY..!
PANT
PANT
...IT IS REALLY AMAZING...!

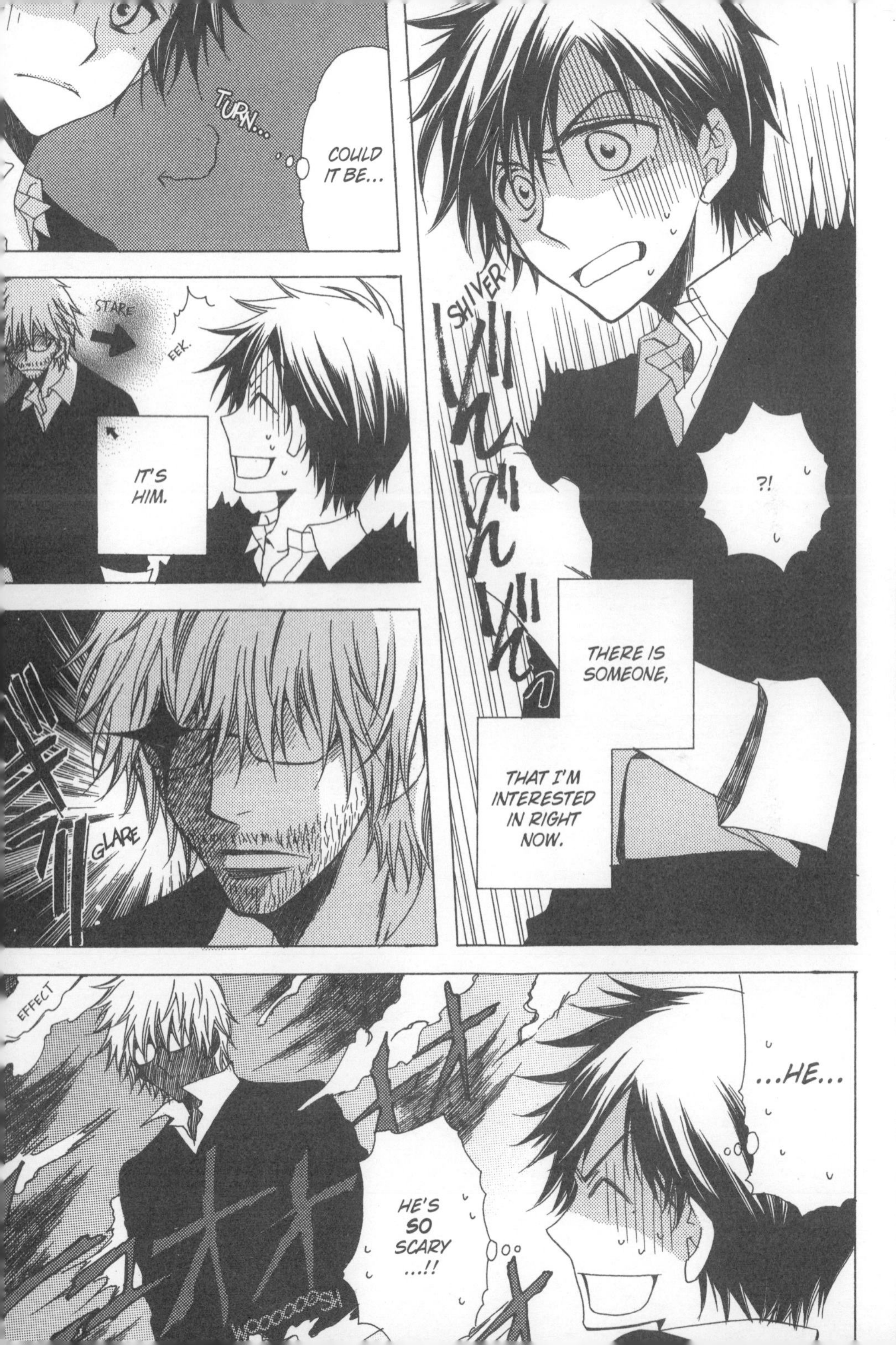
SHIVER
?!
THERE IS SOMEONE,
THAT I'M INTERESTED IN RIGHT NOW.
TURN...
COULD IT BE...
STARE
EEK.
IT'S HIM.
GLARE
...HE...
HE'S SO SCARY ...!!
EFFECT

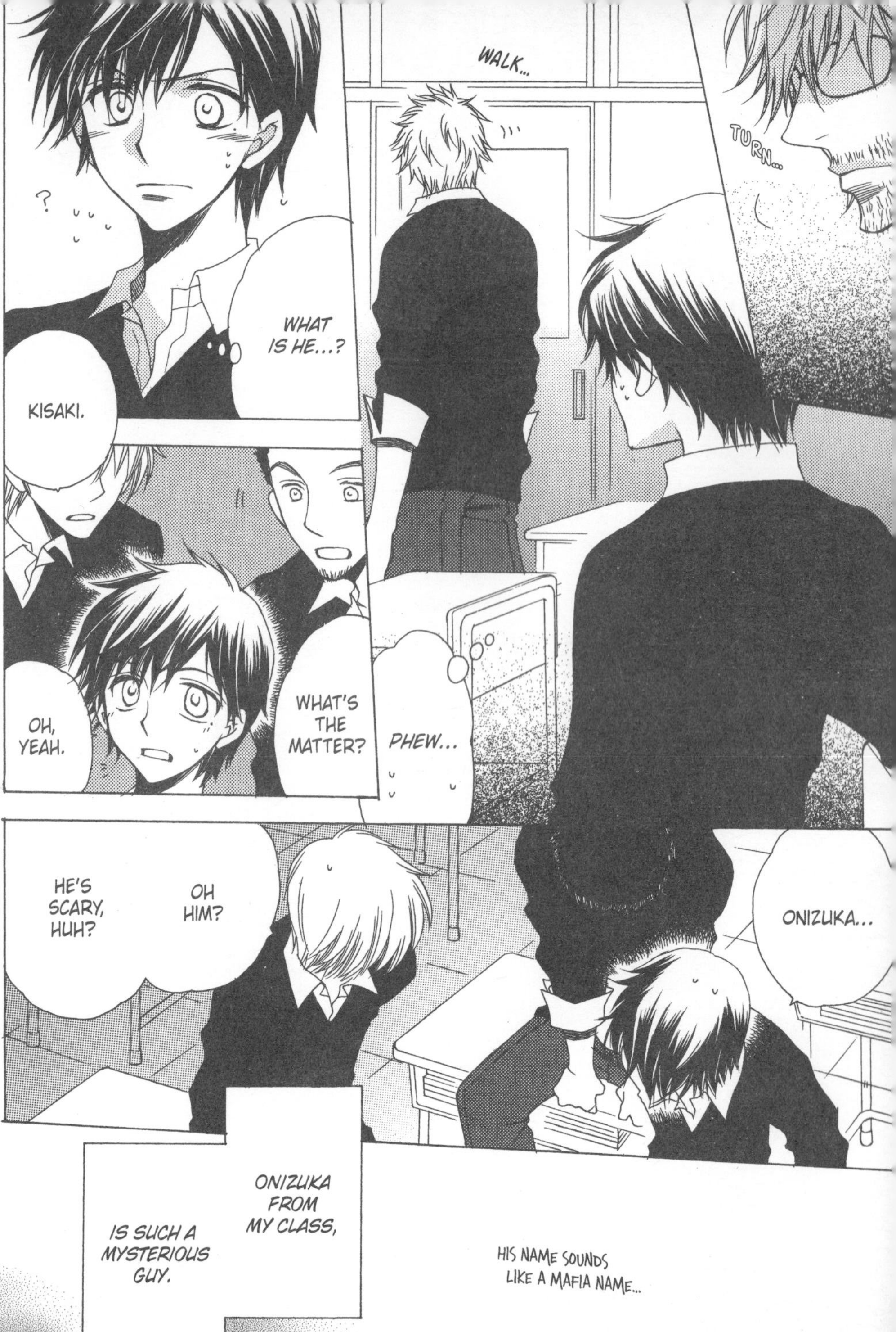
TURN...
WALK...
PHEW...
?
WHAT IS HE...?
KISAKI.
WHAT'S THE MATTER?
OH, YEAH.
ONIZUKA...
OH HIM?
HE'S SCARY, HUH?
ONIZUKA FROM MY CLASS,
IS SUCH A MYSTERIOUS GUY.
HIS NAME SOUNDS LIKE A MAFIA NAME...

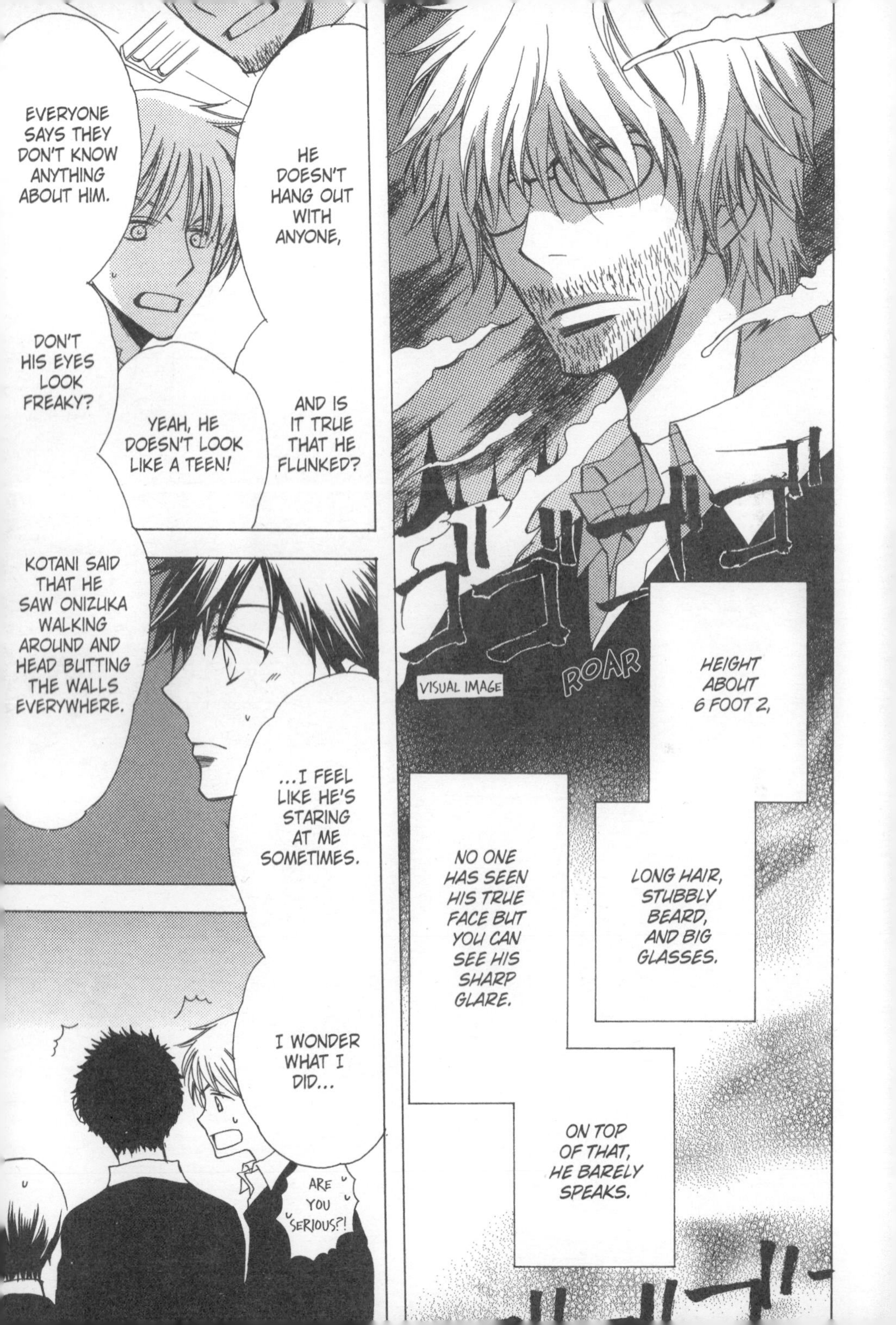
ROAR
VISUAL IMAGE
HEIGHT ABOUT 6 FOOT 2,
LONG HAIR, STUBBLY BEARD, AND BIG GLASSES.
NO ONE HAS SEEN HIS TRUE FACE BUT YOU CAN SEE HIS SHARP GLARE.
ON TOP OF THAT, HE BARELY SPEAKS.
HE DOESN'T HANG OUT WITH ANYONE,
EVERYONE SAYS THEY DON'T KNOW ANYTHING ABOUT HIM.
AND IS IT TRUE THAT HE FLUNKED?
YEAH, HE DOESN'T LOOK LIKE A TEEN!
DON'T HIS EYES LOOK FREAKY?
KOTANI SAID THAT HE SAW ONIZUKA WALKING AROUND AND HEAD BUTTING THE WALLS EVERYWHERE.
...I FEEL LIKE HE'S STARING AT ME SOMETIMES.
I WONDER WHAT I DID...
ARE YOU SERIOUS?!

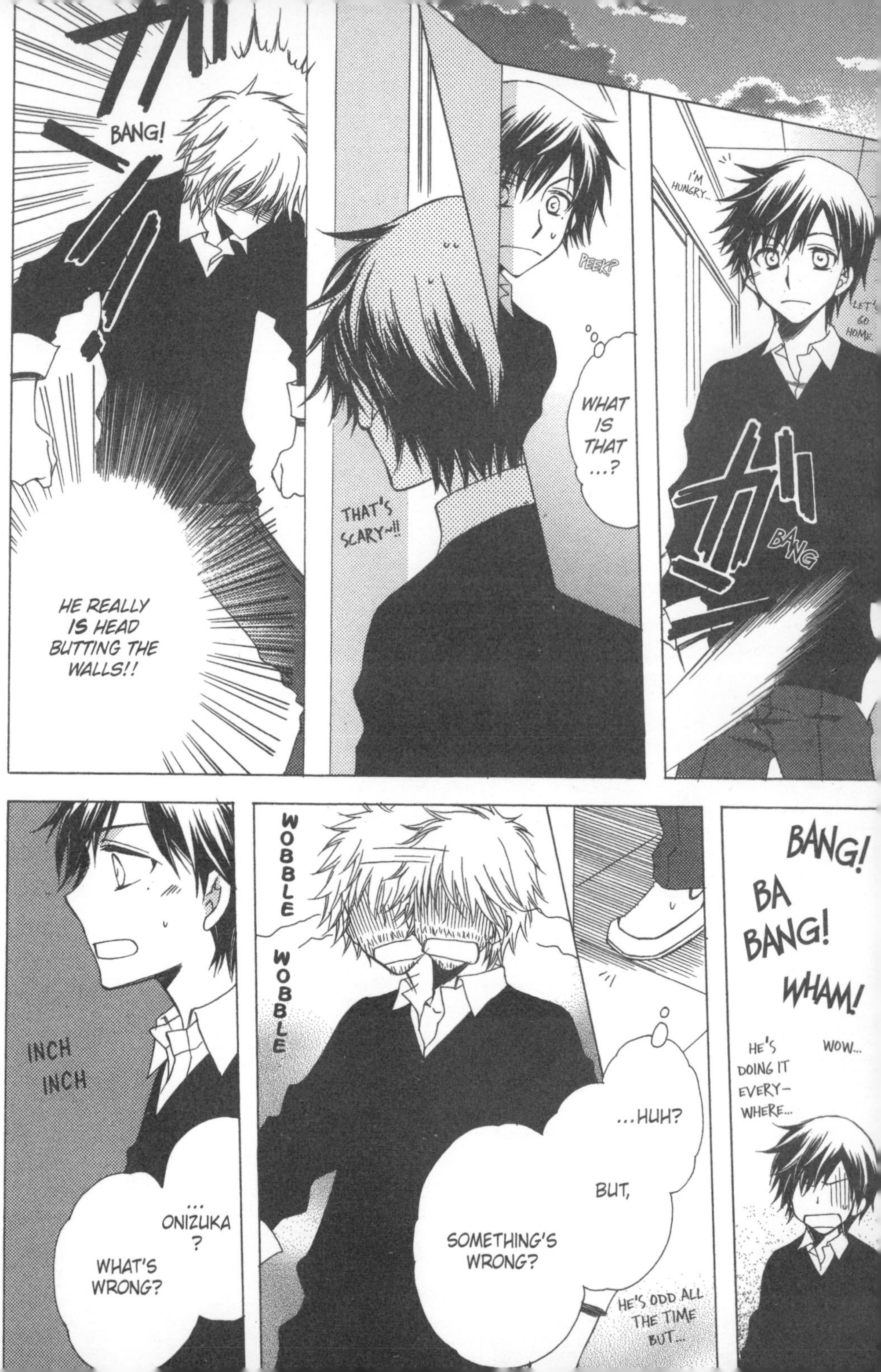
I'M HUNGRY...
LET'S GO HOME
BANG
PEEK?
WHAT IS THAT ...?
THAT'S SCARY~!!
BANG!
HE REALLY IS HEAD BUTTING THE WALLS!!
BANG!
BA BANG!
WHAM!
WOW...
HE'S DOING IT EVERY-WHERE...
...HUH?
BUT,
SOMETHING'S WRONG?
HE'S ODD ALL THE TIME BUT...
WOBBLE WOBBLE
INCH INCH
... ONIZUKA ?
WHAT'S WRONG?

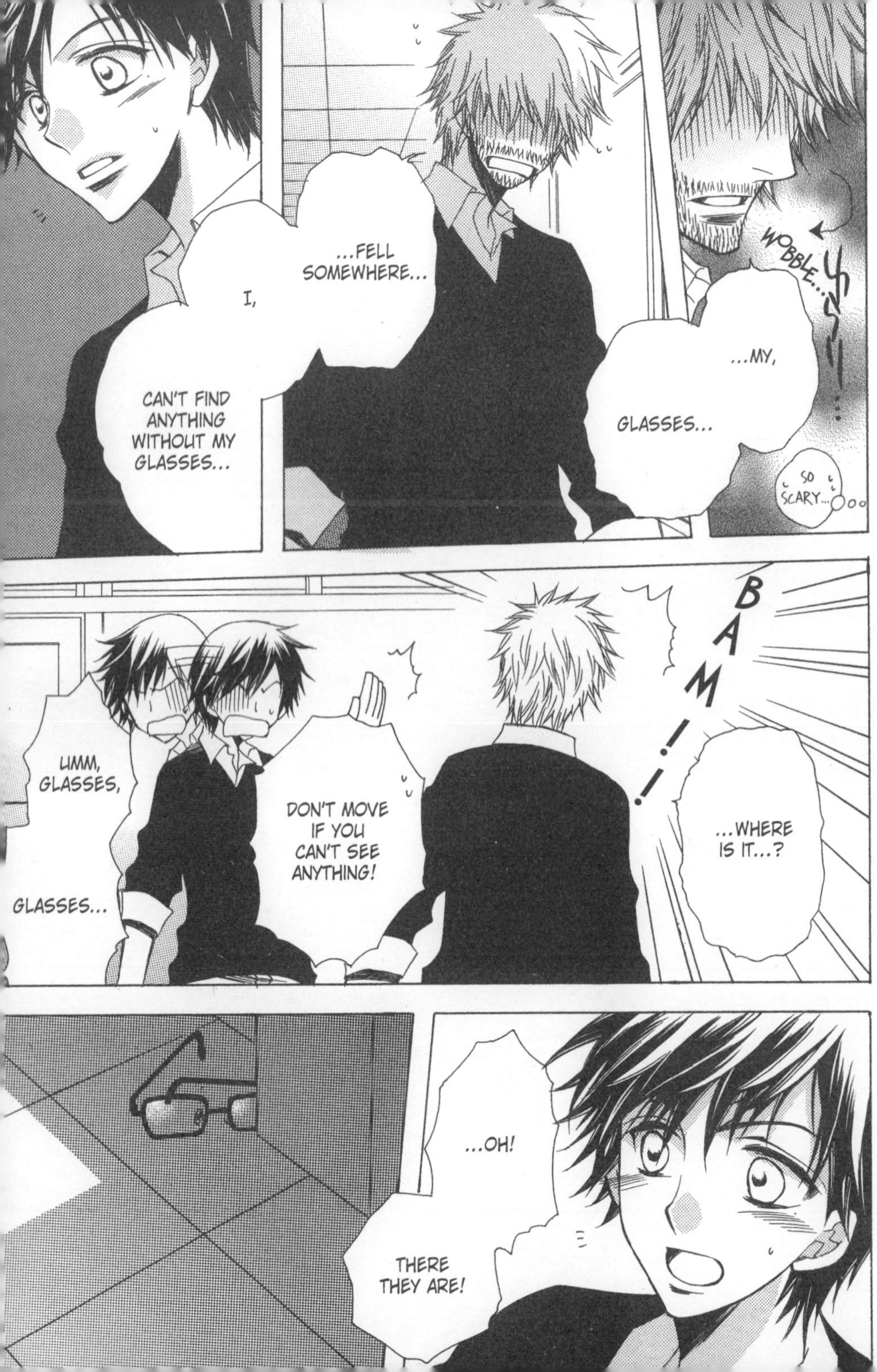
...MY,
GLASSES...
WOBBLE...
SO SCARY...
...FELL SOMEWHERE...
I,
CAN'T FIND ANYTHING WITHOUT MY GLASSES...
BAM!!
...WHERE IS IT...?
DON'T MOVE IF YOU CAN'T SEE ANYTHING!
UMM, GLASSES,
GLASSES...
...OH!
THERE THEY ARE!

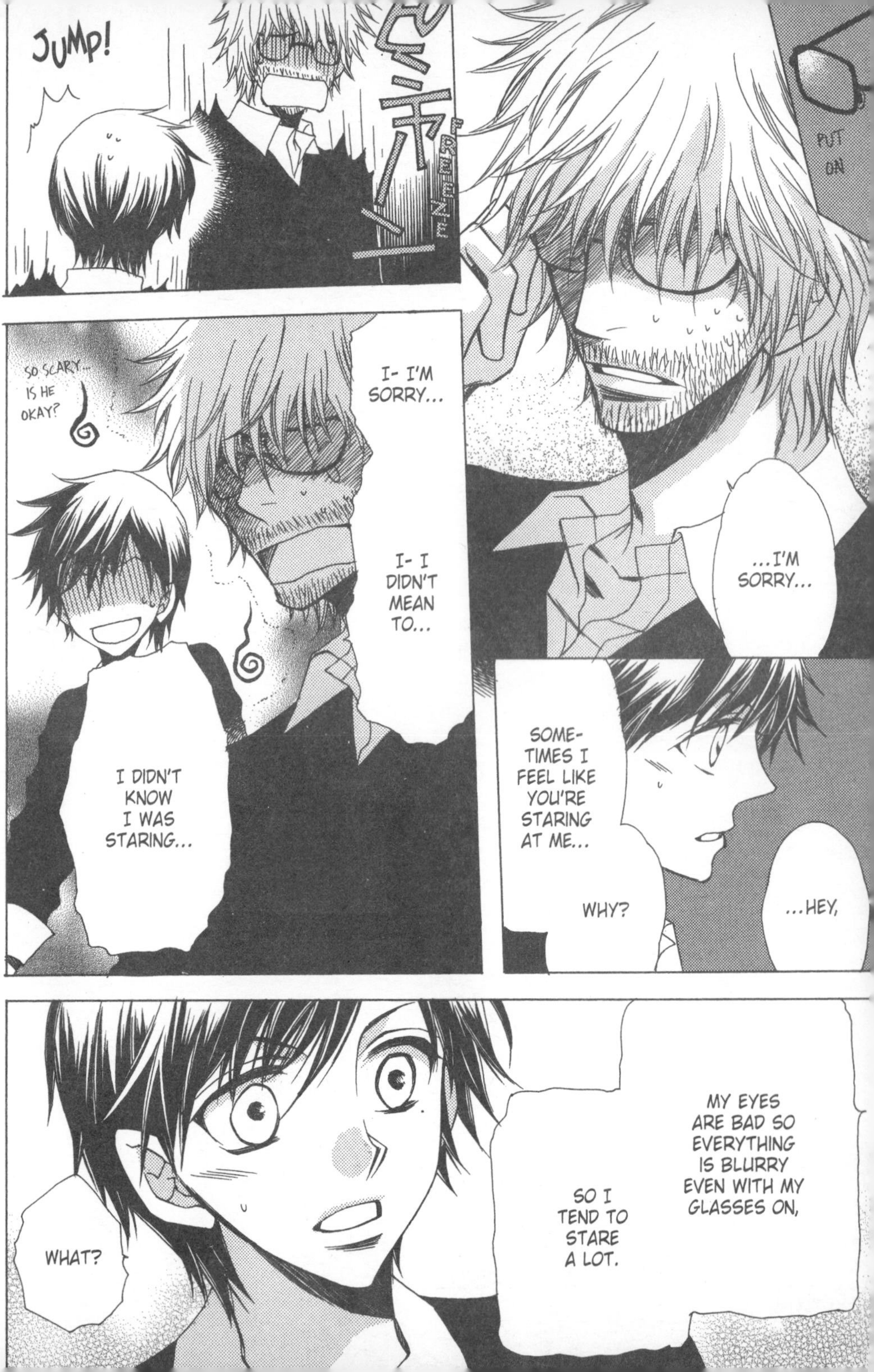
PUT ON
...I'M SORRY...
JUMP!
FREEZE
...HEY,
SOME-TIMES I FEEL LIKE YOU'RE STARING AT ME...
WHY?
I- I'M SORRY...
I- I DIDN'T MEAN TO...
SO SCARY... IS HE OKAY?
I DIDN'T KNOW I WAS STARING...
MY EYES ARE BAD SO EVERYTHING IS BLURRY EVEN WITH MY GLASSES ON,
SO I TEND TO STARE A LOT.
WHAT?

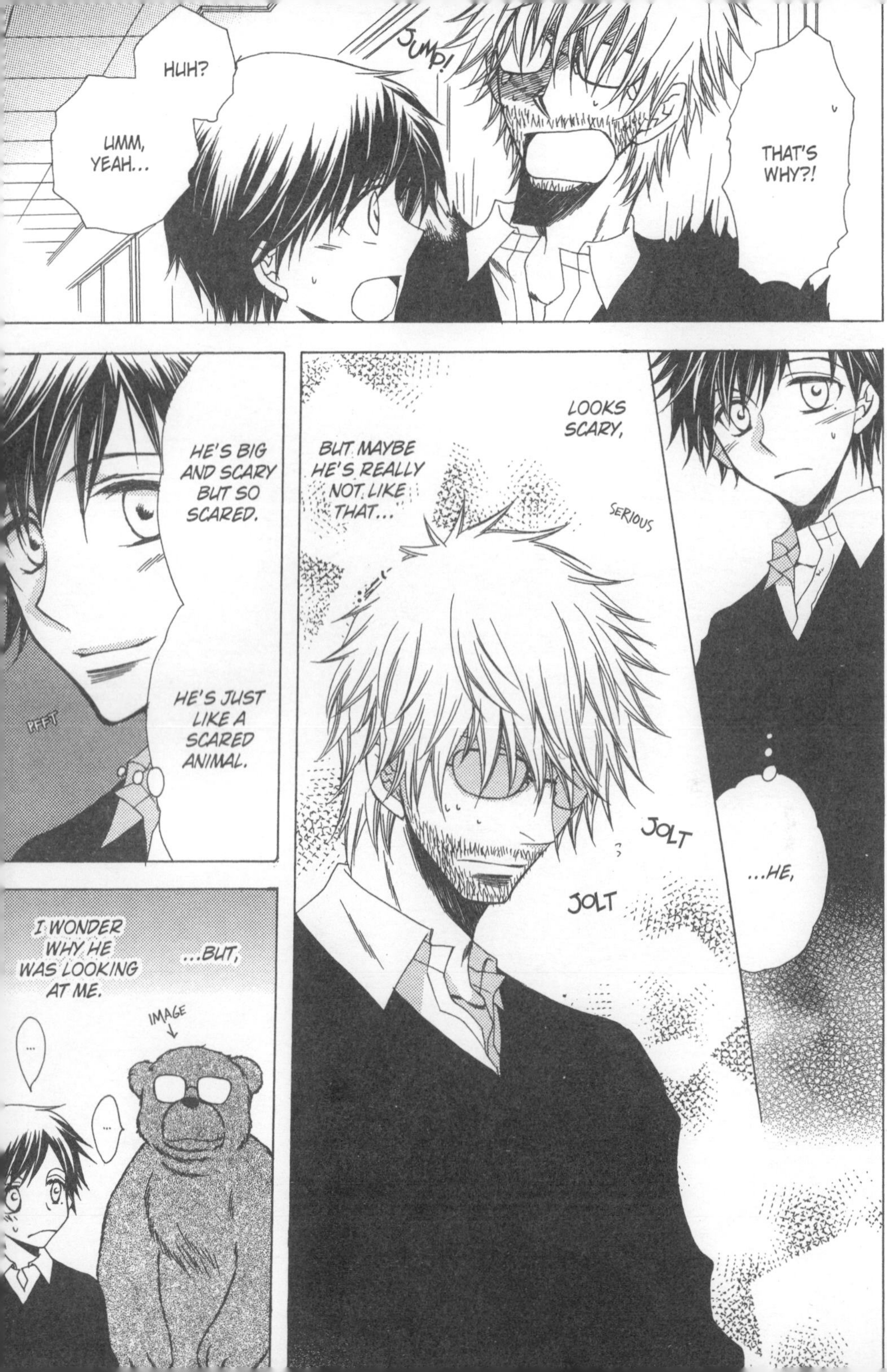
THAT'S WHY?!
JUMP!
HUH?
UMM, YEAH...
...HE,
LOOKS SCARY,
SERIOUS
BUT MAYBE HE'S REALLY NOT LIKE THAT...
JOLT
JOLT
HE'S BIG AND SCARY BUT SO SCARED.
HE'S JUST LIKE A SCARED ANIMAL.
PFFT
...BUT,
I WONDER WHY HE WAS LOOKING AT ME.
IMAGE
...
...

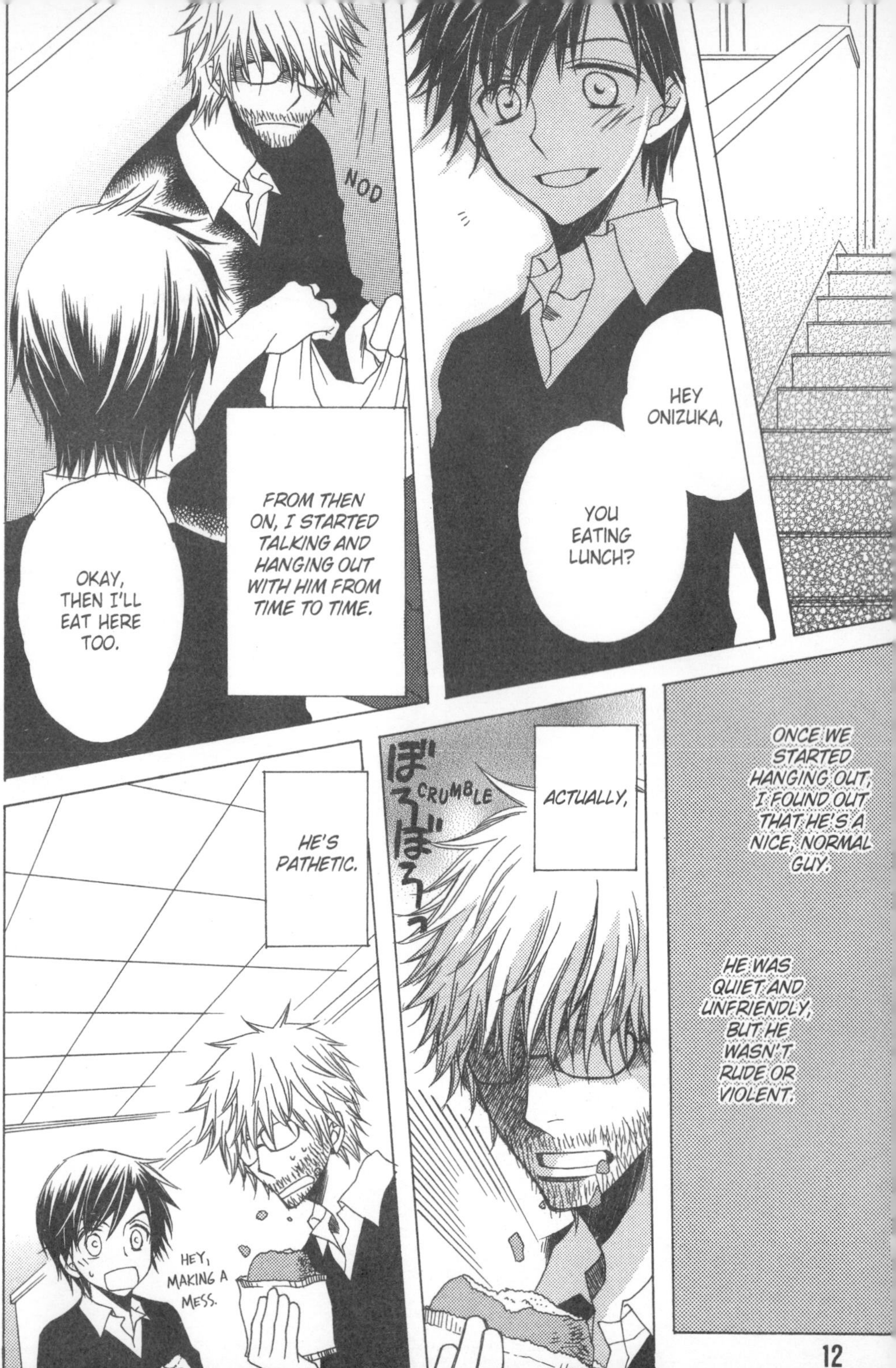

HEY ONIZUKA,
YOU EATING LUNCH?
NOD
FROM THEN ON, I STARTED TALKING AND HANGING OUT WITH HIM FROM TIME TO TIME.
OKAY, THEN I'LL EAT HERE TOO.
ONCE WE STARTED HANGING OUT, I FOUND OUT THAT HE'S A NICE, NORMAL GUY.
HE WAS QUIET AND UNFRIENDLY, BUT HE WASN'T RUDE OR VIOLENT.
ACTUALLY,
ぼろぼろっ
CRUMBLE
HE'S PATHETIC.
HEY, MAKING A MESS.

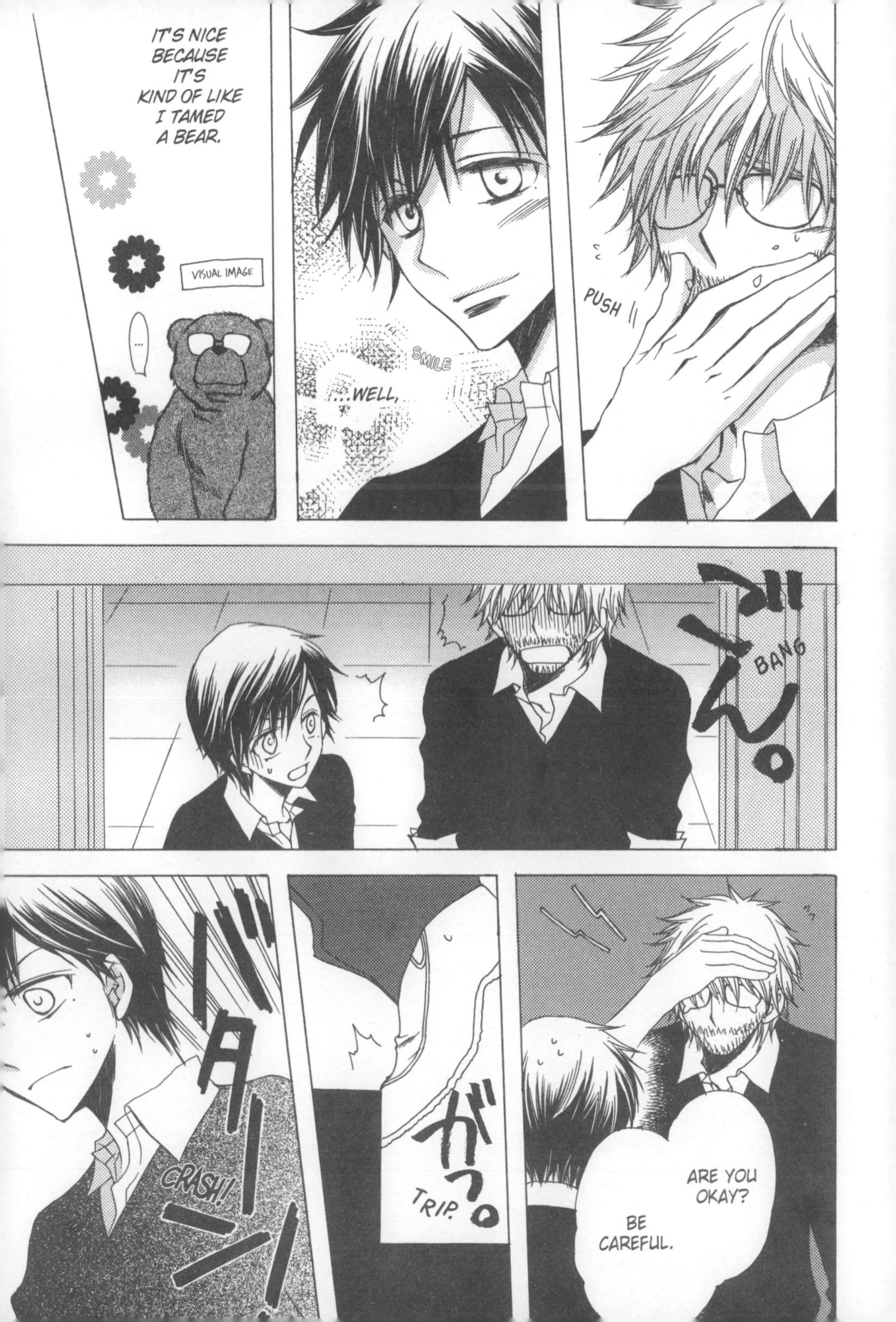
PUSH
SMILE
...WELL,
IT'S NICE BECAUSE IT'S KIND OF LIKE I TAMED A BEAR.
VISUAL IMAGE
...
BANG
ARE YOU OKAY?
BE CAREFUL.
TRIP.
CRASH!

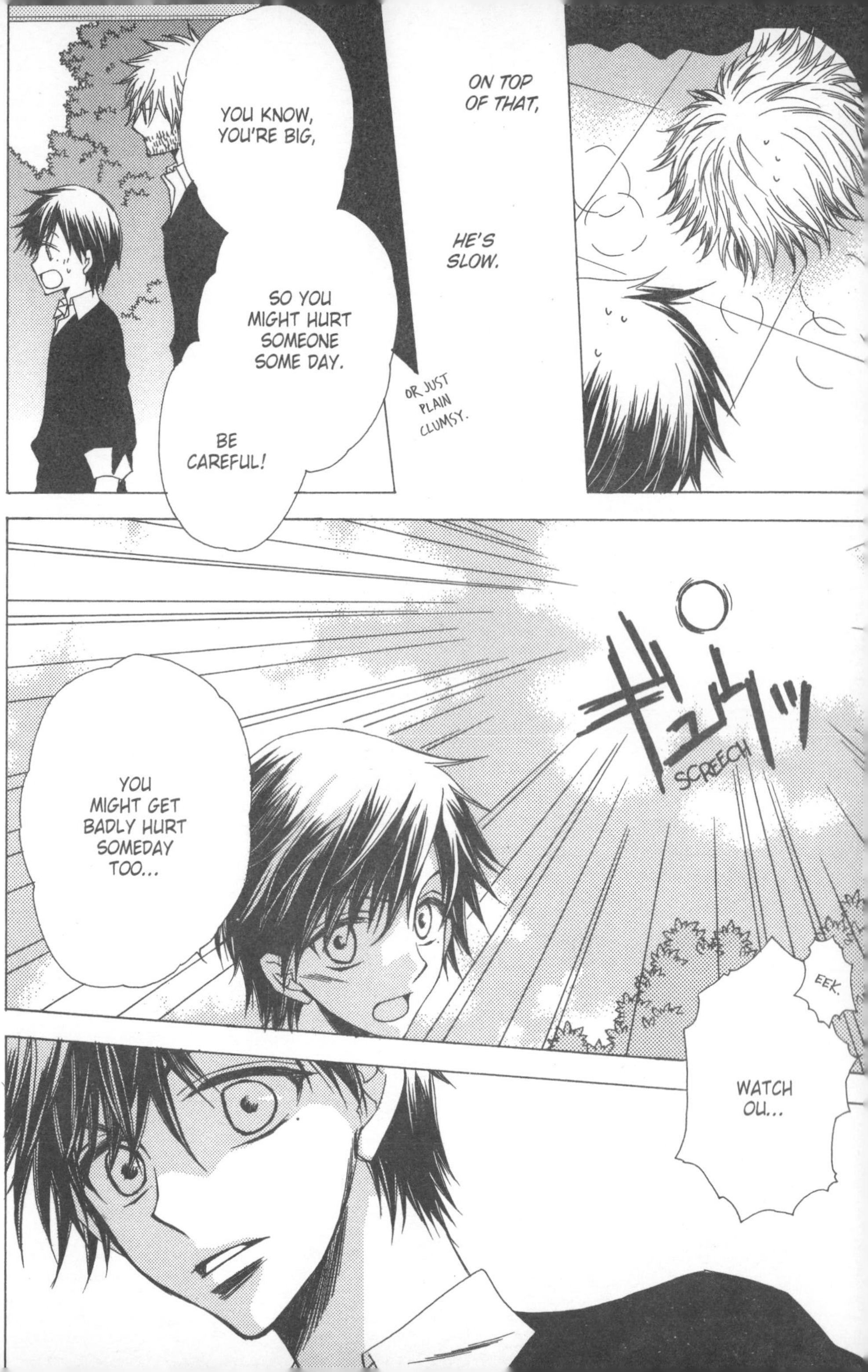

ON TOP OF THAT,
HE'S SLOW.
OR JUST PLAIN CLUMSY.
YOU KNOW, YOU'RE BIG,
SO YOU MIGHT HURT SOMEONE SOME DAY.
BE CAREFUL!
SCREECH
EEK.
WATCH OU...
YOU MIGHT GET BADLY HURT SOMEDAY TOO...

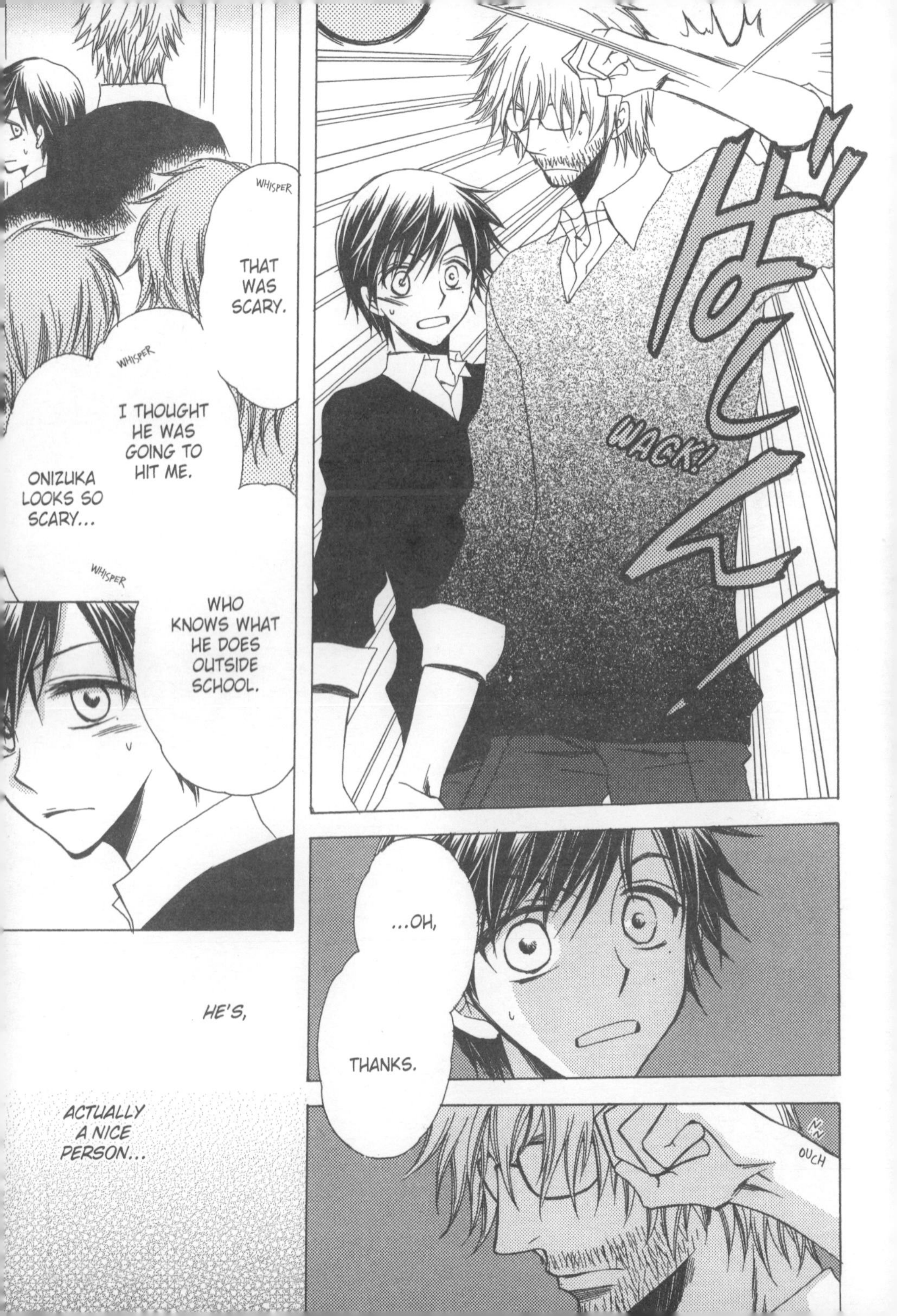
WACK!
WHISPER
THAT WAS SCARY.
WHISPER
I THOUGHT HE WAS GOING TO HIT ME.
ONIZUKA LOOKS SO SCARY...
WHISPER
WHO KNOWS WHAT HE DOES OUTSIDE SCHOOL.
...OH,
THANKS.
NN
OUCH
HE'S,
ACTUALLY A NICE PERSON...

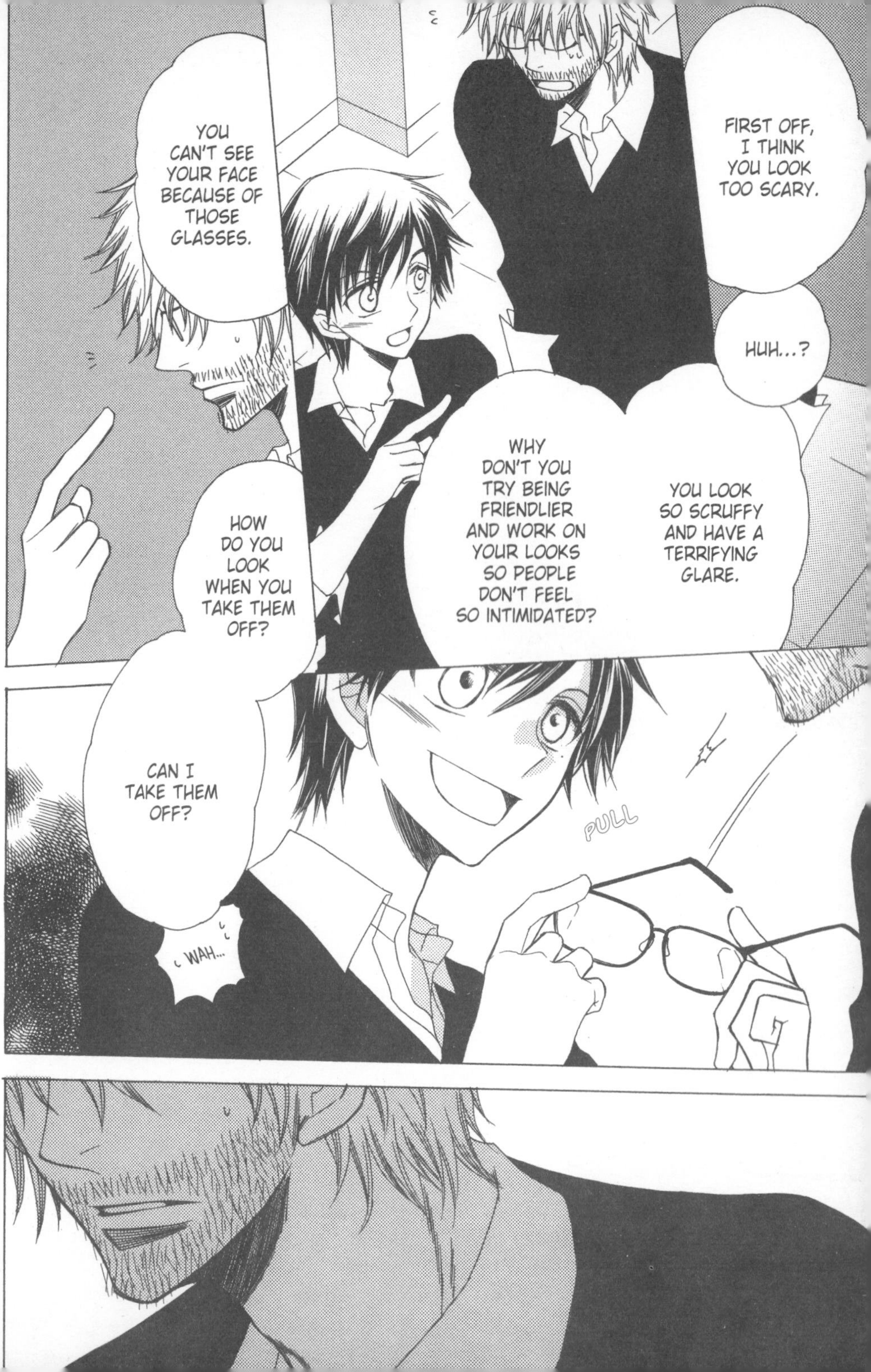
FIRST OFF, I THINK YOU LOOK TOO SCARY.
HUH...?
YOU LOOK SO SCRUFFY AND HAVE A TERRIFYING GLARE.
WHY DON'T YOU TRY BEING FRIENDLIER AND WORK ON YOUR LOOKS SO PEOPLE DON'T FEEL SO INTIMIDATED?
YOU CAN'T SEE YOUR FACE BECAUSE OF THOSE GLASSES.
HOW DO YOU LOOK WHEN YOU TAKE THEM OFF?
CAN I TAKE THEM OFF?
PULL
WAH...

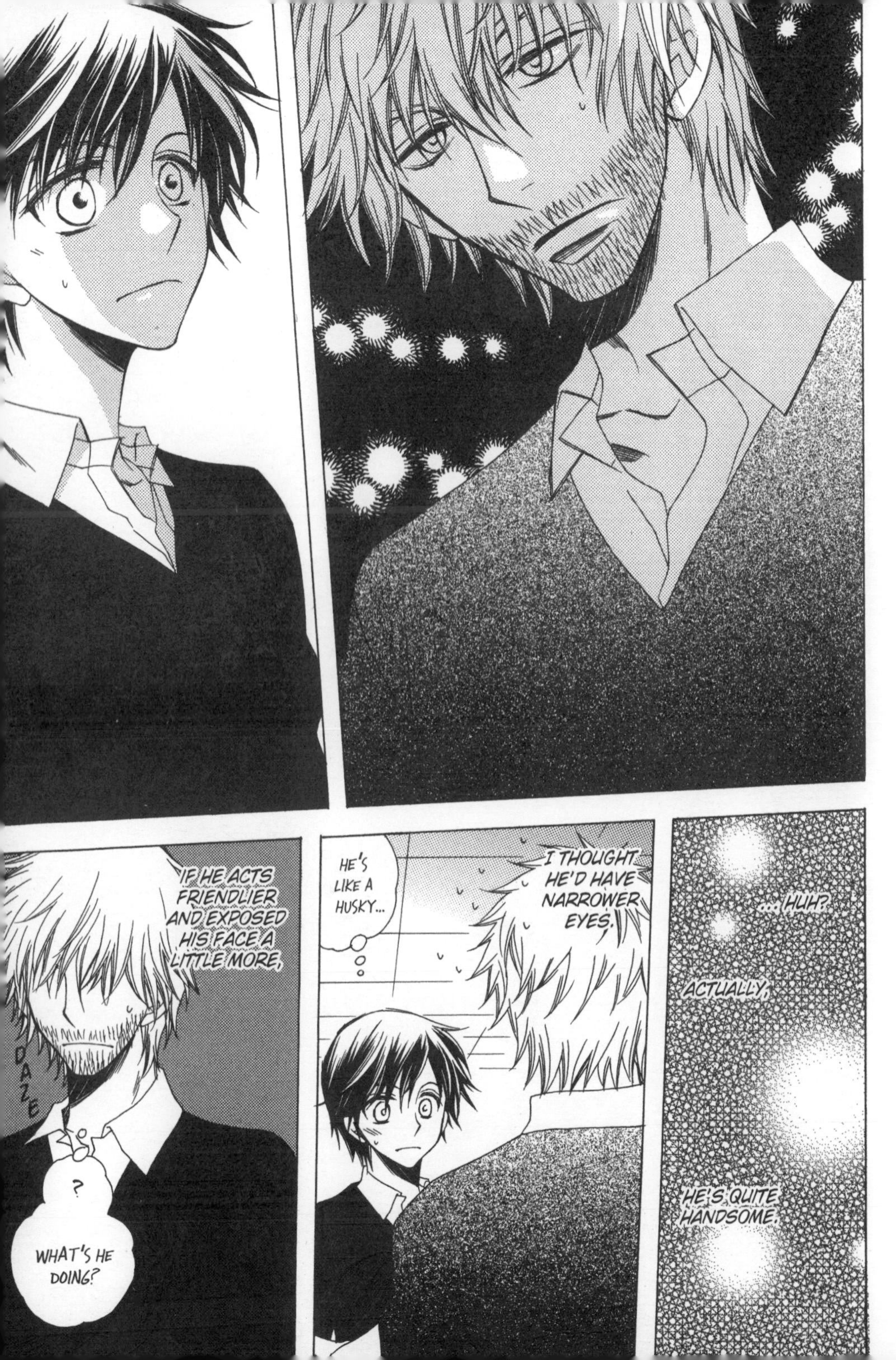
...HUH?
ACTUALLY,
HE'S QUITE HANDSOME.
I THOUGHT HE'D HAVE NARROWER EYES.
HE'S LIKE A HUSKY...
IF HE ACTS FRIENDLIER AND EXPOSED HIS FACE A LITTLE MORE,
DAZE
?
WHAT'S HE DOING?

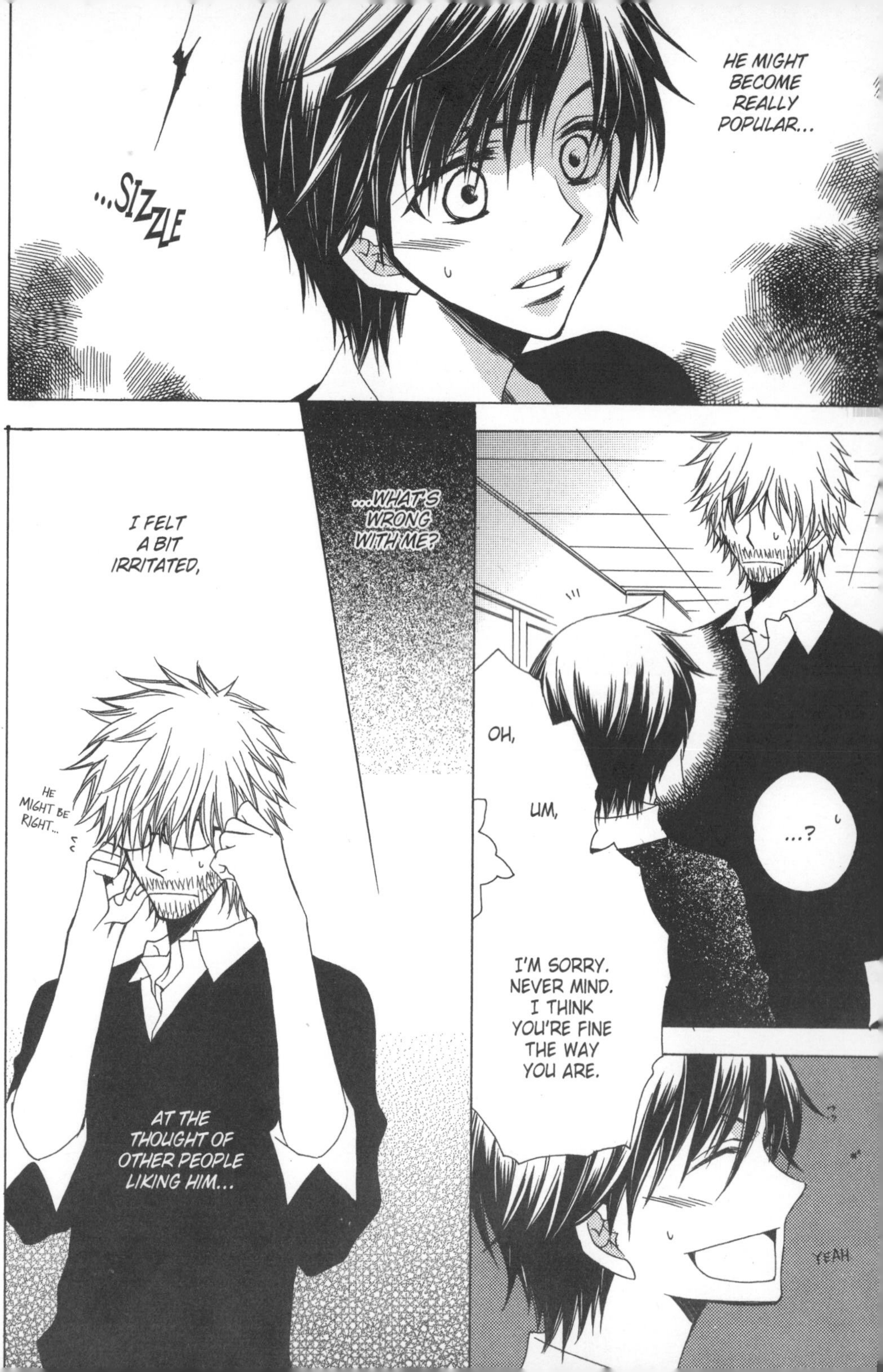
HE MIGHT BECOME REALLY POPULAR...
...SIZZLE
OH,
UM,
...?
I'M SORRY. NEVER MIND. I THINK YOU'RE FINE THE WAY YOU ARE.
YEAH
...WHAT'S WRONG WITH ME?
I FELT A BIT IRRITATED,
HE MIGHT BE RIGHT...
AT THE THOUGHT OF OTHER PEOPLE LIKING HIM...

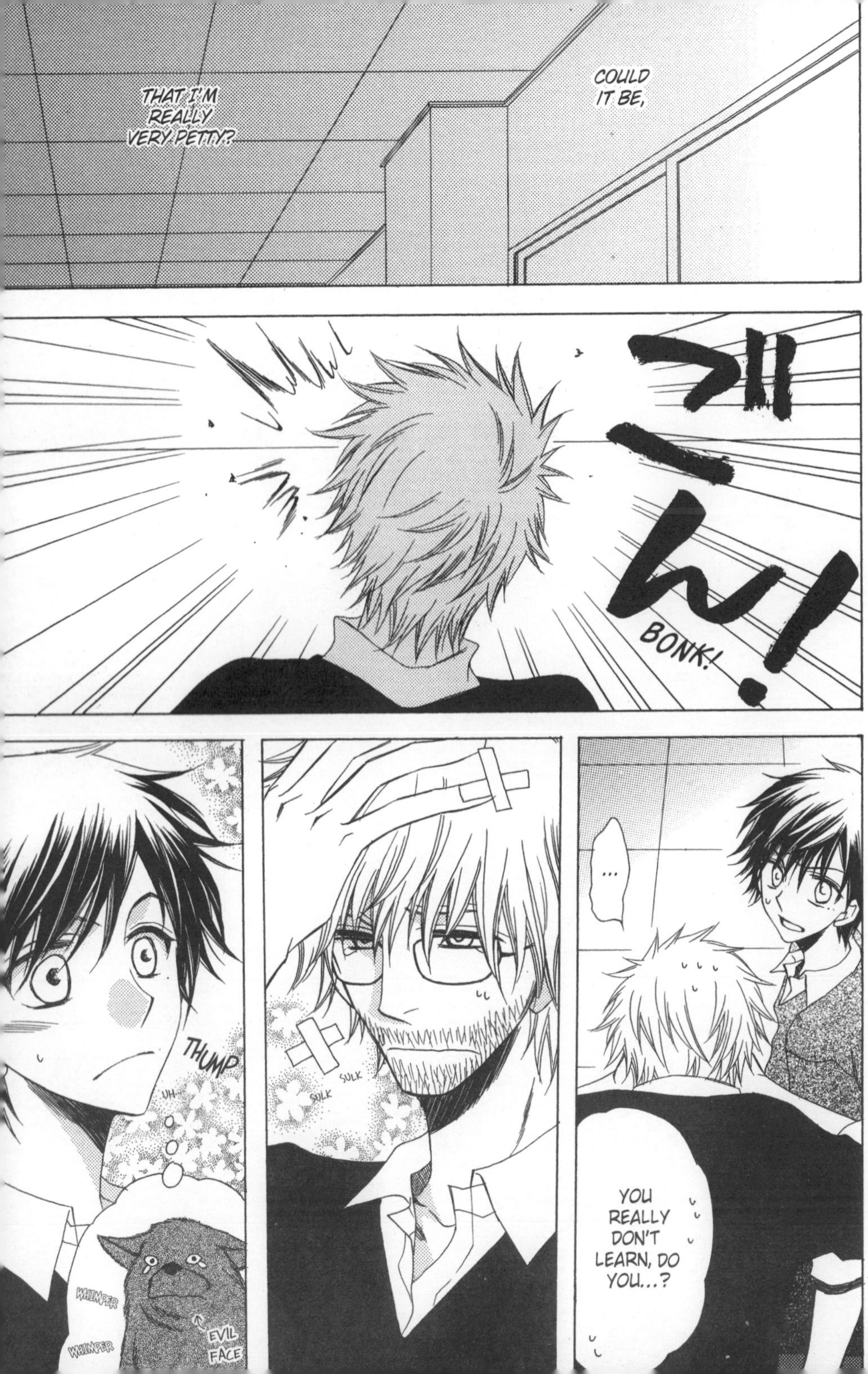
COULD IT BE,
THAT I'M REALLY VERY PETTY?
BONK!
...
YOU REALLY DON'T LEARN, DO YOU...?
SULK
SULK
THUMP
UH
WHIMPER
WHIMPER
EVIL FACE

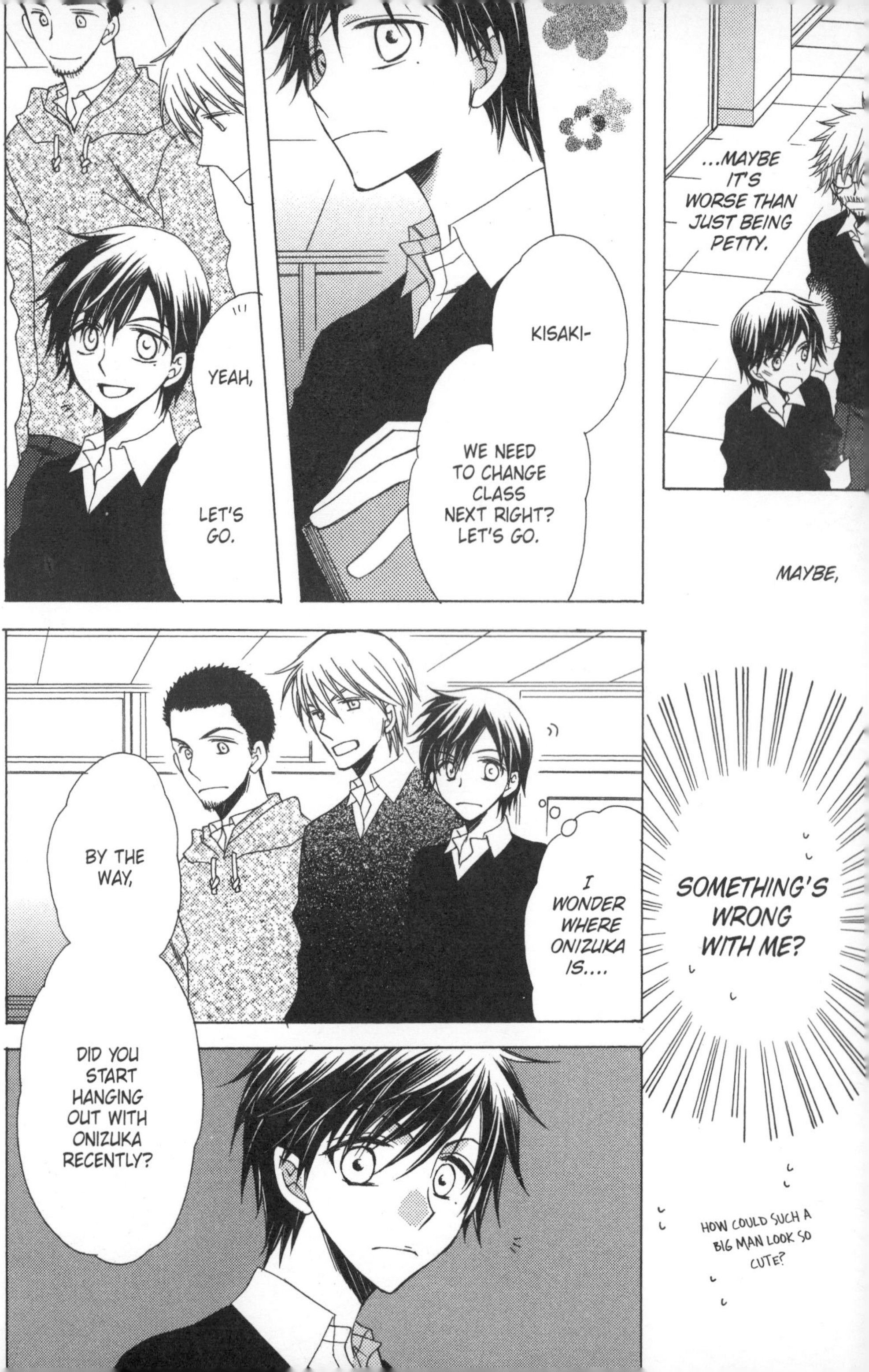
...MAYBE IT'S WORSE THAN JUST BEING PETTY.
KISAKI-
WE NEED TO CHANGE CLASS NEXT RIGHT? LET'S GO.
YEAH,
LET'S GO.
MAYBE,
SOMETHING'S WRONG WITH ME?
I WONDER WHERE ONIZUKA IS....
BY THE WAY,
HOW COULD SUCH A BIG MAN LOOK SO CUTE?
DID YOU START HANGING OUT WITH ONIZUKA RECENTLY?

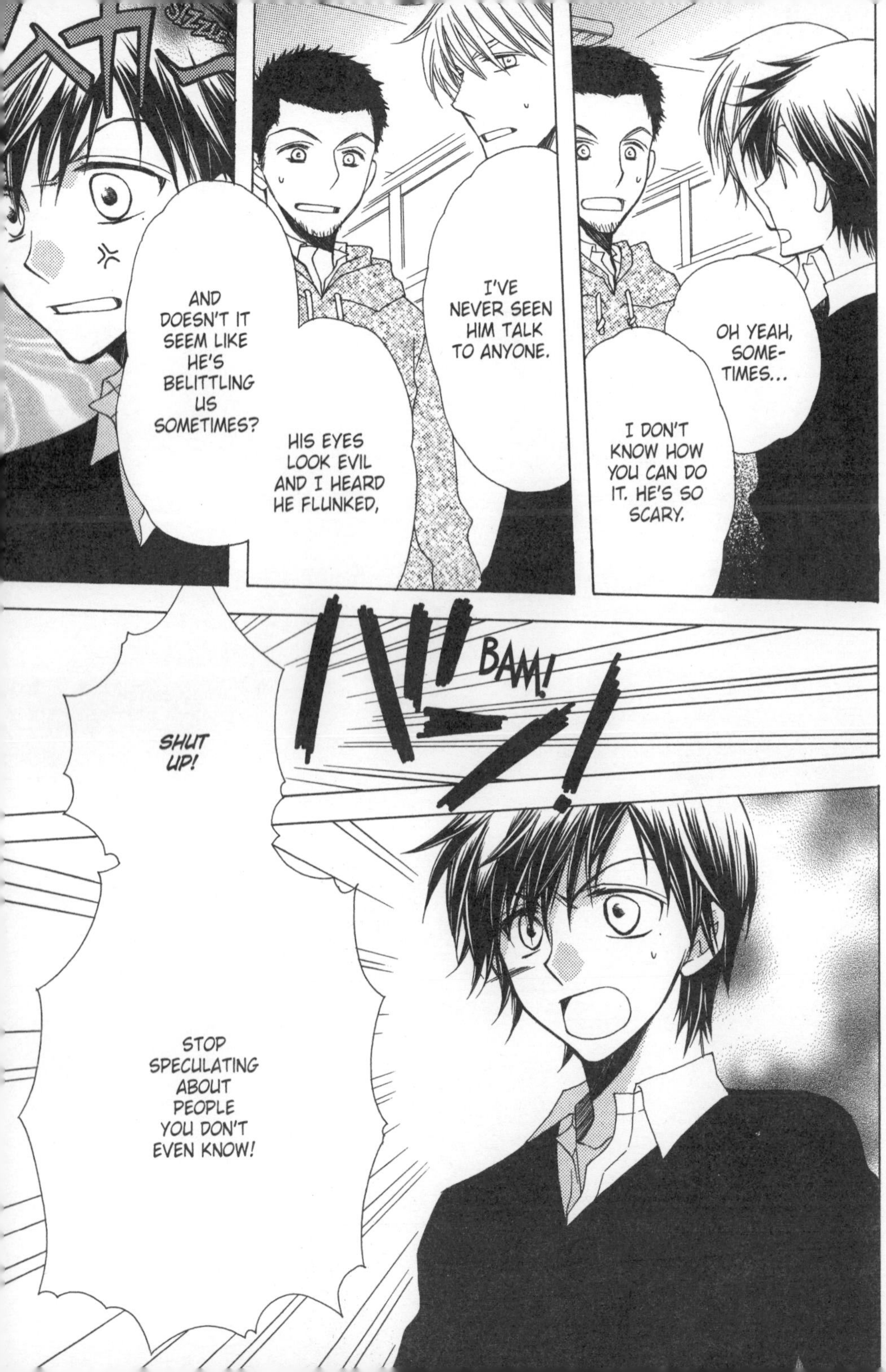
OH YEAH, SOME-TIMES...
I DON'T KNOW HOW YOU CAN DO IT. HE'S SO SCARY.
I'VE NEVER SEEN HIM TALK TO ANYONE.
HIS EYES LOOK EVIL AND I HEARD HE FLUNKED,
AND DOESN'T IT SEEM LIKE HE'S BELITTLING US SOMETIMES?
BAM!
SHUT UP!
STOP SPECULATING ABOUT PEOPLE YOU DON'T EVEN KNOW!

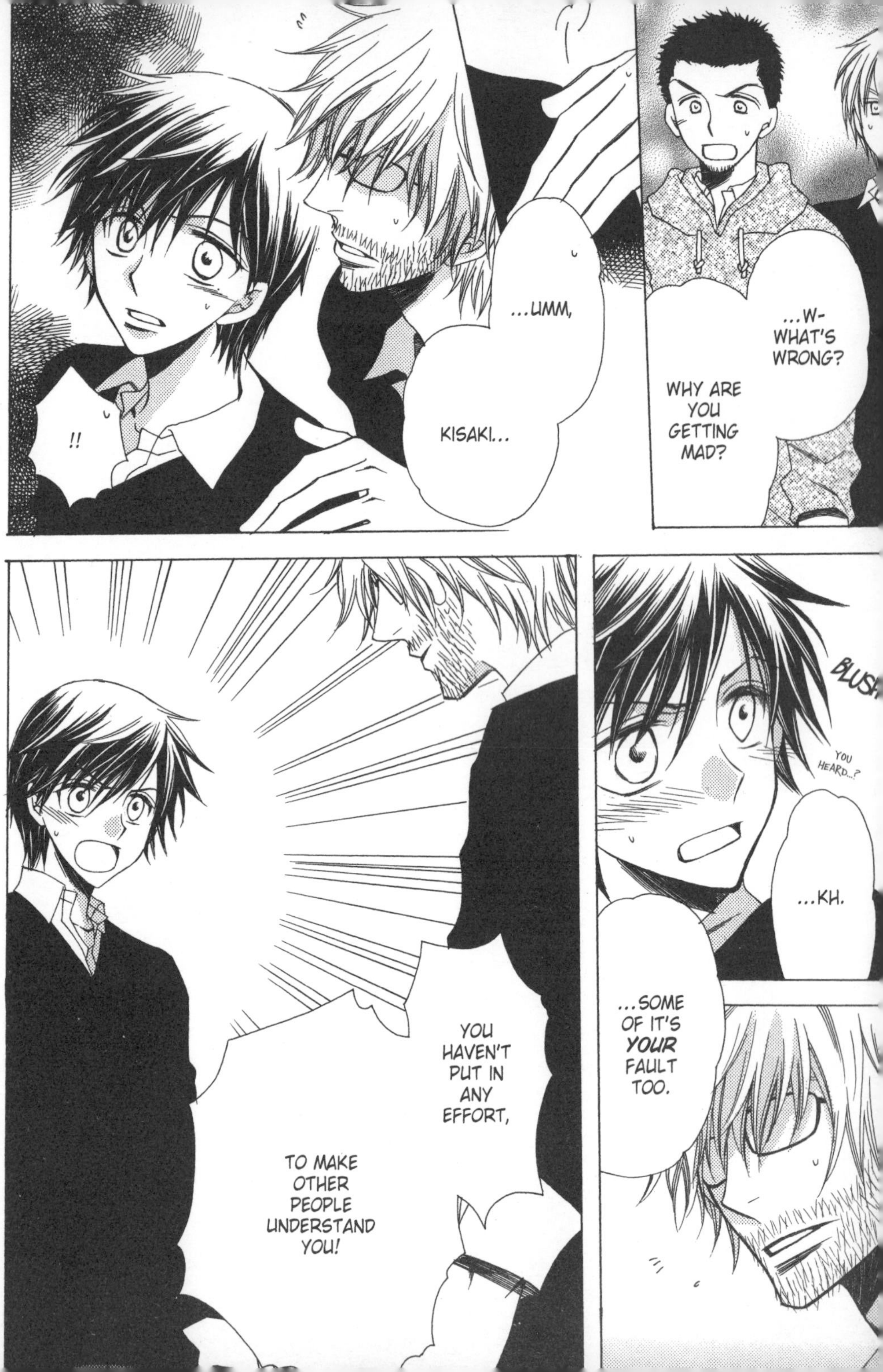
...W-WHAT'S WRONG?
WHY ARE YOU GETTING MAD?
...UMM,
KISAKI...
!!
BLUSH
YOU HEARD...?
...KH.
...SOME OF IT'S ***YOUR*** FAULT TOO.
YOU HAVEN'T PUT IN ANY EFFORT,
TO MAKE OTHER PEOPLE UNDERSTAND YOU!

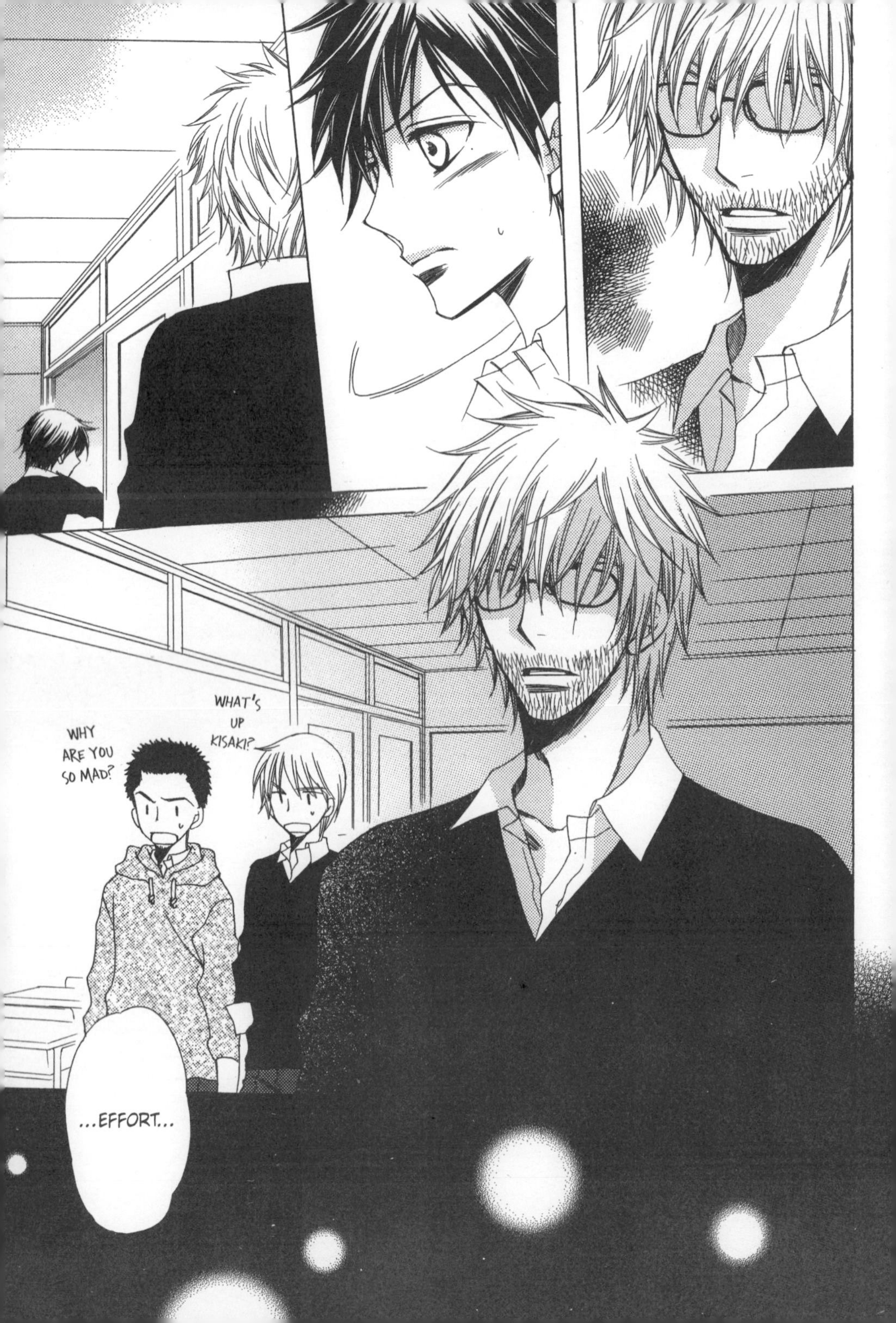
WHAT'S UP KISAKI?
WHY ARE YOU SO MAD?
...EFFORT...

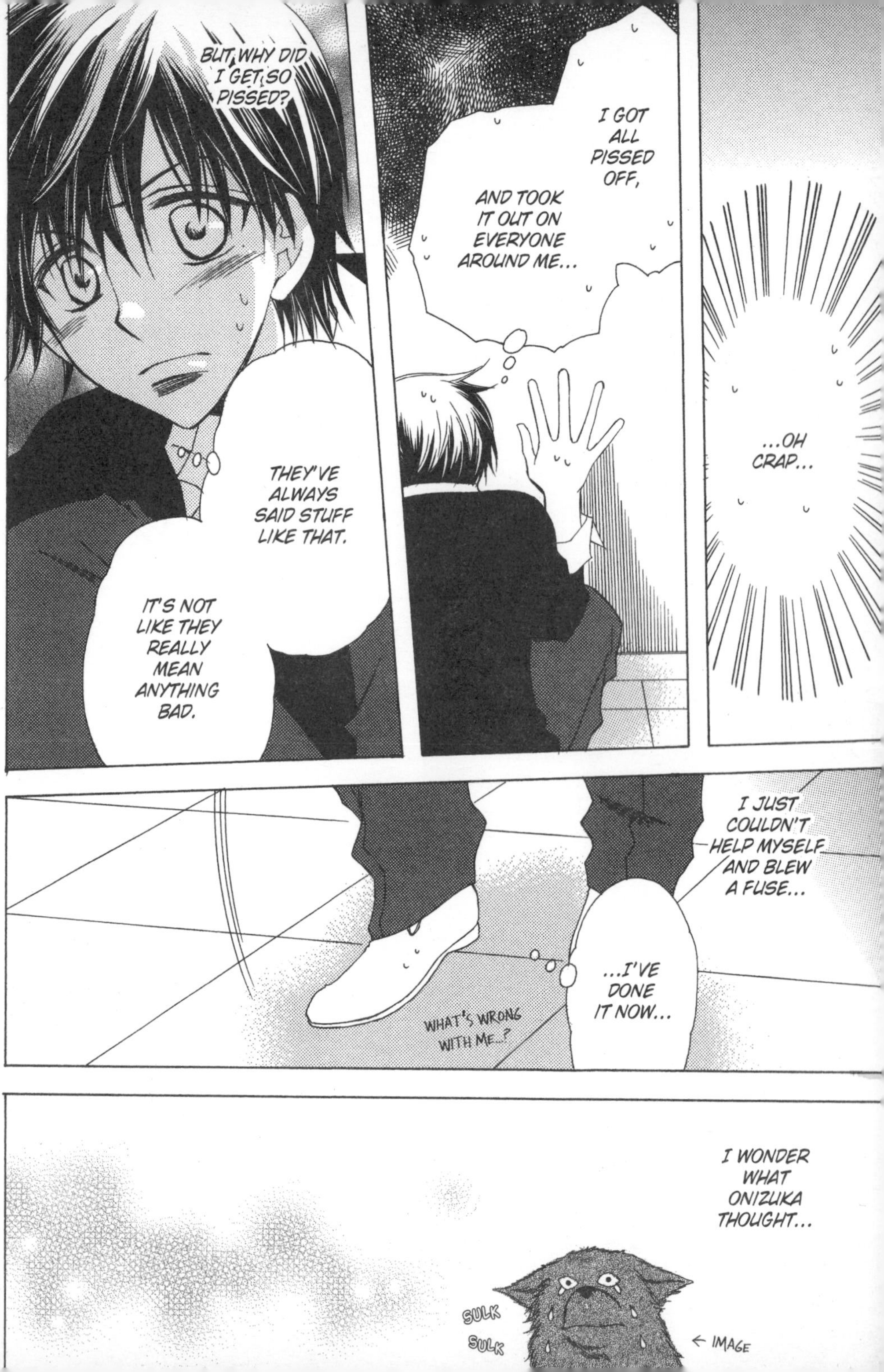
...OH CRAP...
I GOT ALL PISSED OFF,
AND TOOK IT OUT ON EVERYONE AROUND ME...
BUT, WHY DID I GET SO PISSED?
THEY'VE ALWAYS SAID STUFF LIKE THAT.
IT'S NOT LIKE THEY REALLY MEAN ANYTHING BAD.
I JUST COULDN'T HELP MYSELF AND BLEW A FUSE...
...I'VE DONE IT NOW...
WHAT'S WRONG WITH ME...?
I WONDER WHAT ONIZUKA THOUGHT...
SULK
SULK
← IMAGE

UMM... WHO IS THAT?

WAS THERE A GUY LIKE THAT IN OUR GRADE?

IS HE A FOREIGNER?

HE'S JAPANESE...

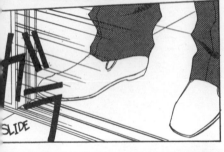

ISN'T HE HANDSOME...?

STEP STEP STEP

SLIDE

BONK

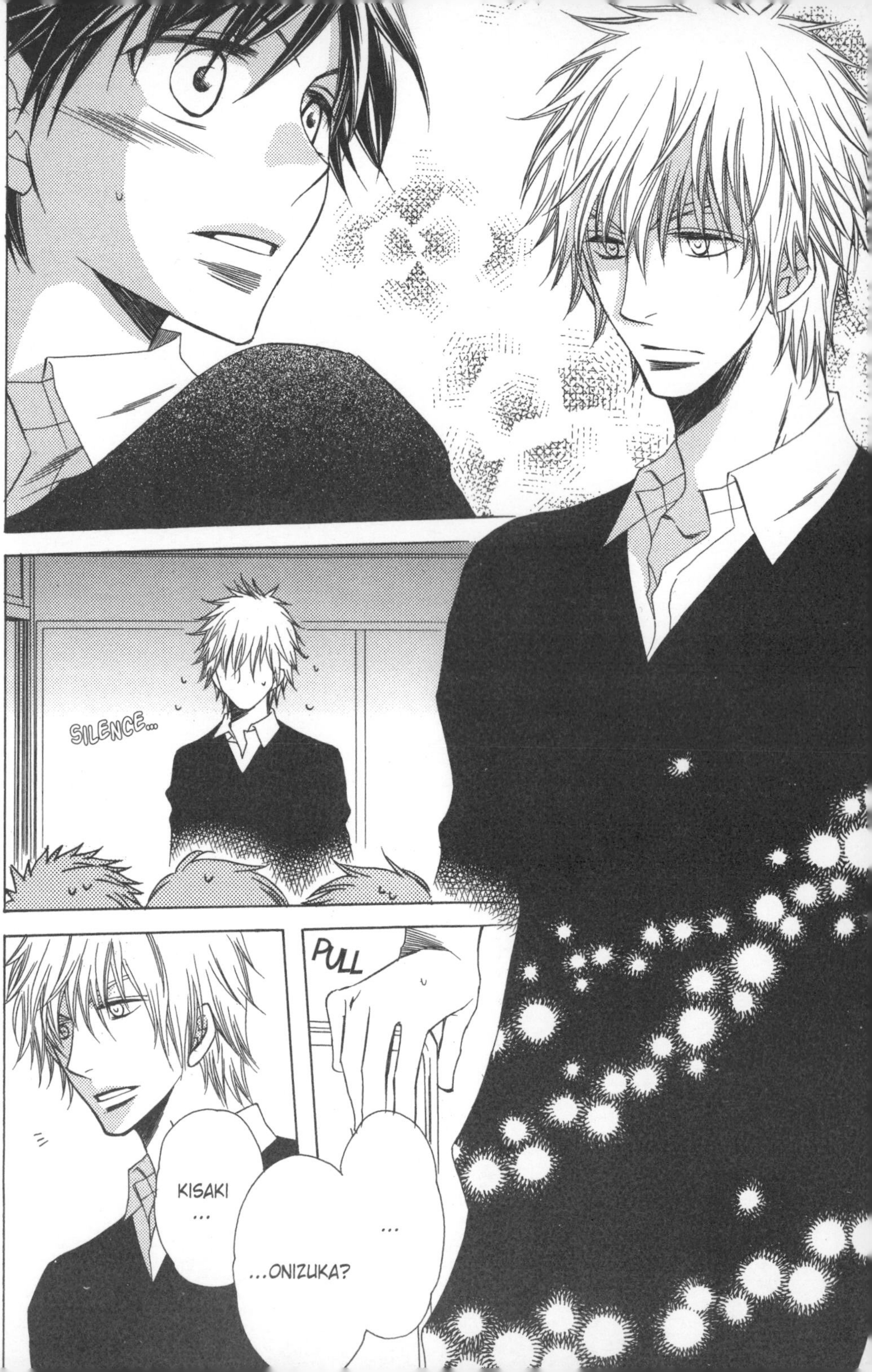
SILENCE...
PULL
... ...ONIZUKA?
KISAKI ...

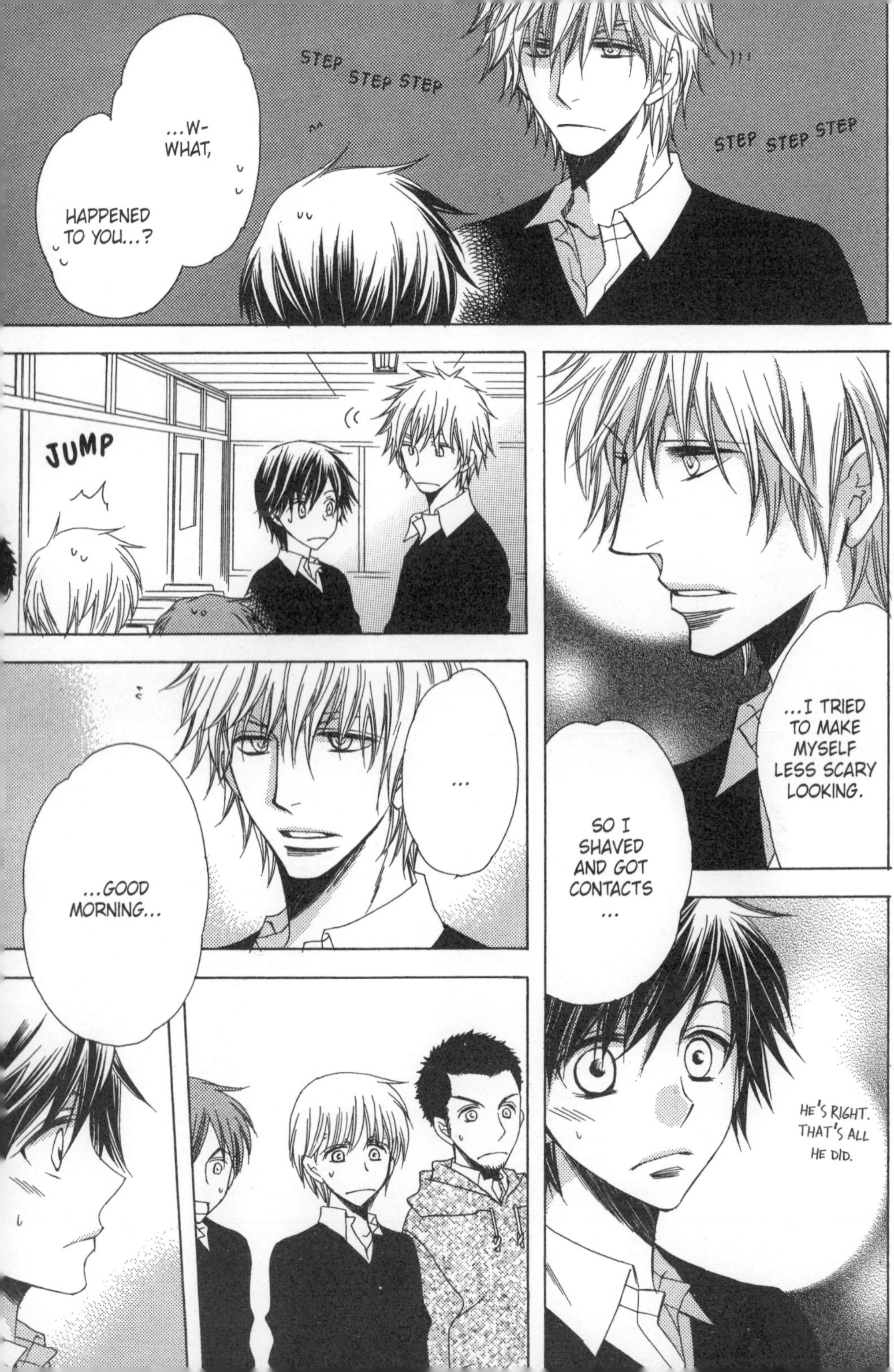
STEP STEP STEP
STEP STEP STEP
...W- WHAT, HAPPENED TO YOU...?
JUMP
...
...GOOD MORNING...
...I TRIED TO MAKE MYSELF LESS SCARY LOOKING.
SO I SHAVED AND GOT CONTACTS ...
HE'S RIGHT. THAT'S ALL HE DID.

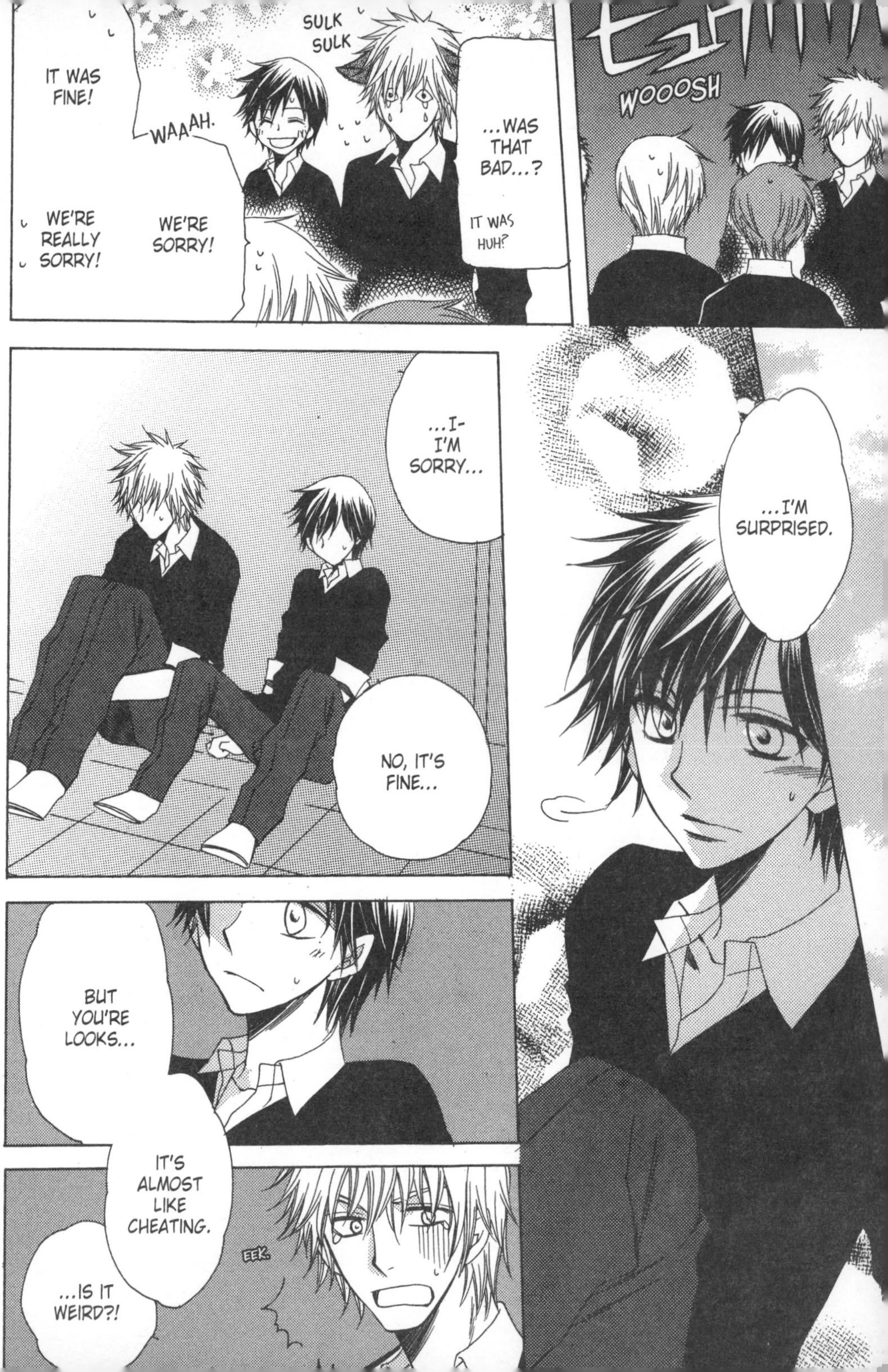
WOOOSH
...WAS THAT BAD...?
IT WAS HUH?
SULK SULK
IT WAS FINE!
WAAAH.
WE'RE SORRY!
WE'RE REALLY SORRY!
...I'M SURPRISED.
...I- I'M SORRY...
NO, IT'S FINE...
BUT YOU'RE LOOKS...
IT'S ALMOST LIKE CHEATING.
EEK.
...IS IT WEIRD?!

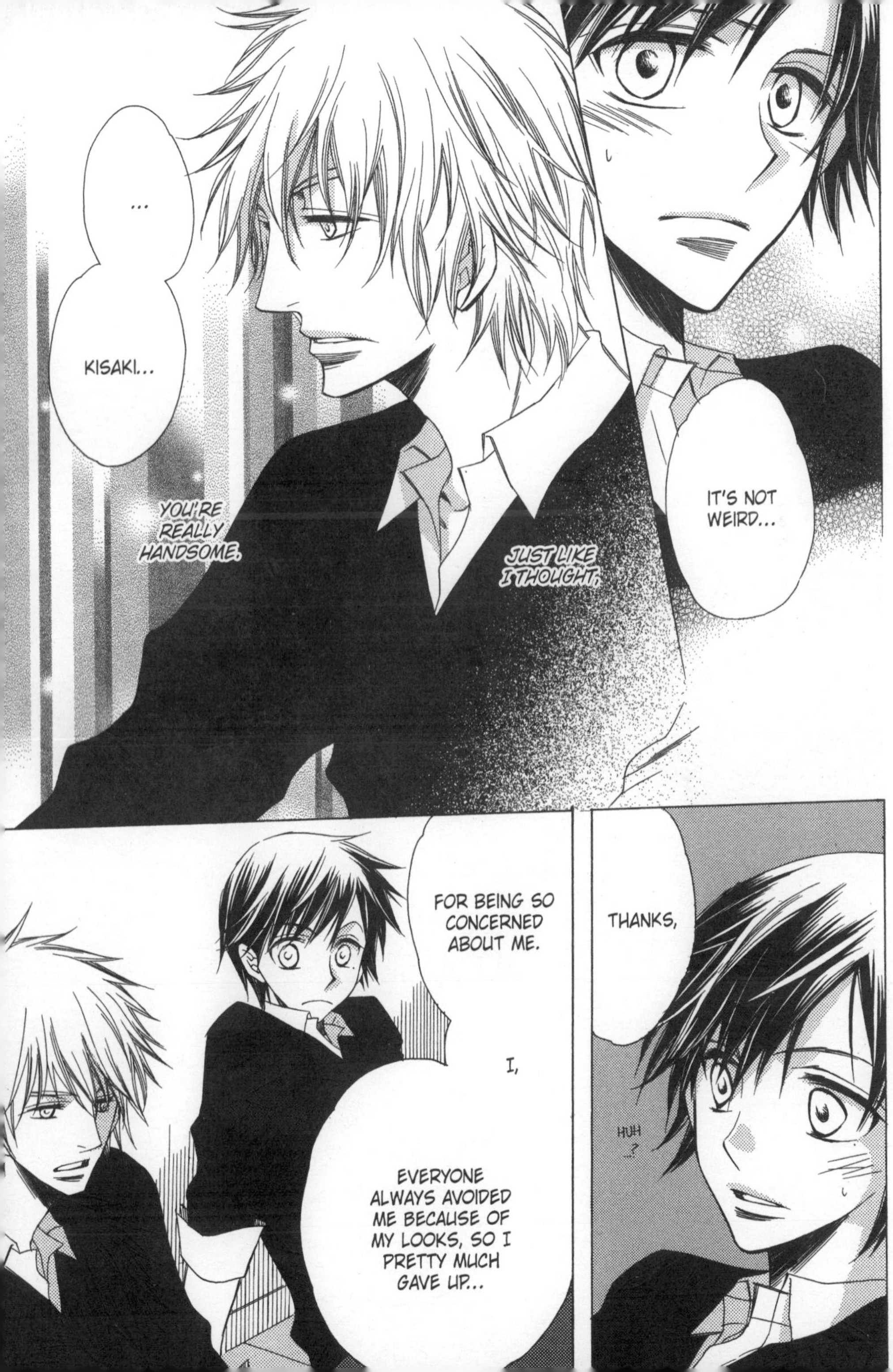
IT'S NOT WEIRD...
...
KISAKI...
YOU'RE REALLY HANDSOME.
JUST LIKE I THOUGHT.
THANKS,
HUH ...?
FOR BEING SO CONCERNED ABOUT ME.
I,
EVERYONE ALWAYS AVOIDED ME BECAUSE OF MY LOOKS, SO I PRETTY MUCH GAVE UP...

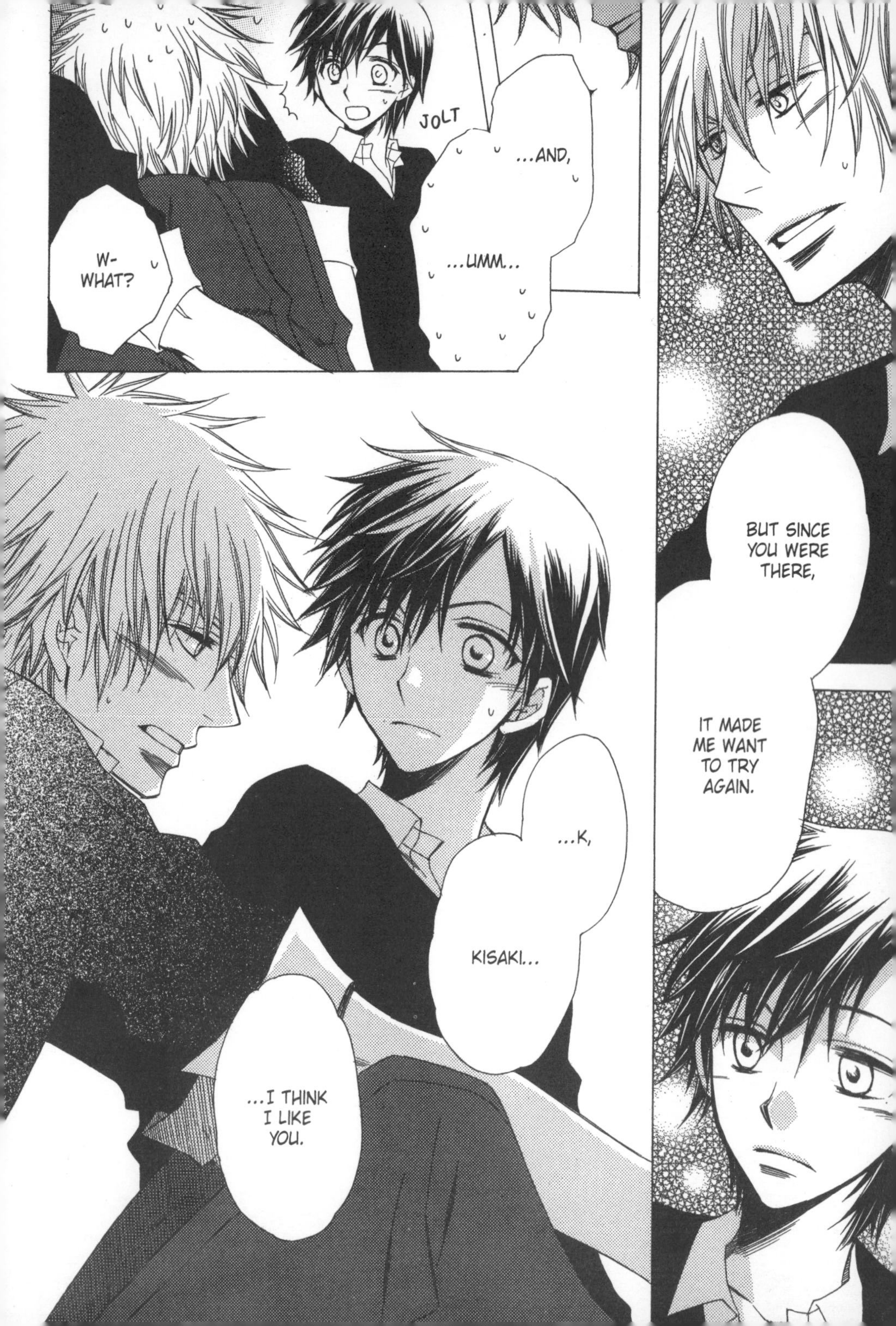
BUT SINCE YOU WERE THERE,
IT MADE ME WANT TO TRY AGAIN.
JOLT
...AND,
...UMM...
W-WHAT?
...K,
KISAKI...
...I THINK I LIKE YOU.

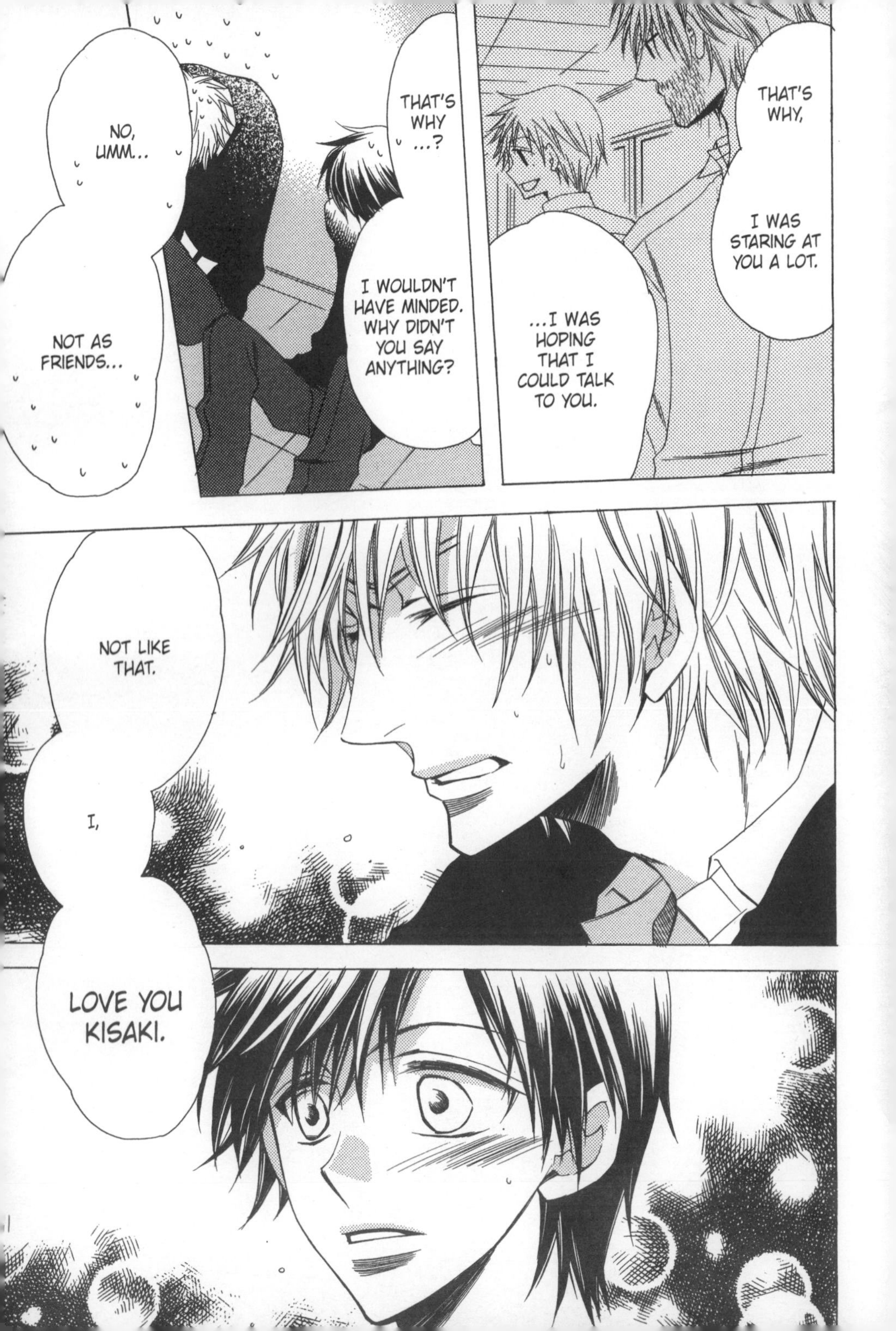
THAT'S WHY,
I WAS STARING AT YOU A LOT.
...I WAS HOPING THAT I COULD TALK TO YOU.
THAT'S WHY ...?
I WOULDN'T HAVE MINDED. WHY DIDN'T YOU SAY ANYTHING?
NO, UMM...
NOT AS FRIENDS...
NOT LIKE THAT.
I,
LOVE YOU KISAKI.

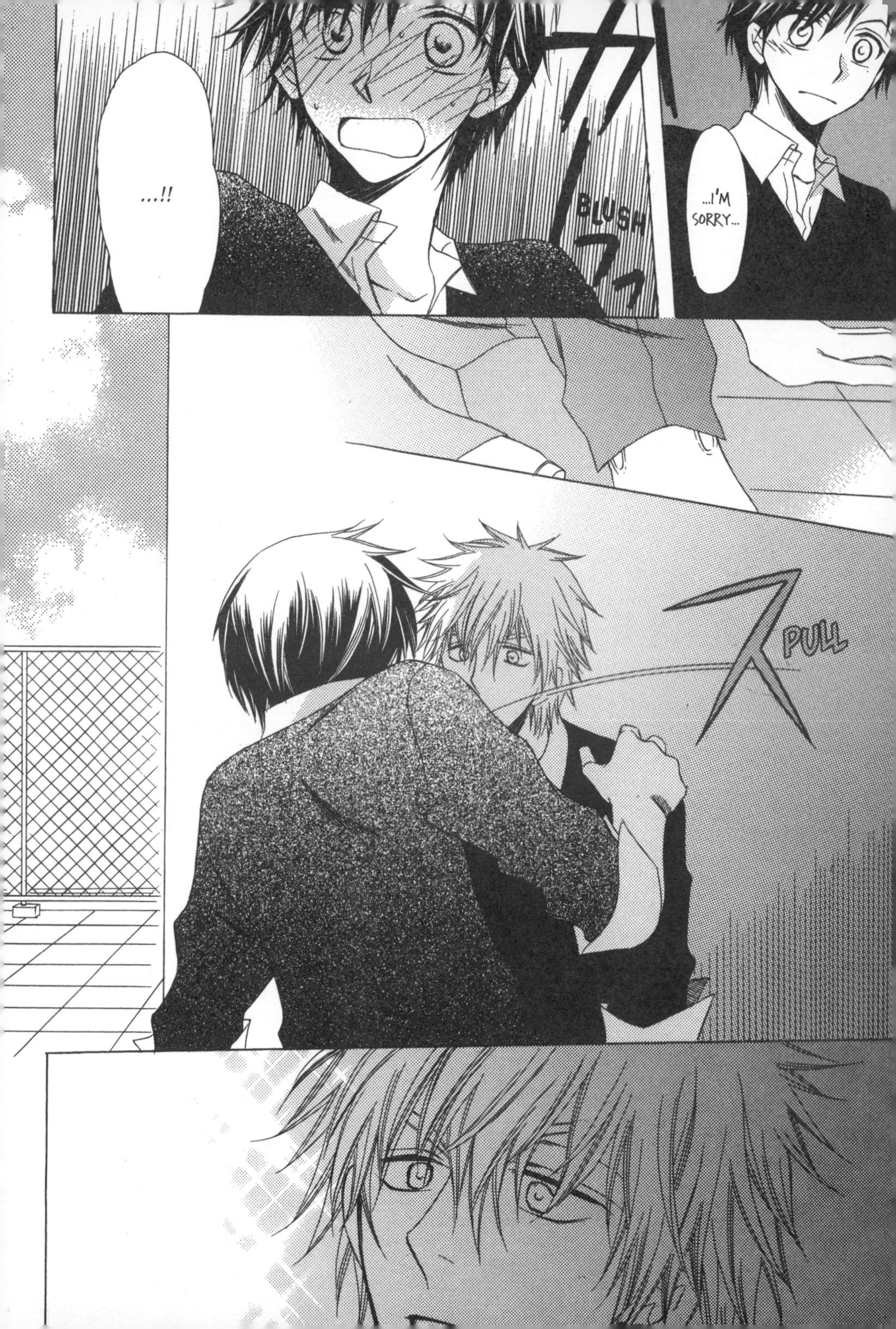
...I'M SORRY...
BLUSH
...!!
PULL

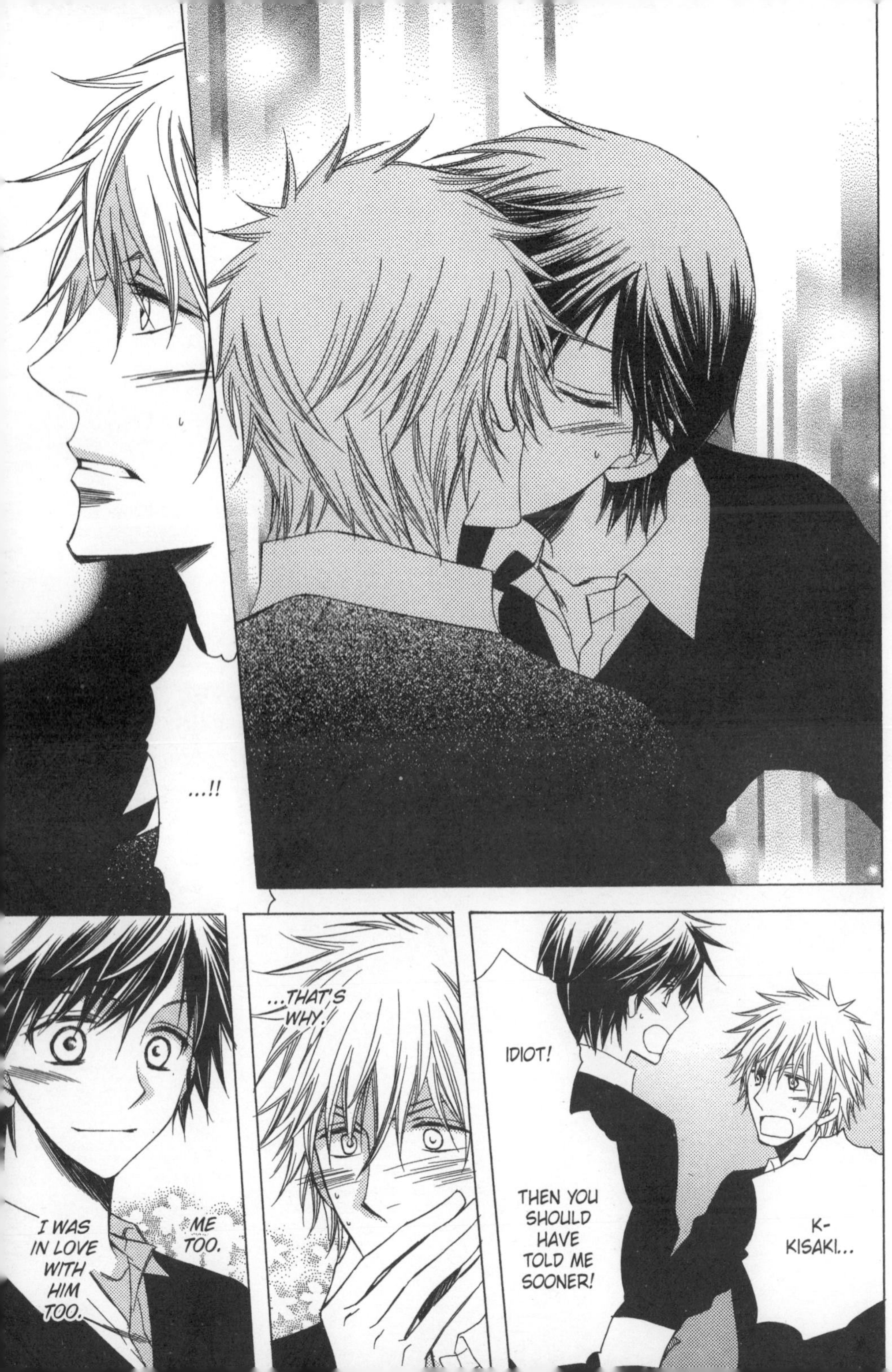
...!!
IDIOT!
THEN YOU SHOULD HAVE TOLD ME SOONER!
K-KISAKI...
...THAT'S WHY.
ME TOO.
I WAS IN LOVE WITH HIM TOO.

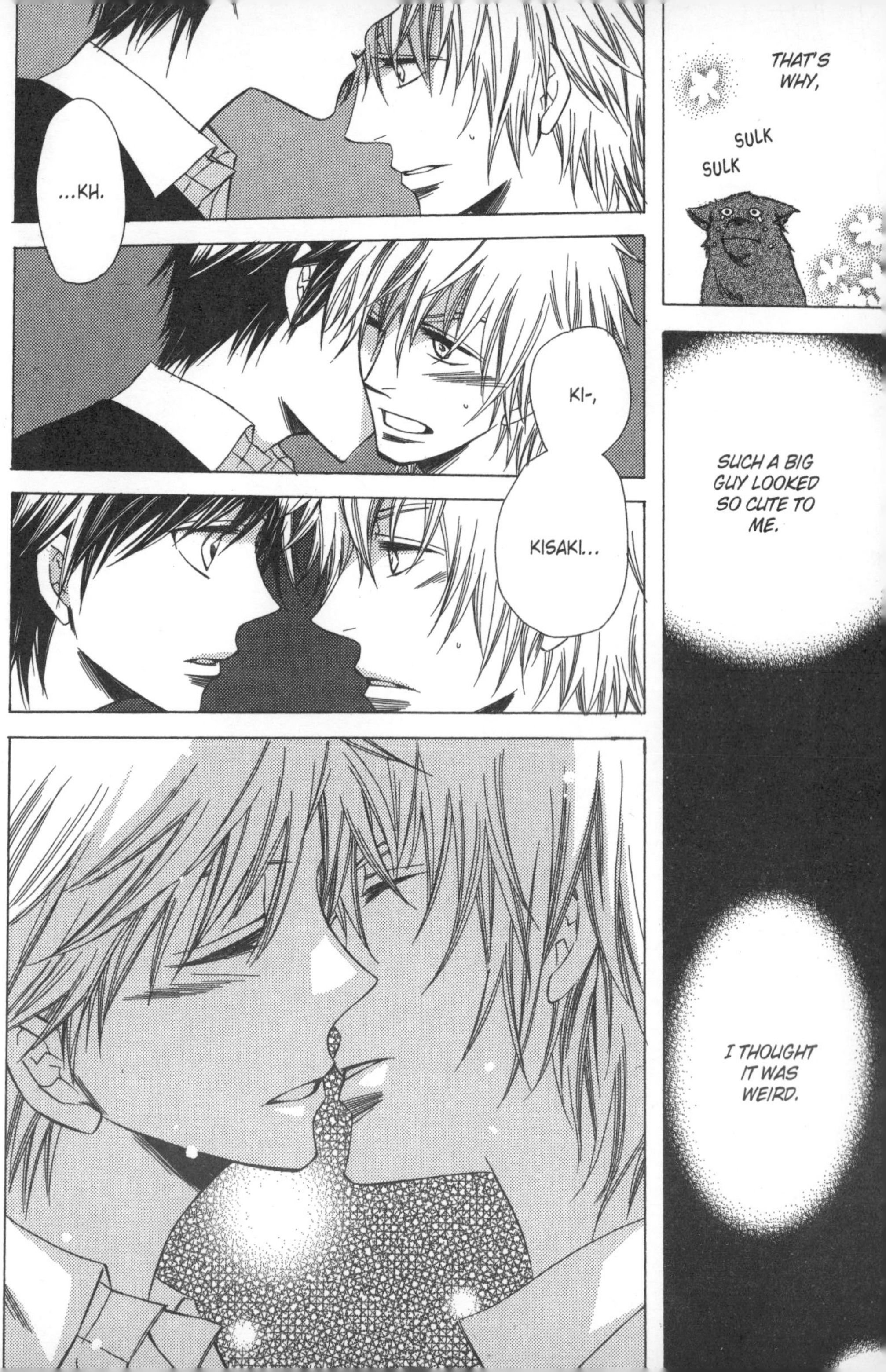
THAT'S WHY,
SULK
SULK
SUCH A BIG GUY LOOKED SO CUTE TO ME.
I THOUGHT IT WAS WEIRD.
...KH.
KI-,
KISAKI...

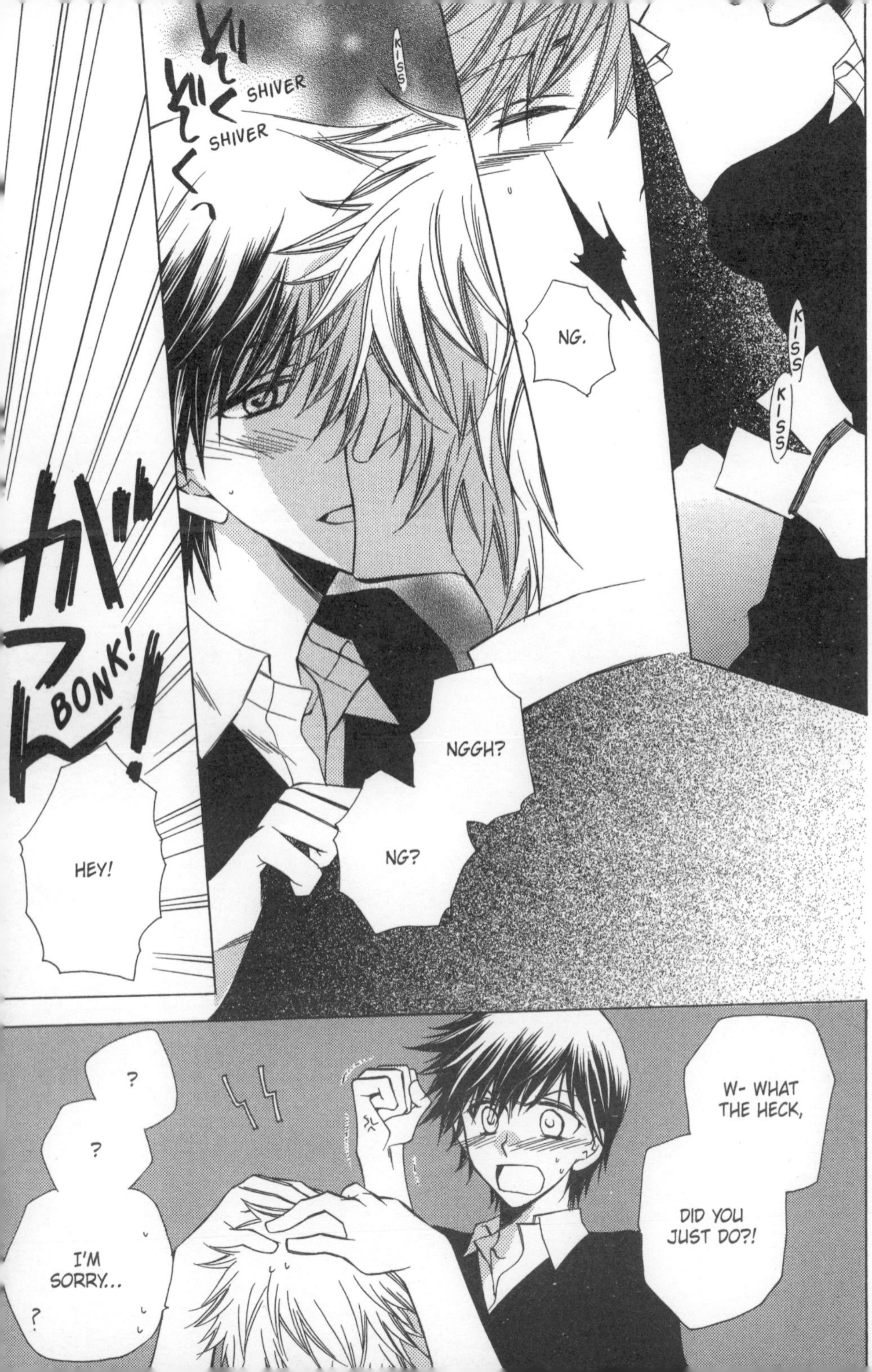
KISS
KISS
NG.
KISS
ぞくぞくっ
SHIVER
SHIVER
NGGH?
NG?
ガツン!
BONK!
HEY!
W- WHAT THE HECK,
DID YOU JUST DO?!
?
?
I'M SORRY...
?

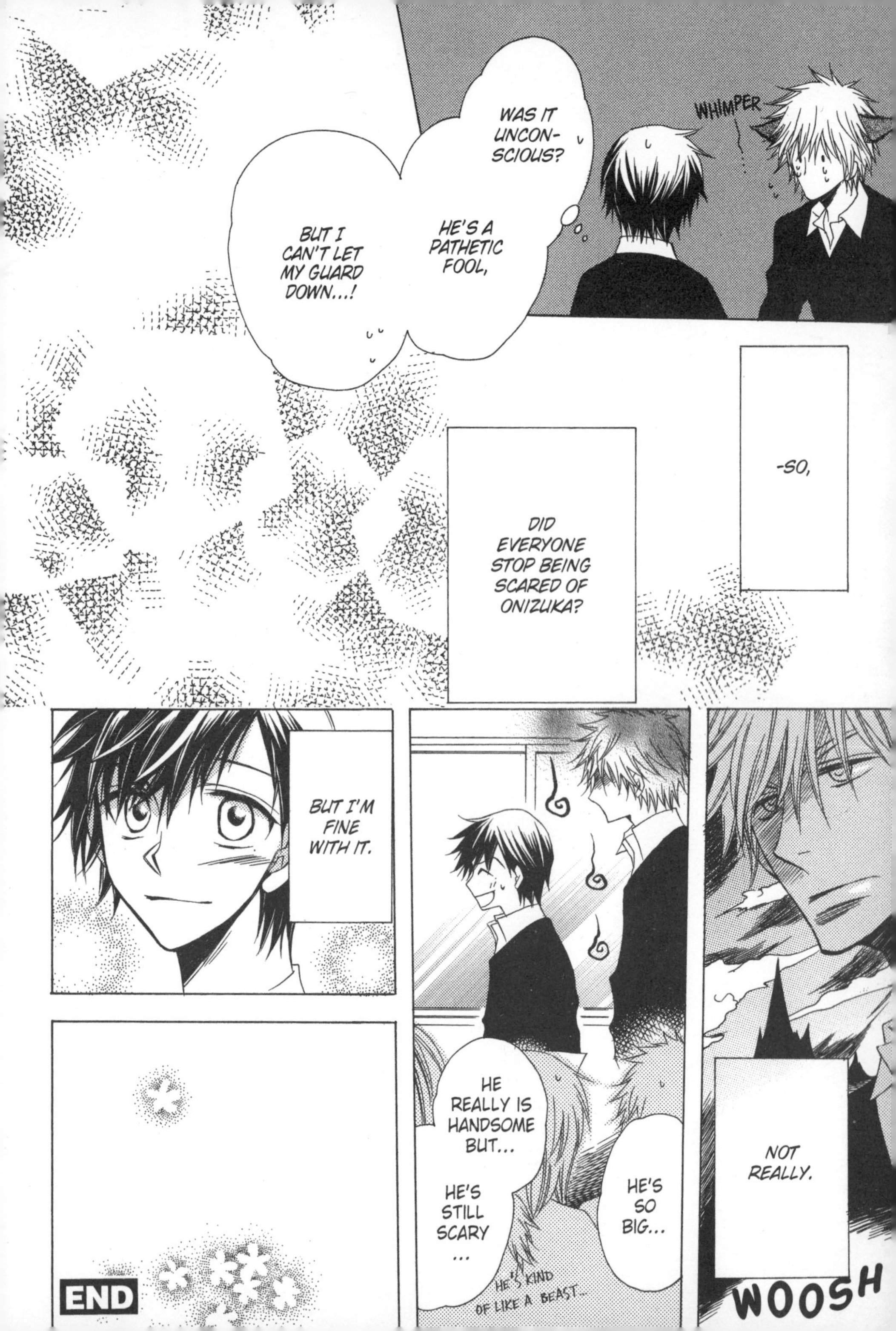
WHIMPER
WAS IT UNCONSCIOUS?
HE'S A PATHETIC FOOL,
BUT I CAN'T LET MY GUARD DOWN...!
-SO,
DID EVERYONE STOP BEING SCARED OF ONIZUKA?
NOT REALLY.
WOOSH
HE REALLY IS HANDSOME BUT...
HE'S SO BIG...
HE'S STILL SCARY ...
HE'S KIND OF LIKE A BEAST..
BUT I'M FINE WITH IT.
END

王子様の本気

THE PRINCE'S COMMITMENT

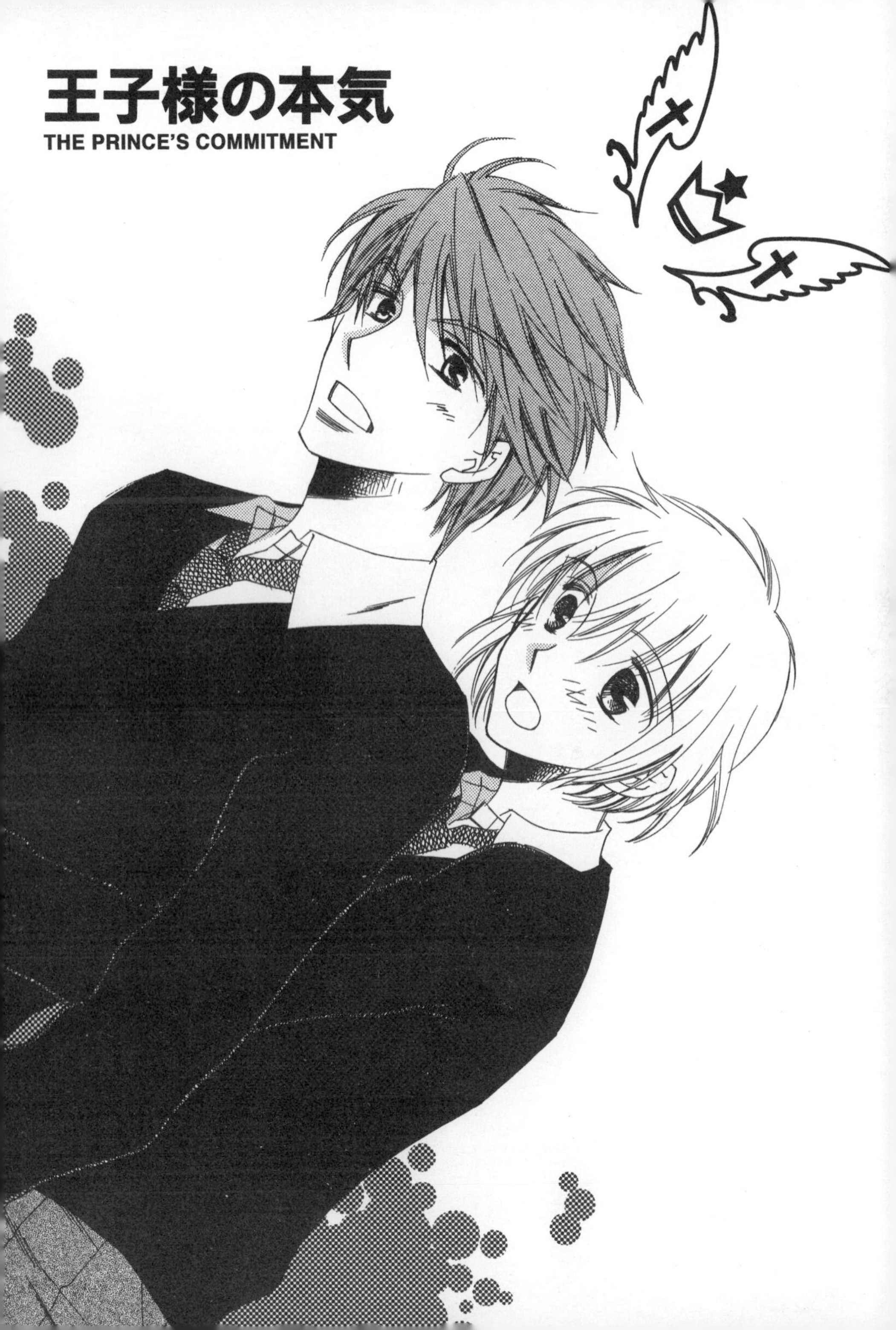

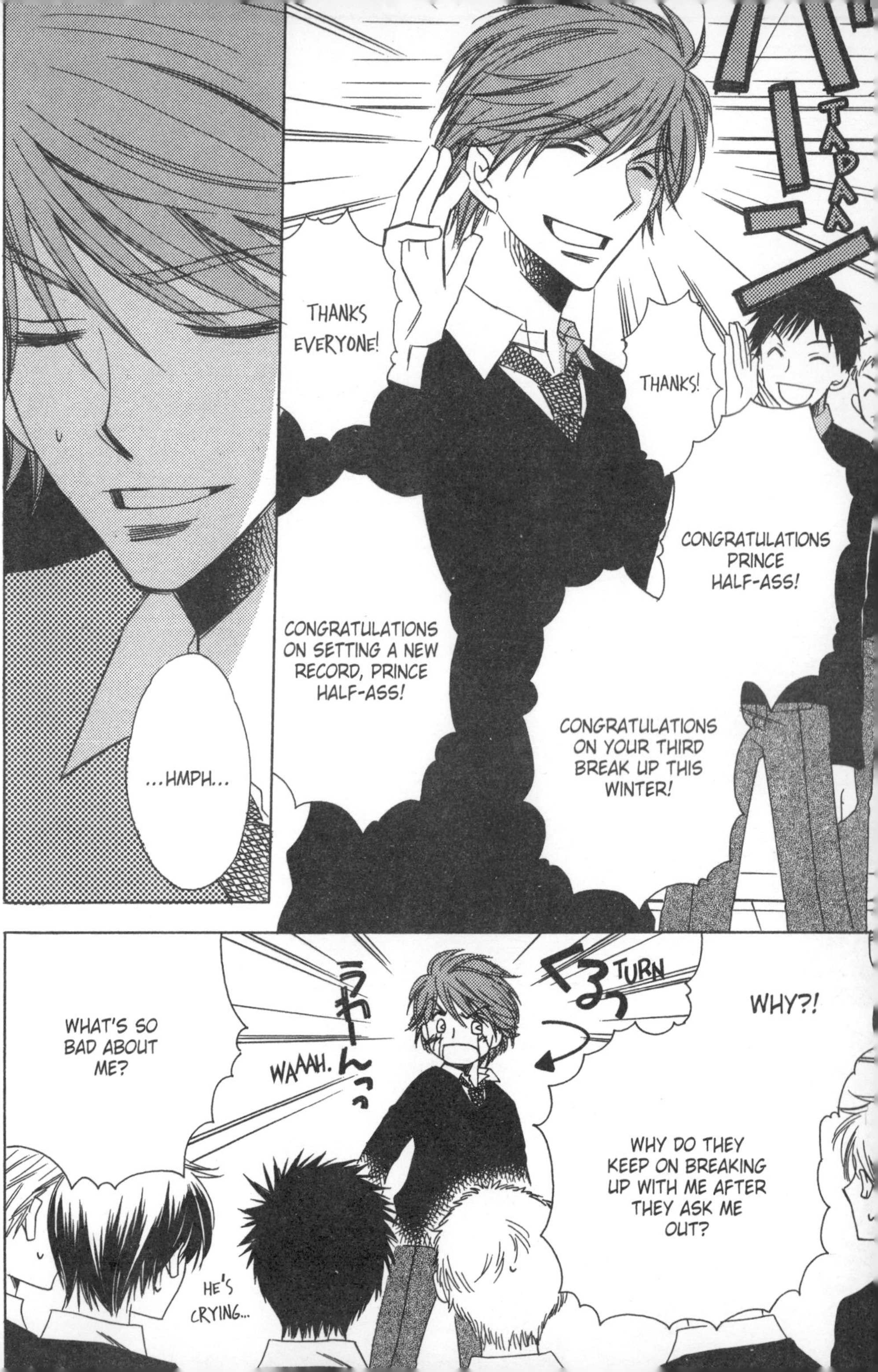
TAPAA
THANKS!
THANKS EVERYONE!
CONGRATULATIONS PRINCE HALF-ASS!
CONGRATULATIONS ON SETTING A NEW RECORD, PRINCE HALF-ASS!
CONGRATULATIONS ON YOUR THIRD BREAK UP THIS WINTER!
...HMPH...
WHY?!
TURN
WHY DO THEY KEEP ON BREAKING UP WITH ME AFTER THEY ASK ME OUT?
WAAAH.
WHAT'S SO BAD ABOUT ME?
HE'S CRYING...

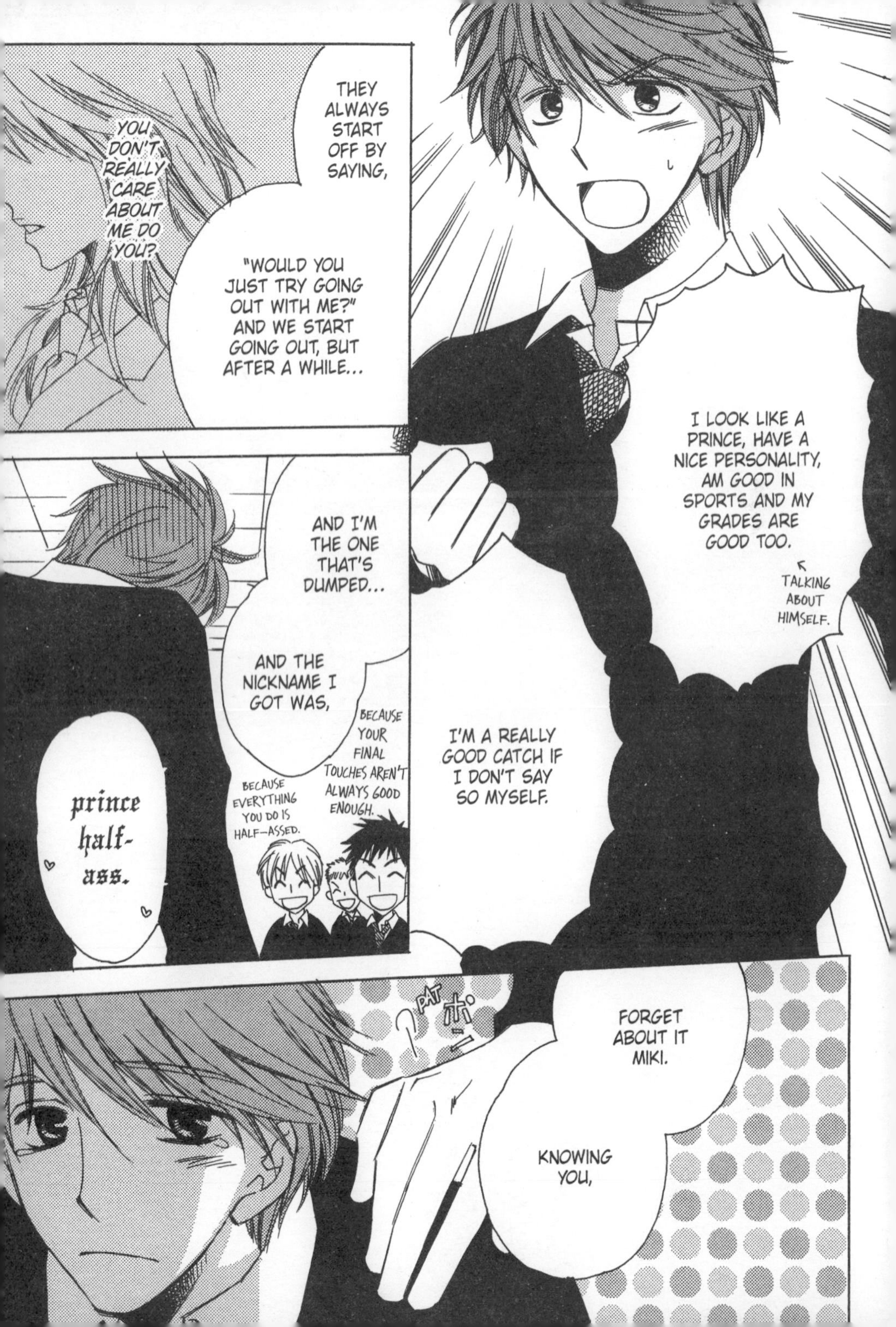
I LOOK LIKE A PRINCE, HAVE A NICE PERSONALITY, AM GOOD IN SPORTS AND MY GRADES ARE GOOD TOO.
TALKING ABOUT HIMSELF.
I'M A REALLY GOOD CATCH IF I DON'T SAY SO MYSELF.
THEY ALWAYS START OFF BY SAYING,
"WOULD YOU JUST TRY GOING OUT WITH ME?" AND WE START GOING OUT, BUT AFTER A WHILE...
YOU DON'T REALLY CARE ABOUT ME DO YOU?
AND I'M THE ONE THAT'S DUMPED...
AND THE NICKNAME I GOT WAS,
BECAUSE YOUR FINAL TOUCHES AREN'T ALWAYS GOOD ENOUGH.
BECAUSE EVERYTHING YOU DO IS HALF-ASSED.
prince half-ass.
PAT
FORGET ABOUT IT MIKI.
KNOWING YOU,

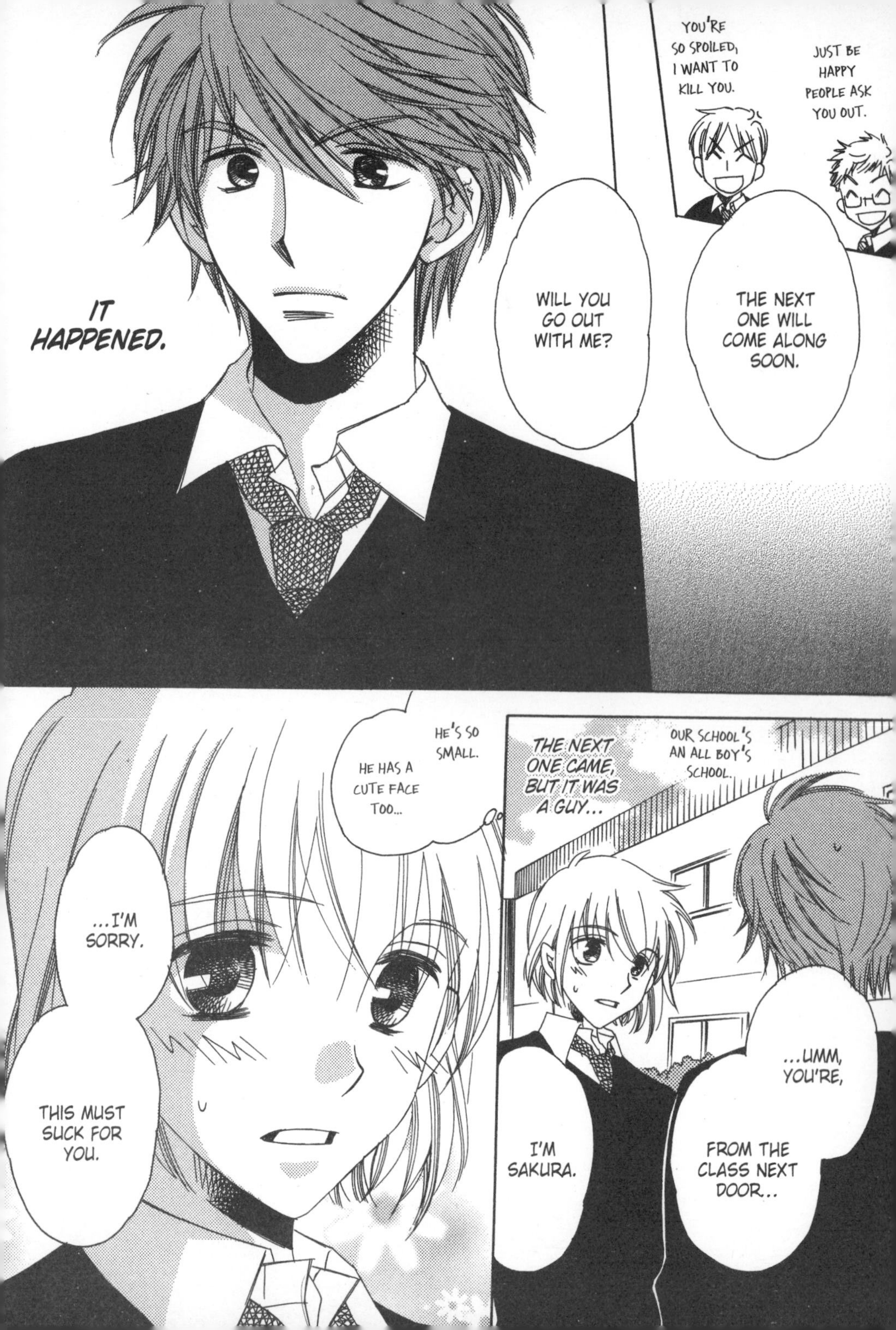
JUST BE HAPPY PEOPLE ASK YOU OUT.
YOU'RE SO SPOILED, I WANT TO KILL YOU.
THE NEXT ONE WILL COME ALONG SOON.
WILL YOU GO OUT WITH ME?
IT HAPPENED.
OUR SCHOOL'S AN ALL BOY'S SCHOOL.
THE NEXT ONE CAME, BUT IT WAS A GUY...
...UMM, YOU'RE,
FROM THE CLASS NEXT DOOR...
I'M SAKURA.
HE'S SO SMALL.
HE HAS A CUTE FACE TOO...
...I'M SORRY.
THIS MUST SUCK FOR YOU.

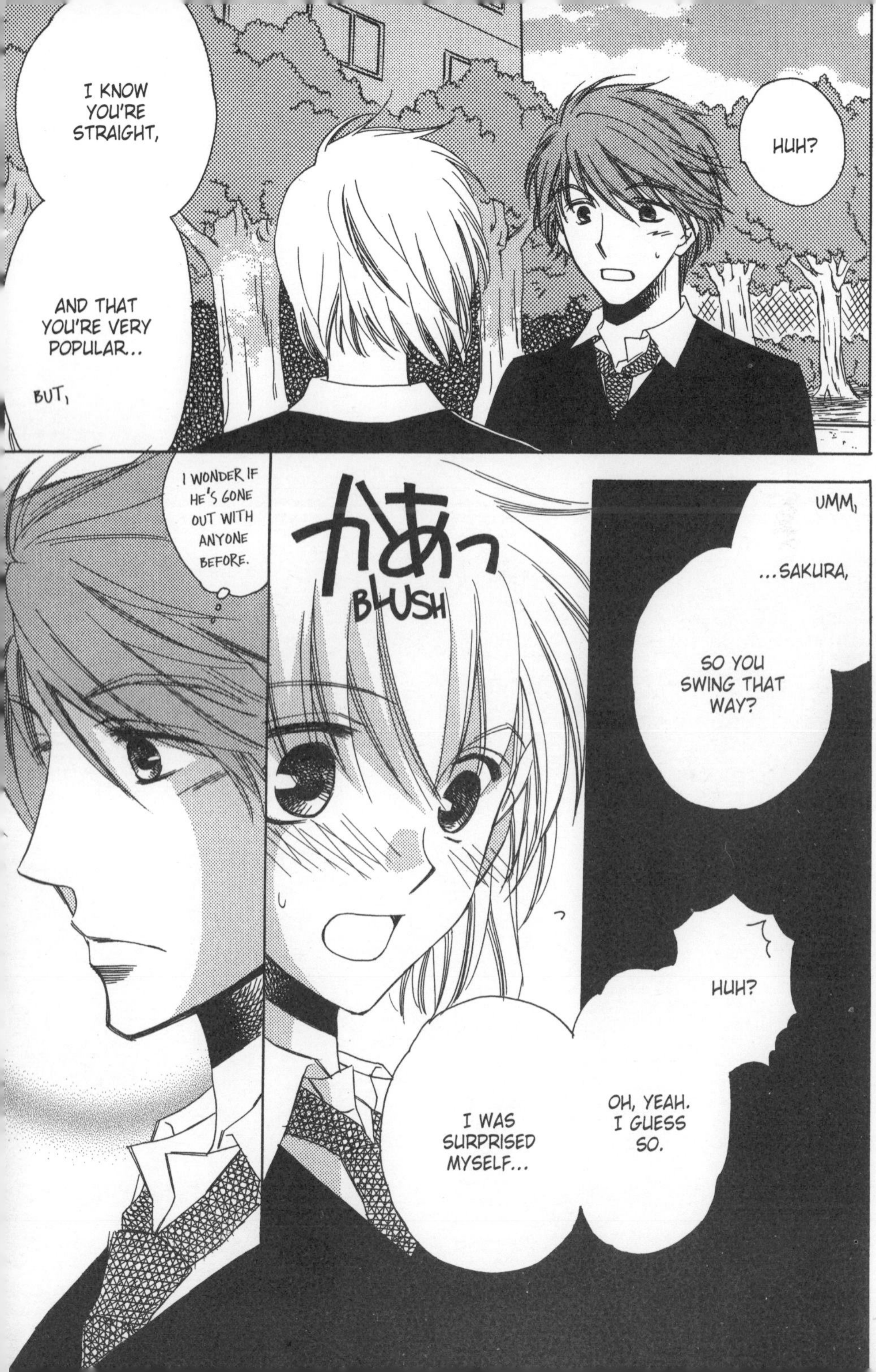
I KNOW YOU'RE STRAIGHT,
AND THAT YOU'RE VERY POPULAR...
BUT,
HUH?
UMM,
...SAKURA,
SO YOU SWING THAT WAY?
HUH?
OH, YEAH. I GUESS SO.
I WAS SURPRISED MYSELF...
かあっ
BLUSH
I WONDER IF HE'S GONE OUT WITH ANYONE BEFORE.

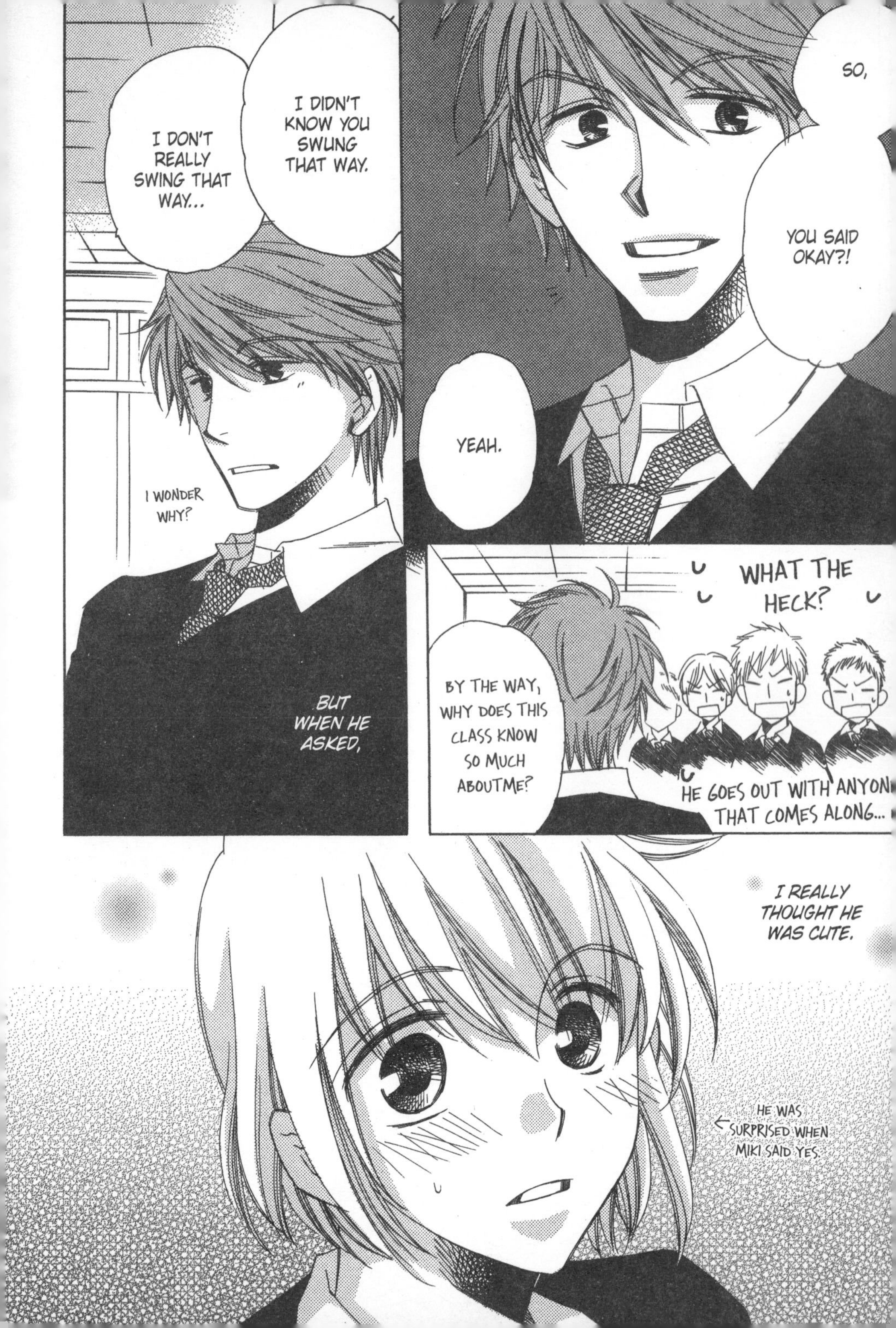
SO,
YOU SAID OKAY?!
YEAH.
WHAT THE HECK?
HE GOES OUT WITH ANYON
THAT COMES ALONG...
BY THE WAY, WHY DOES THIS CLASS KNOW SO MUCH ABOUTME?
I DIDN'T KNOW YOU SWUNG THAT WAY.
I DON'T REALLY SWING THAT WAY...
I WONDER WHY?
BUT WHEN HE ASKED,
I REALLY THOUGHT HE WAS CUTE.
HE WAS SURPRISED WHEN MIKI SAID YES.

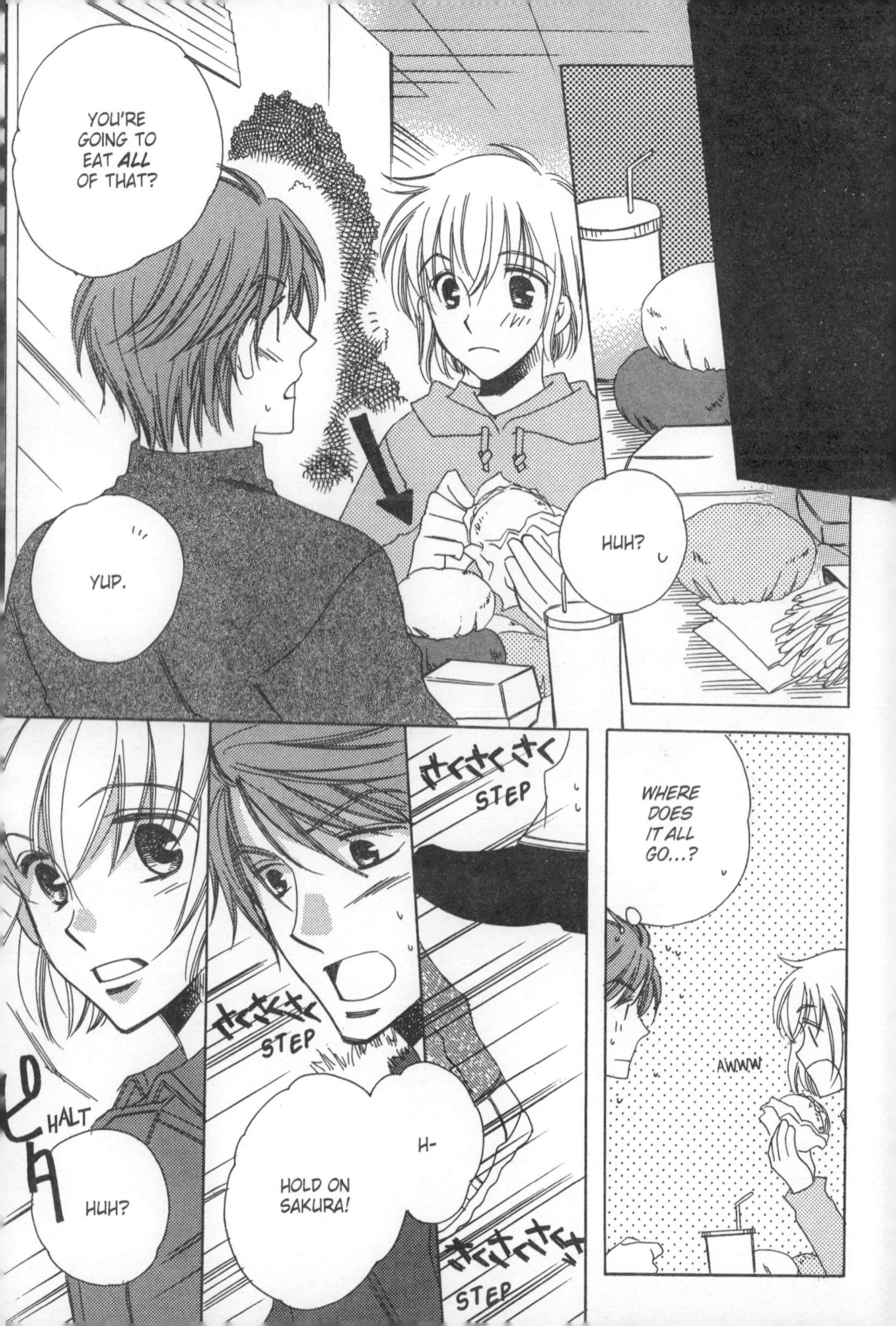
YOU'RE GOING TO EAT ALL OF THAT?
HUH?
YUP.
WHERE DOES IT ALL GO...?
AWWW
STEP
STEP
H-
HOLD ON SAKURA!
STEP
HALT
HUH?

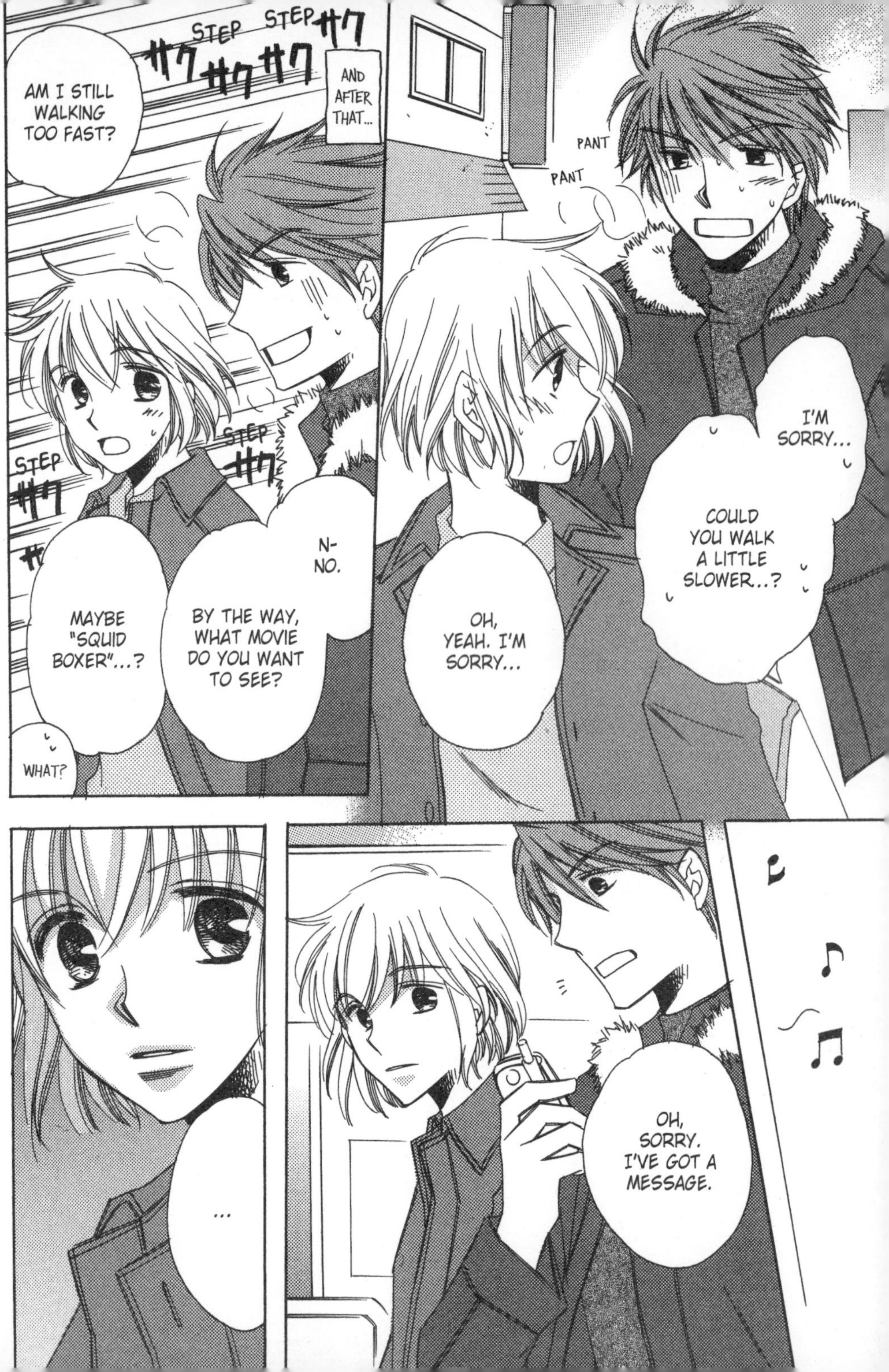
PANT
PANT
I'M SORRY...
COULD YOU WALK A LITTLE SLOWER...?
OH, YEAH. I'M SORRY...
AND AFTER THAT...
STEP STEP
サクサクサク
AM I STILL WALKING TOO FAST?
N-NO.
BY THE WAY, WHAT MOVIE DO YOU WANT TO SEE?
STEP
サク
STEP
サク
MAYBE "SQUID BOXER"...?
WHAT?
OH, SORRY. I'VE GOT A MESSAGE.
...

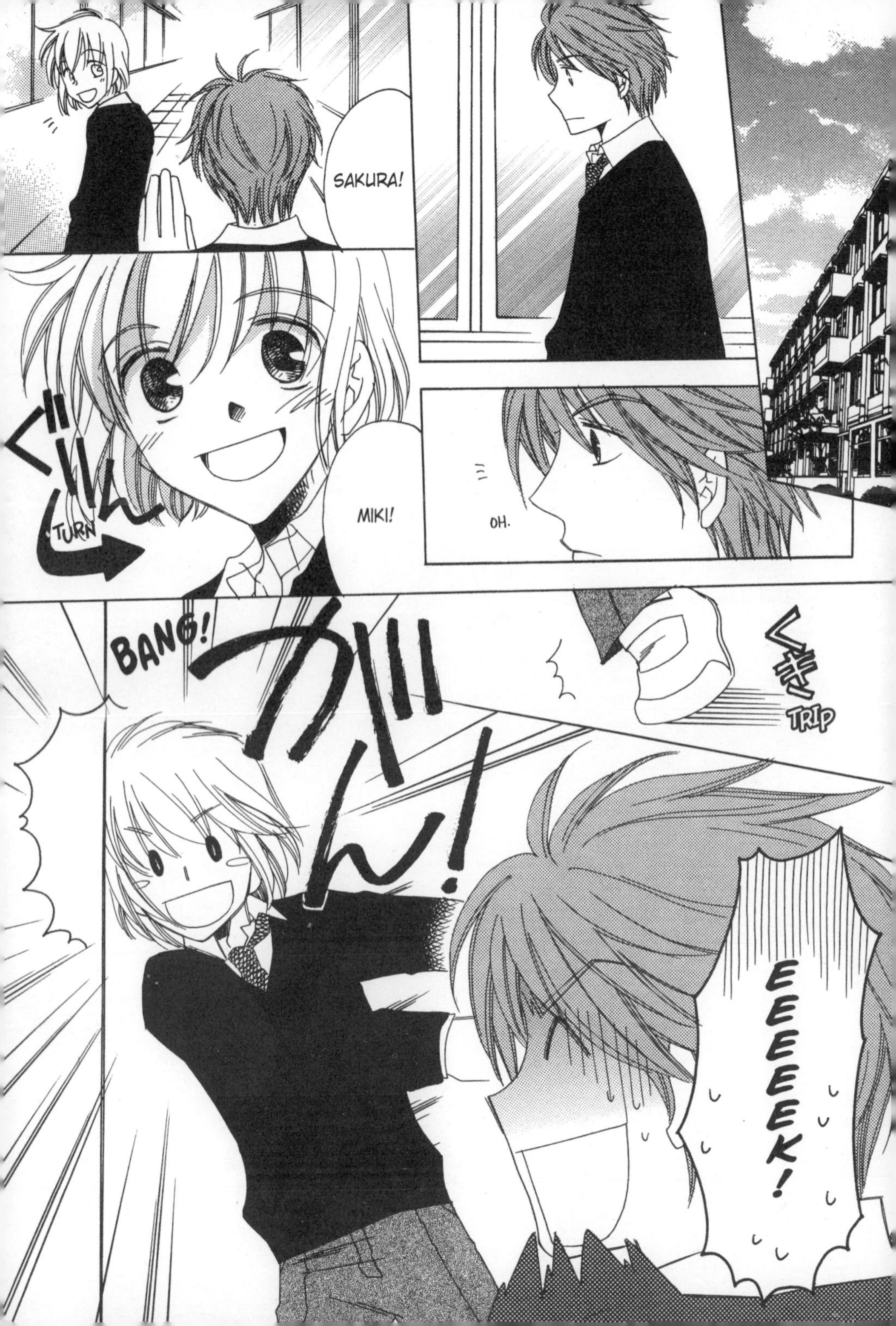

SAKURA!
OH.
MIKI!
ぐりん
TURN
くき
TRIP
BANG!
がーん!
EEEEEEK!

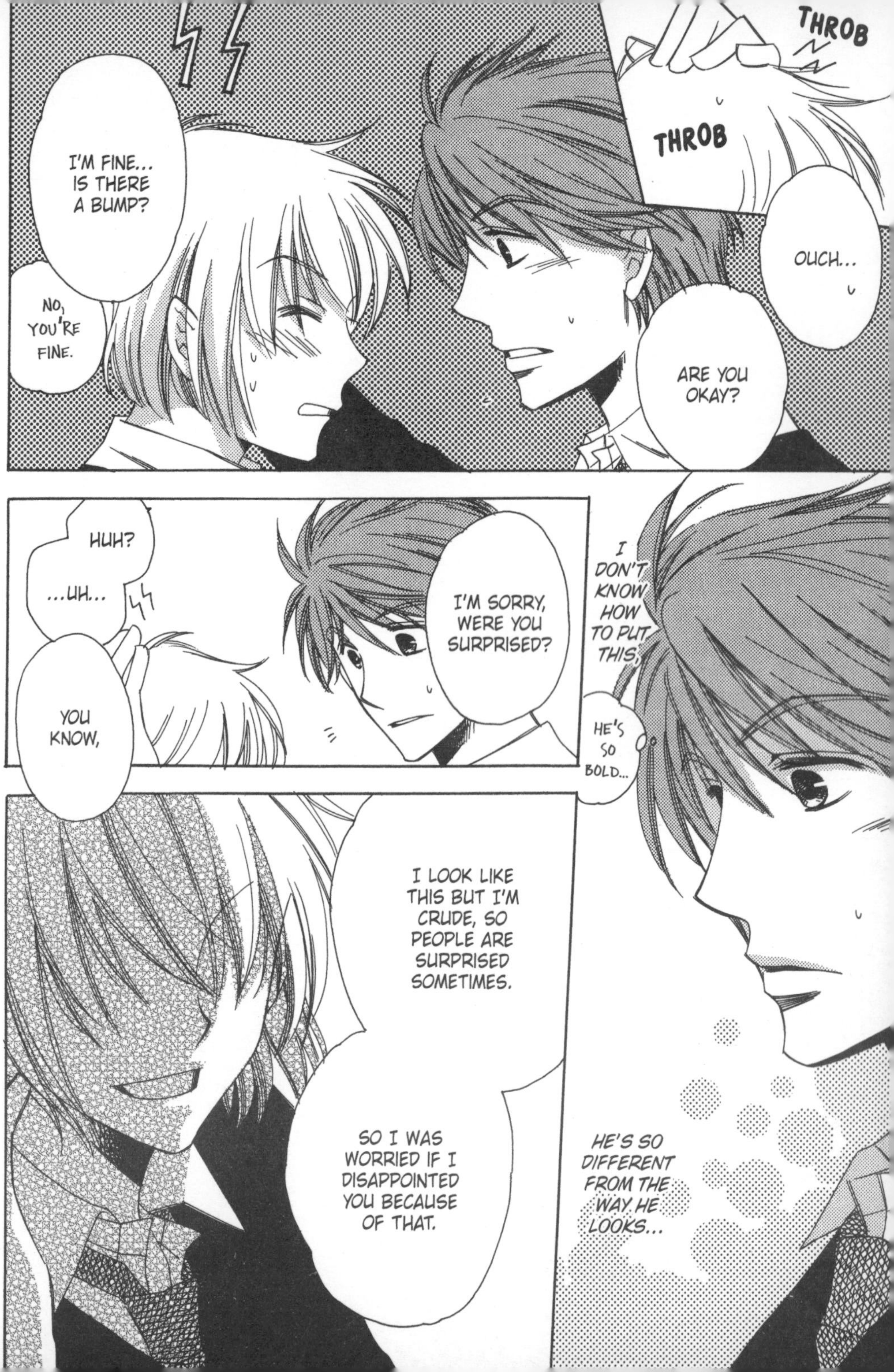
THROB
THROB
OUCH...
ARE YOU OKAY?
I'M FINE... IS THERE A BUMP?
NO, YOU'RE FINE.
I DON'T KNOW HOW TO PUT THIS,
HE'S SO BOLD...
HE'S SO DIFFERENT FROM THE WAY HE LOOKS...
I'M SORRY, WERE YOU SURPRISED?
HUH?
...UH...
YOU KNOW,
I LOOK LIKE THIS BUT I'M CRUDE, SO PEOPLE ARE SURPRISED SOMETIMES.
SO I WAS WORRIED IF I DISAPPOINTED YOU BECAUSE OF THAT.

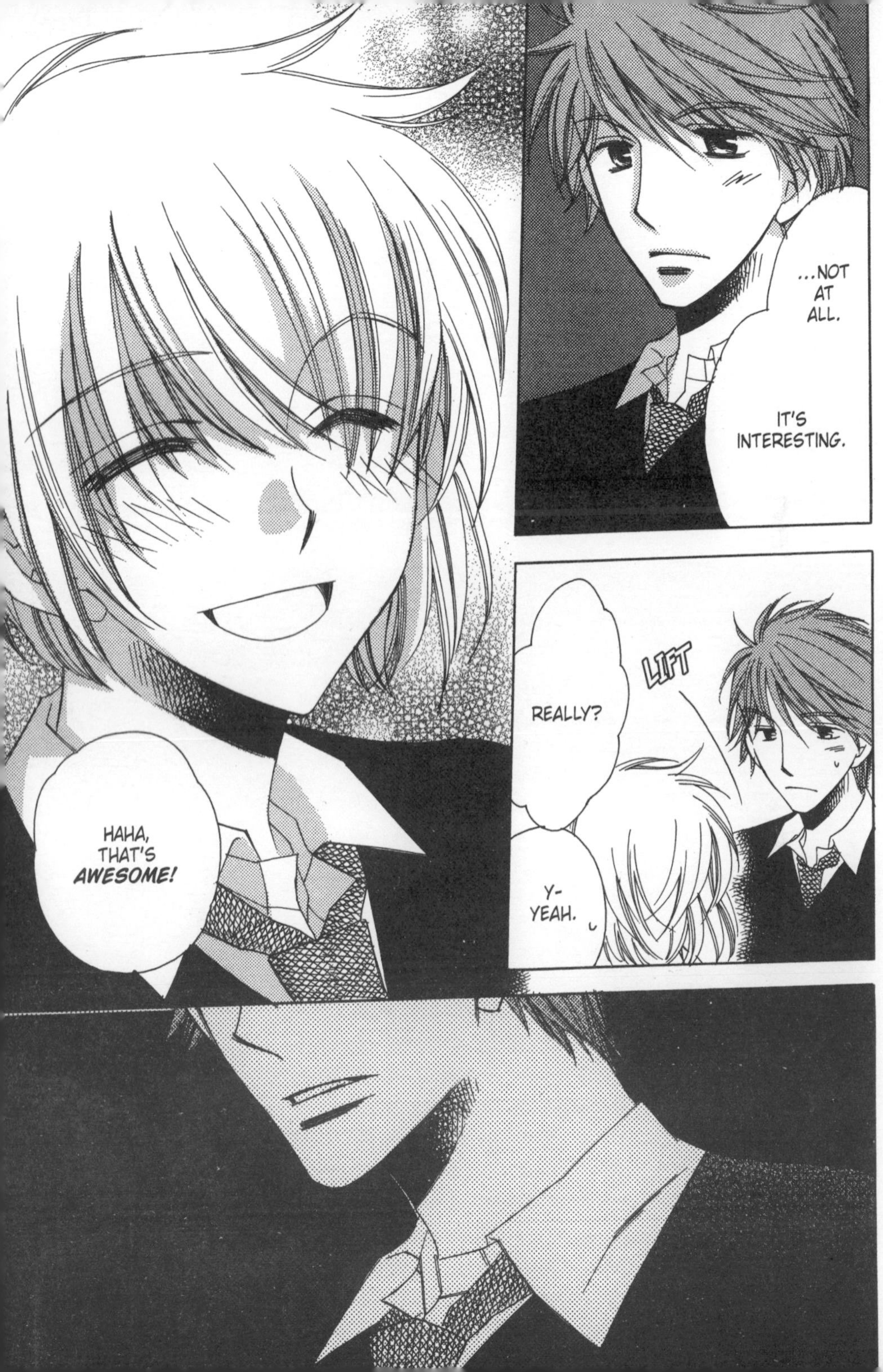
...NOT AT ALL.
IT'S INTERESTING.
LIFT
REALLY?
Y-YEAH.
HAHA, THAT'S **AWESOME!**

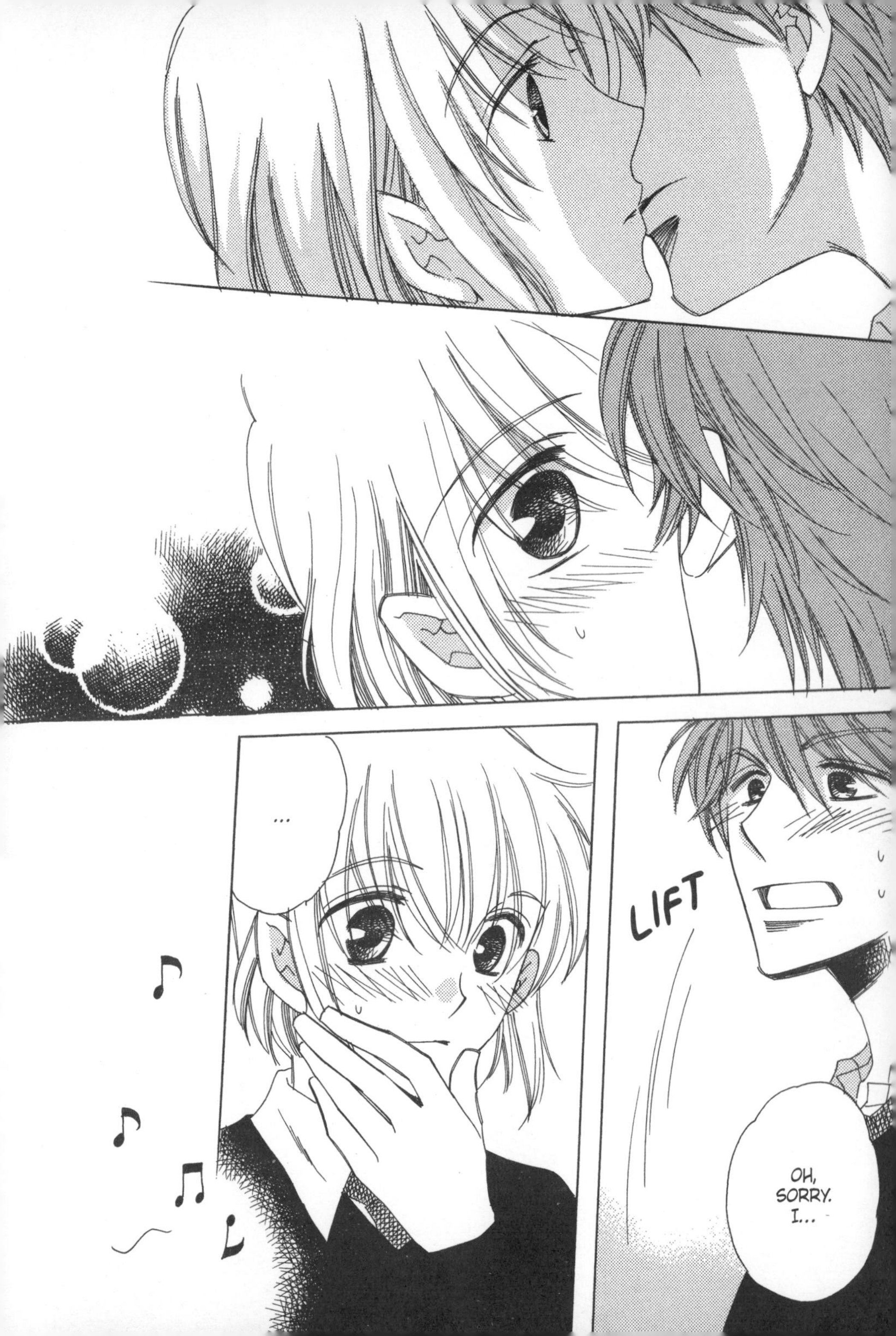
LIFT
OH, SORRY. I...
...

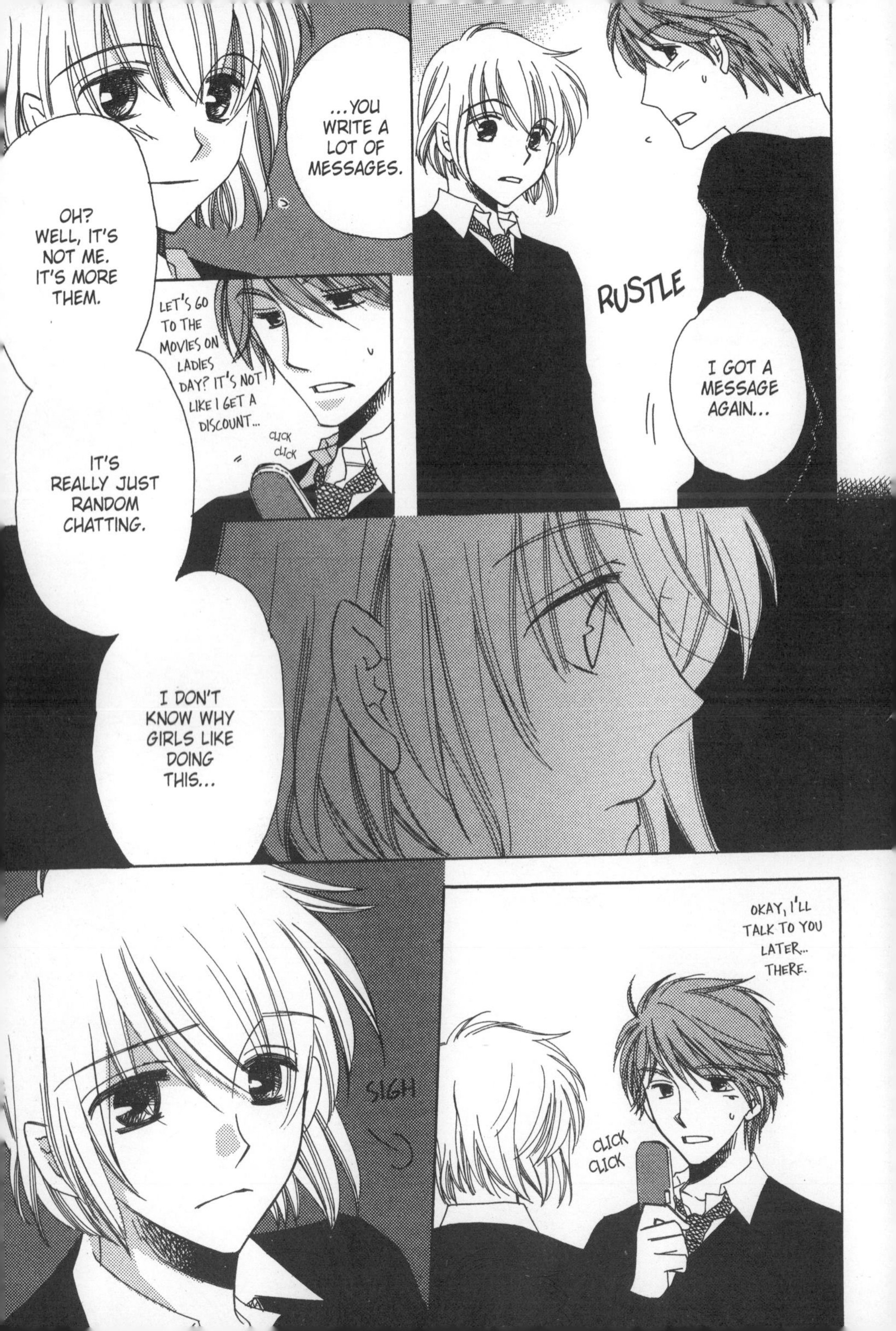
RUSTLE
I GOT A MESSAGE AGAIN...
...YOU WRITE A LOT OF MESSAGES.
OH? WELL, IT'S NOT ME. IT'S MORE THEM.
LET'S GO TO THE MOVIES ON LADIES DAY? IT'S NOT LIKE I GET A DISCOUNT...
CLICK CLICK
IT'S REALLY JUST RANDOM CHATTING.
I DON'T KNOW WHY GIRLS LIKE DOING THIS...
OKAY, I'LL TALK TO YOU LATER... THERE.
CLICK CLICK
SIGH

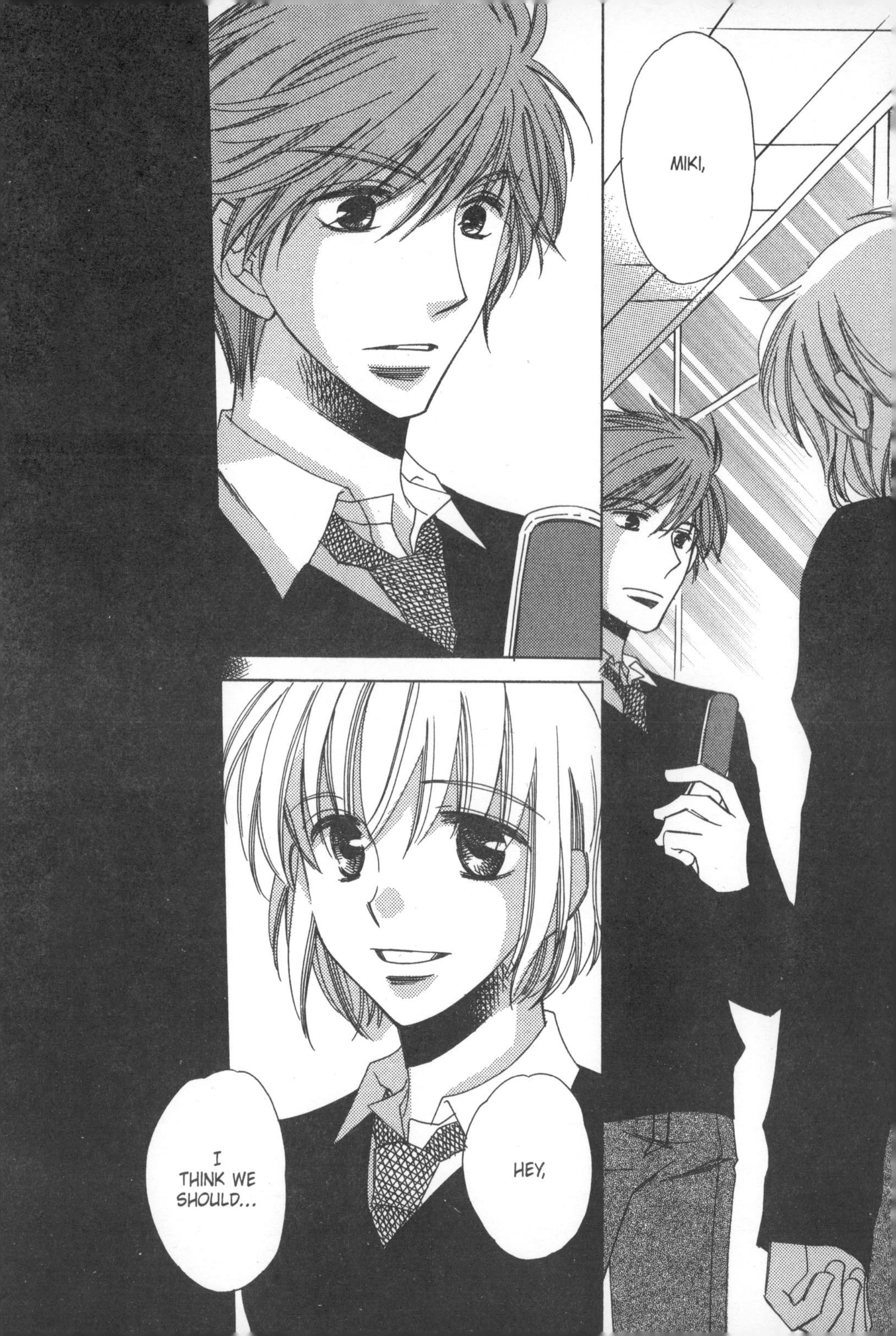
MIKI,
HEY,
I THINK WE SHOULD...

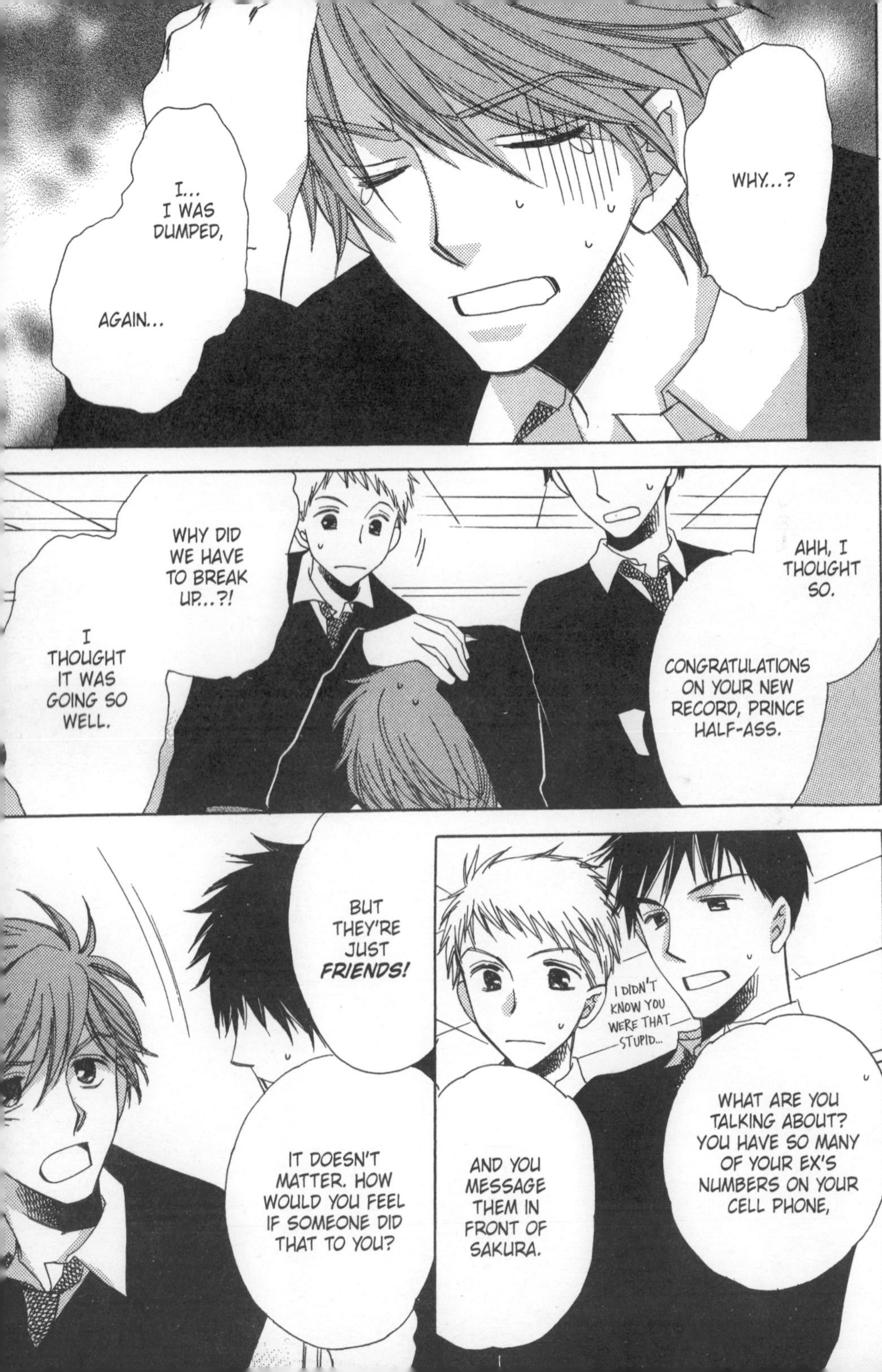
WHY...?
I... I WAS DUMPED,
AGAIN...
AHH, I THOUGHT SO.
CONGRATULATIONS ON YOUR NEW RECORD, PRINCE HALF-ASS.
WHY DID WE HAVE TO BREAK UP...?!
I THOUGHT IT WAS GOING SO WELL.
I DIDN'T KNOW YOU WERE THAT STUPID...
WHAT ARE YOU TALKING ABOUT? YOU HAVE SO MANY OF YOUR EX'S NUMBERS ON YOUR CELL PHONE,
AND YOU MESSAGE THEM IN FRONT OF SAKURA.
BUT THEY'RE JUST FRIENDS!
IT DOESN'T MATTER. HOW WOULD YOU FEEL IF SOMEONE DID THAT TO YOU?

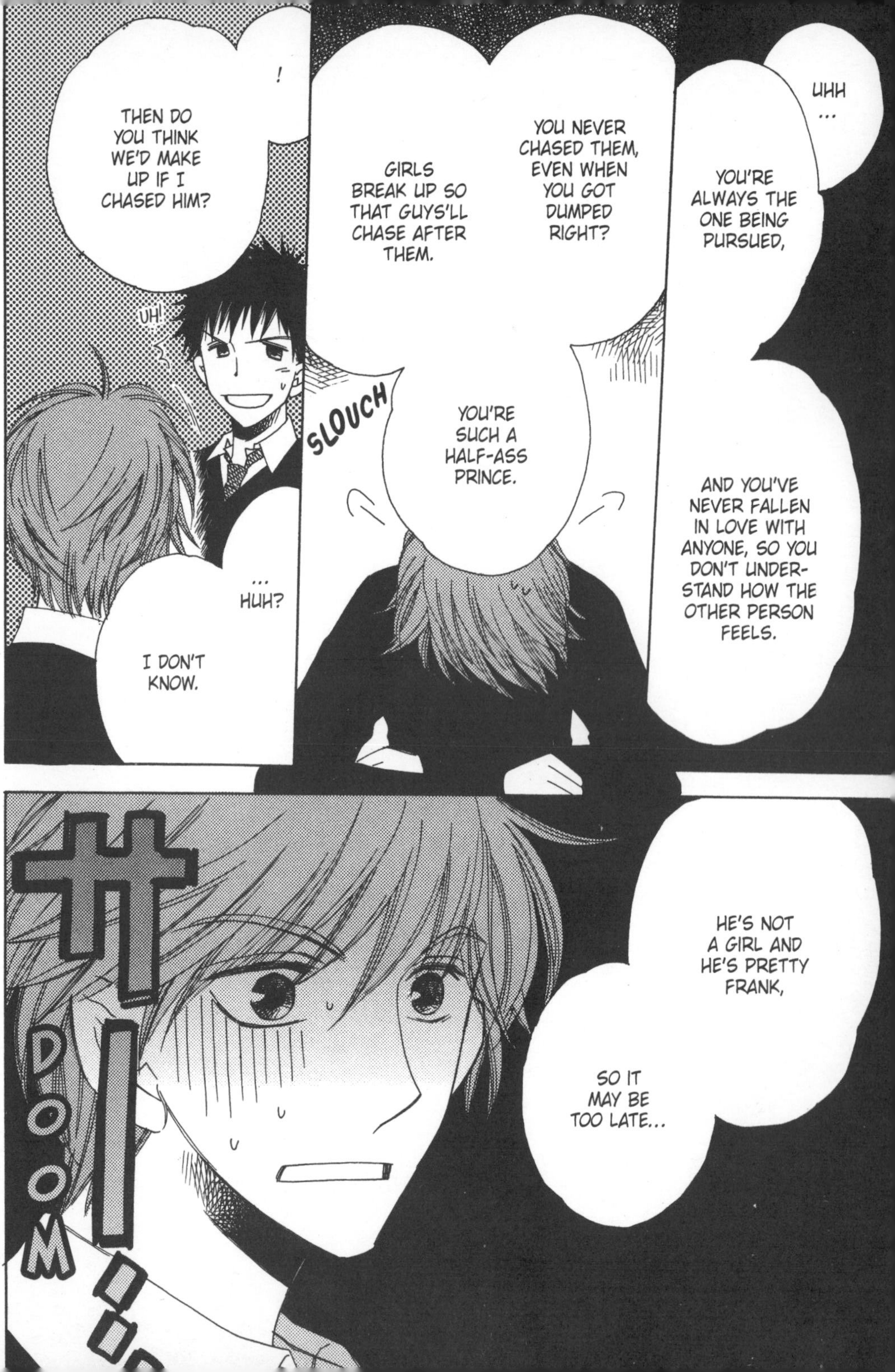
UHH ...
YOU'RE ALWAYS THE ONE BEING PURSUED,
AND YOU'VE NEVER FALLEN IN LOVE WITH ANYONE, SO YOU DON'T UNDER-STAND HOW THE OTHER PERSON FEELS.
YOU NEVER CHASED THEM, EVEN WHEN YOU GOT DUMPED RIGHT?
GIRLS BREAK UP SO THAT GUYS'LL CHASE AFTER THEM.
SLOUCH
YOU'RE SUCH A HALF-ASS PRINCE.
!
THEN DO YOU THINK WE'D MAKE UP IF I CHASED HIM?
UH!
... HUH?
I DON'T KNOW.
HE'S NOT A GIRL AND HE'S PRETTY FRANK,
SO IT MAY BE TOO LATE...
DOOM

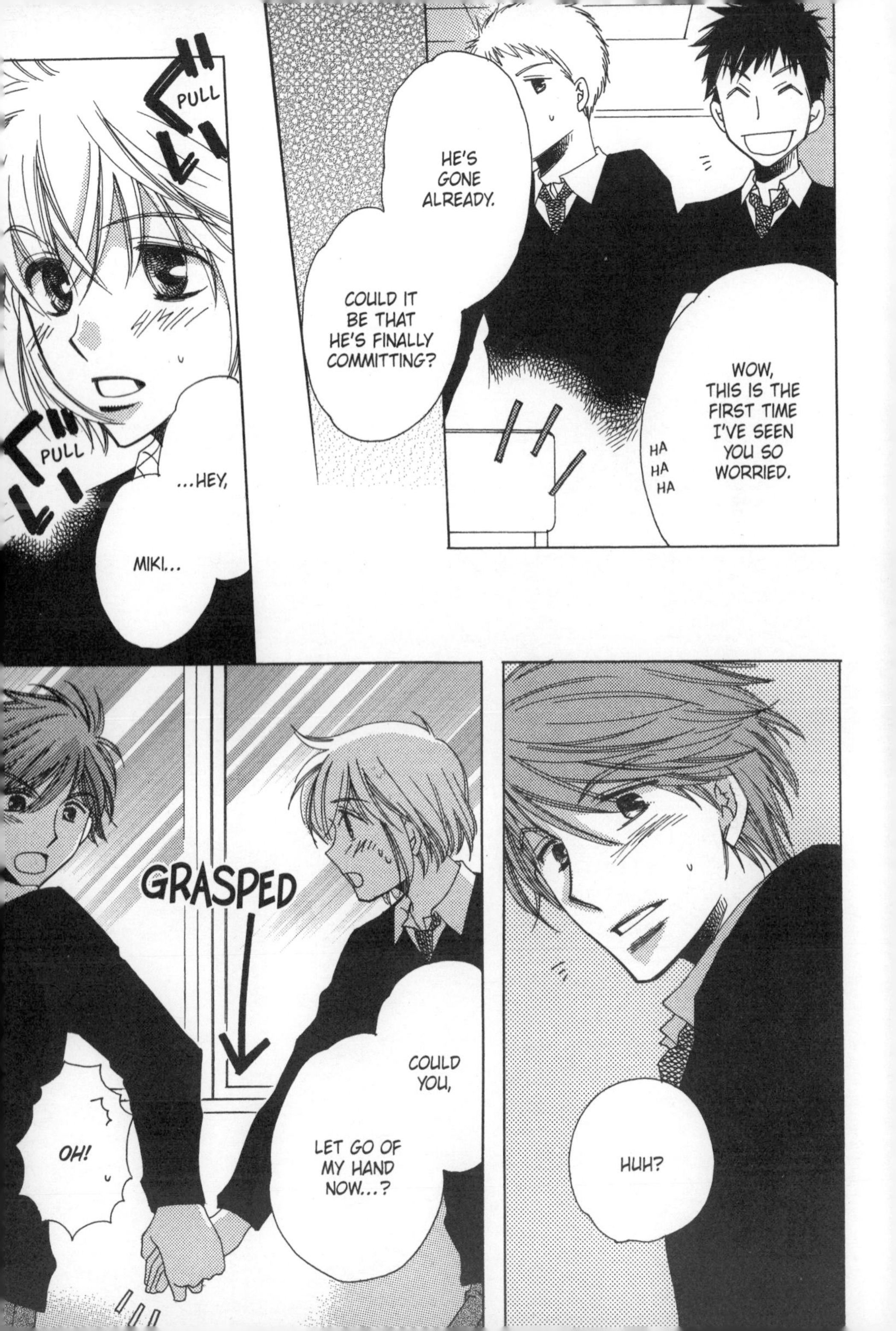
HE'S GONE ALREADY.
COULD IT BE THAT HE'S FINALLY COMMITTING?
WOW, THIS IS THE FIRST TIME I'VE SEEN YOU SO WORRIED.
HA HA HA
PULL
PULL
...HEY,
MIKI...
HUH?
GRASPED
COULD YOU,
LET GO OF MY HAND NOW...?
OH!

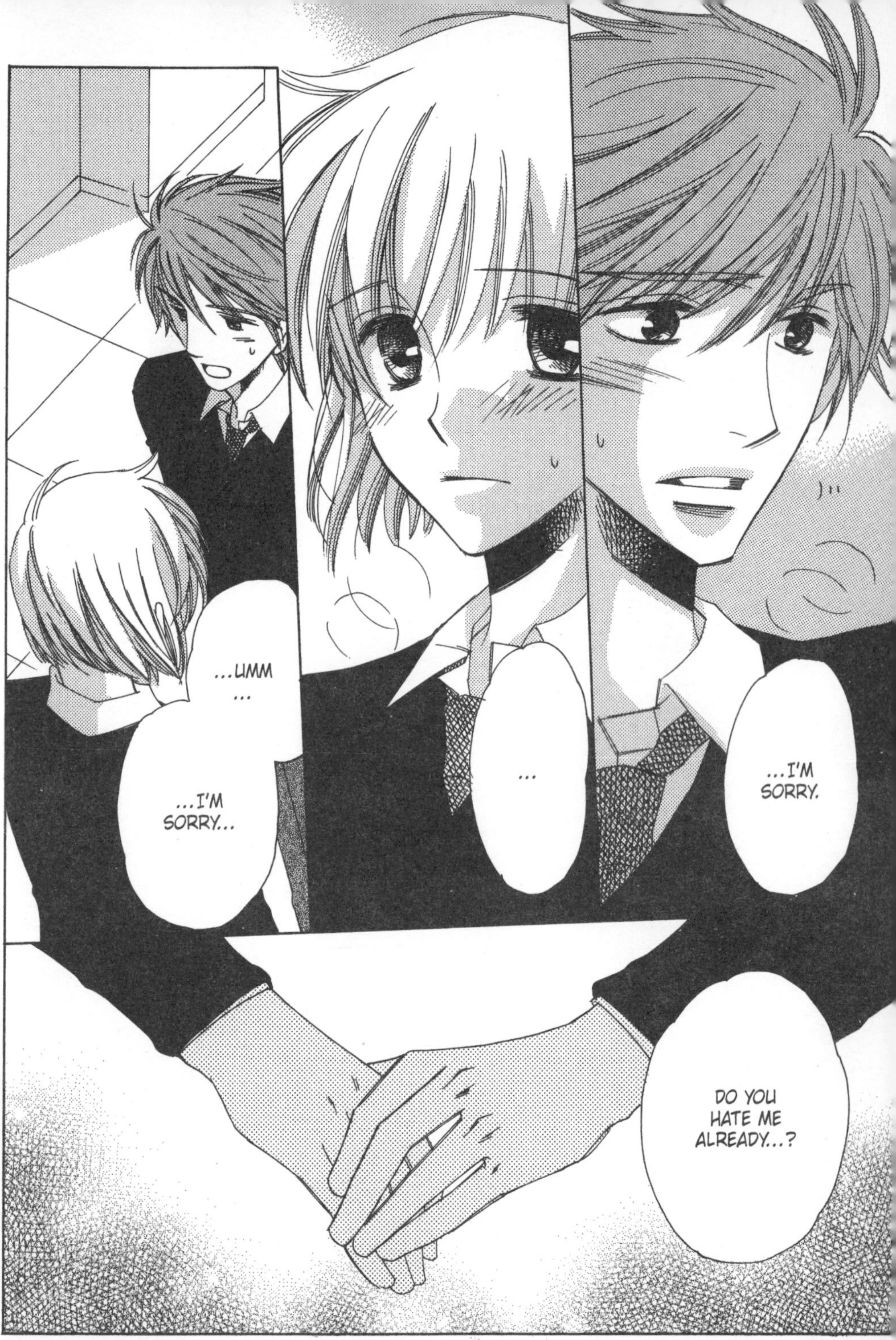
...I'M SORRY.
...
...UMM ...
...I'M SORRY...
DO YOU HATE ME ALREADY...?

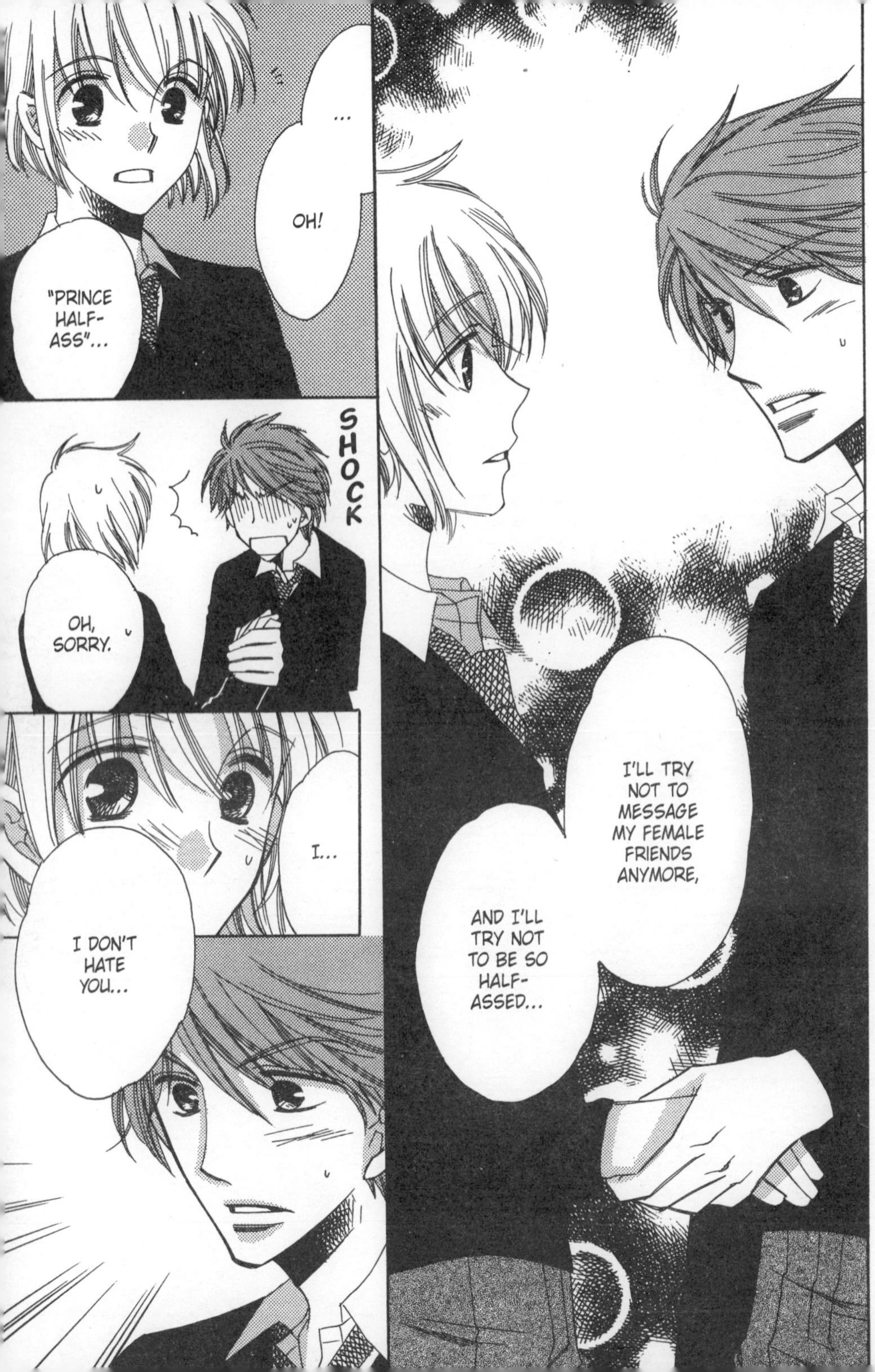
...
OH!
"PRINCE HALF-ASS"...
SHOCK
OH, SORRY.
I...
I DON'T HATE YOU...
I'LL TRY NOT TO MESSAGE MY FEMALE FRIENDS ANYMORE,
AND I'LL TRY NOT TO BE SO HALF-ASSED...

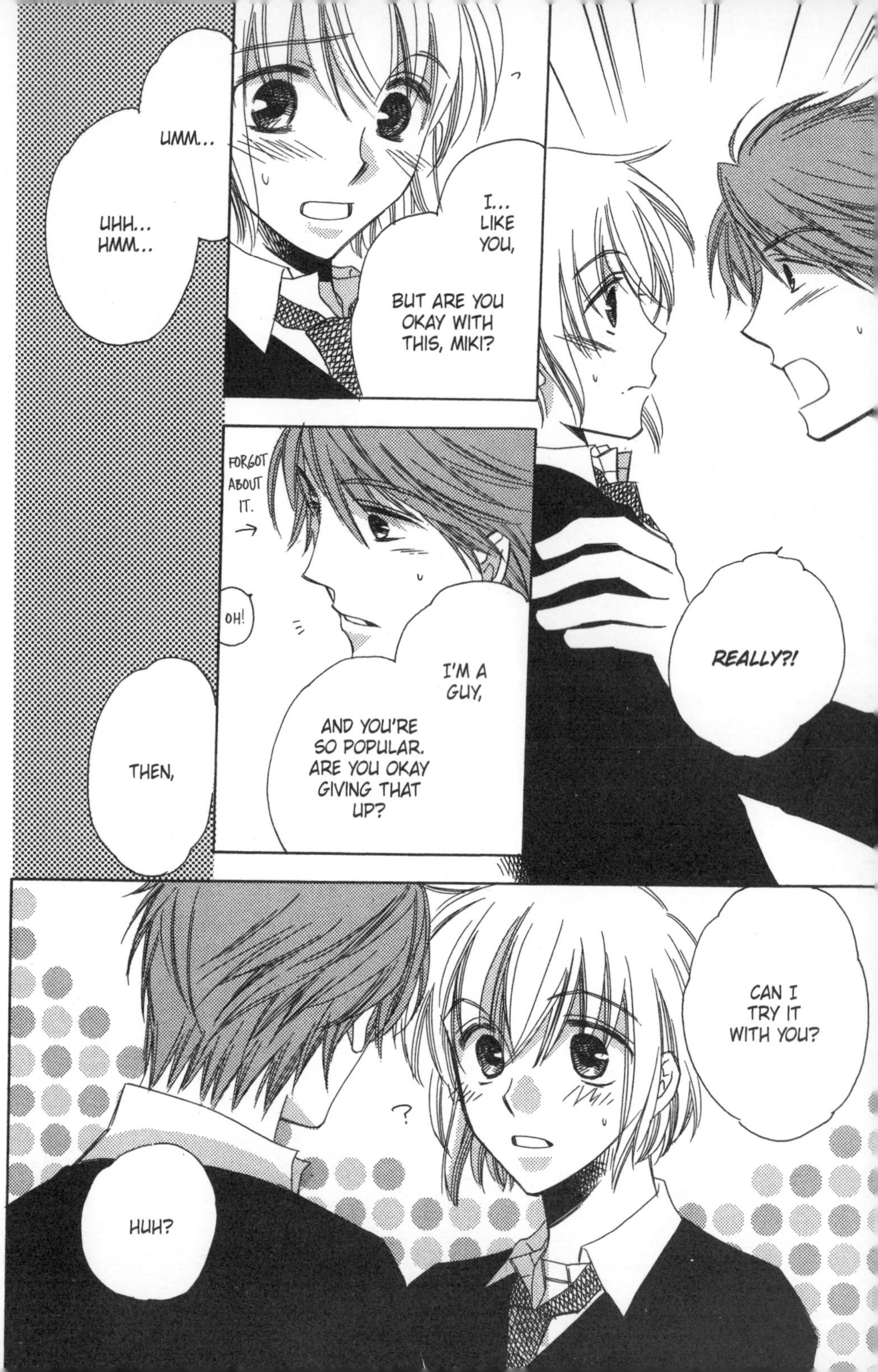
REALLY?!
I... LIKE YOU,
BUT ARE YOU OKAY WITH THIS, MIKI?
FORGOT ABOUT IT. →
OH!
I'M A GUY,
AND YOU'RE SO POPULAR. ARE YOU OKAY GIVING THAT UP?
UMM...
UHH... HMM...
THEN,
CAN I TRY IT WITH YOU?
HUH?

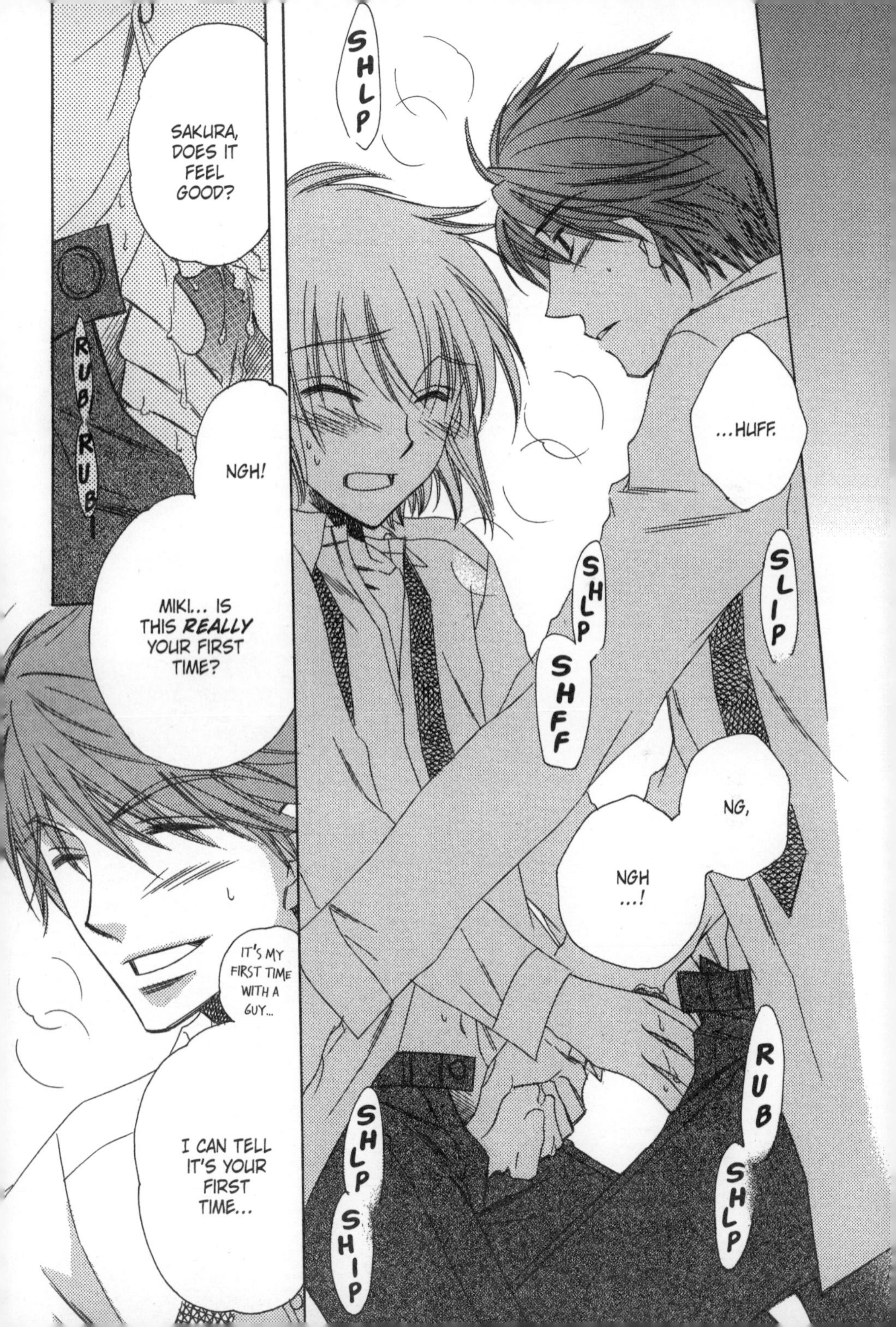
SHLP
...HUFF.
SLIP
SHLP
SHFF
NG,
NGH ...!
RUB
SHLP
SHLP
SHIP
SAKURA, DOES IT FEEL GOOD?
RUB RUB
NGH!
MIKI... IS THIS ***REALLY*** YOUR FIRST TIME?
IT'S MY FIRST TIME WITH A GUY...
I CAN TELL IT'S YOUR FIRST TIME...

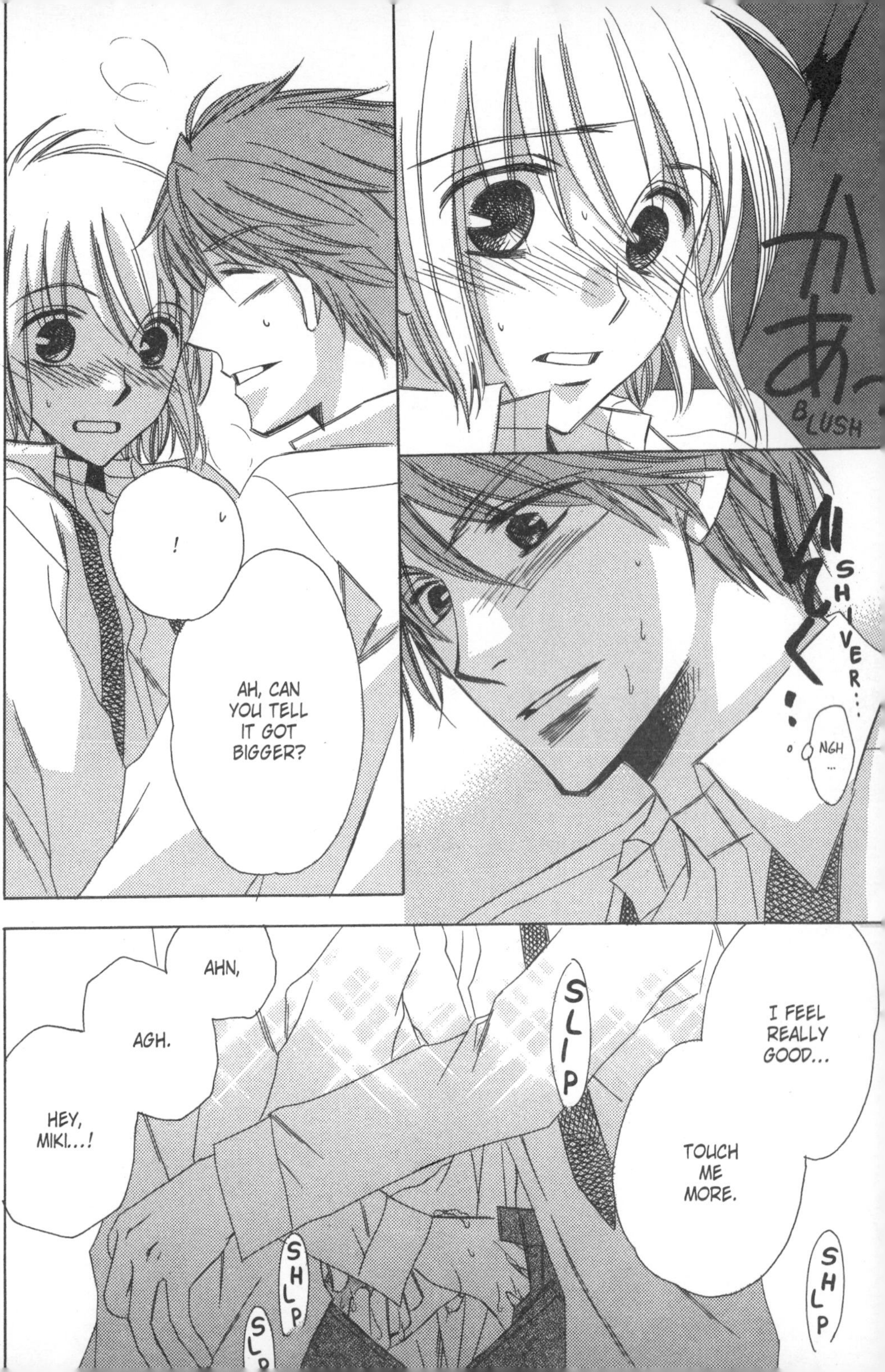
かあっ
BLUSH
SHIVER...
NGH...
!
AH, CAN YOU TELL IT GOT BIGGER?
I FEEL REALLY GOOD...
TOUCH ME MORE.
SHLP
SLIP
AHN,
AGH.
HEY, MIKI...!
SHLP
SLP

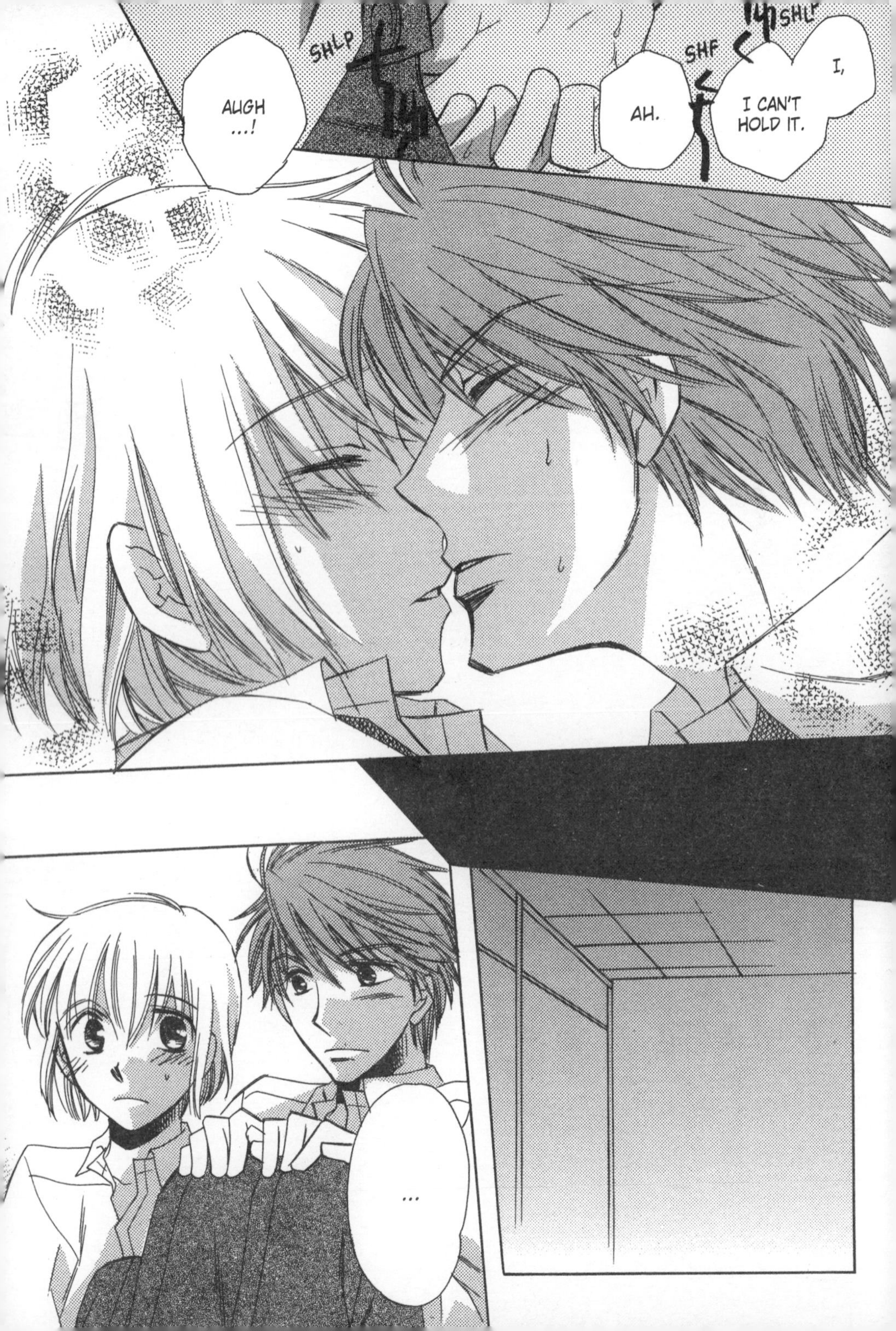
SHLP
I,
I CAN'T HOLD IT.
SHF
AH.
SHLP
AUGH ...!
...

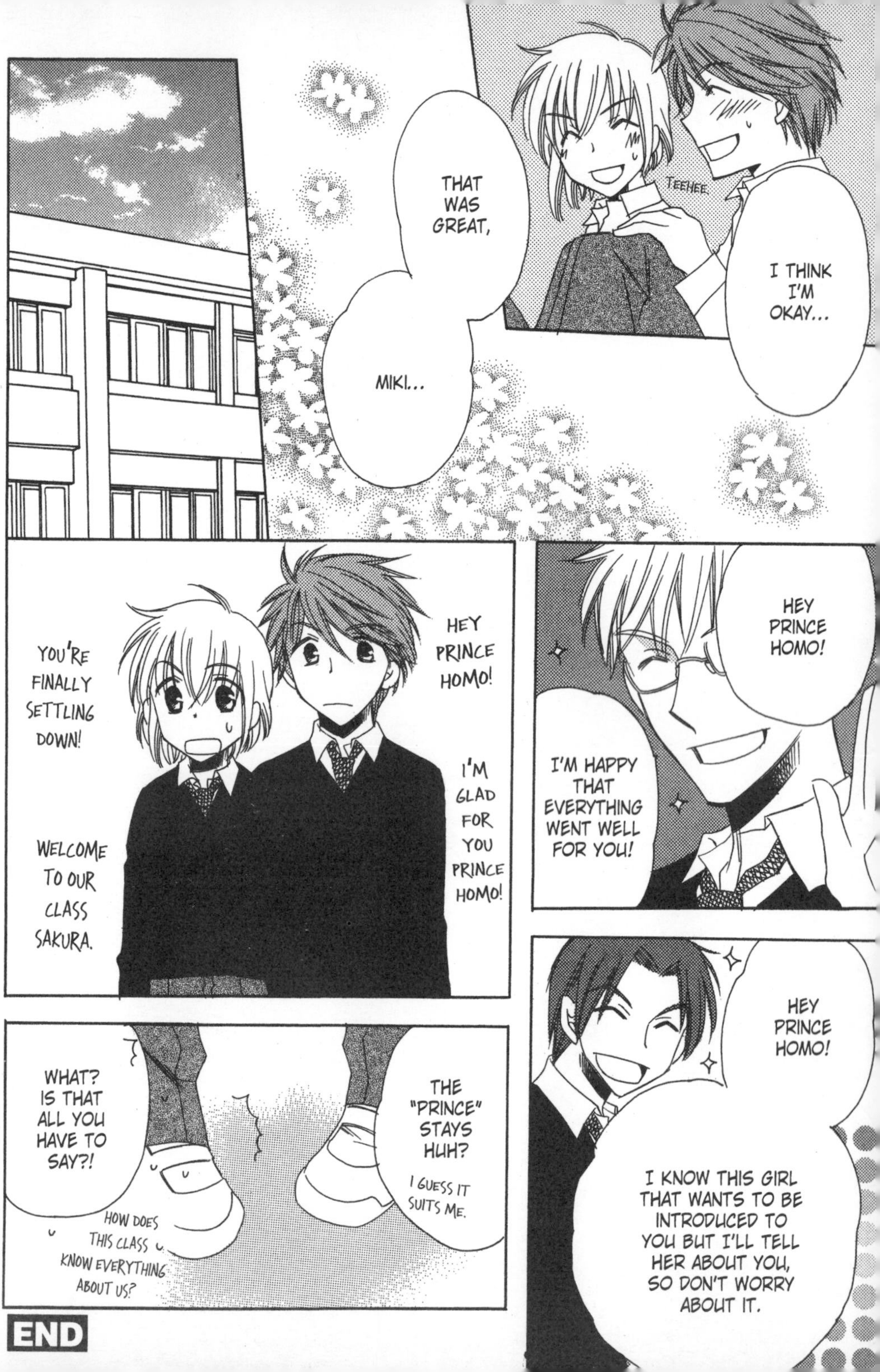
THAT WAS GREAT,
MIKI...
TEEHEE
I THINK I'M OKAY...
HEY PRINCE HOMO!
I'M HAPPY THAT EVERYTHING WENT WELL FOR YOU!
HEY PRINCE HOMO!
I'M GLAD FOR YOU PRINCE HOMO!
YOU'RE FINALLY SETTLING DOWN!
WELCOME TO OUR CLASS SAKURA.
HEY PRINCE HOMO!
I KNOW THIS GIRL THAT WANTS TO BE INTRODUCED TO YOU BUT I'LL TELL HER ABOUT YOU, SO DON'T WORRY ABOUT IT.
THE "PRINCE" STAYS HUH?
I GUESS IT SUITS ME.
WHAT? IS THAT ALL YOU HAVE TO SAY?!
HOW DOES THIS CLASS KNOW EVERYTHING ABOUT US?

END

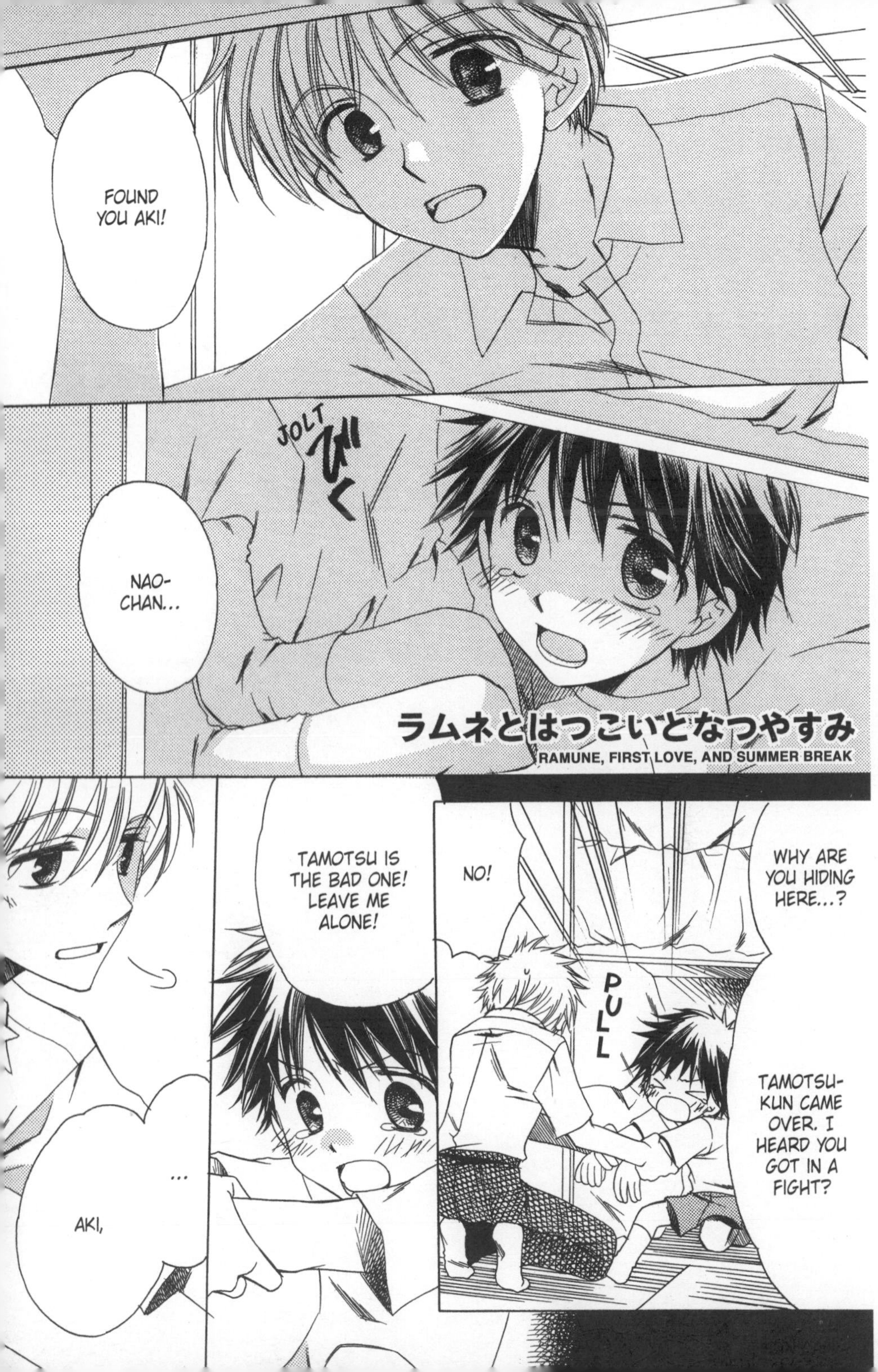
FOUND YOU AKI!
JOLT
びく
NAO-CHAN...
ラムネとはつこいとなつやすみ
RAMUNE, FIRST LOVE, AND SUMMER BREAK
WHY ARE YOU HIDING HERE...?
TAMOTSU-KUN CAME OVER. I HEARD YOU GOT IN A FIGHT?
PULL
NO!
TAMOTSU IS THE BAD ONE! LEAVE ME ALONE!
...
AKI,

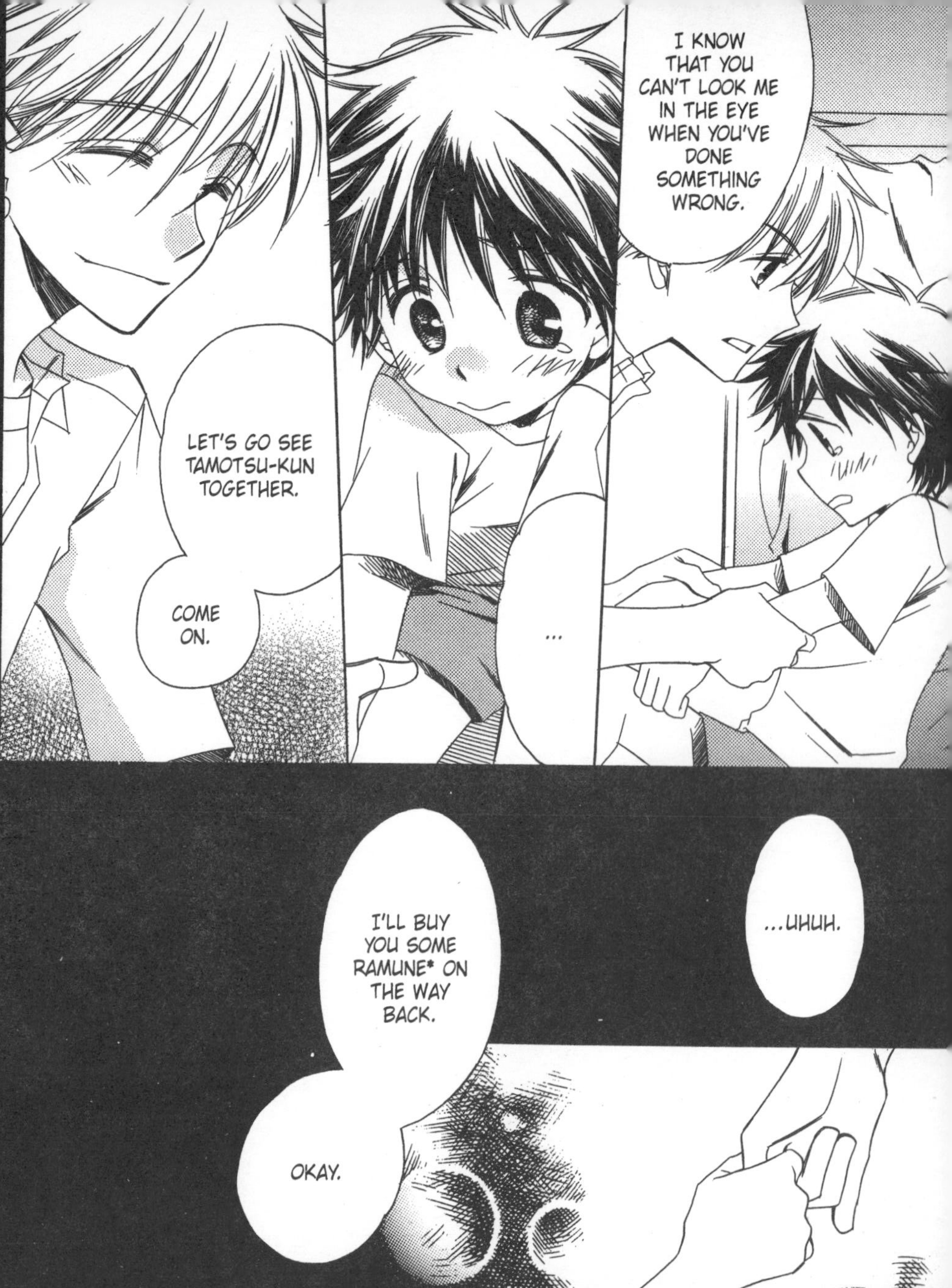
I KNOW THAT YOU CAN'T LOOK ME IN THE EYE WHEN YOU'VE DONE SOMETHING WRONG.
...
LET'S GO SEE TAMOTSU-KUN TOGETHER.
COME ON.
...UHUH.
I'LL BUY YOU SOME RAMUNE* ON THE WAY BACK.
OKAY.

*NOTE: RAMUNE = A CARBONATED SOFT DRINK.

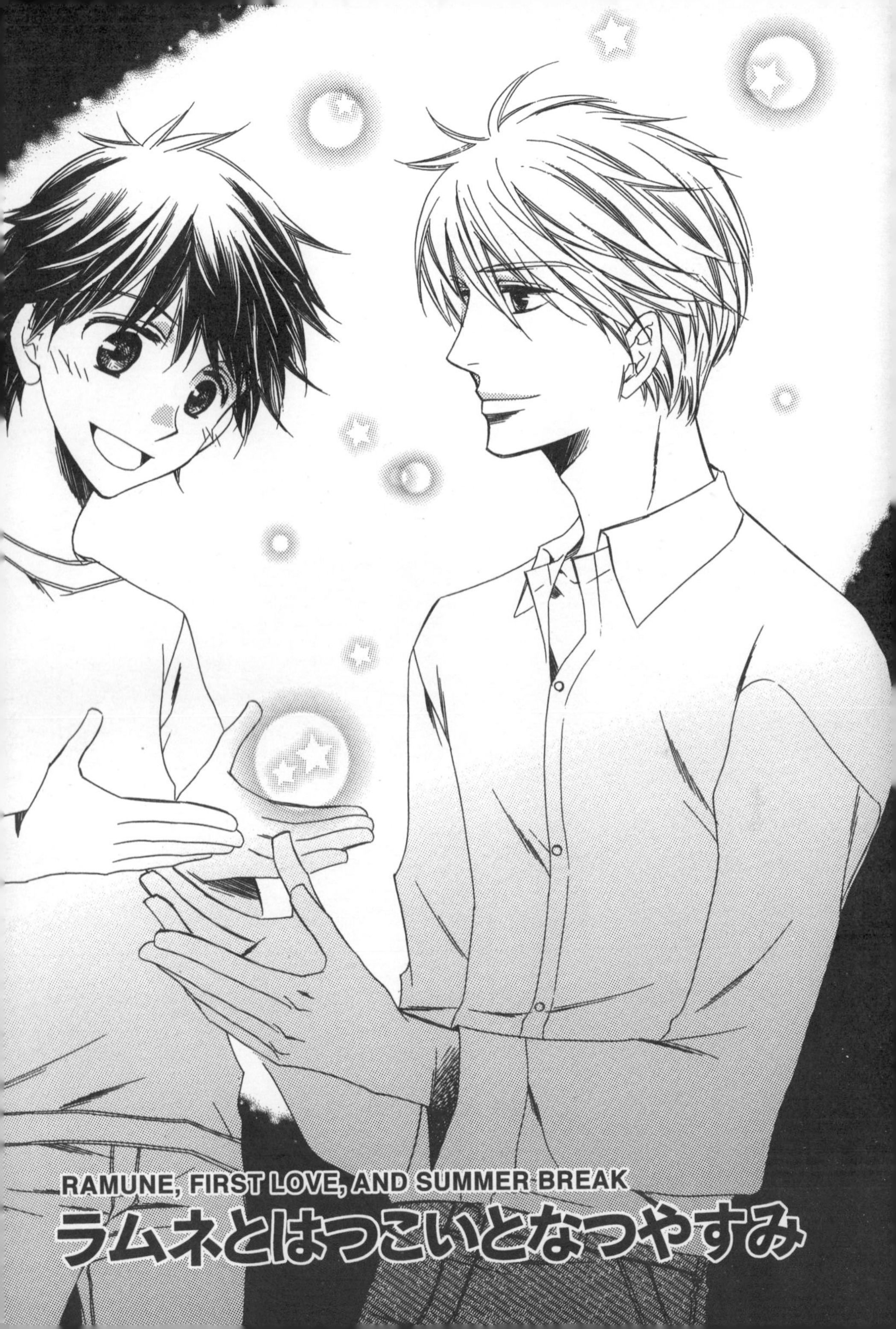

RAMUNE, FIRST LOVE, AND SUMMER BREAK
ラムネとはつこいとなつやすみ

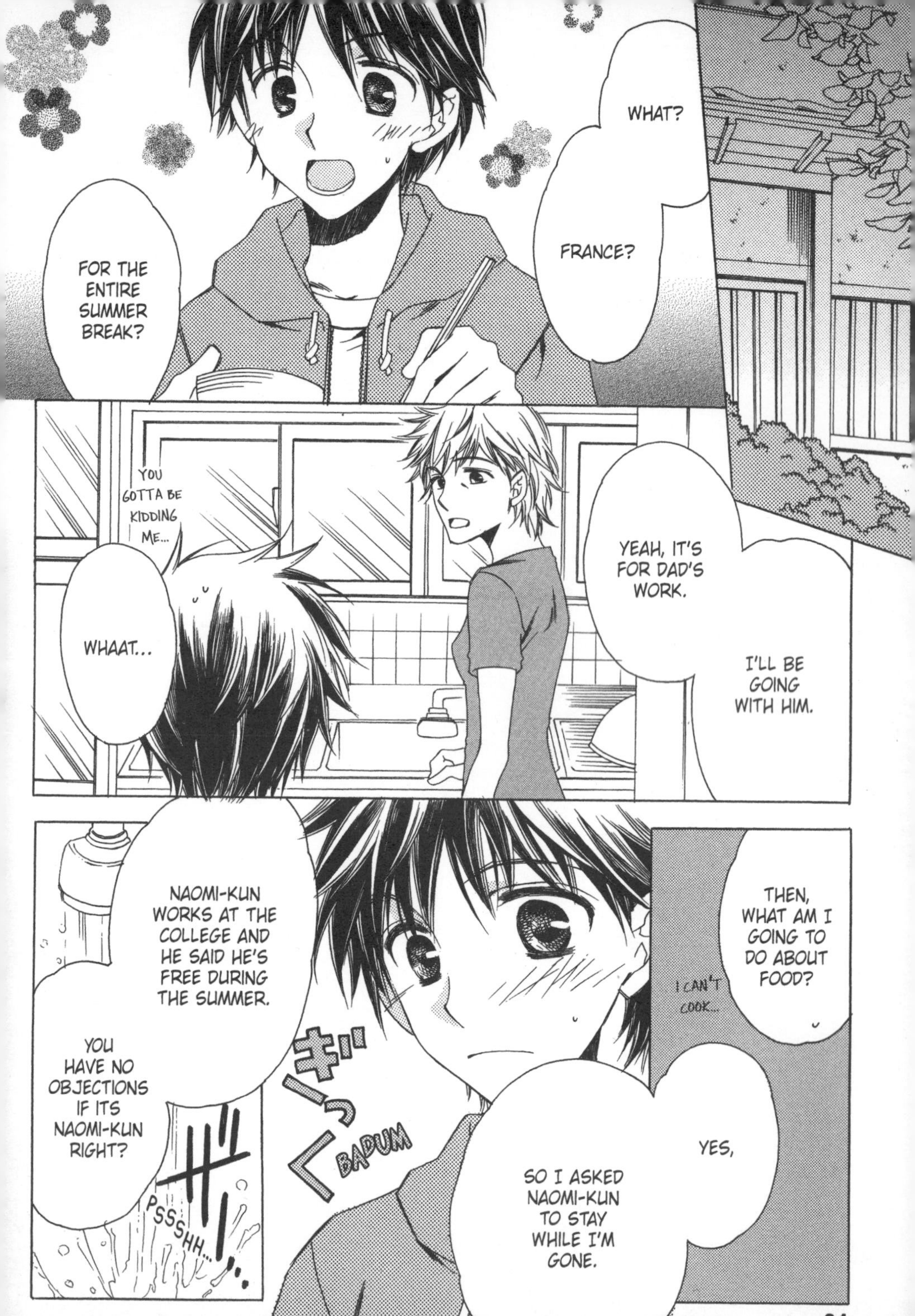
WHAT?
FRANCE?
FOR THE ENTIRE SUMMER BREAK?
YEAH, IT'S FOR DAD'S WORK.
I'LL BE GOING WITH HIM.
YOU GOTTA BE KIDDING ME...
WHAAT...
THEN, WHAT AM I GOING TO DO ABOUT FOOD?
I CAN'T COOK...
YES,
SO I ASKED NAOMI-KUN TO STAY WHILE I'M GONE.
NAOMI-KUN WORKS AT THE COLLEGE AND HE SAID HE'S FREE DURING THE SUMMER.
YOU HAVE NO OBJECTIONS IF ITS NAOMI-KUN RIGHT?
BADUM
PSSSHH...

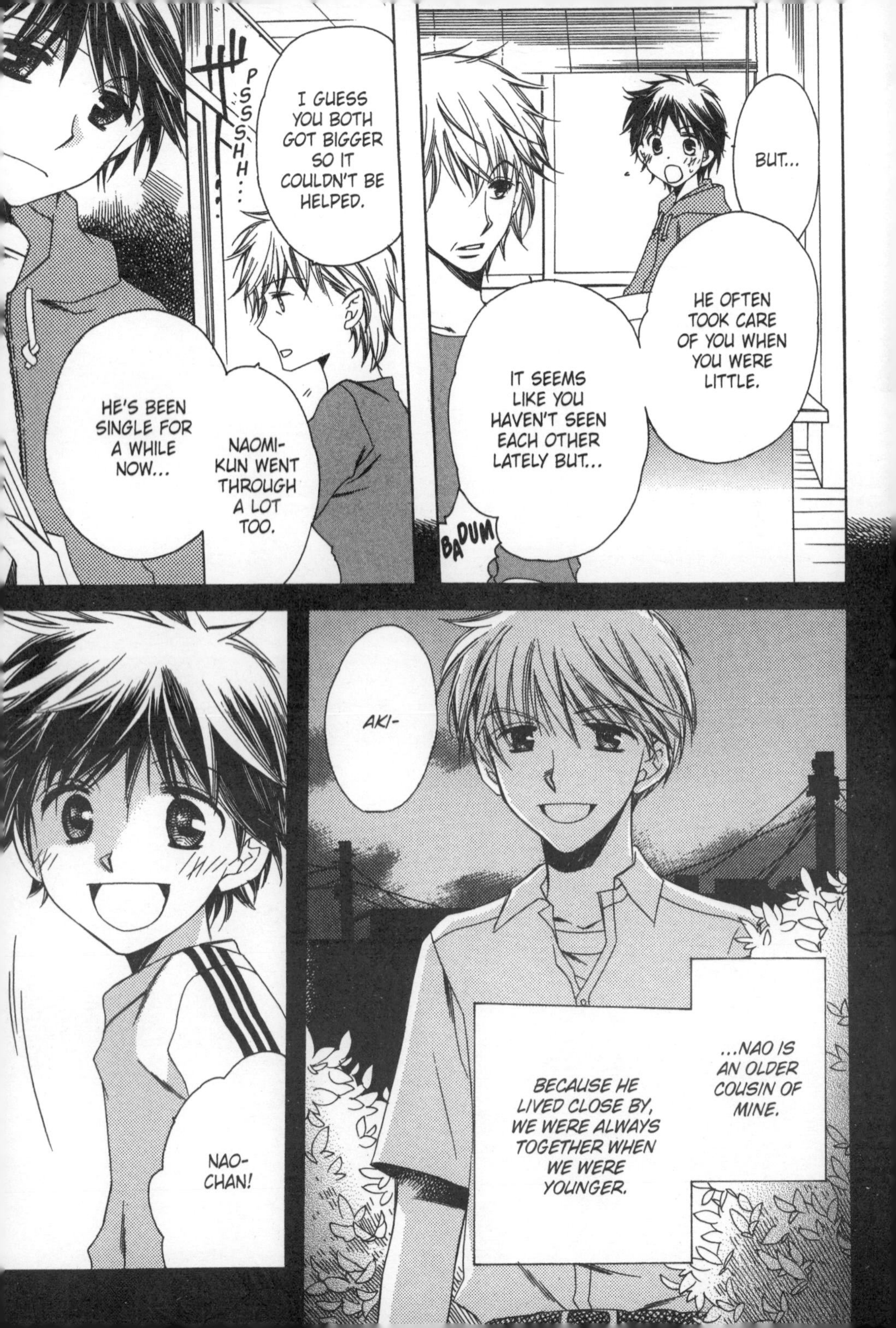
BUT...
HE OFTEN TOOK CARE OF YOU WHEN YOU WERE LITTLE.
IT SEEMS LIKE YOU HAVEN'T SEEN EACH OTHER LATELY BUT...
BADUM
I GUESS YOU BOTH GOT BIGGER SO IT COULDN'T BE HELPED.
PSSSHH...
NAOMI-KUN WENT THROUGH A LOT TOO.
HE'S BEEN SINGLE FOR A WHILE NOW...
...NAO IS AN OLDER COUSIN OF MINE.
BECAUSE HE LIVED CLOSE BY, WE WERE ALWAYS TOGETHER WHEN WE WERE YOUNGER.
AKI-
NAO-CHAN!

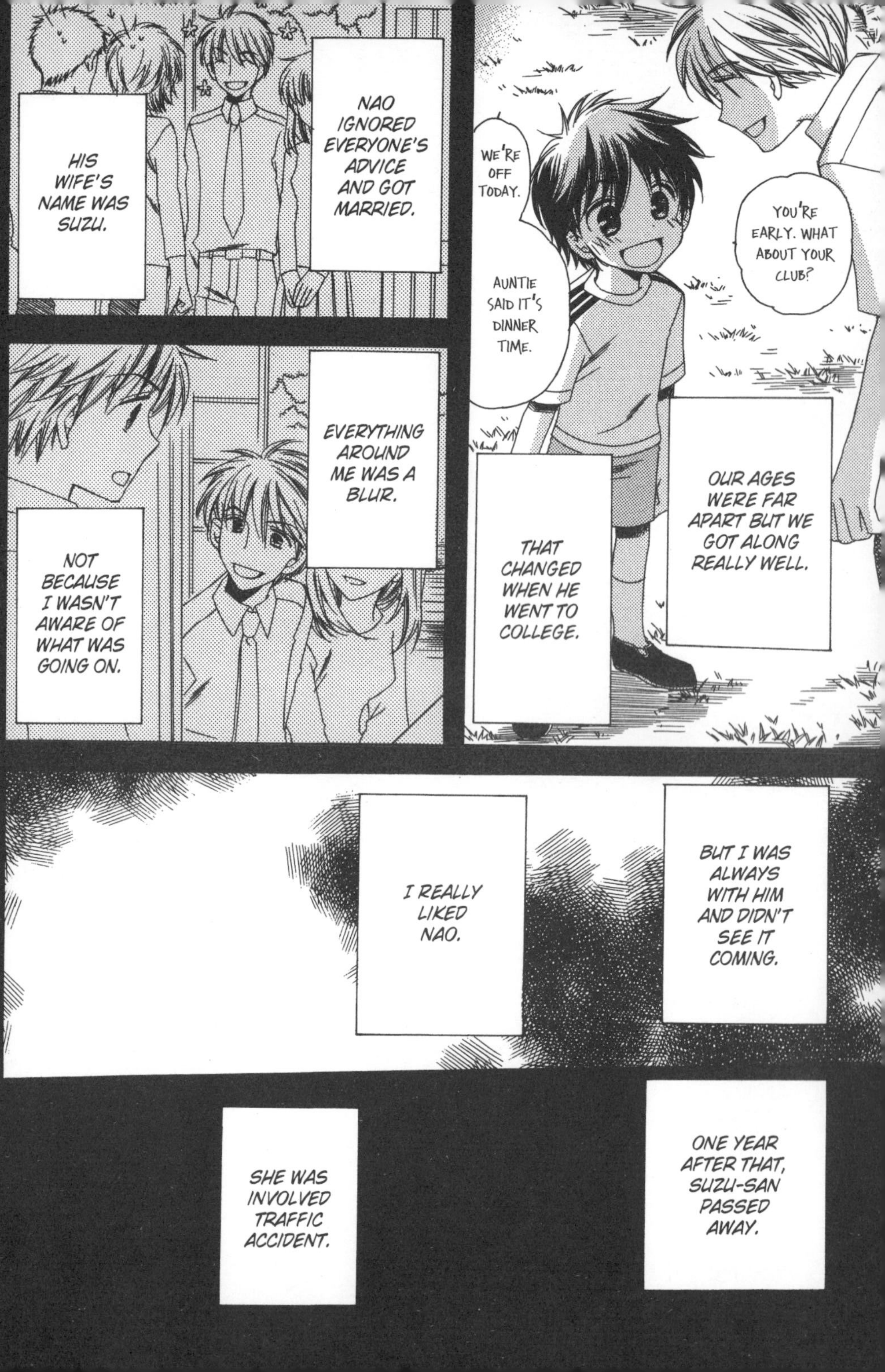
YOU'RE EARLY. WHAT ABOUT YOUR CLUB?
WE'RE OFF TODAY.
AUNTIE SAID IT'S DINNER TIME.
OUR AGES WERE FAR APART BUT WE GOT ALONG REALLY WELL.
THAT CHANGED WHEN HE WENT TO COLLEGE.
NAO IGNORED EVERYONE'S ADVICE AND GOT MARRIED.
HIS WIFE'S NAME WAS SUZU.
EVERYTHING AROUND ME WAS A BLUR.
NOT BECAUSE I WASN'T AWARE OF WHAT WAS GOING ON.
BUT I WAS ALWAYS WITH HIM AND DIDN'T SEE IT COMING.
I REALLY LIKED NAO.
ONE YEAR AFTER THAT, SUZU-SAN PASSED AWAY.
SHE WAS INVOLVED TRAFFIC ACCIDENT.

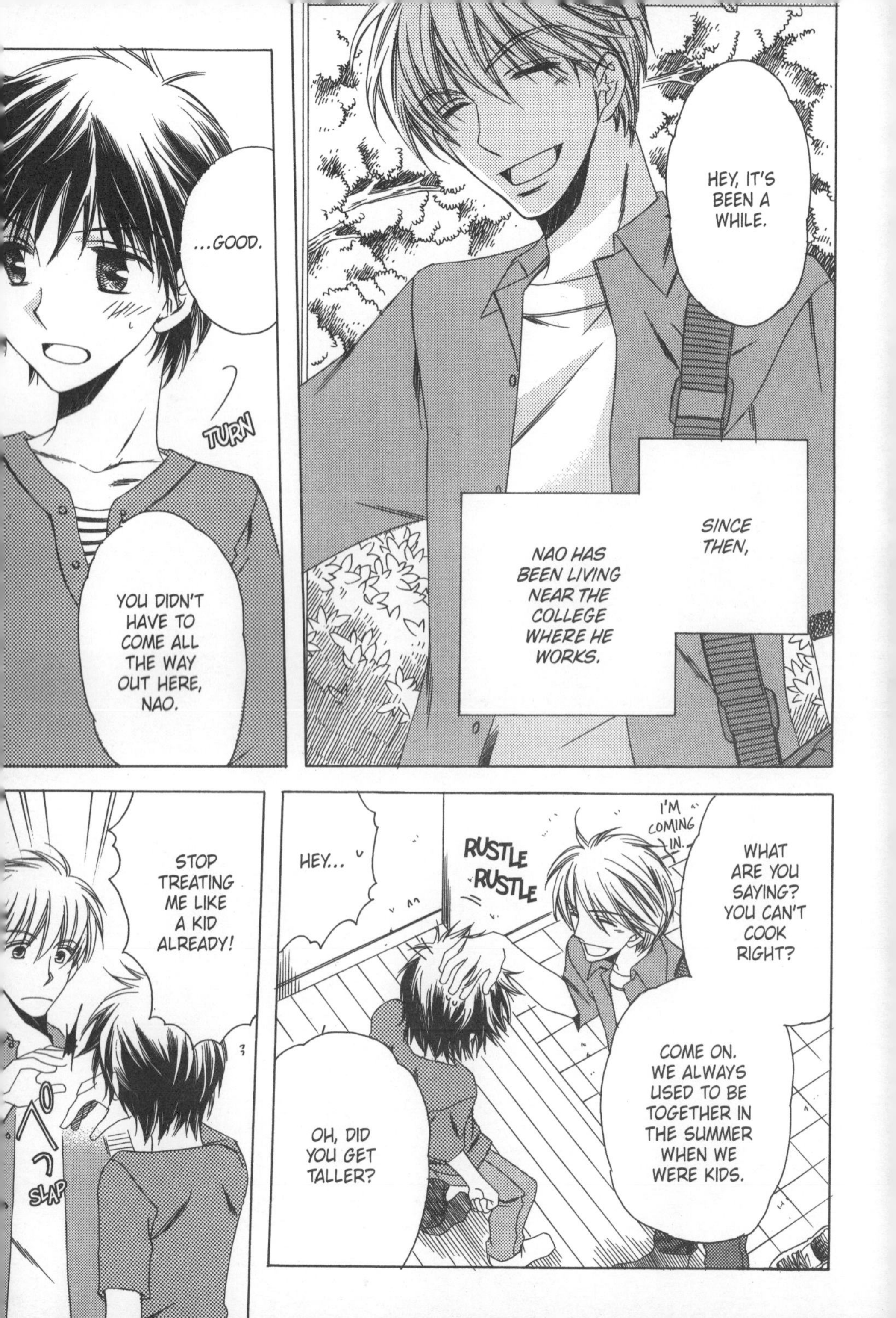
HEY, IT'S BEEN A WHILE.
SINCE THEN,
NAO HAS BEEN LIVING NEAR THE COLLEGE WHERE HE WORKS.
...GOOD.
TURN
YOU DIDN'T HAVE TO COME ALL THE WAY OUT HERE, NAO.
I'M COMING IN.
WHAT ARE YOU SAYING? YOU CAN'T COOK RIGHT?
COME ON. WE ALWAYS USED TO BE TOGETHER IN THE SUMMER WHEN WE WERE KIDS.
RUSTLE RUSTLE
HEY...
OH, DID YOU GET TALLER?
STOP TREATING ME LIKE A KID ALREADY!
SLAP

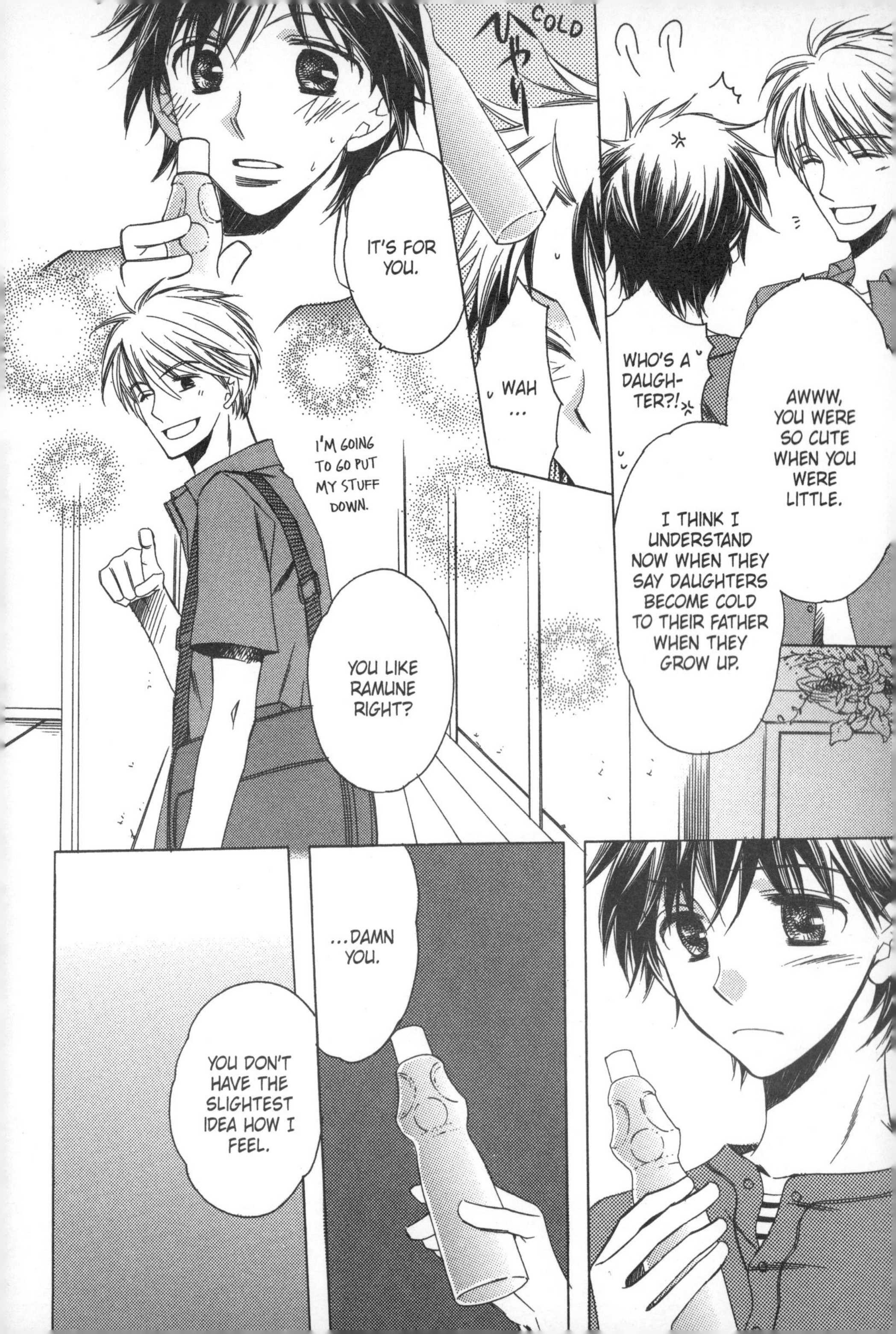
AWWW, YOU WERE SO CUTE WHEN YOU WERE LITTLE.
WHO'S A DAUGHTER?!
I THINK I UNDERSTAND NOW WHEN THEY SAY DAUGHTERS BECOME COLD TO THEIR FATHER WHEN THEY GROW UP.
COLD
WAH ...
IT'S FOR YOU.
I'M GOING TO GO PUT MY STUFF DOWN.
YOU LIKE RAMUNE RIGHT?
...DAMN YOU.
YOU DON'T HAVE THE SLIGHTEST IDEA HOW I FEEL.

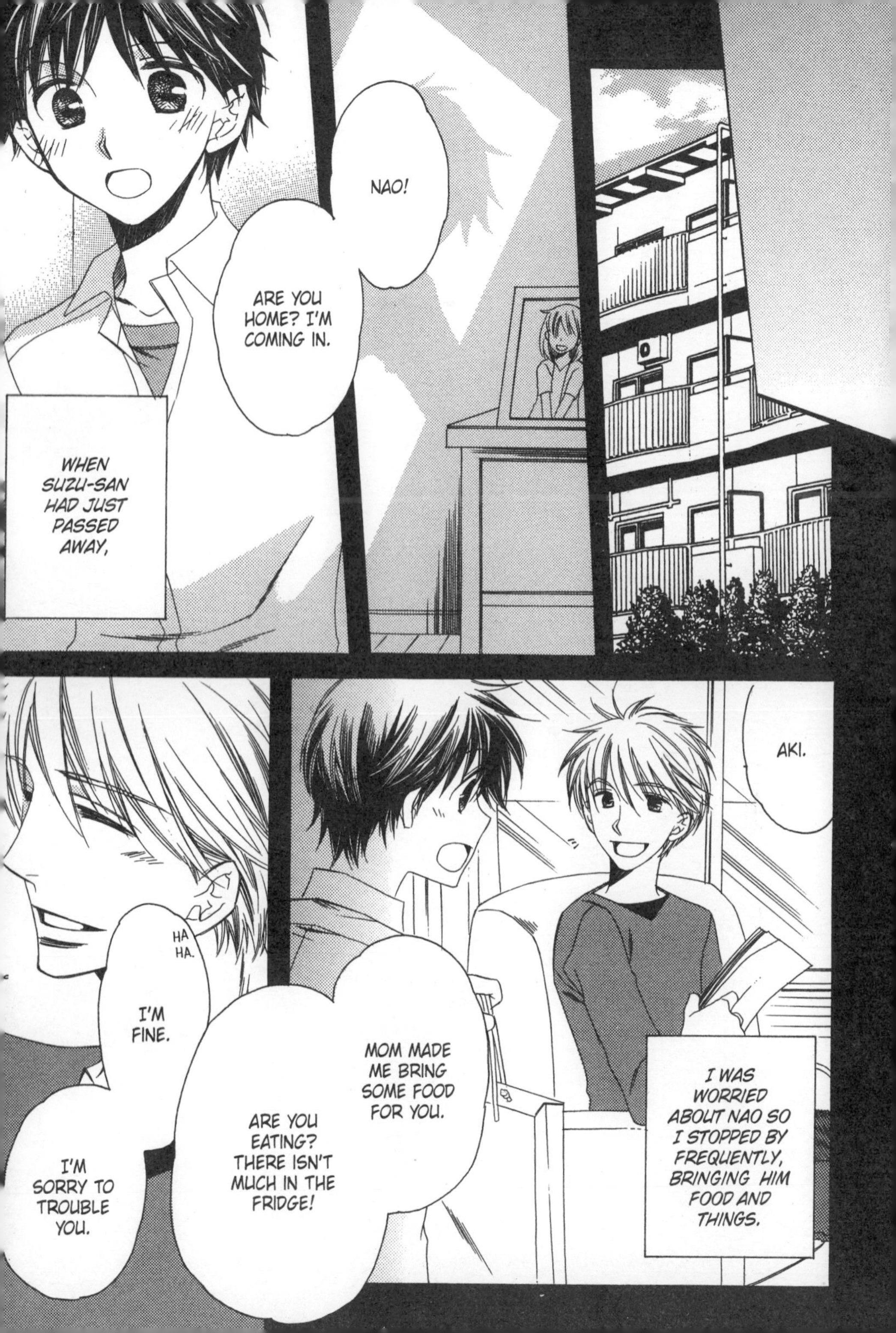
NAO!
ARE YOU HOME? I'M COMING IN.
WHEN SUZU-SAN HAD JUST PASSED AWAY,
AKI.
I WAS WORRIED ABOUT NAO SO I STOPPED BY FREQUENTLY, BRINGING HIM FOOD AND THINGS.
MOM MADE ME BRING SOME FOOD FOR YOU.
ARE YOU EATING? THERE ISN'T MUCH IN THE FRIDGE!
HA HA.
I'M FINE.
I'M SORRY TO TROUBLE YOU.

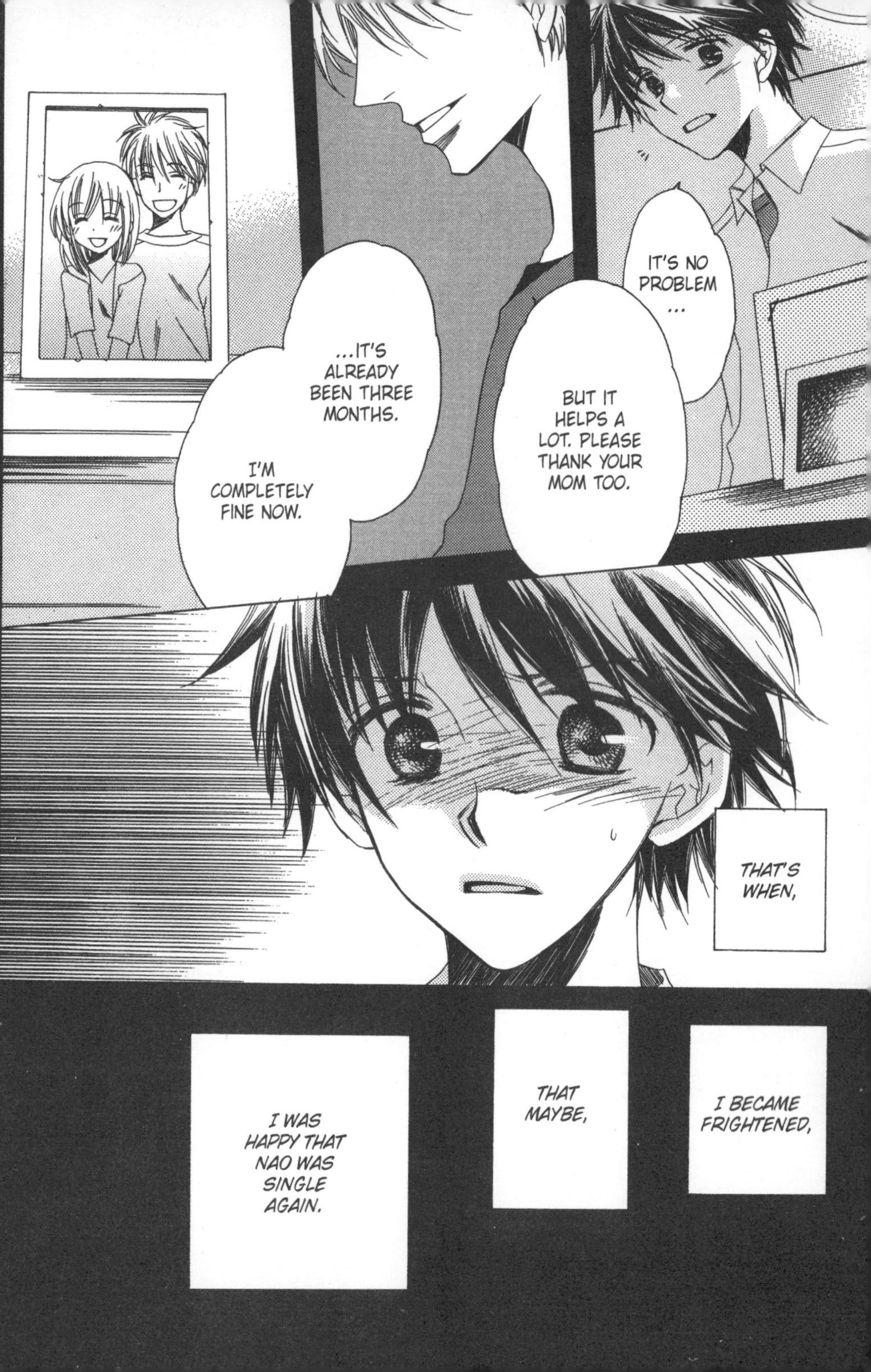
IT'S NO PROBLEM ...
BUT IT HELPS A LOT. PLEASE THANK YOUR MOM TOO.
...IT'S ALREADY BEEN THREE MONTHS.
I'M COMPLETELY FINE NOW.
THAT'S WHEN,
I BECAME FRIGHTENED,
THAT MAYBE,
I WAS HAPPY THAT NAO WAS SINGLE AGAIN.

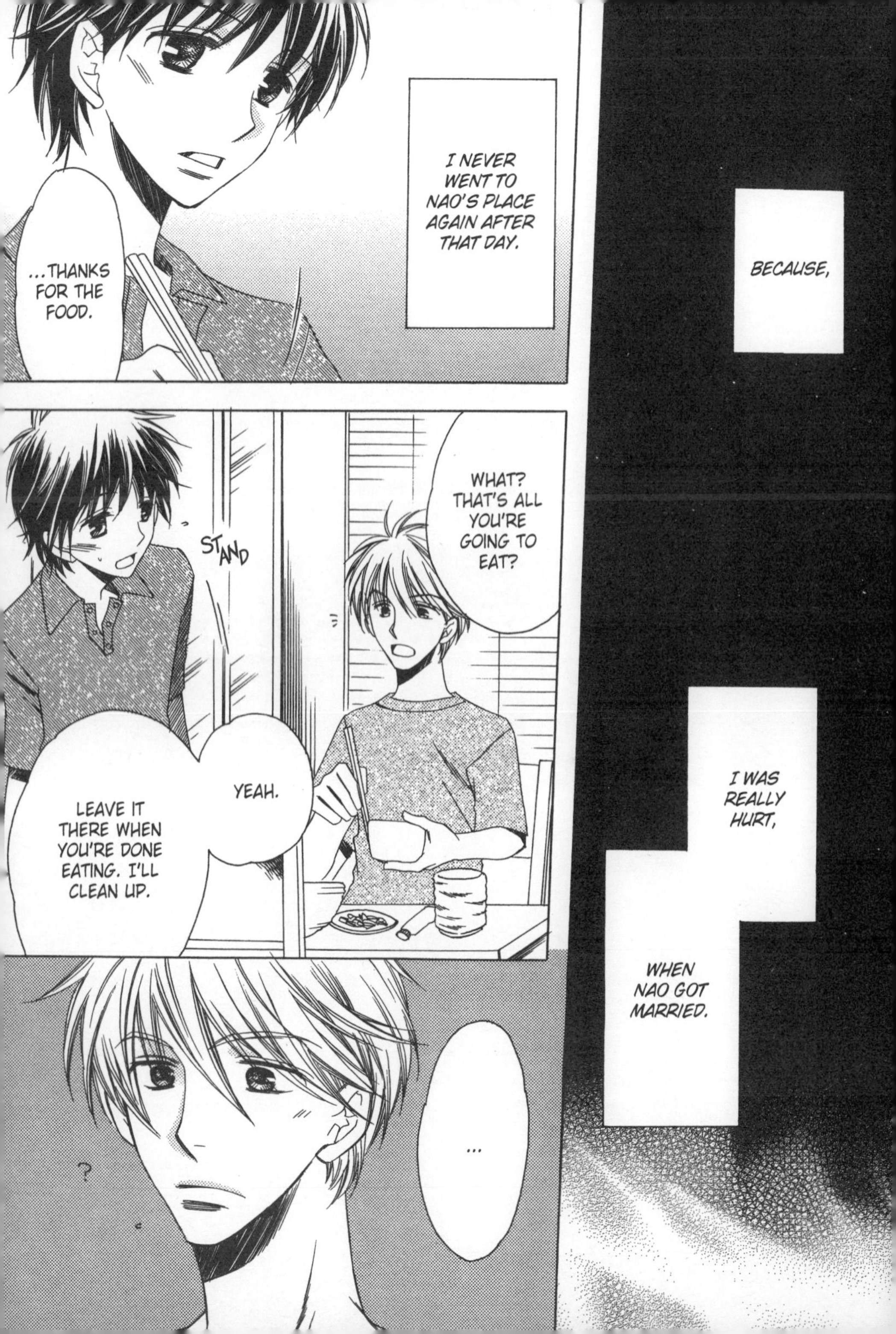
BECAUSE,
I WAS REALLY HURT,
WHEN NAO GOT MARRIED.
I NEVER WENT TO NAO'S PLACE AGAIN AFTER THAT DAY.
...THANKS FOR THE FOOD.
WHAT? THAT'S ALL YOU'RE GOING TO EAT?
STAND
YEAH.
LEAVE IT THERE WHEN YOU'RE DONE EATING. I'LL CLEAN UP.
...
?

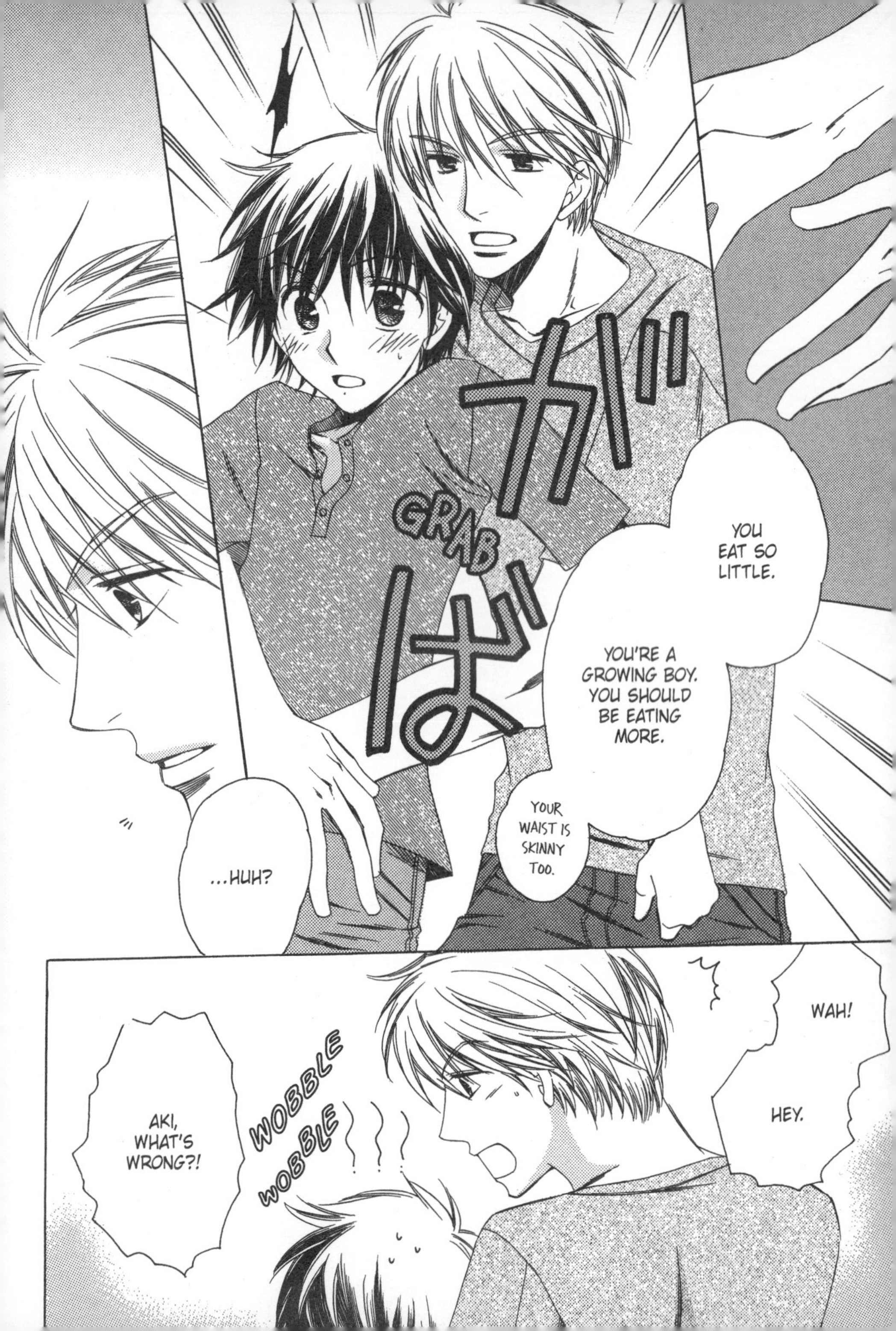
ガば
GRAB
YOU EAT SO LITTLE.
YOU'RE A GROWING BOY. YOU SHOULD BE EATING MORE.
YOUR WAIST IS SKINNY TOO.
...HUH?
WAH!
HEY.
WOBBLE WOBBLE
AKI, WHAT'S WRONG?!

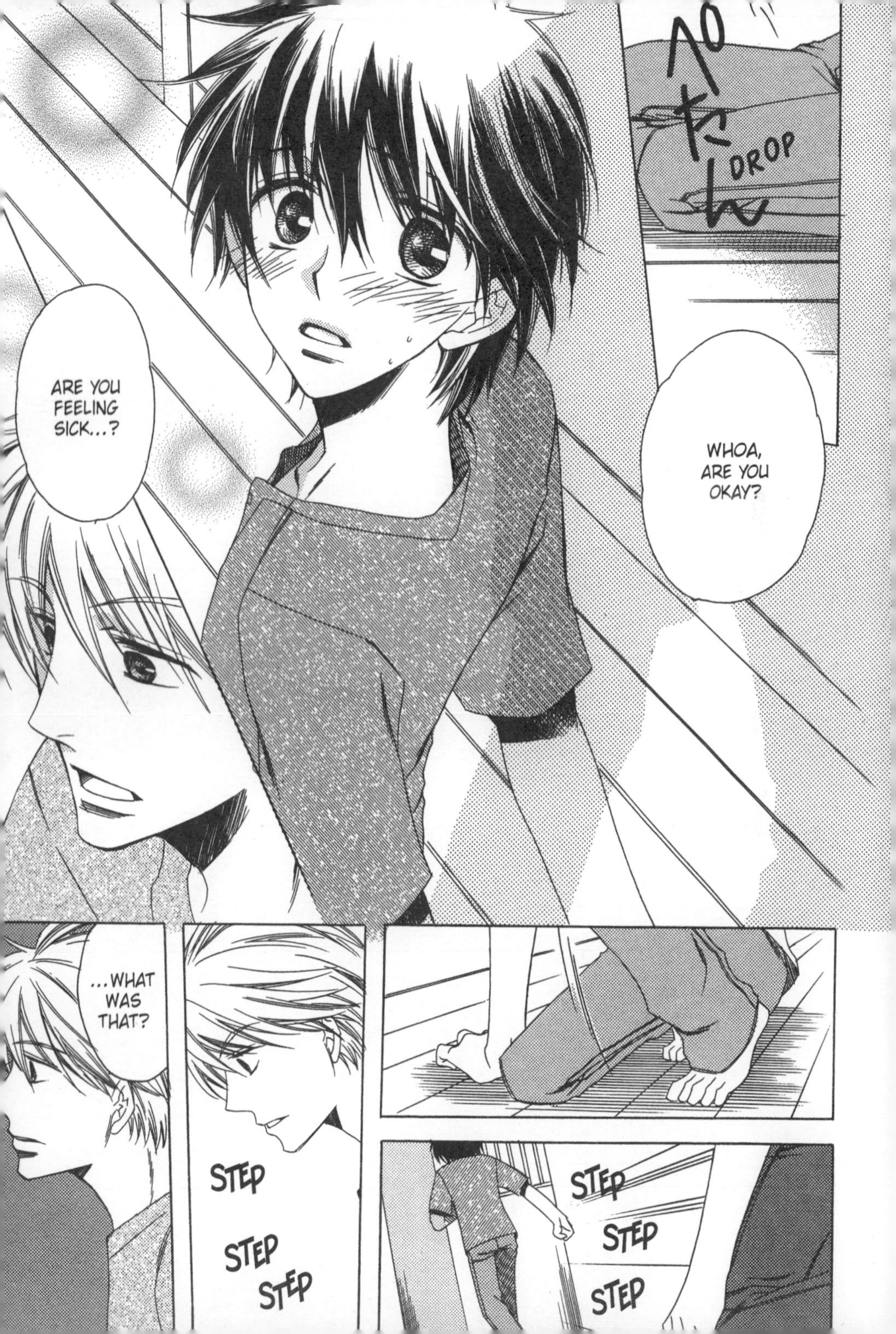
DROP
WHOA, ARE YOU OKAY?
ARE YOU FEELING SICK...?
STEP
STEP
STEP
STEP
STEP
STEP
...WHAT WAS THAT?

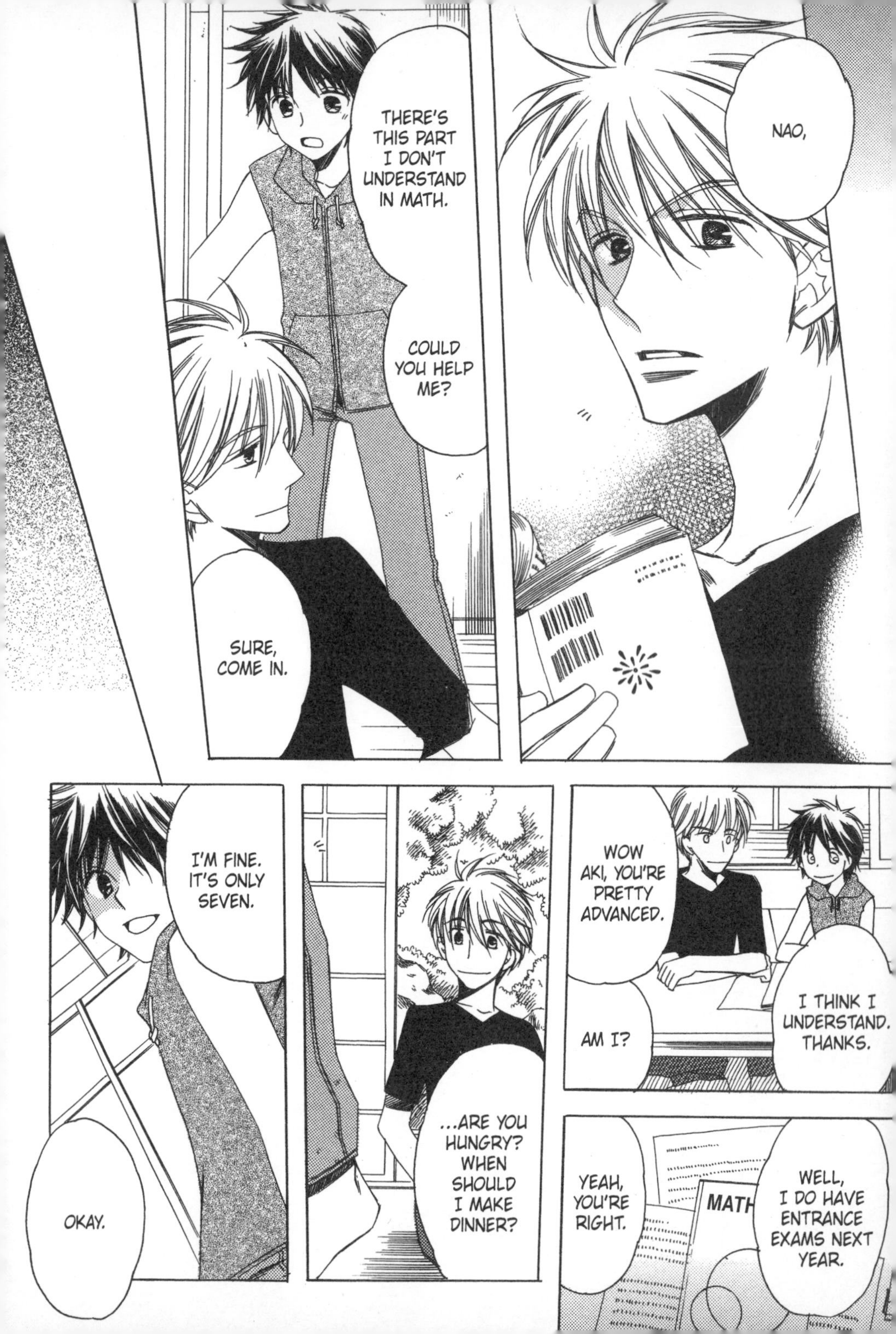
NAO,
THERE'S THIS PART I DON'T UNDERSTAND IN MATH.
COULD YOU HELP ME?
SURE, COME IN.
I THINK I UNDERSTAND. THANKS.
WOW AKI, YOU'RE PRETTY ADVANCED.
AM I?
WELL, I DO HAVE ENTRANCE EXAMS NEXT YEAR.
YEAH, YOU'RE RIGHT.
MATH
...ARE YOU HUNGRY? WHEN SHOULD I MAKE DINNER?
I'M FINE. IT'S ONLY SEVEN.
OKAY.

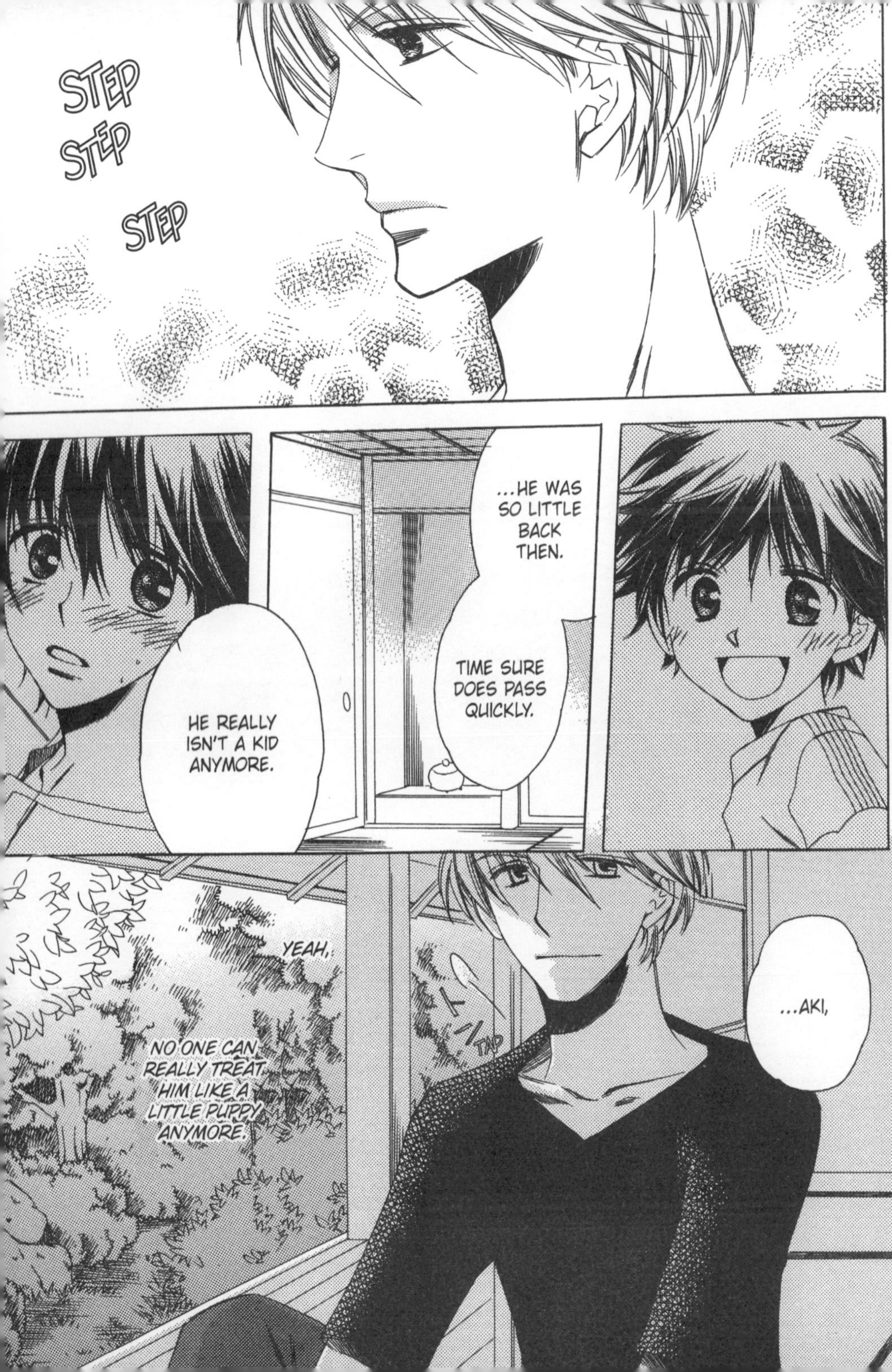
STEP
STEP
STEP
...HE WAS SO LITTLE BACK THEN.
TIME SURE DOES PASS QUICKLY.
HE REALLY ISN'T A KID ANYMORE.
...AKI,
TAP
YEAH,
NO ONE CAN REALLY TREAT HIM LIKE A LITTLE PUPPY ANYMORE.

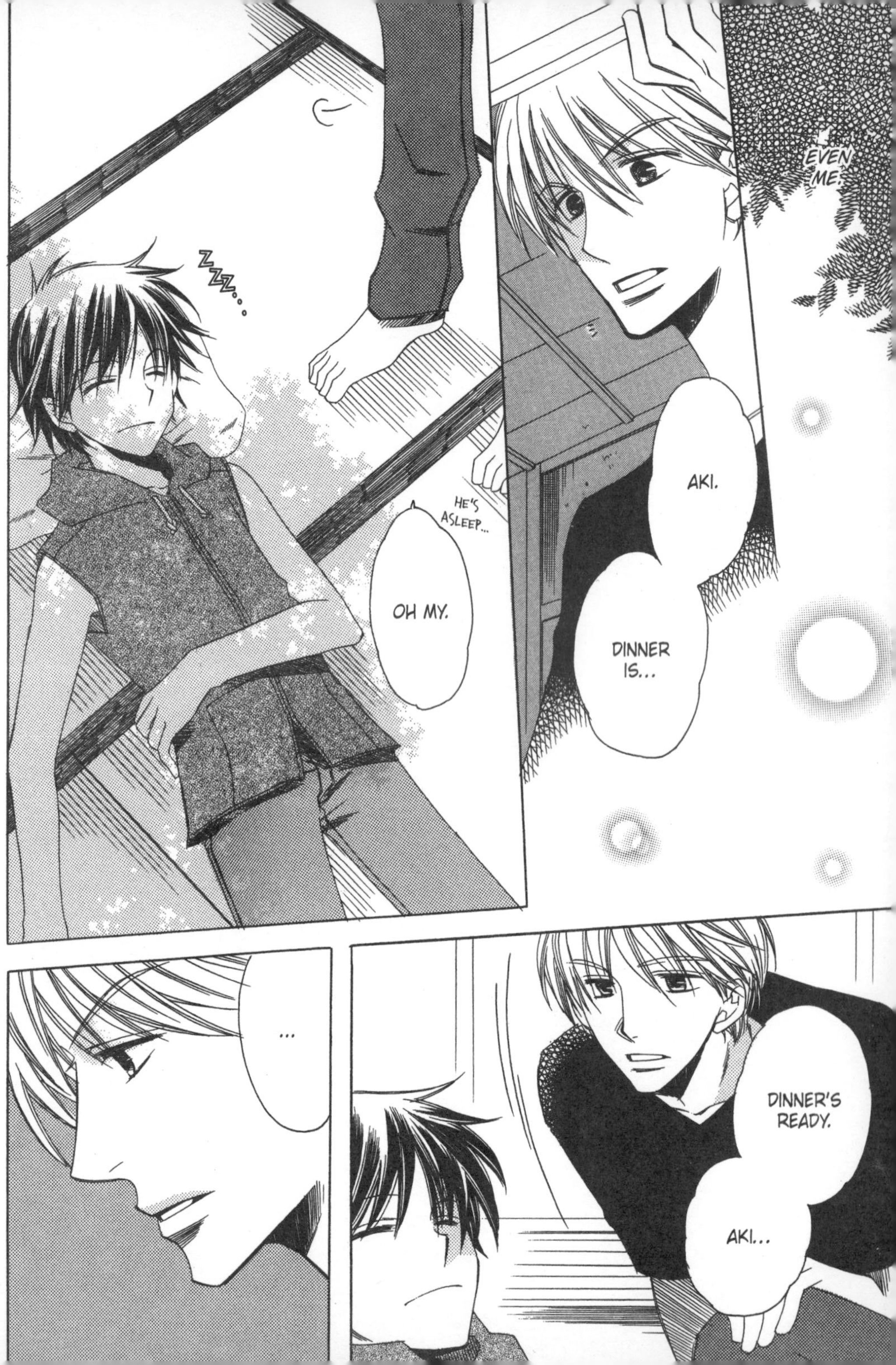
EVEN ME.
AKI.
DINNER IS...
OH MY.
HE'S ASLEEP...
ZZZ...
DINNER'S READY.
AKI...
...

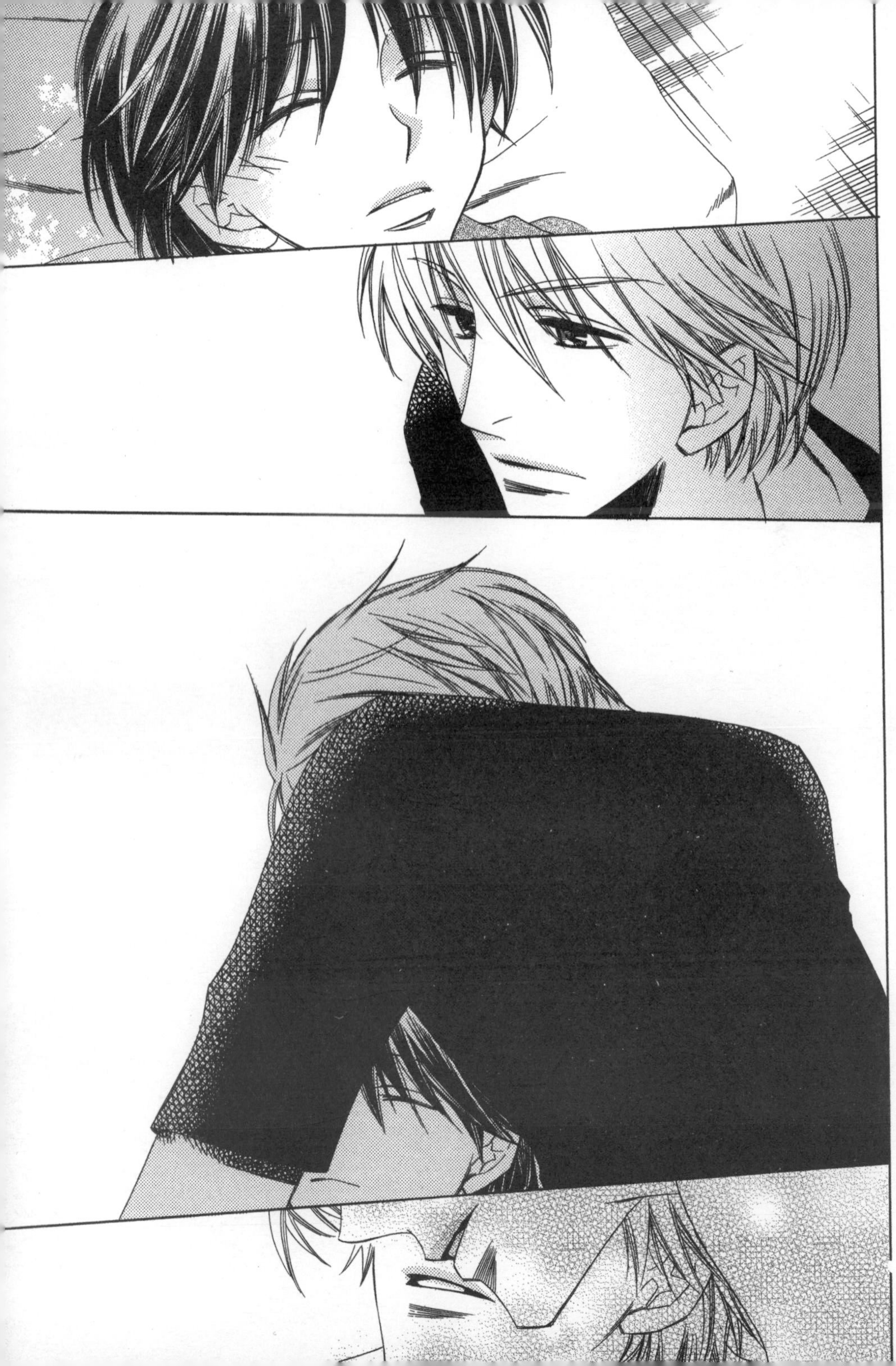

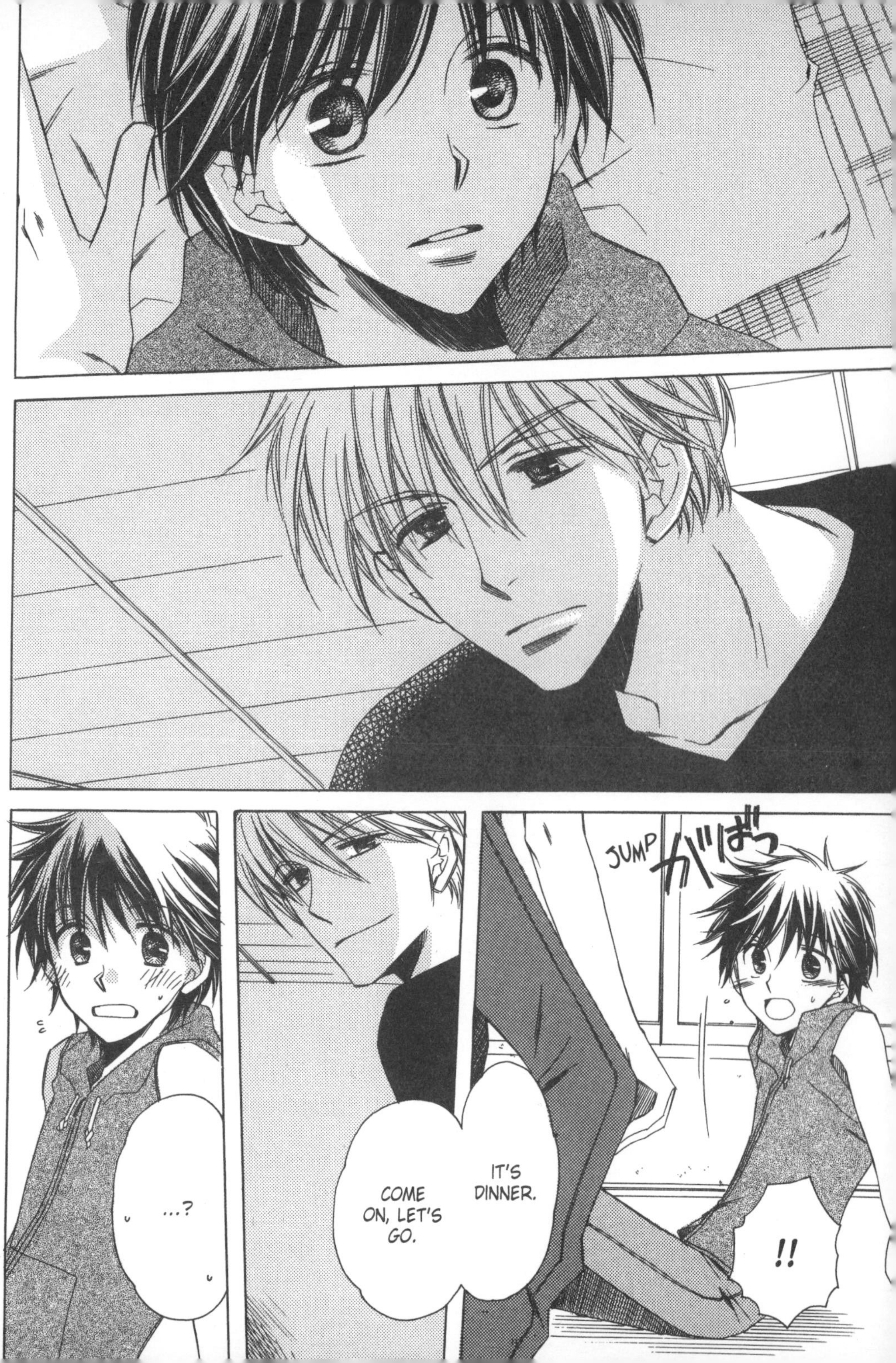
JUMP
がばっ
!!
IT'S DINNER.
COME ON, LET'S GO.
...?

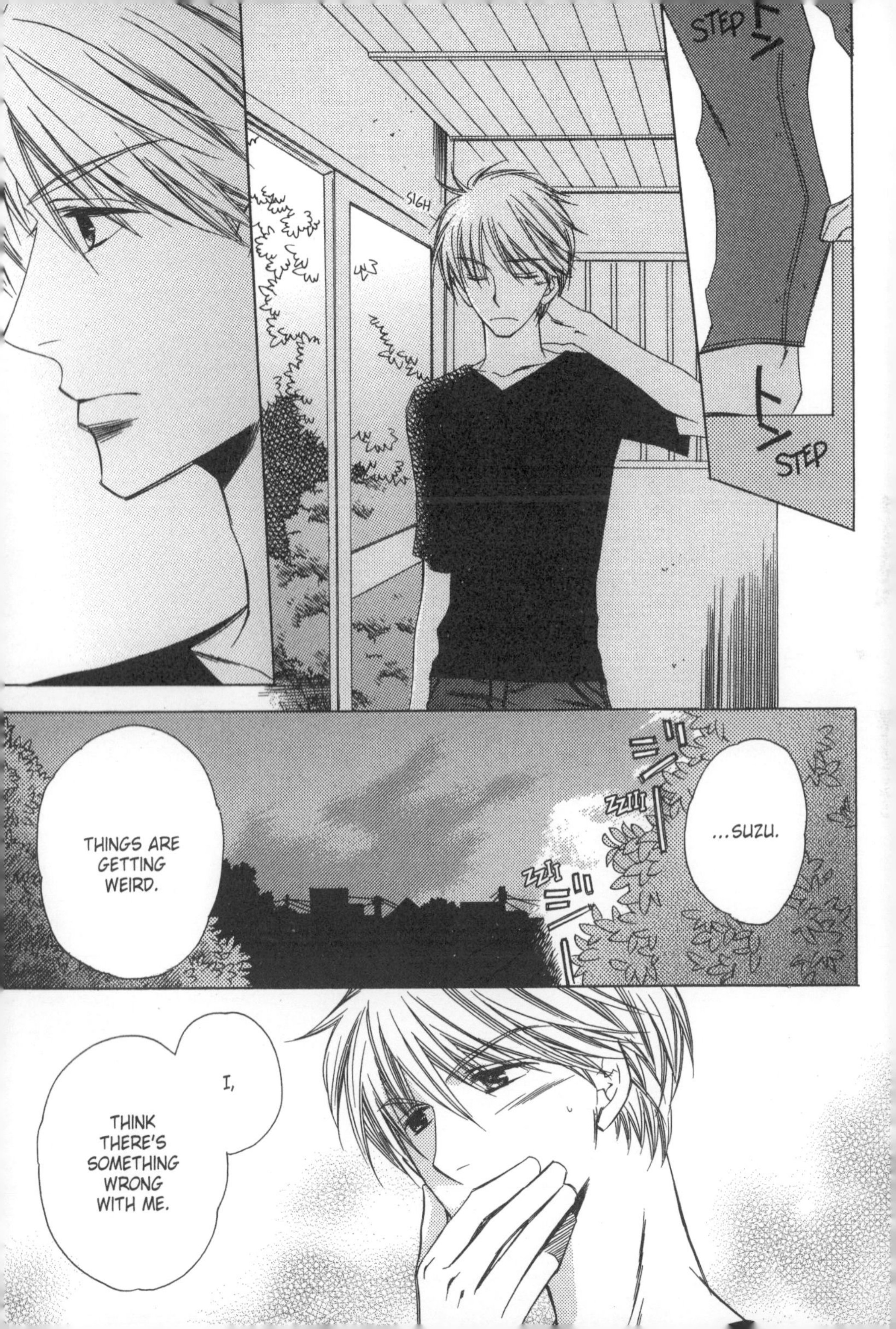
STEP
STEP
SIGH
...SUZU.
ZZII
ZZII
THINGS ARE GETTING WEIRD.
I,
THINK THERE'S SOMETHING WRONG WITH ME.

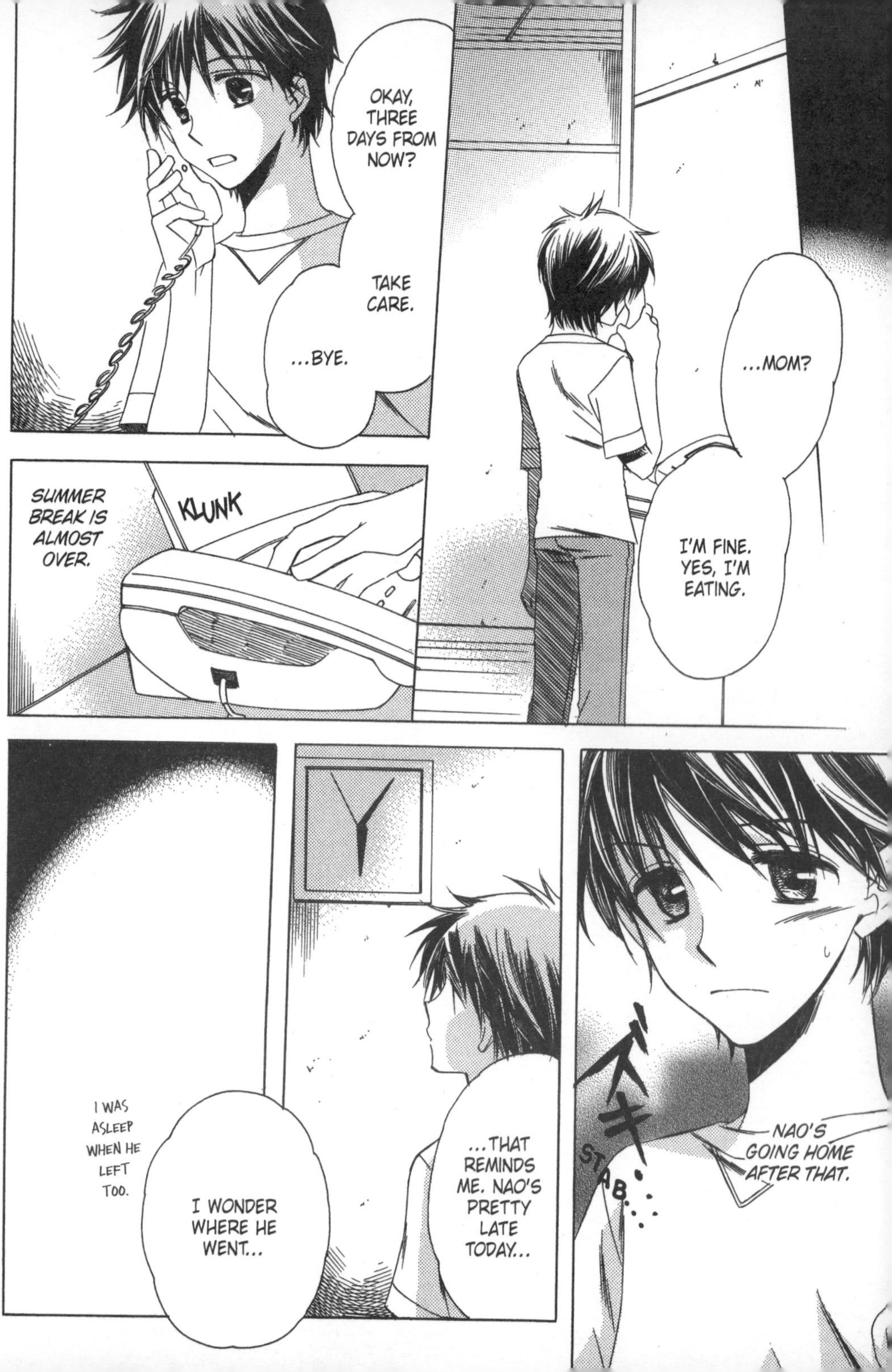
...MOM?
I'M FINE. YES, I'M EATING.
OKAY, THREE DAYS FROM NOW?
TAKE CARE.
...BYE.
KLUNK
SUMMER BREAK IS ALMOST OVER.
NAO'S GOING HOME AFTER THAT.
ズキ
STAB...
...THAT REMINDS ME. NAO'S PRETTY LATE TODAY...
I WONDER WHERE HE WENT...
I WAS ASLEEP WHEN HE LEFT TOO.

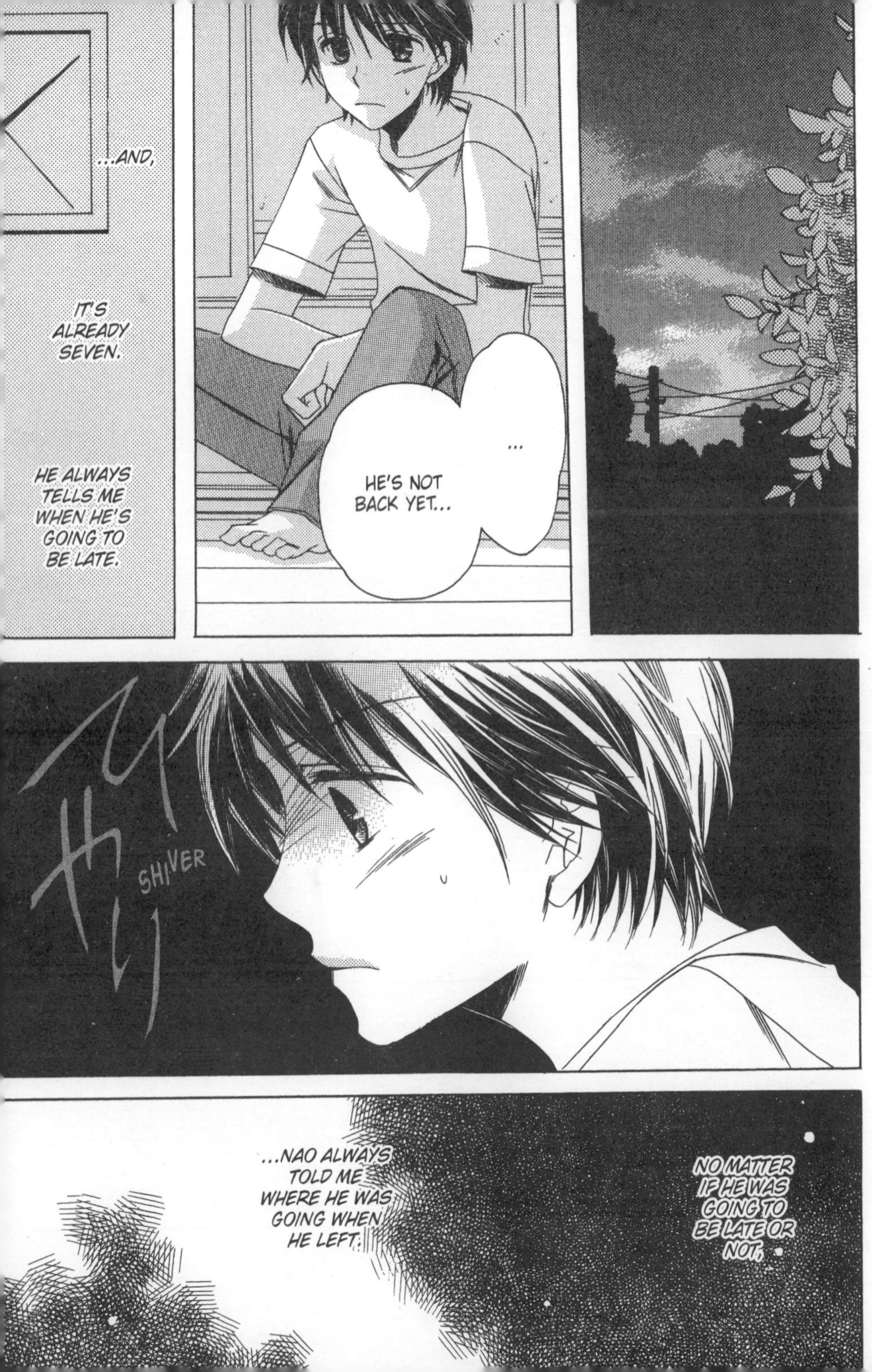
...
HE'S NOT BACK YET...
...AND,
IT'S ALREADY SEVEN.
HE ALWAYS TELLS ME WHEN HE'S GOING TO BE LATE.
SHIVER
NO MATTER IF HE WAS GOING TO BE LATE OR NOT,
...NAO ALWAYS TOLD ME WHERE HE WAS GOING WHEN HE LEFT.

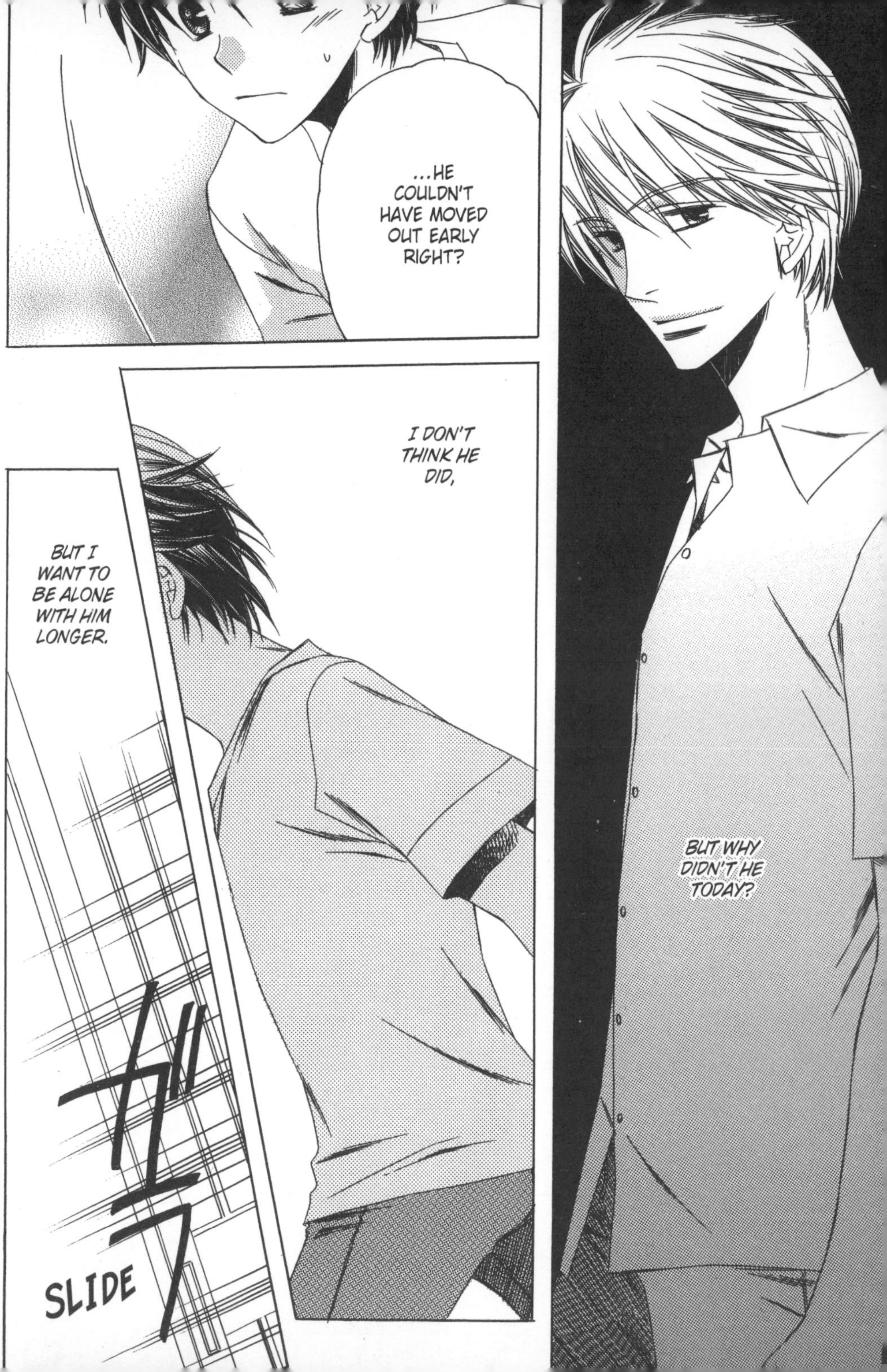
...HE COULDN'T HAVE MOVED OUT EARLY RIGHT?
I DON'T THINK HE DID,
BUT I WANT TO BE ALONE WITH HIM LONGER.
SLIDE
BUT WHY DIDN'T HE TODAY?

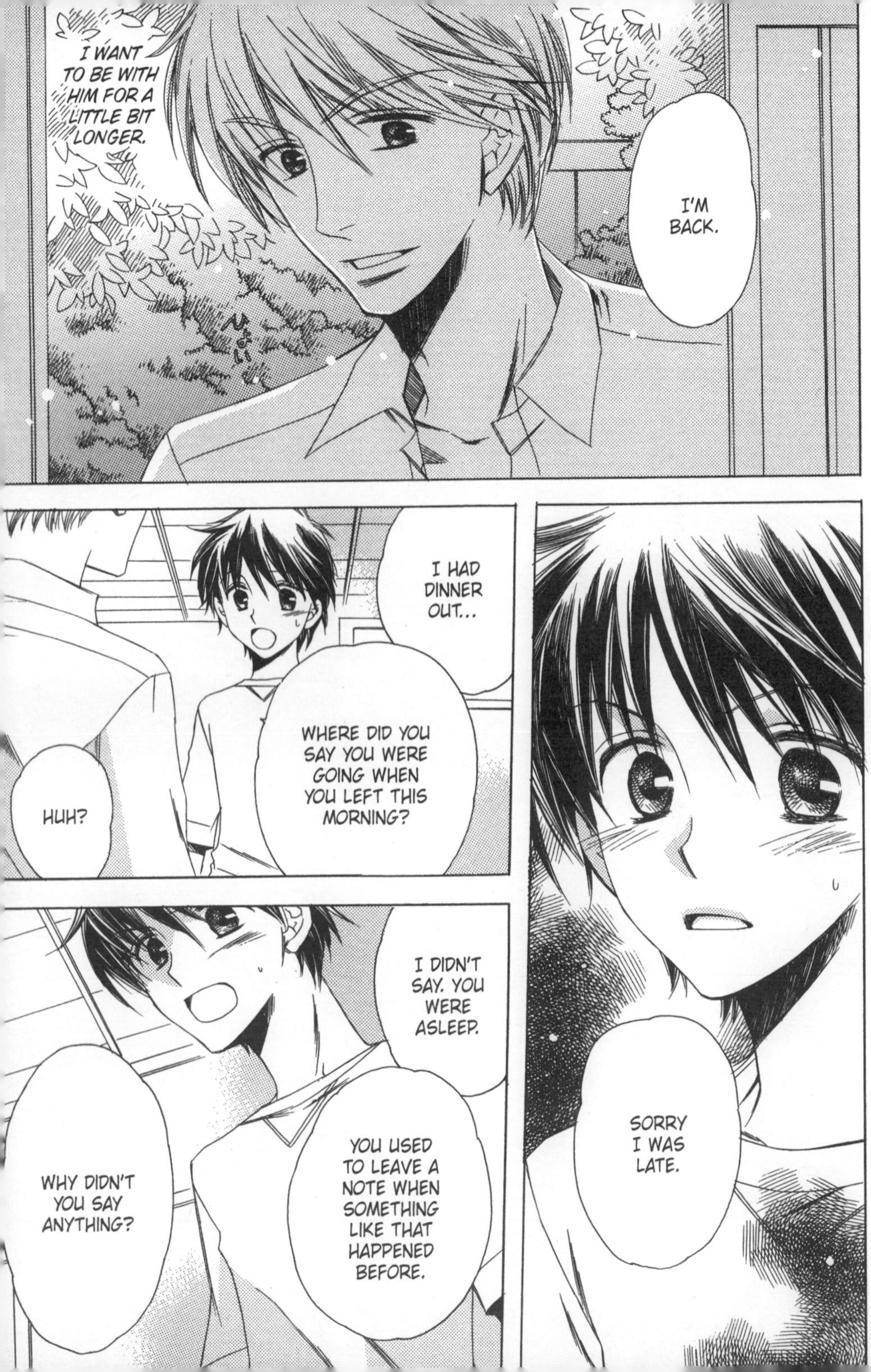
I'M BACK.
I WANT TO BE WITH HIM FOR A LITTLE BIT LONGER.
SORRY I WAS LATE.
I HAD DINNER OUT...
WHERE DID YOU SAY YOU WERE GOING WHEN YOU LEFT THIS MORNING?
HUH?
I DIDN'T SAY. YOU WERE ASLEEP.
YOU USED TO LEAVE A NOTE WHEN SOMETHING LIKE THAT HAPPENED BEFORE.
WHY DIDN'T YOU SAY ANYTHING?

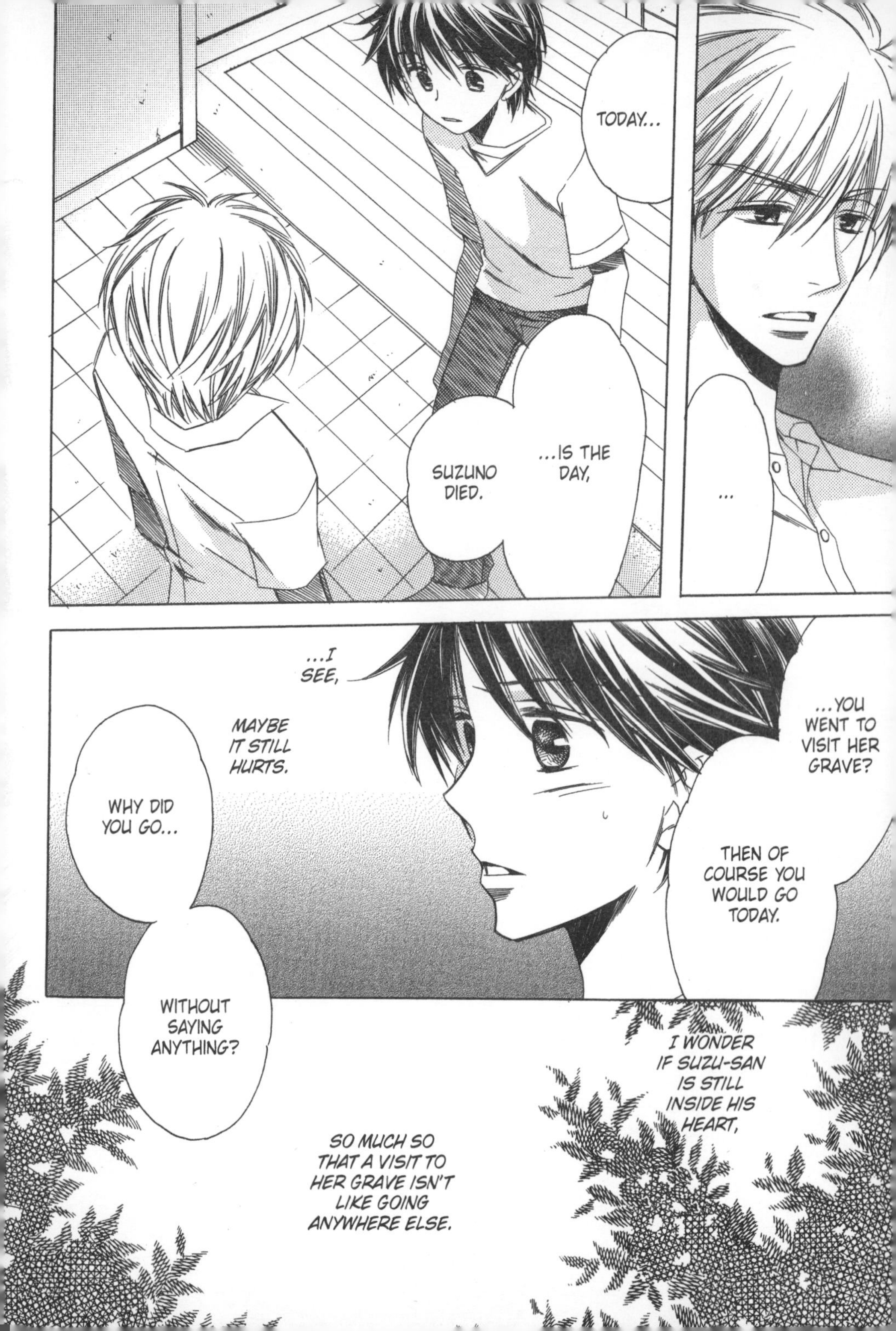

TODAY...
...IS THE DAY,
SUZUNO DIED.
...
...YOU WENT TO VISIT HER GRAVE?
THEN OF COURSE YOU WOULD GO TODAY.
...I SEE,
MAYBE IT STILL HURTS.
WHY DID YOU GO...
WITHOUT SAYING ANYTHING?
I WONDER IF SUZU-SAN IS STILL INSIDE HIS HEART,
SO MUCH SO THAT A VISIT TO HER GRAVE ISN'T LIKE GOING ANYWHERE ELSE.

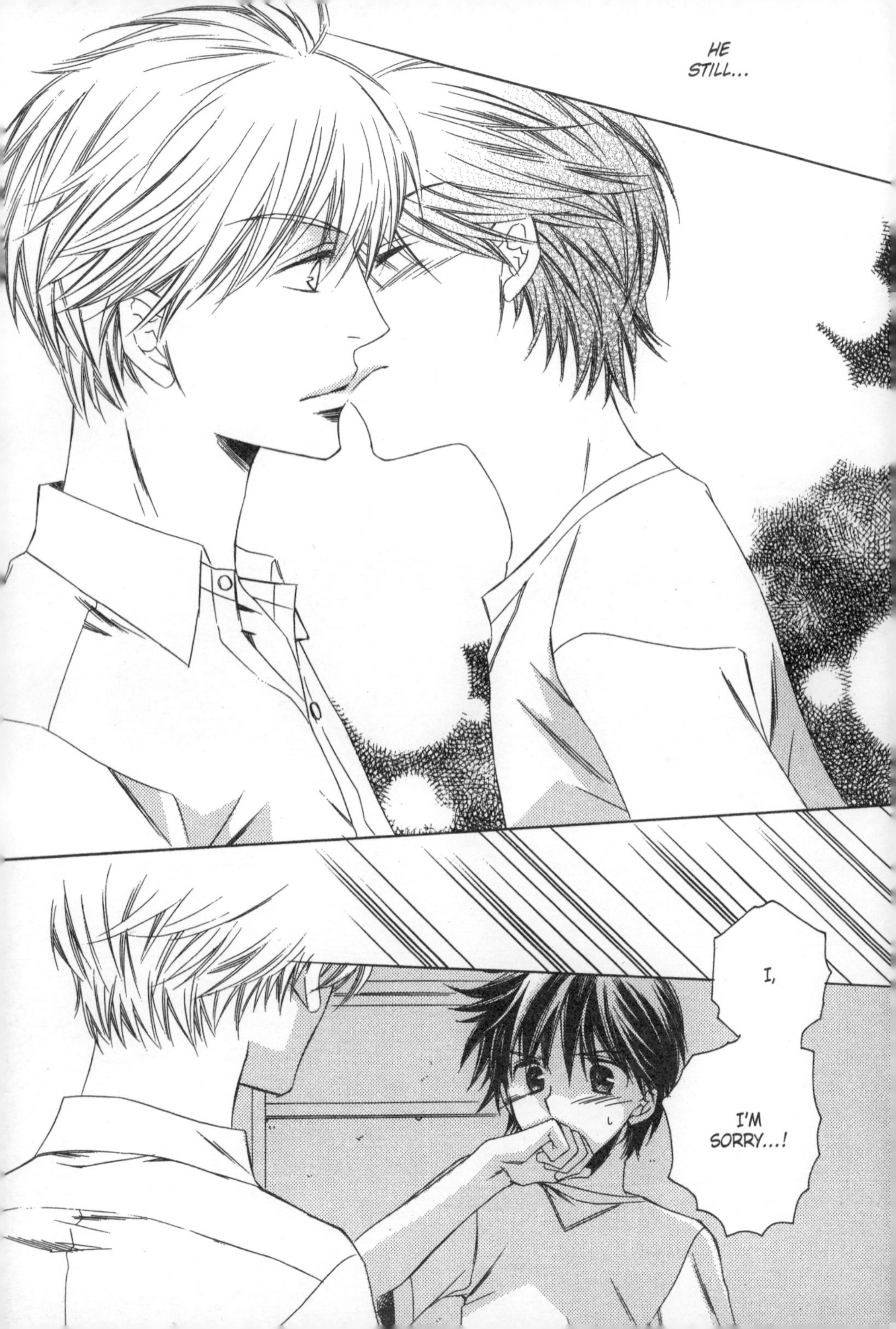
HE STILL...
I,
I'M SORRY...!

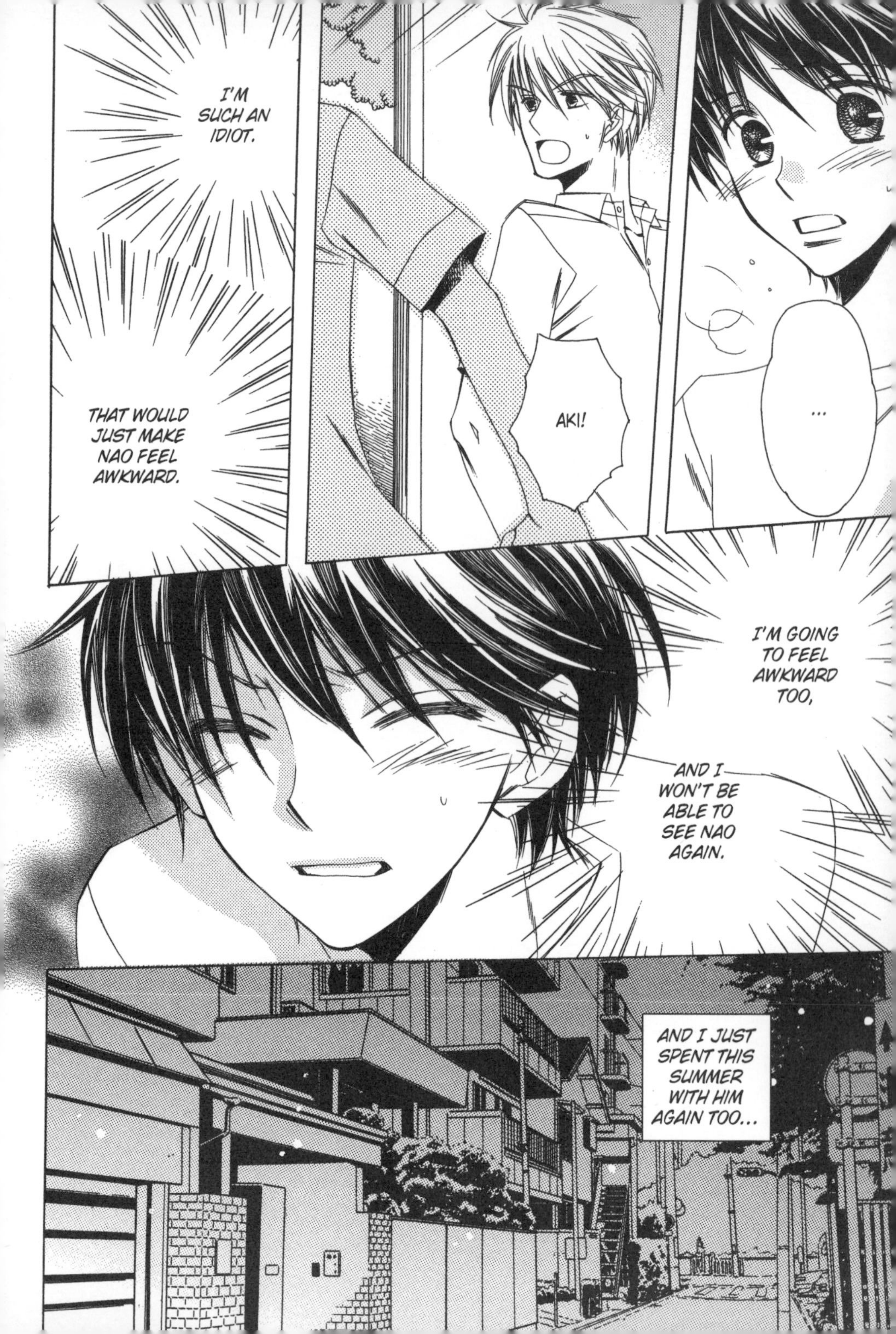
...
AKI!
I'M SUCH AN IDIOT.
THAT WOULD JUST MAKE NAO FEEL AWKWARD.
I'M GOING TO FEEL AWKWARD TOO,
AND I WON'T BE ABLE TO SEE NAO AGAIN.
AND I JUST SPENT THIS SUMMER WITH HIM AGAIN TOO...

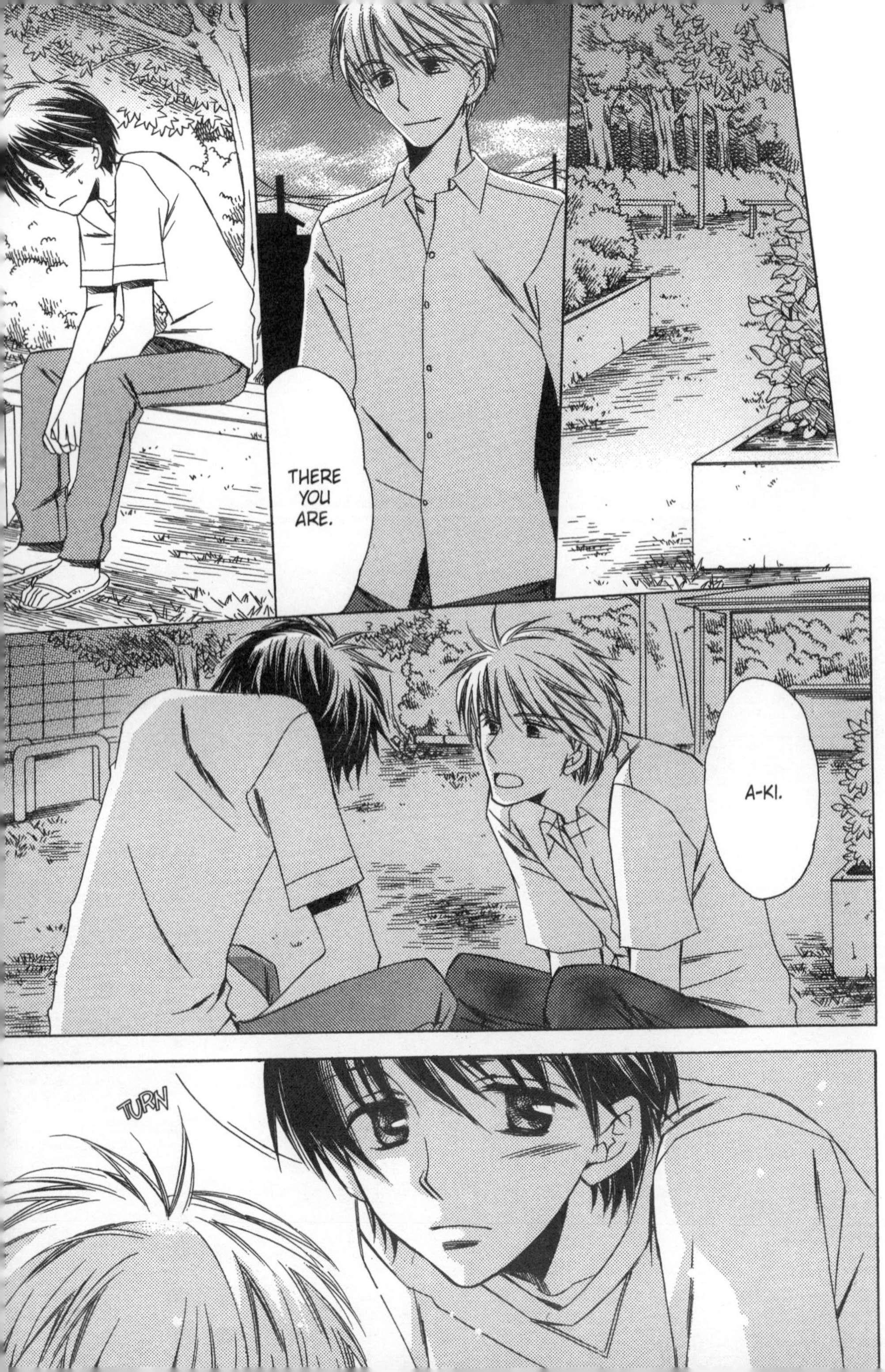
THERE YOU ARE.
A-KI.
TURN

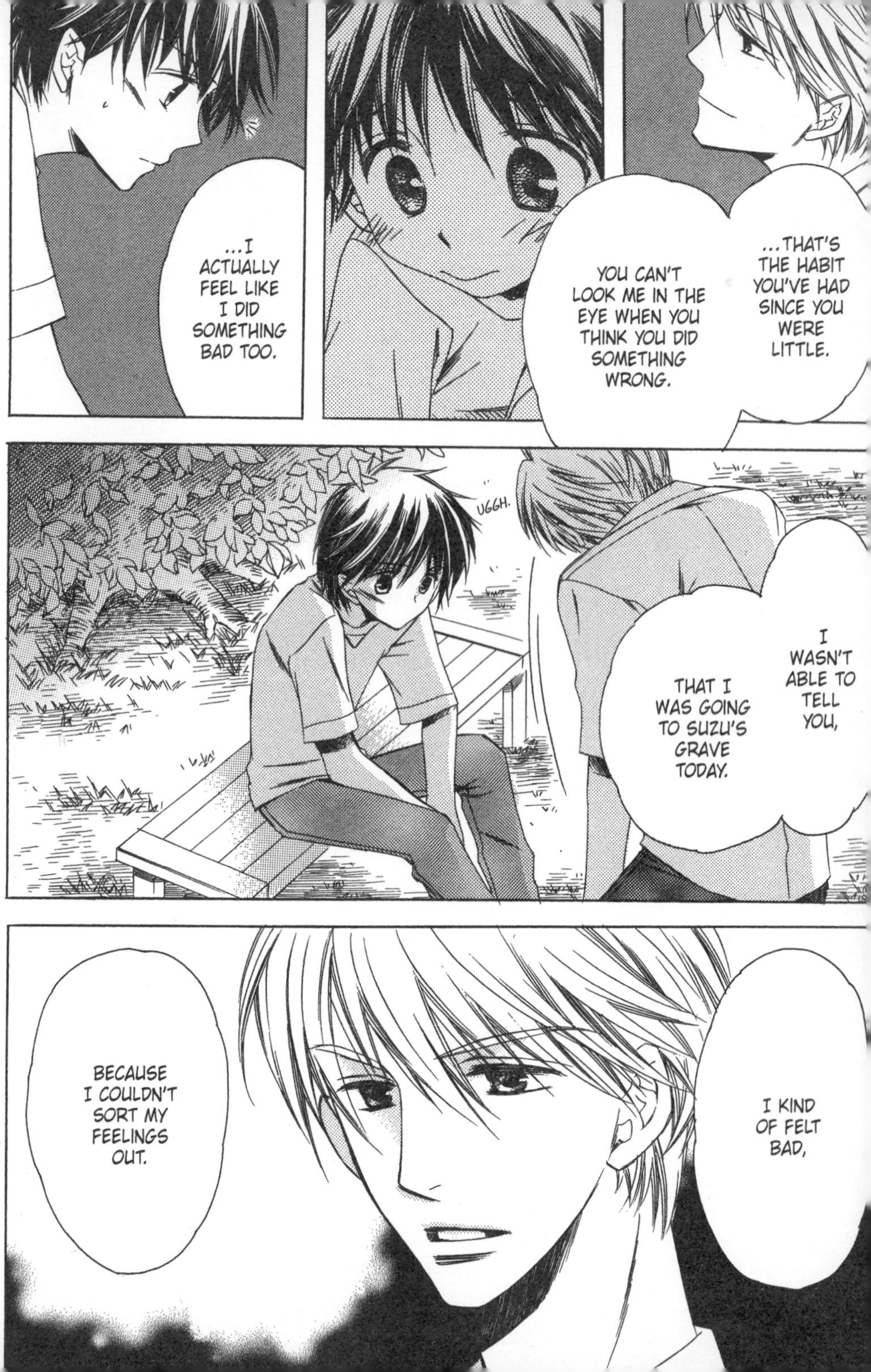
...THAT'S THE HABIT YOU'VE HAD SINCE YOU WERE LITTLE.
YOU CAN'T LOOK ME IN THE EYE WHEN YOU THINK YOU DID SOMETHING WRONG.
...I ACTUALLY FEEL LIKE I DID SOMETHING BAD TOO.
I WASN'T ABLE TO TELL YOU,
THAT I WAS GOING TO SUZU'S GRAVE TODAY.
UGGH.
I KIND OF FELT BAD,
BECAUSE I COULDN'T SORT MY FEELINGS OUT.

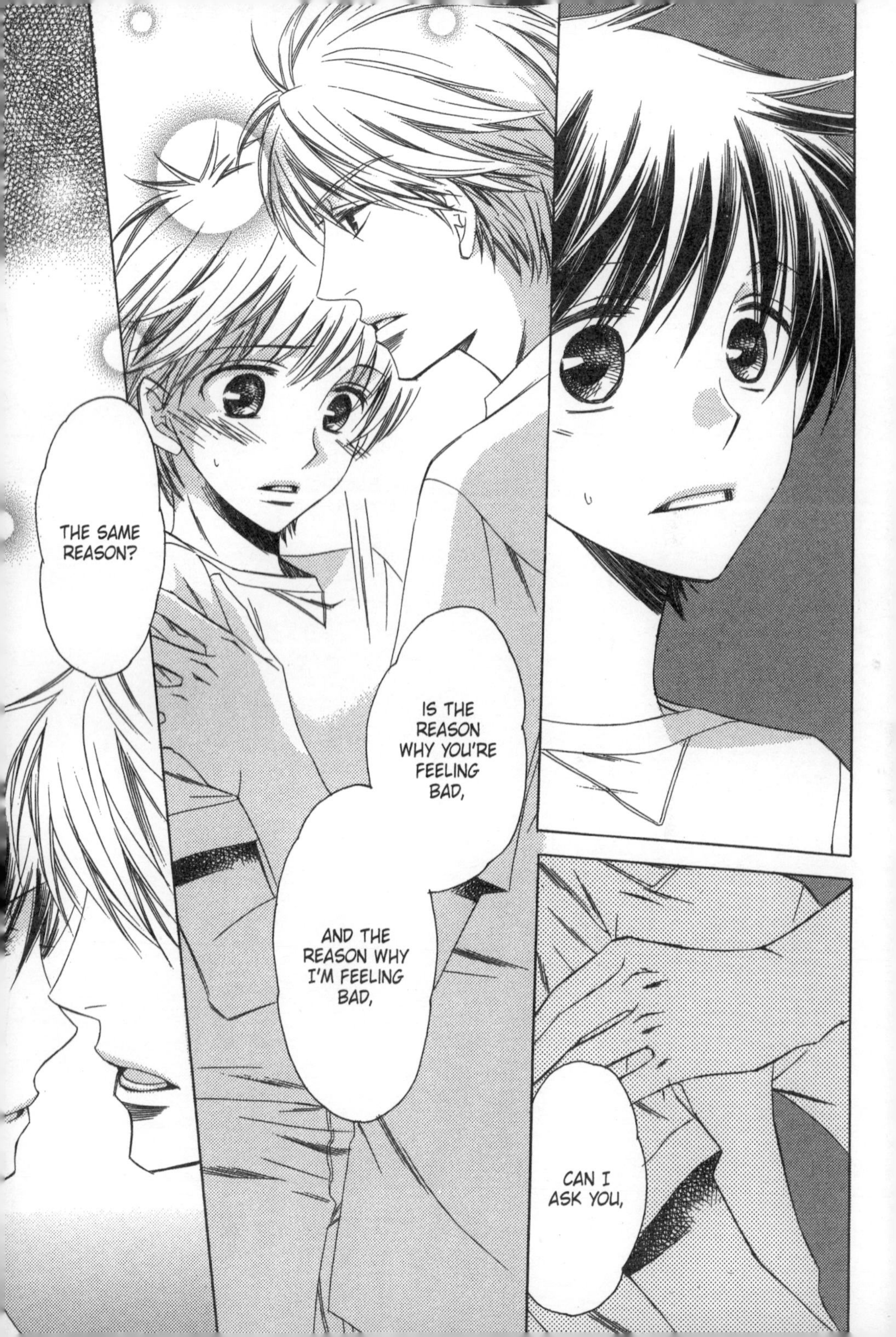
IS THE REASON WHY YOU'RE FEELING BAD,
AND THE REASON WHY I'M FEELING BAD,
CAN I ASK YOU,
THE SAME REASON?

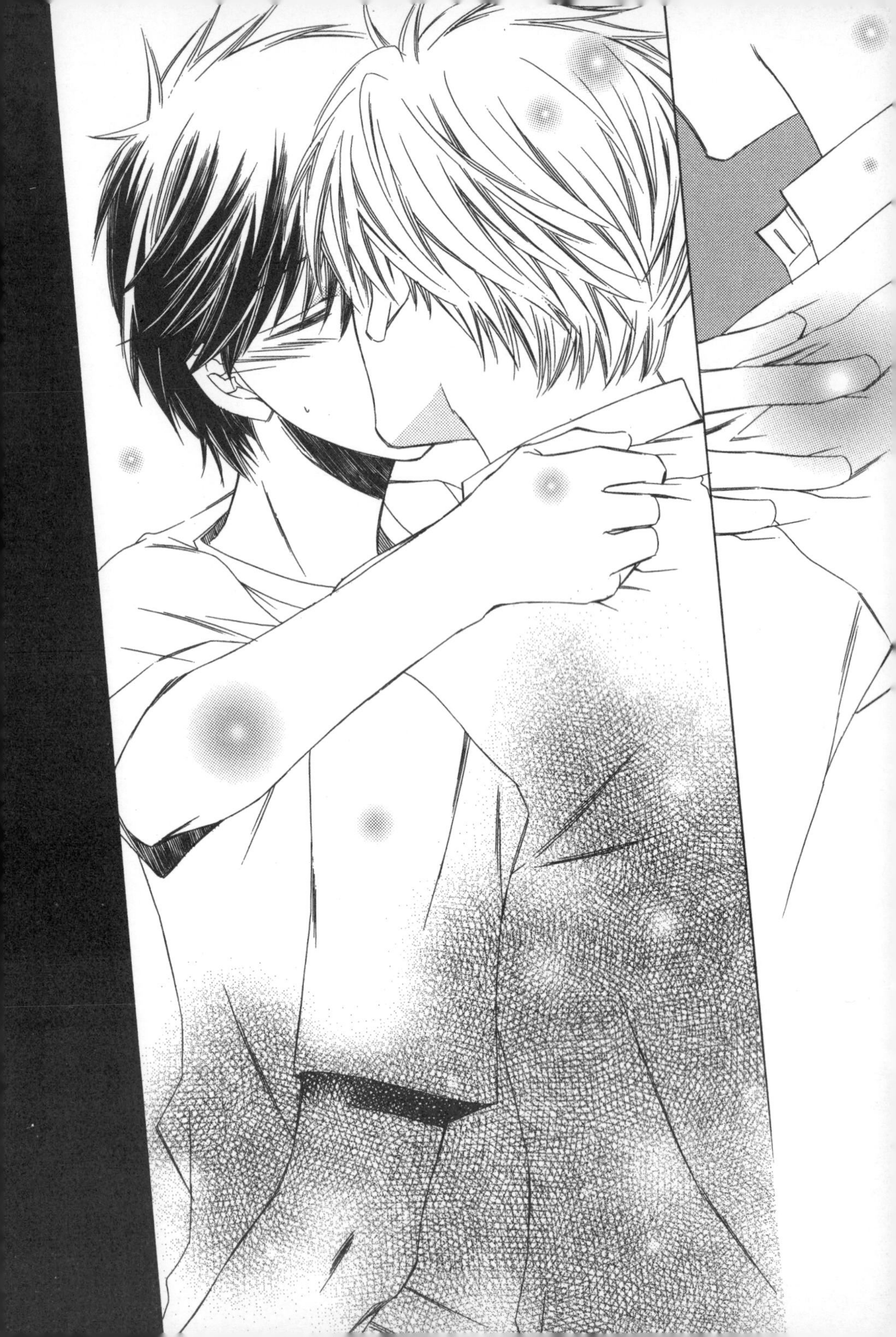

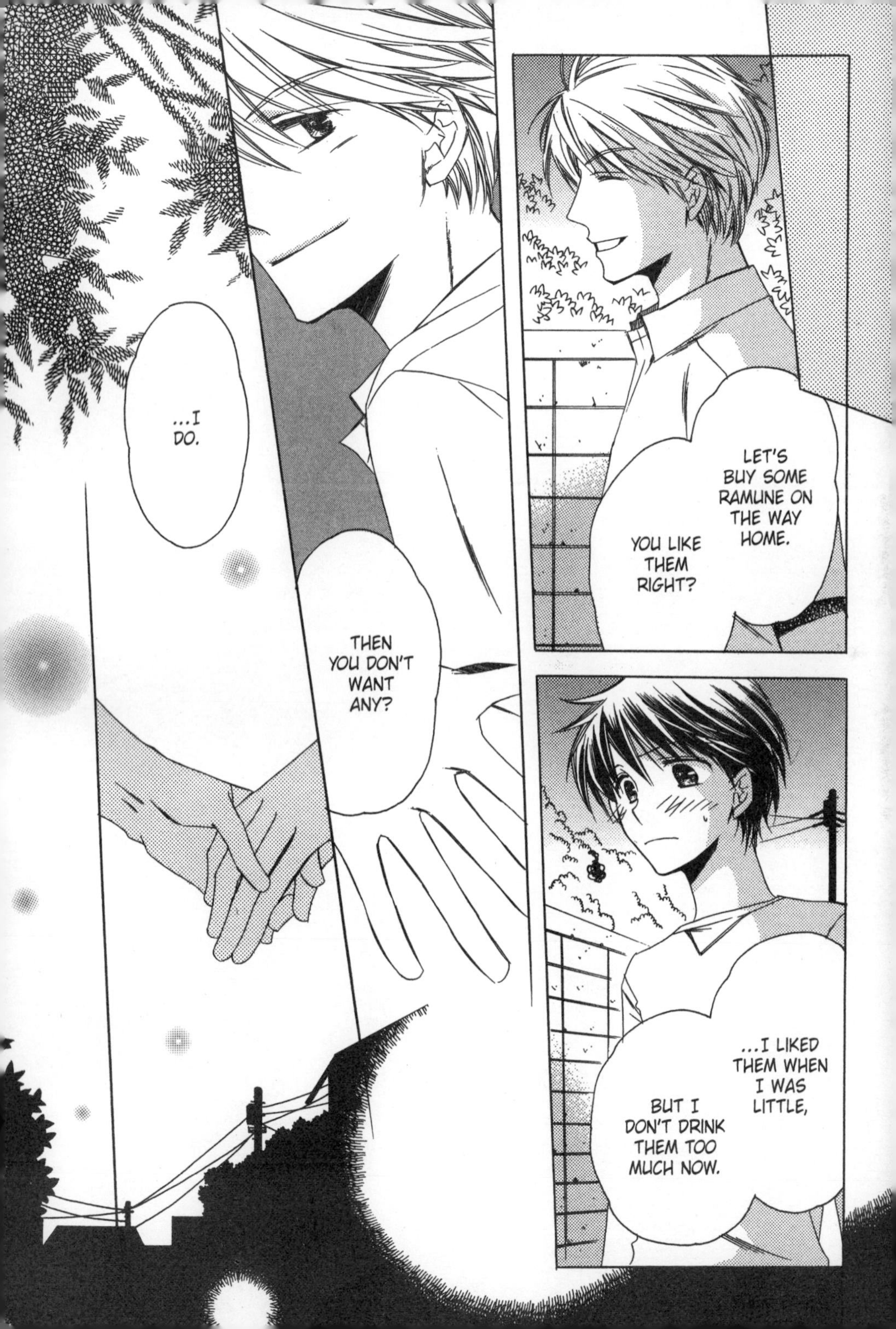
LET'S BUY SOME RAMUNE ON THE WAY HOME.
YOU LIKE THEM RIGHT?
...I LIKED THEM WHEN I WAS LITTLE,
BUT I DON'T DRINK THEM TOO MUCH NOW.
THEN YOU DON'T WANT ANY?
...I DO.

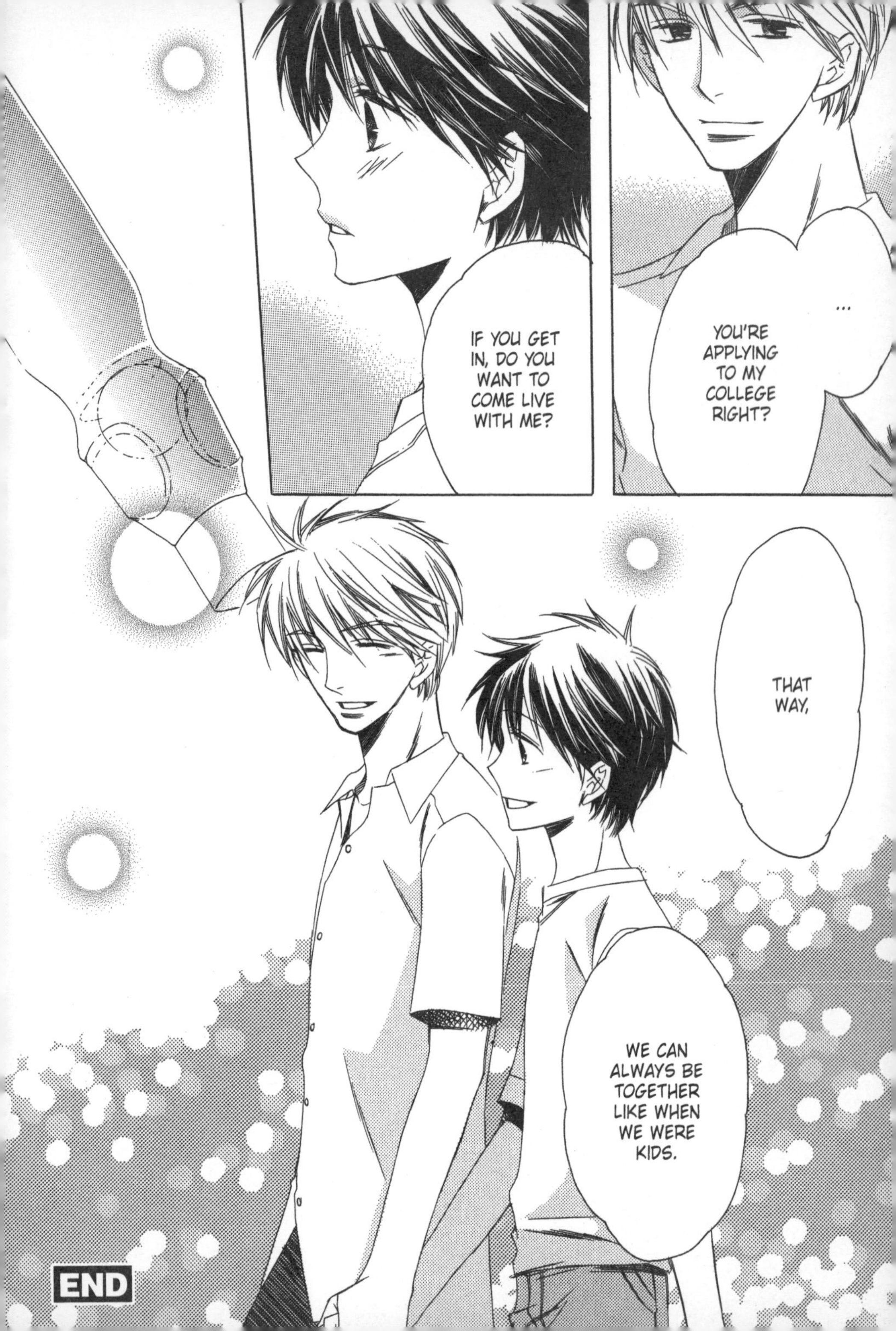
...
YOU'RE APPLYING TO MY COLLEGE RIGHT?
IF YOU GET IN, DO YOU WANT TO COME LIVE WITH ME?
THAT WAY,
WE CAN ALWAYS BE TOGETHER LIKE WHEN WE WERE KIDS.
END

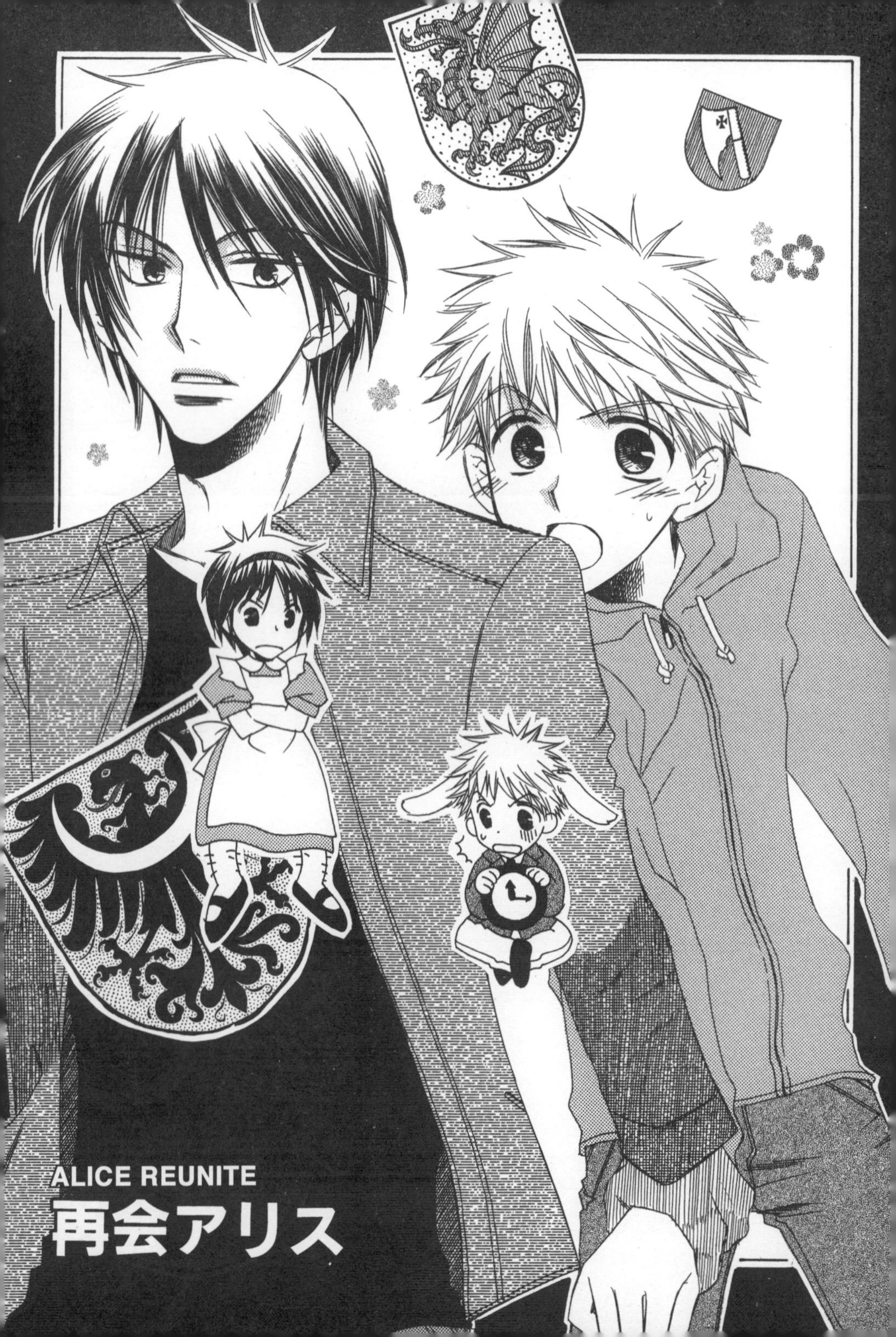

ALICE REUNITE
再会アリス

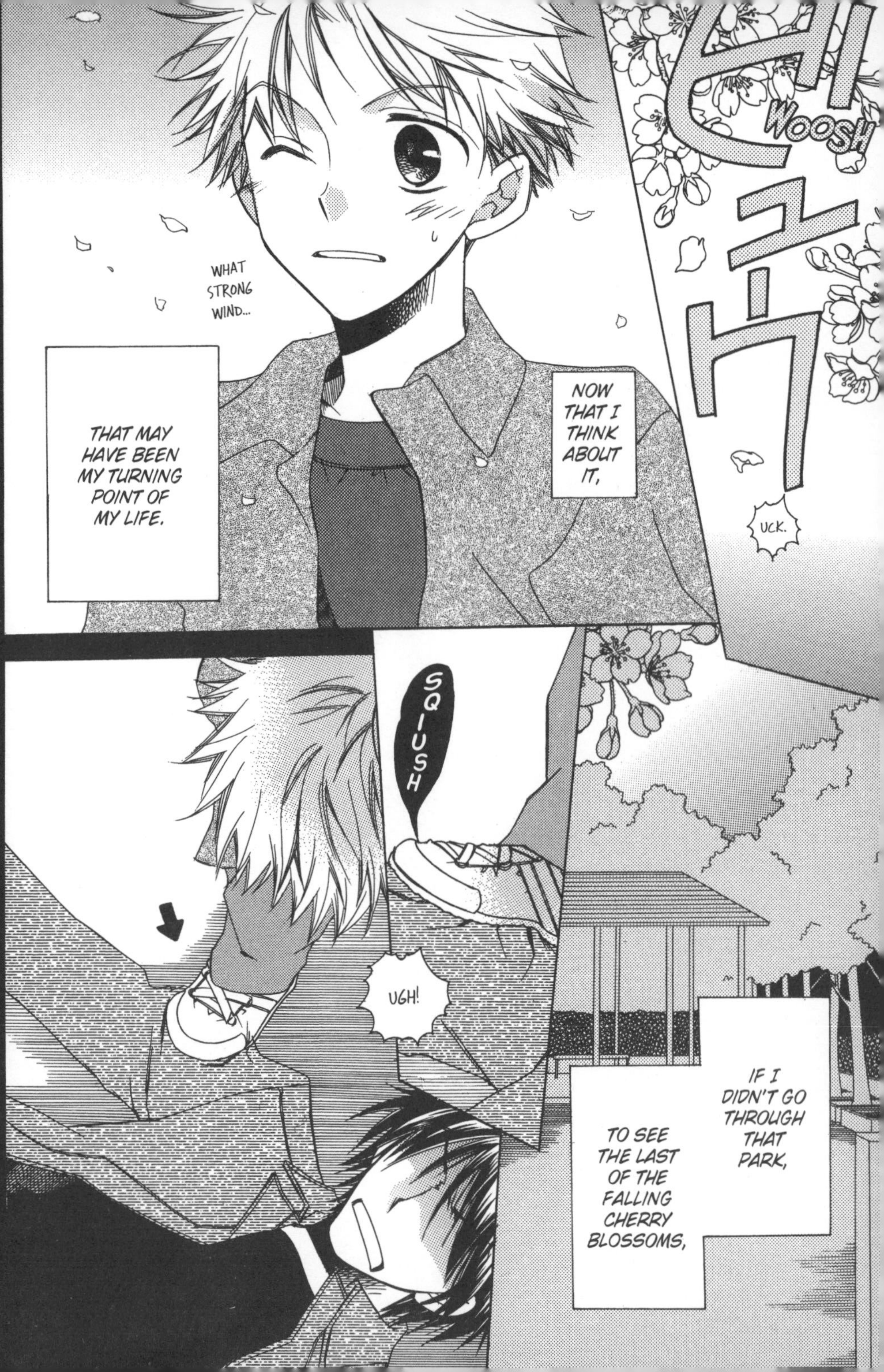
WOOSH
UCK.
WHAT STRONG WIND...
NOW THAT I THINK ABOUT IT,
THAT MAY HAVE BEEN MY TURNING POINT OF MY LIFE.
IF I DIDN'T GO THROUGH THAT PARK,
TO SEE THE LAST OF THE FALLING CHERRY BLOSSOMS,
SQIUSH
UGH!

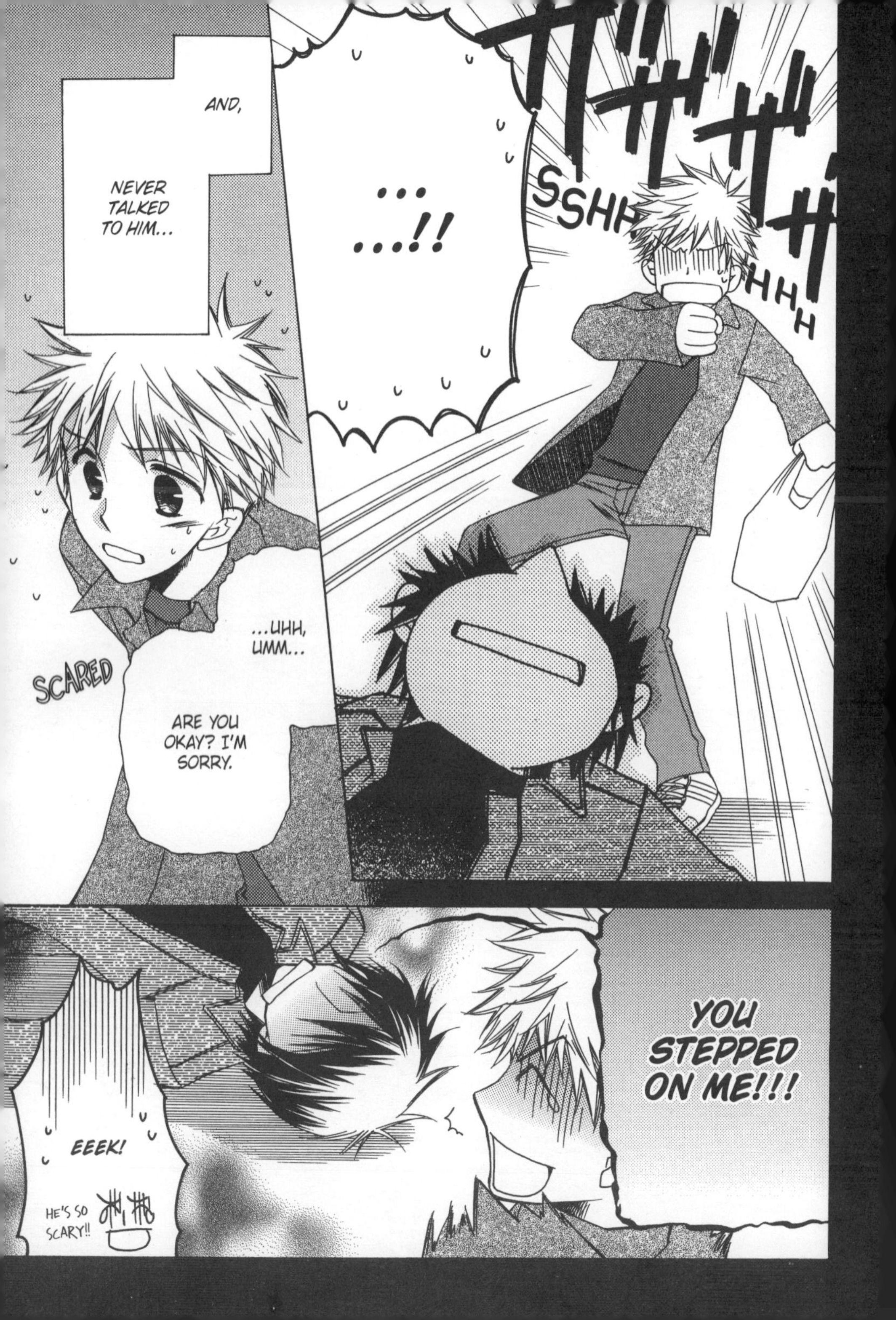
SSHH
HHHH
......!!
AND,
NEVER TALKED TO HIM...
...UHH, UMM...
SCARED
ARE YOU OKAY? I'M SORRY.
YOU STEPPED ON ME!!!
EEEK!
HE'S SO SCARY!!

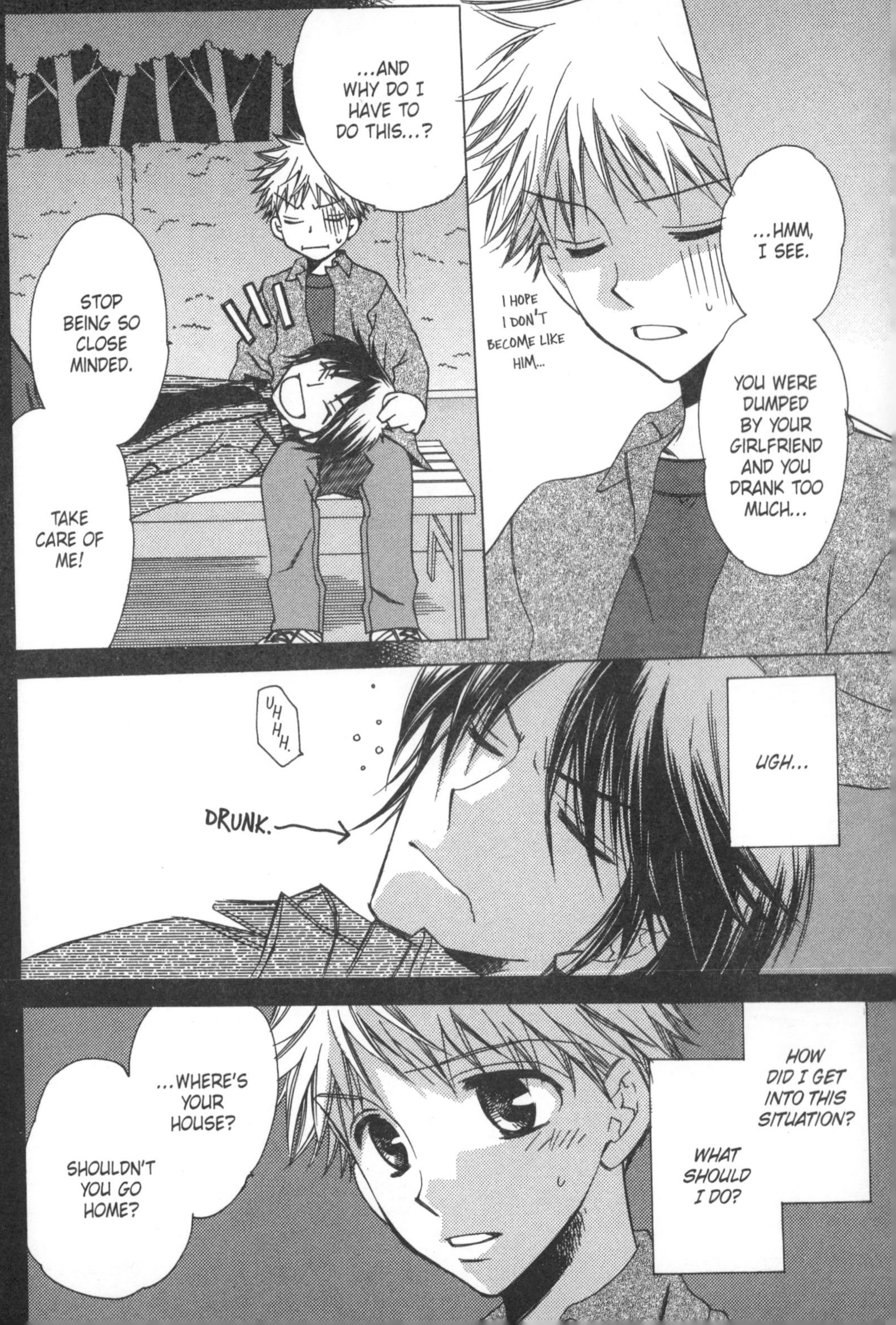
...HMM, I SEE.
YOU WERE DUMPED BY YOUR GIRLFRIEND AND YOU DRANK TOO MUCH...
I HOPE I DON'T BECOME LIKE HIM...
...AND WHY DO I HAVE TO DO THIS...?
STOP BEING SO CLOSE MINDED.
TAKE CARE OF ME!
UGH...
UHHH.
DRUNK.
HOW DID I GET INTO THIS SITUATION?
WHAT SHOULD I DO?
...WHERE'S YOUR HOUSE?
SHOULDN'T YOU GO HOME?

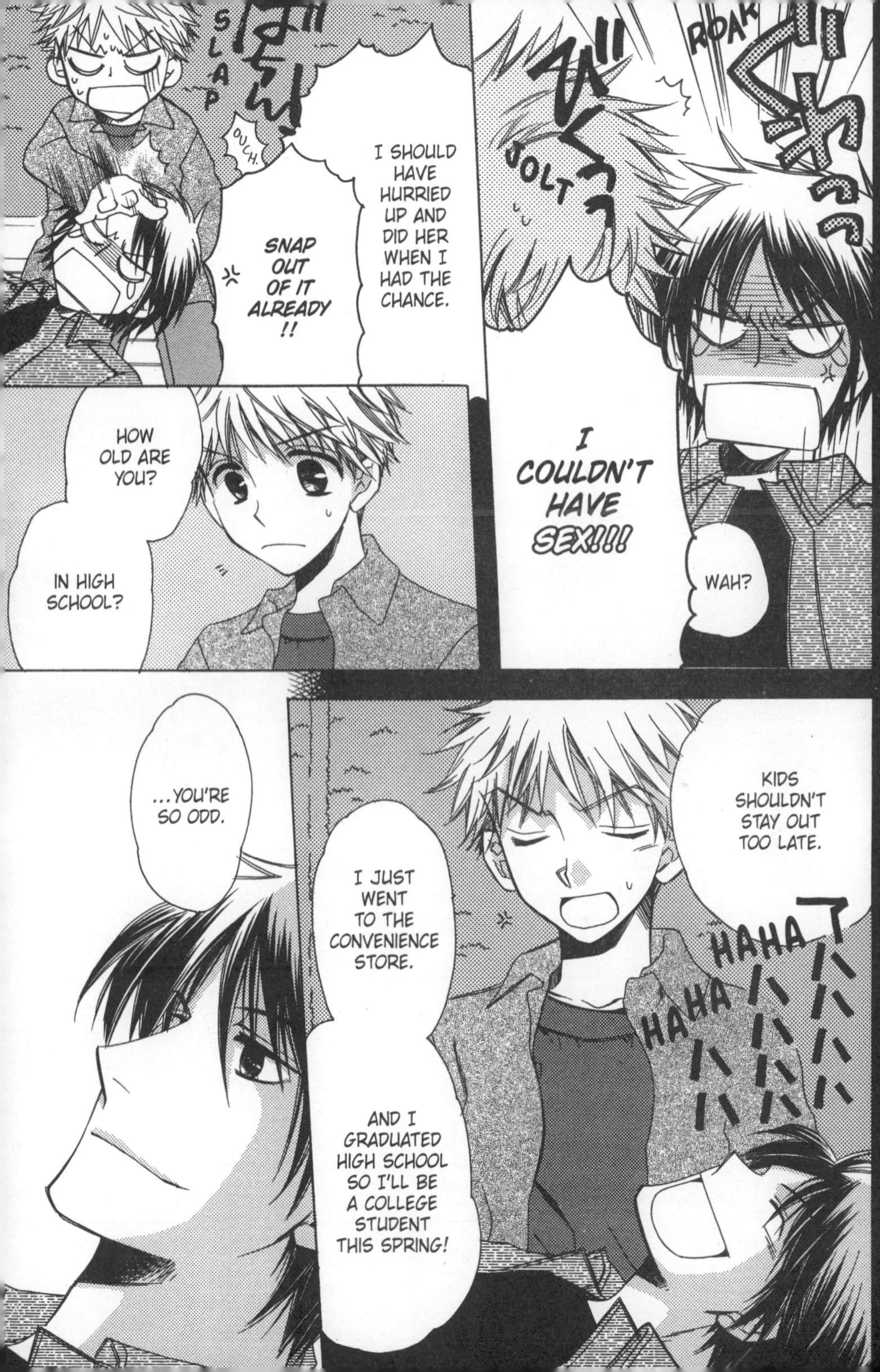
ROAR
JOLT
I COULDN'T HAVE SEX!!!
WAH?
I SHOULD HAVE HURRIED UP AND DID HER WHEN I HAD THE CHANCE.
SNAP OUT OF IT ALREADY !!
SLAP
OUCH.
HOW OLD ARE YOU?
IN HIGH SCHOOL?
KIDS SHOULDN'T STAY OUT TOO LATE.
HAHA HAHA
I JUST WENT TO THE CONVENIENCE STORE.
AND I GRADUATED HIGH SCHOOL SO I'LL BE A COLLEGE STUDENT THIS SPRING!
...YOU'RE SO ODD.

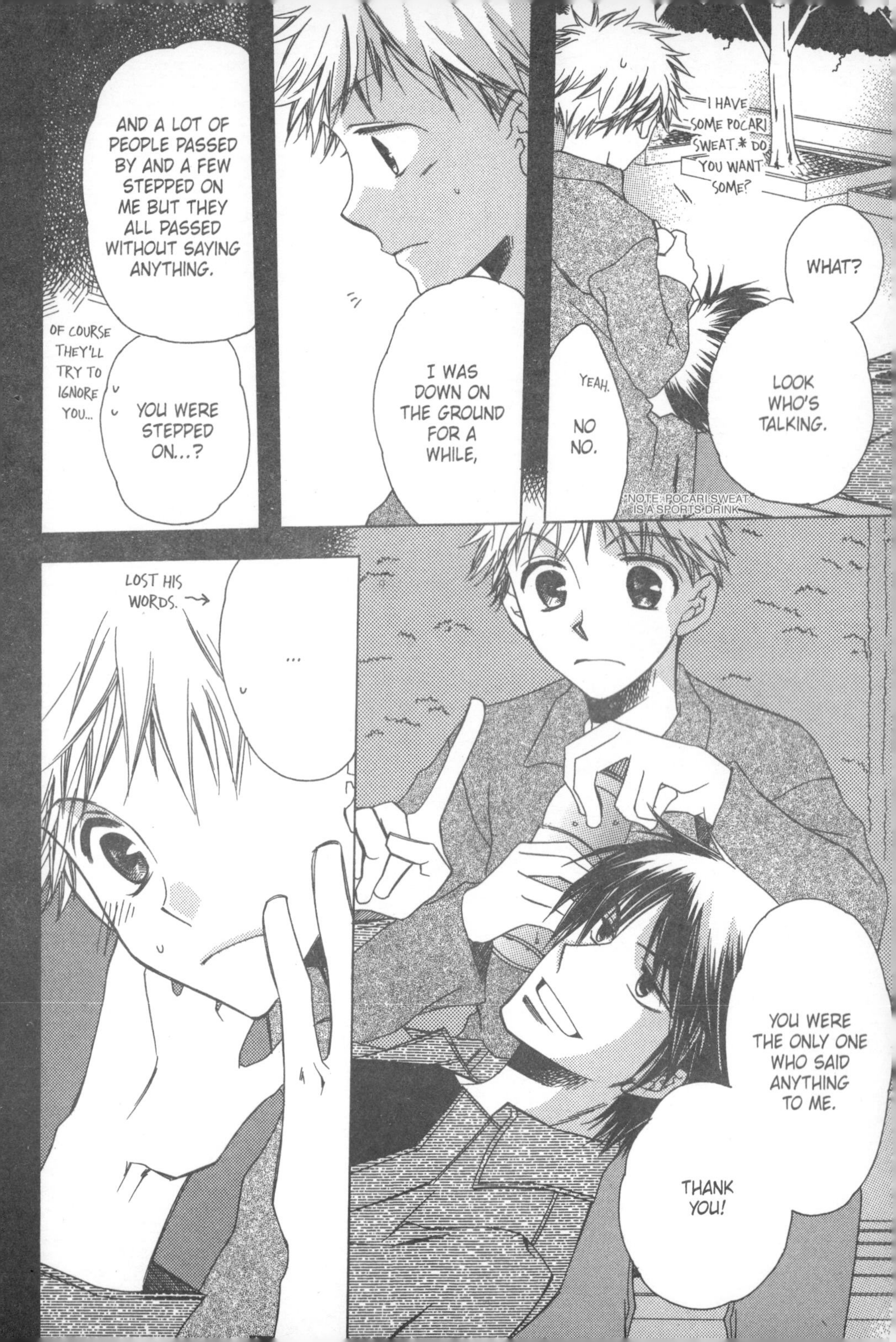
I HAVE SOME POCARI SWEAT.* DO YOU WANT SOME?
WHAT?
LOOK WHO'S TALKING.
YEAH.
NO NO.
*NOTE: POCARI SWEAT IS A SPORTS DRINK
I WAS DOWN ON THE GROUND FOR A WHILE,
AND A LOT OF PEOPLE PASSED BY AND A FEW STEPPED ON ME BUT THEY ALL PASSED WITHOUT SAYING ANYTHING.
YOU WERE STEPPED ON...?
OF COURSE THEY'LL TRY TO IGNORE YOU...
YOU WERE THE ONLY ONE WHO SAID ANYTHING TO ME.
THANK YOU!
...
LOST HIS WORDS.

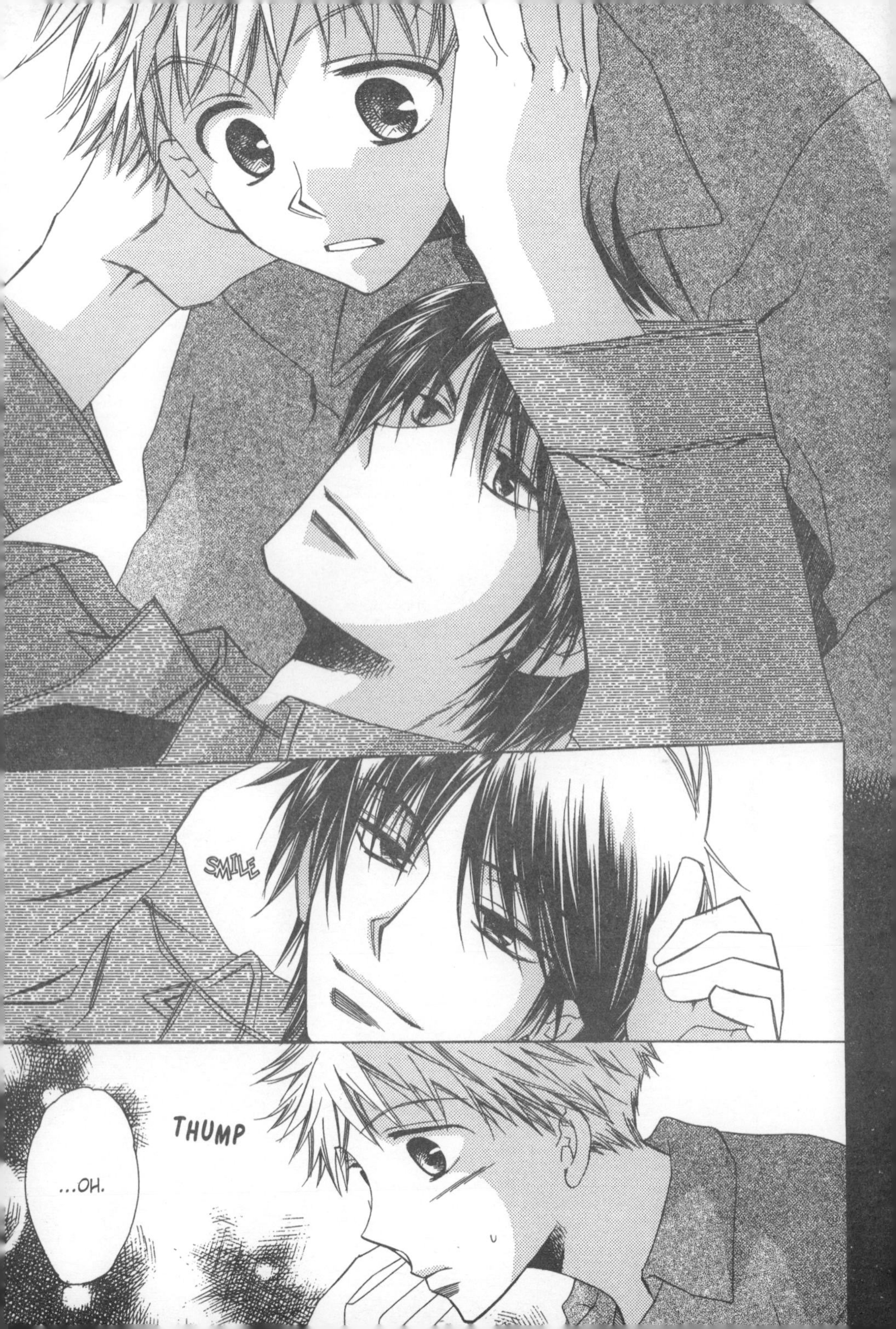
SMILE
THUMP
...OH.

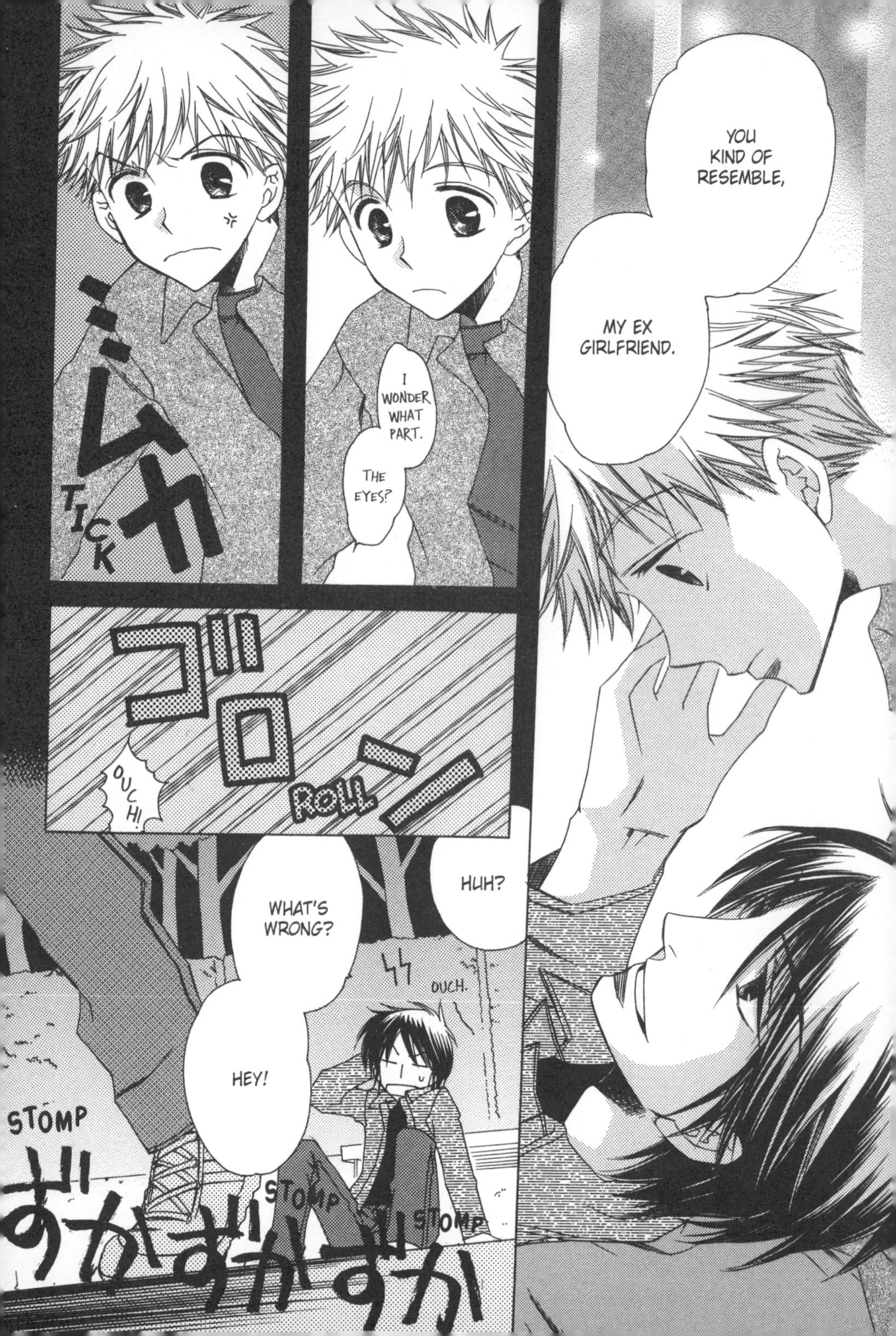
YOU KIND OF RESEMBLE,
MY EX GIRLFRIEND.
I WONDER WHAT PART.
THE EYES?
ムカ
TICK
ゴロ～
ROLL
OUCH!
HUH?
WHAT'S WRONG?
OUCH.
HEY!
STOMP
ずかずかずか
STOMP
STOMP

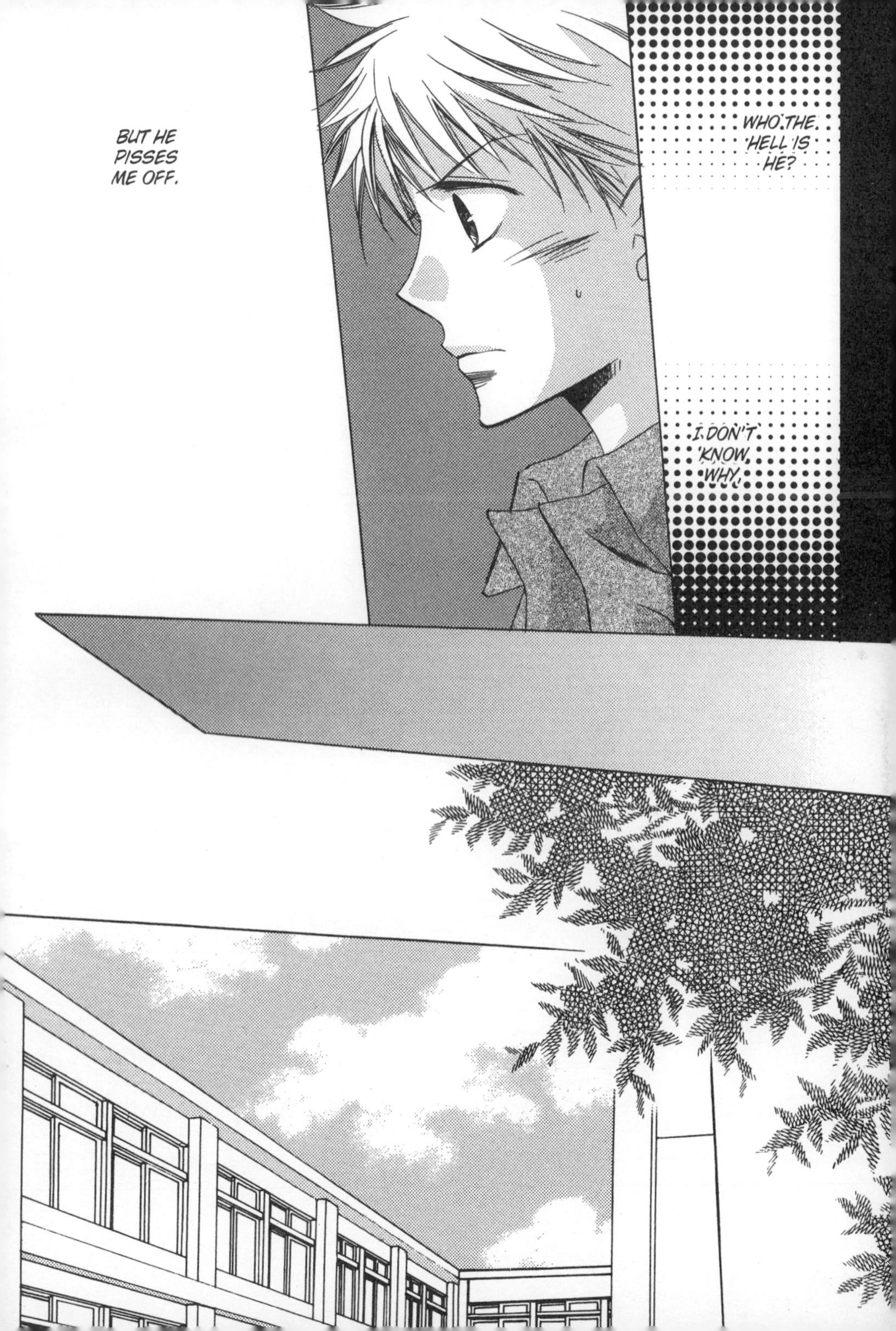
WHO THE HELL IS HE?
I DON'T KNOW WHY,
BUT HE PISSES ME OFF.

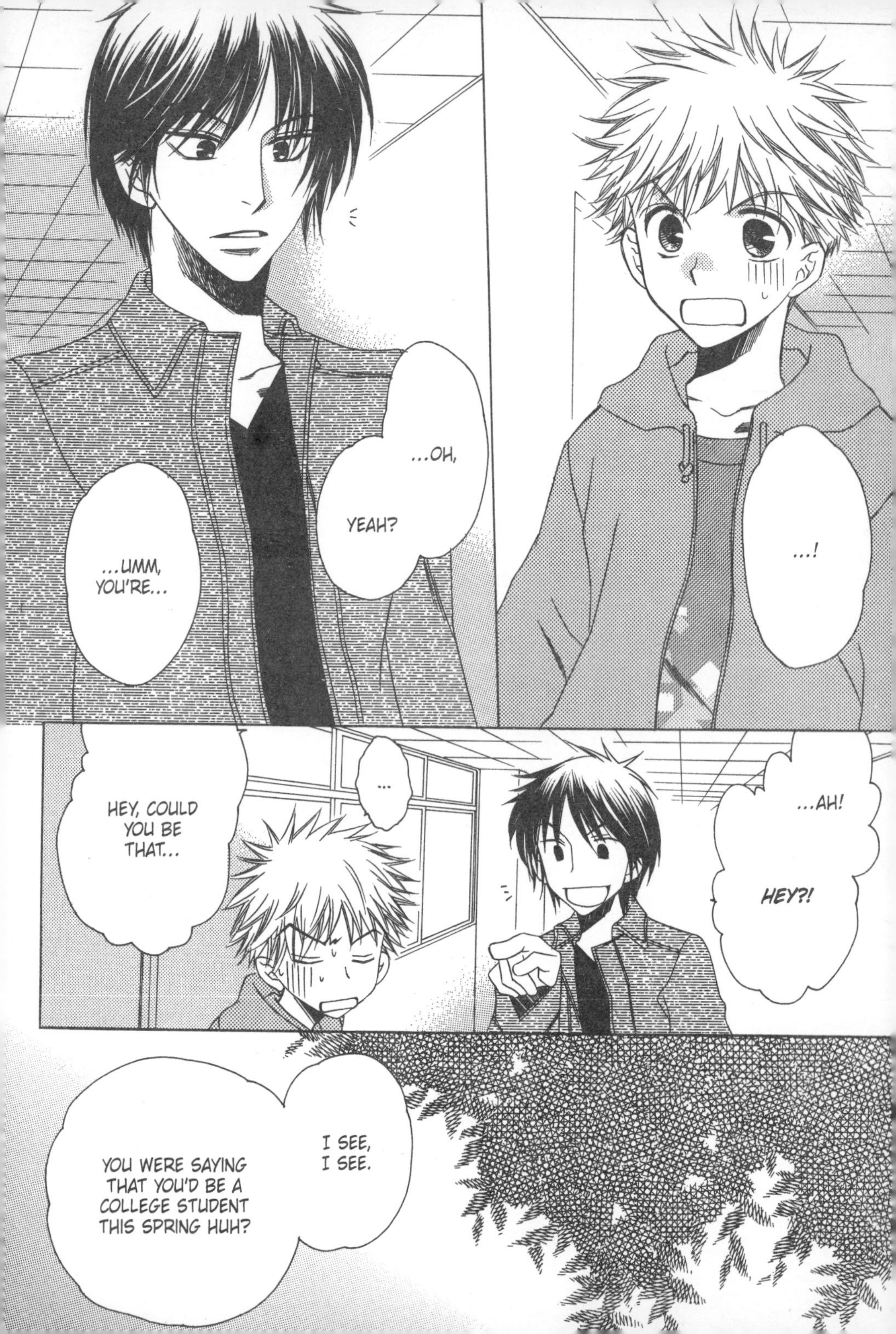
...!
...OH, YEAH?
...UMM, YOU'RE...
...AH! HEY?!
...
HEY, COULD YOU BE THAT...
I SEE, I SEE.
YOU WERE SAYING THAT YOU'D BE A COLLEGE STUDENT THIS SPRING HUH?

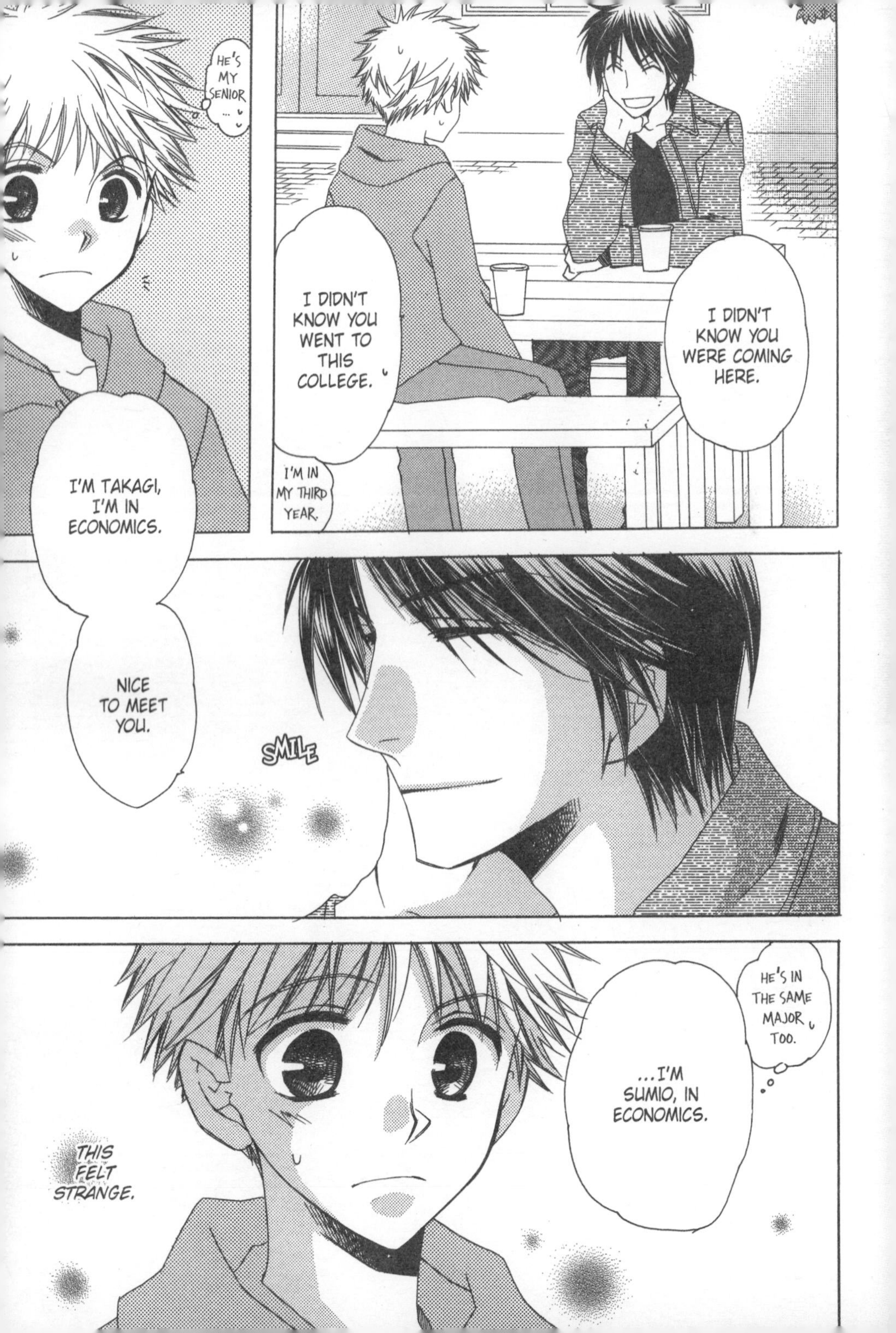
I DIDN'T KNOW YOU WERE COMING HERE.
I DIDN'T KNOW YOU WENT TO THIS COLLEGE.
I'M IN MY THIRD YEAR.
HE'S MY SENIOR...
I'M TAKAGI, I'M IN ECONOMICS.
NICE TO MEET YOU.
SMILE
HE'S IN THE SAME MAJOR TOO.
...I'M SUMIO, IN ECONOMICS.
THIS FELT STRANGE.

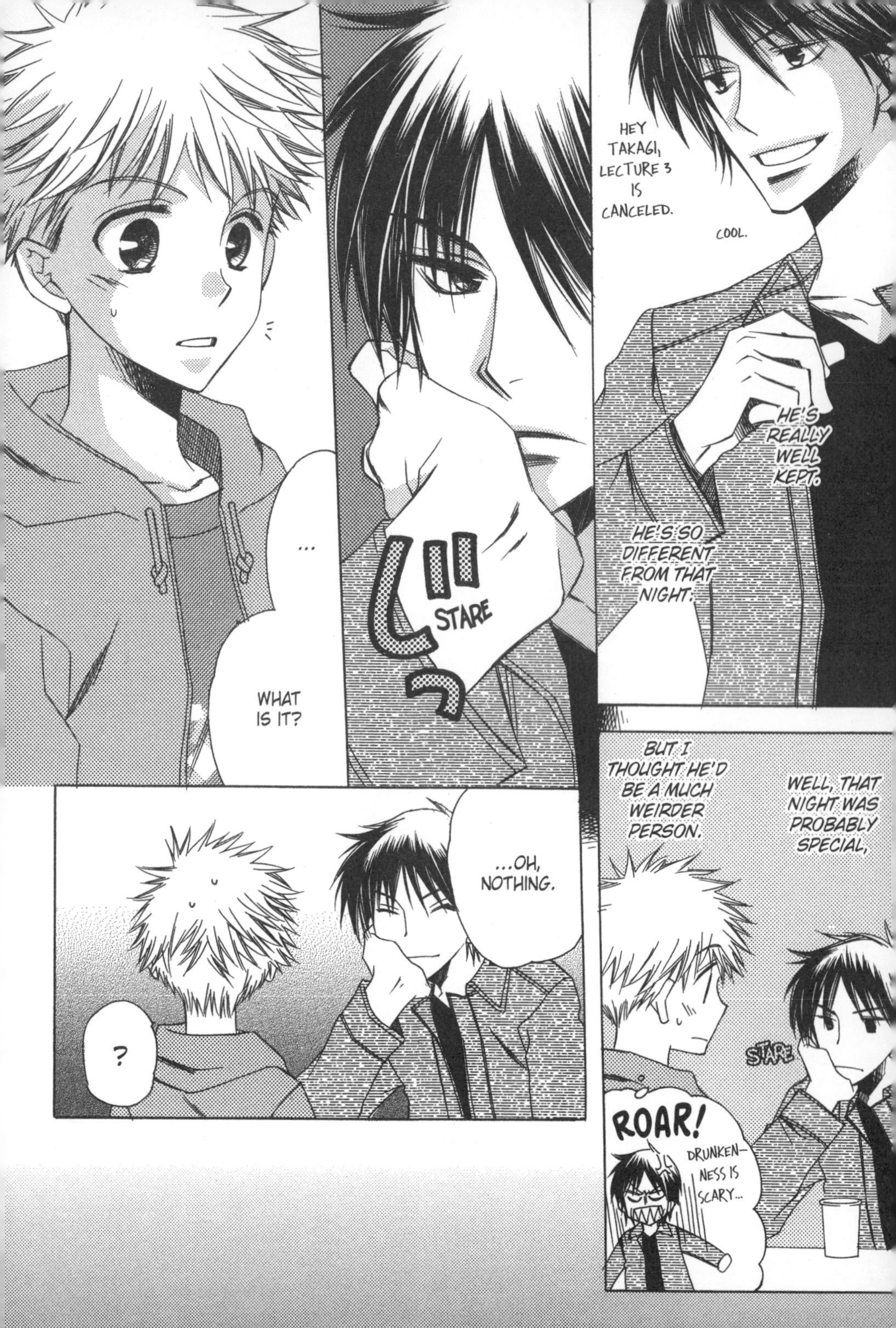
HEY TAKAGI, LECTURE 3 IS CANCELED.
COOL.
HE'S REALLY WELL KEPT.
HE'S SO DIFFERENT FROM THAT NIGHT.
じーっ
STARE
...
WHAT IS IT?
WELL, THAT NIGHT WAS PROBABLY SPECIAL,
BUT I THOUGHT HE'D BE A MUCH WEIRDER PERSON.
STARE
ROAR!
DRUNKEN-NESS IS SCARY...
...OH, NOTHING.
?

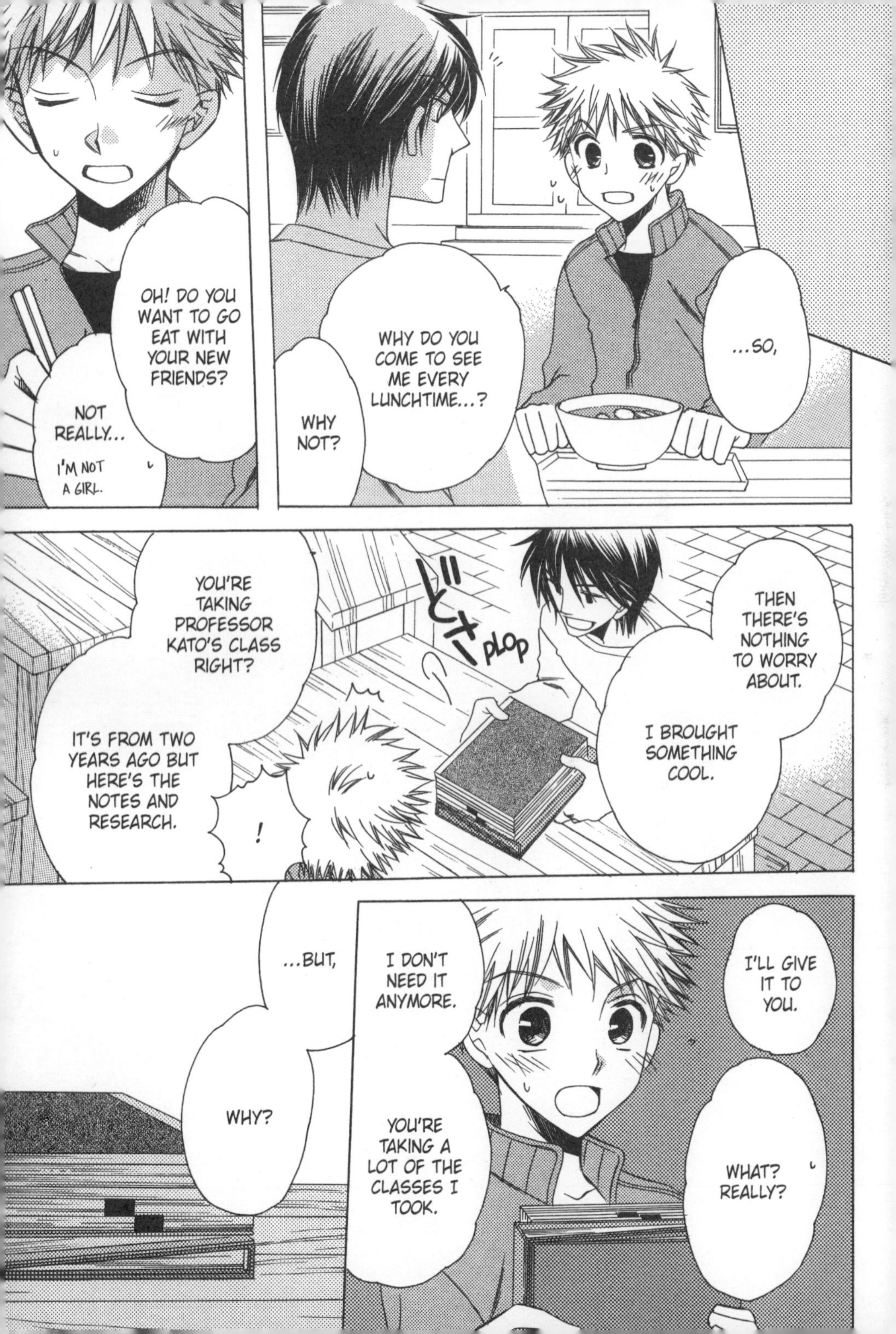
...SO,
WHY DO YOU COME TO SEE ME EVERY LUNCHTIME...?
WHY NOT?
OH! DO YOU WANT TO GO EAT WITH YOUR NEW FRIENDS?
NOT REALLY...
I'M NOT A GIRL.
THEN THERE'S NOTHING TO WORRY ABOUT.
I BROUGHT SOMETHING COOL.
PLOP
YOU'RE TAKING PROFESSOR KATO'S CLASS RIGHT?
IT'S FROM TWO YEARS AGO BUT HERE'S THE NOTES AND RESEARCH.
!
I'LL GIVE IT TO YOU.
WHAT? REALLY?
I DON'T NEED IT ANYMORE.
YOU'RE TAKING A LOT OF THE CLASSES I TOOK.
...BUT,
WHY?

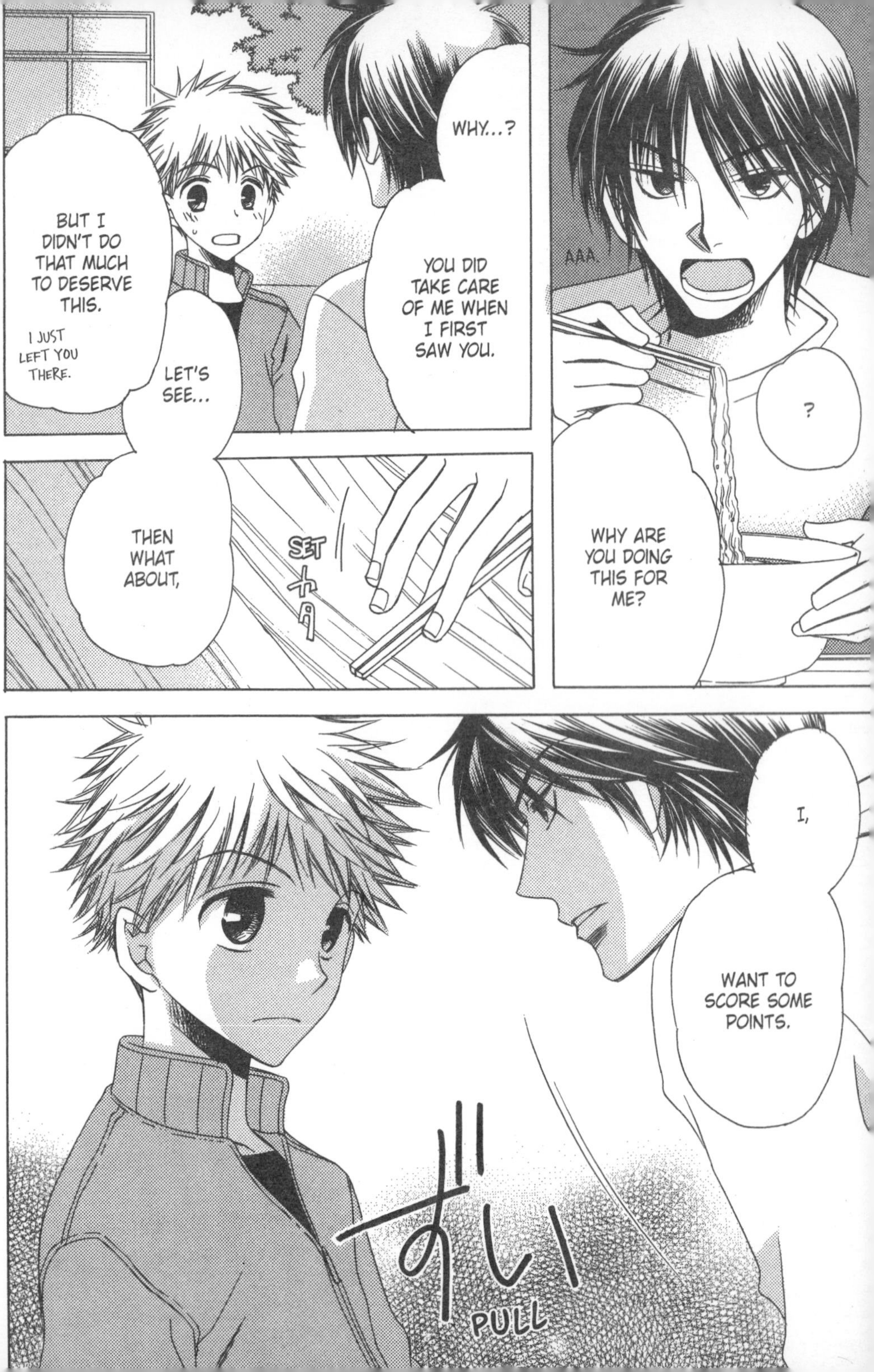
AAA.
?
WHY ARE YOU DOING THIS FOR ME?
WHY...?
YOU DID TAKE CARE OF ME WHEN I FIRST SAW YOU.
BUT I DIDN'T DO THAT MUCH TO DESERVE THIS.
I JUST LEFT YOU THERE.
LET'S SEE...
THEN WHAT ABOUT,
SET
I,
WANT TO SCORE SOME POINTS.
PULL

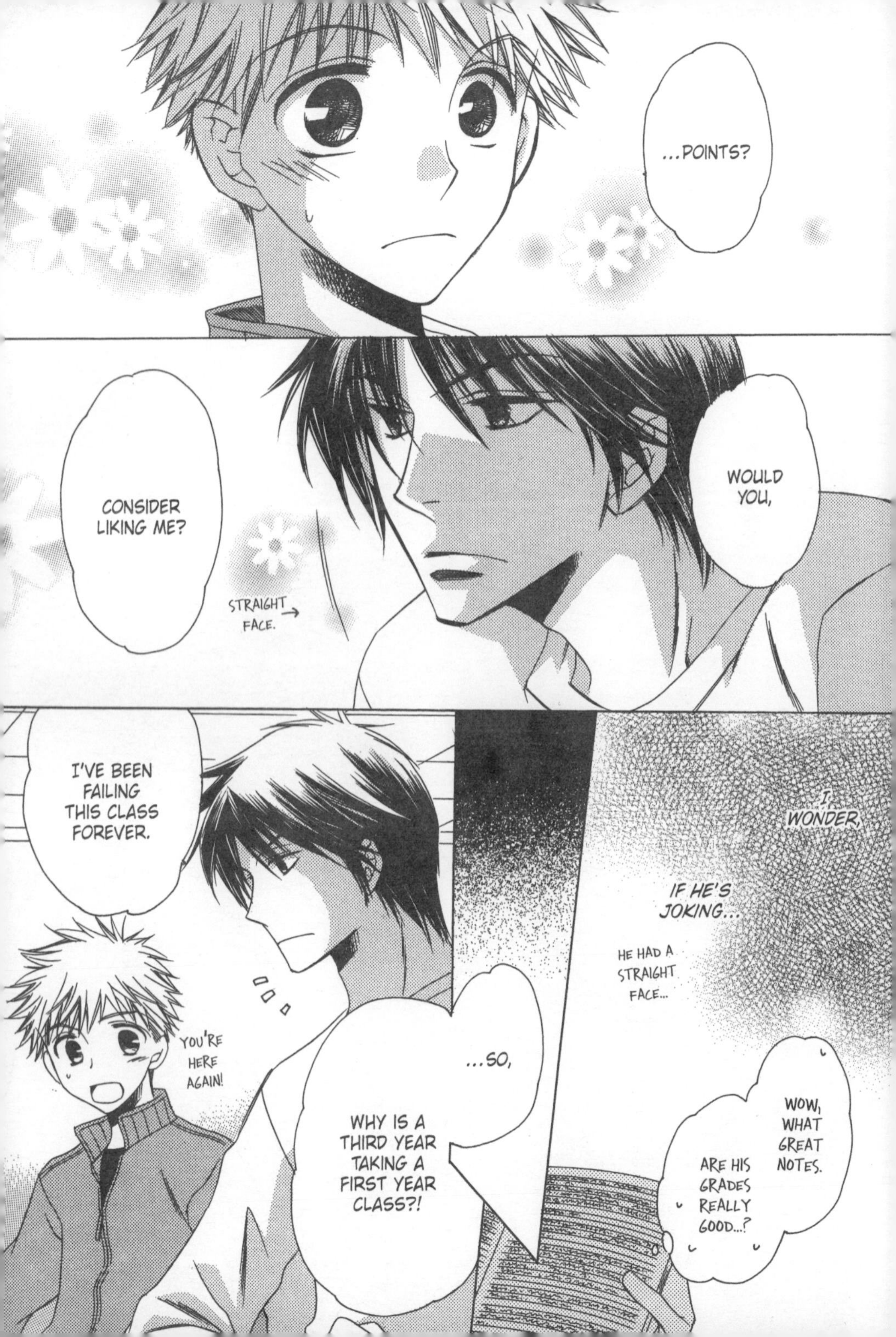
...POINTS?
WOULD YOU,
CONSIDER LIKING ME?
STRAIGHT FACE.
I, WONDER,
IF HE'S JOKING...
HE HAD A STRAIGHT FACE...
WOW, WHAT GREAT NOTES.
ARE HIS GRADES REALLY GOOD...?
...SO,
WHY IS A THIRD YEAR TAKING A FIRST YEAR CLASS?!
I'VE BEEN FAILING THIS CLASS FOREVER.
YOU'RE HERE AGAIN!

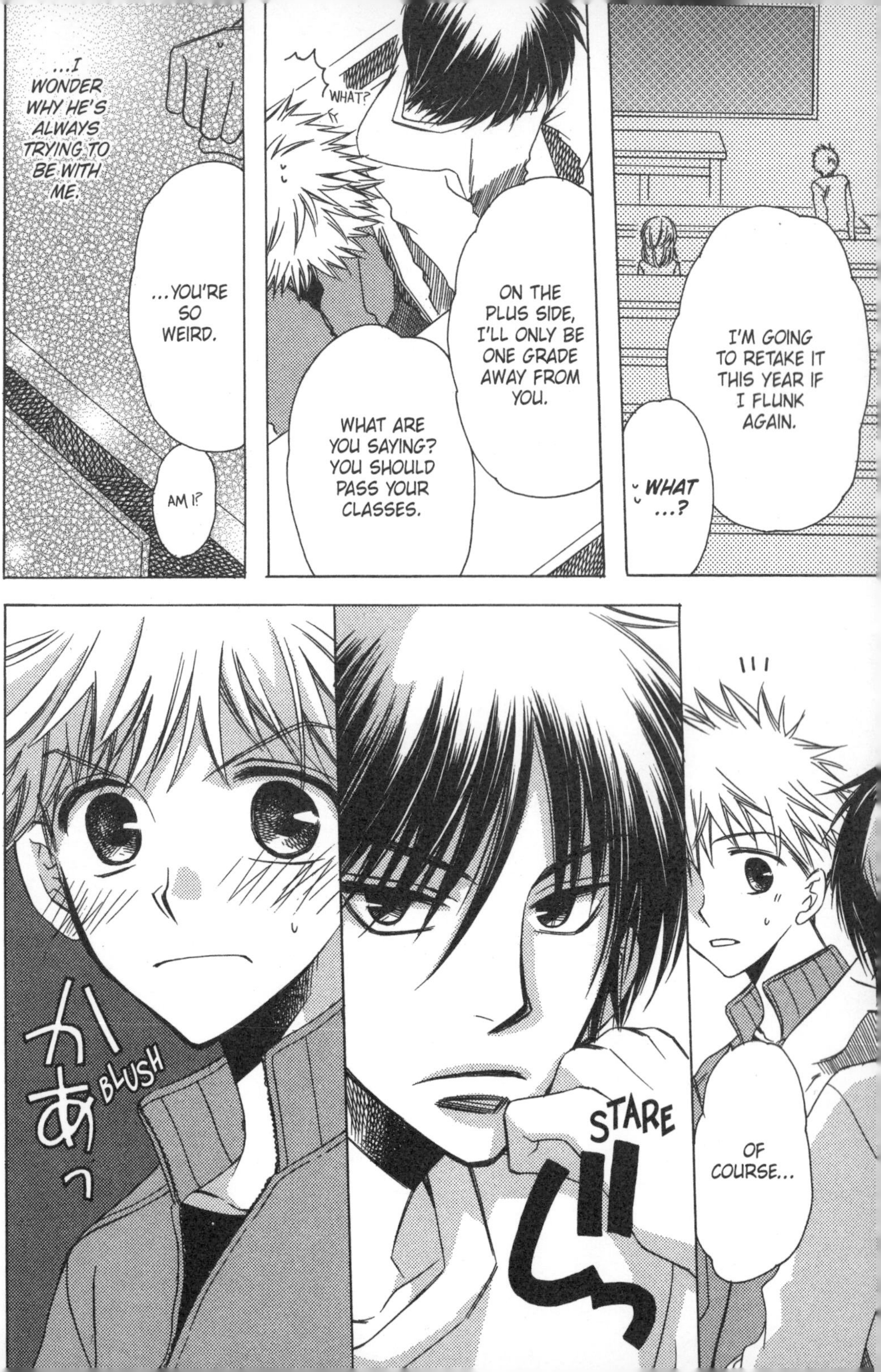
I'M GOING TO RETAKE IT THIS YEAR IF I FLUNK AGAIN.
WHAT ...?
WHAT?
ON THE PLUS SIDE, I'LL ONLY BE ONE GRADE AWAY FROM YOU.
WHAT ARE YOU SAYING? YOU SHOULD PASS YOUR CLASSES.
...I WONDER WHY HE'S ALWAYS TRYING TO BE WITH ME.
...YOU'RE SO WEIRD.
AM I?
OF COURSE...
STARE
かあっ
BLUSH

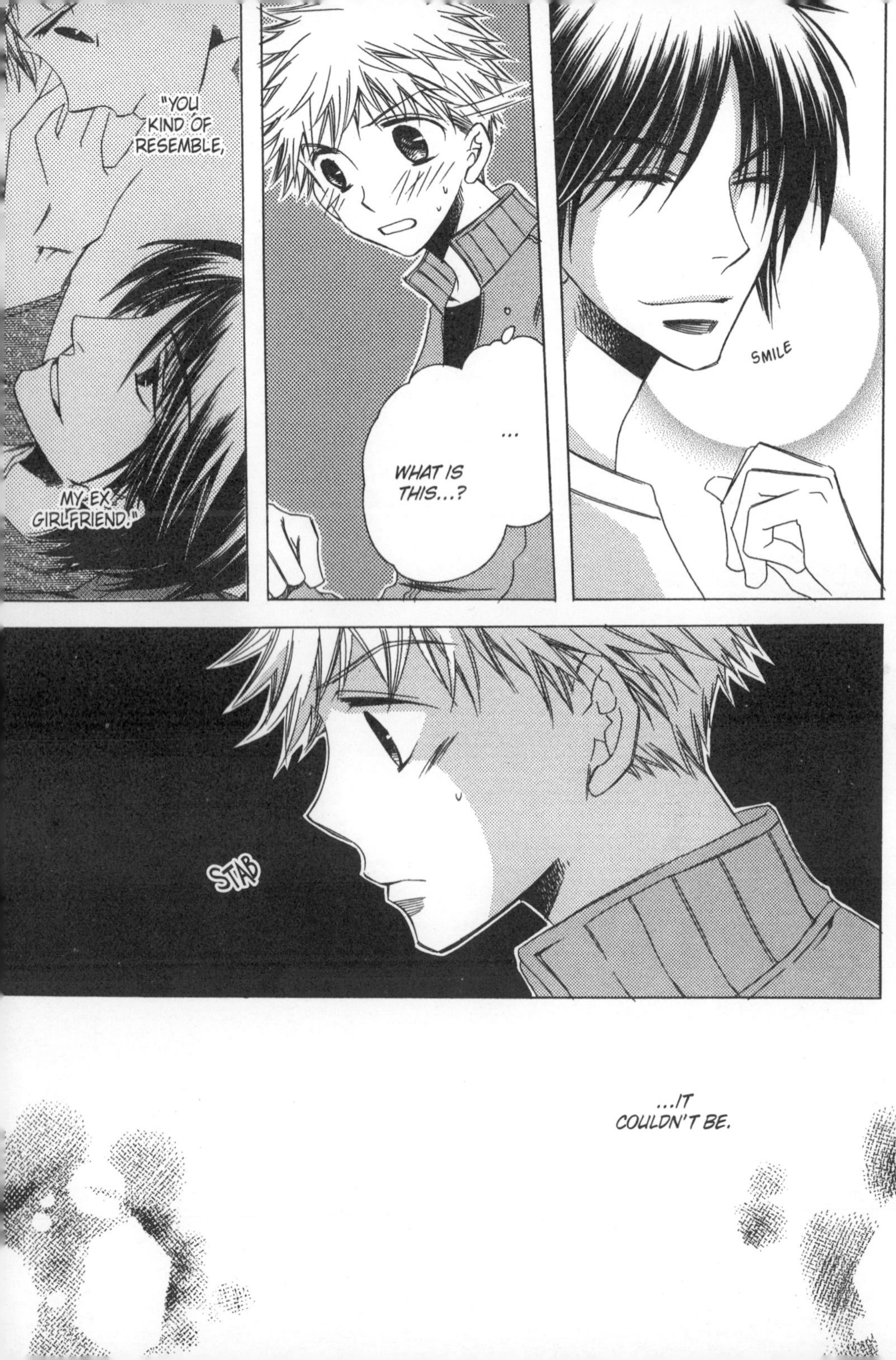
SMILE
...
WHAT IS THIS...?
"YOU KIND OF RESEMBLE,
MY EX GIRLFRIEND."
STAB
...IT COULDN'T BE.

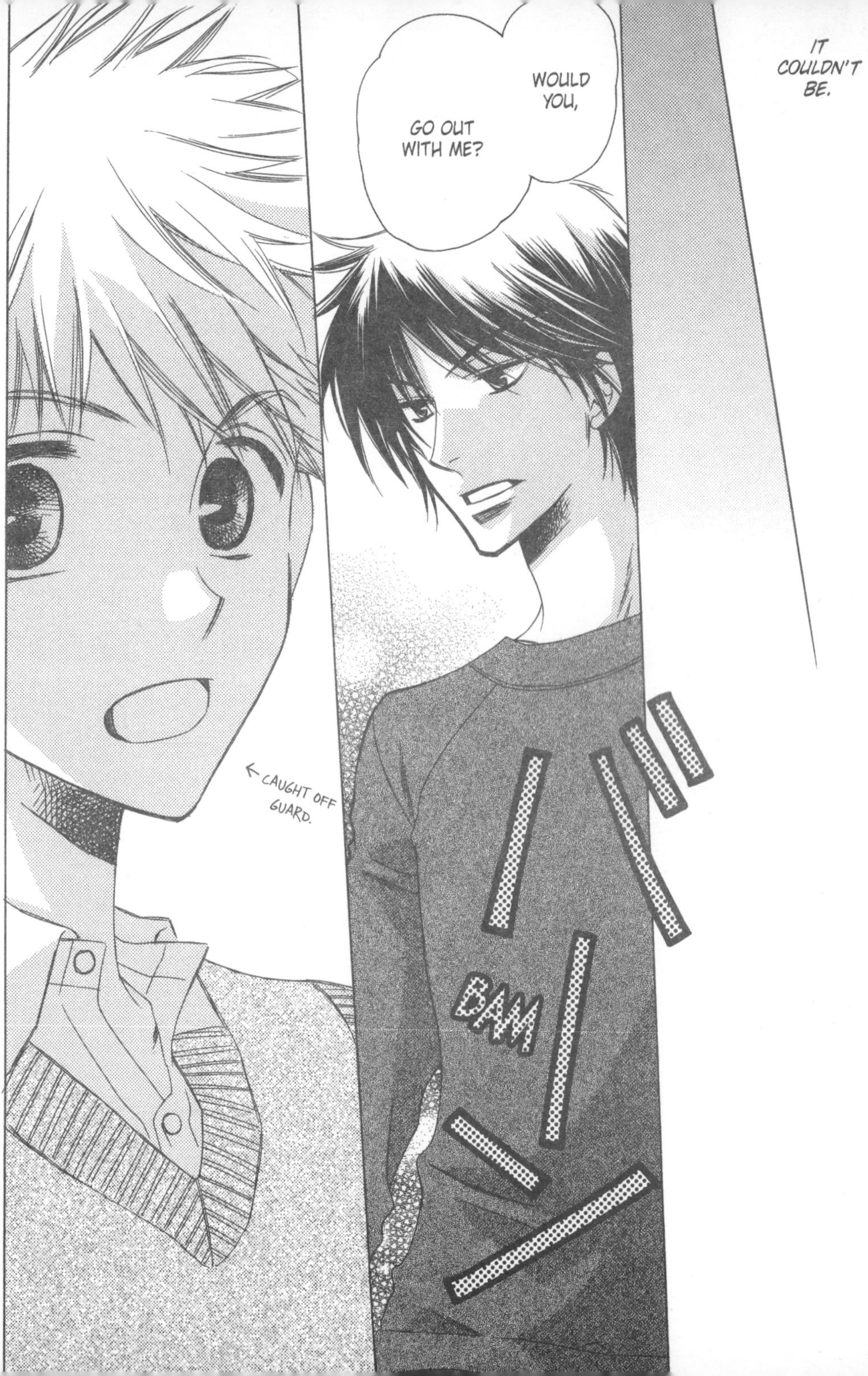
IT COULDN'T BE.
WOULD YOU, GO OUT WITH ME?
BAM
← CAUGHT OFF GUARD.

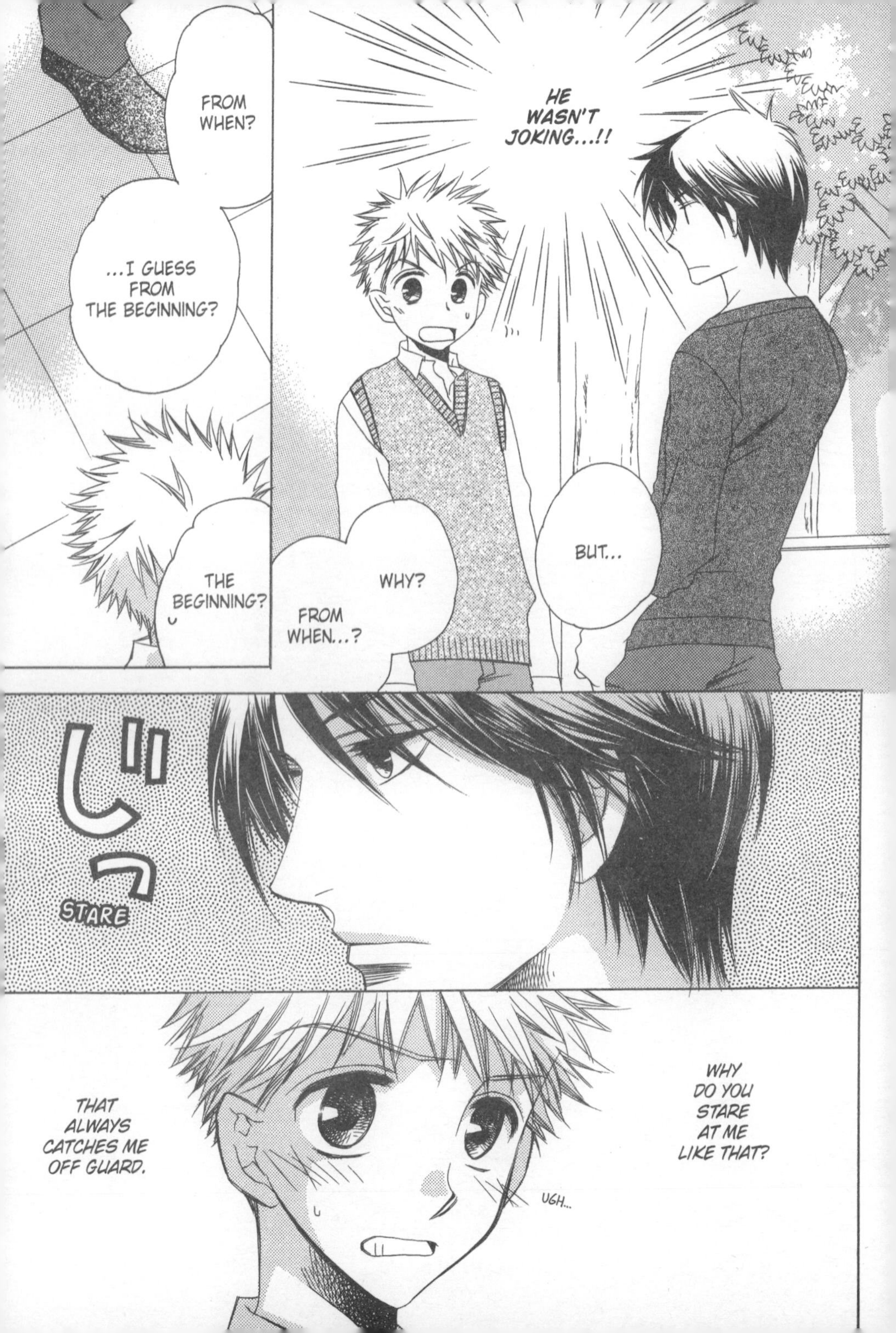
HE WASN'T JOKING...!!
BUT...
WHY? FROM WHEN...?
FROM WHEN?
...I GUESS FROM THE BEGINNING?
THE BEGINNING?
じっ
STARE
WHY DO YOU STARE AT ME LIKE THAT?
UGH...
THAT ALWAYS CATCHES ME OFF GUARD.

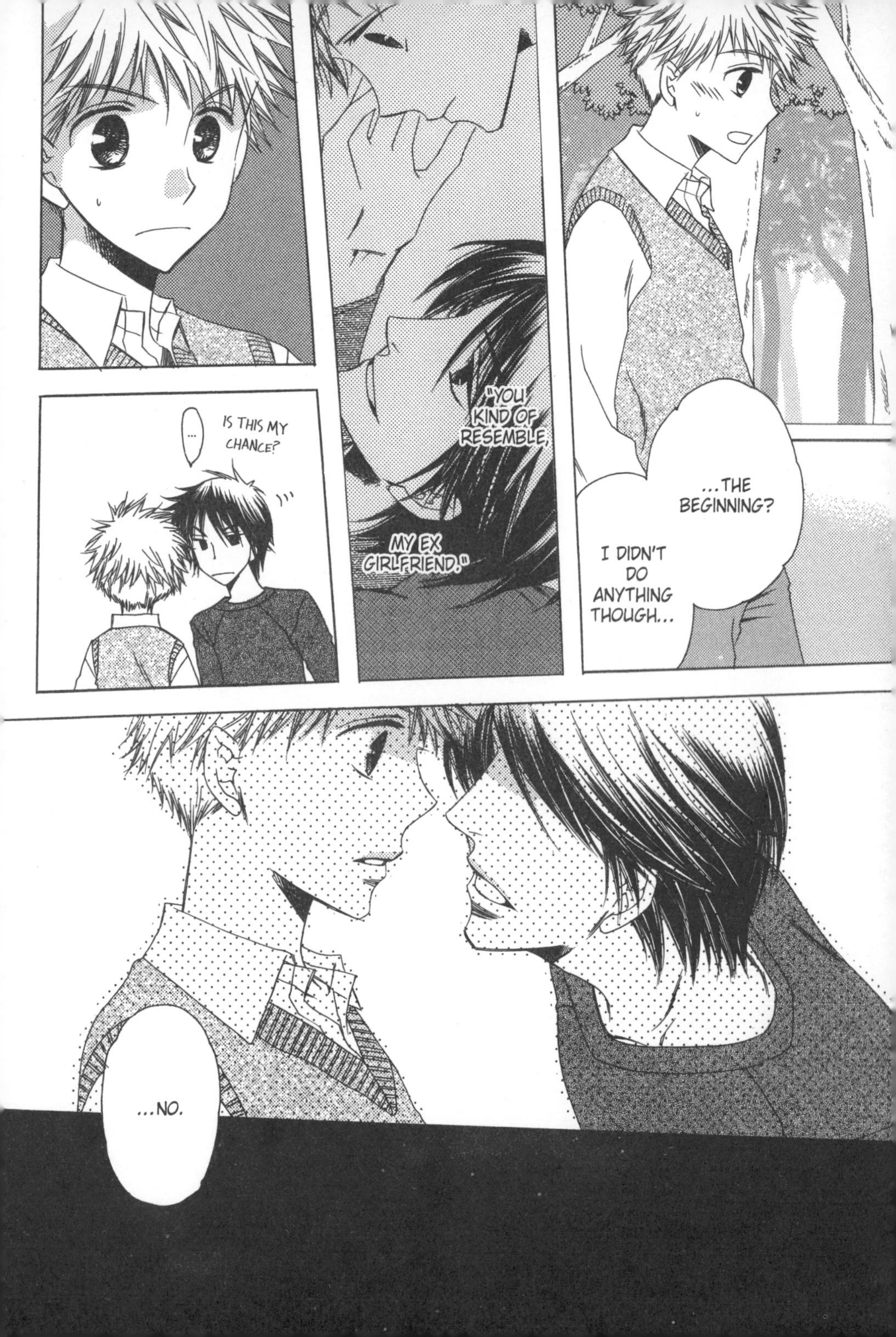
...THE BEGINNING?
I DIDN'T DO ANYTHING THOUGH...
"YOU KIND OF RESEMBLE,
MY EX GIRLFRIEND."
...
IS THIS MY CHANCE?
...NO.

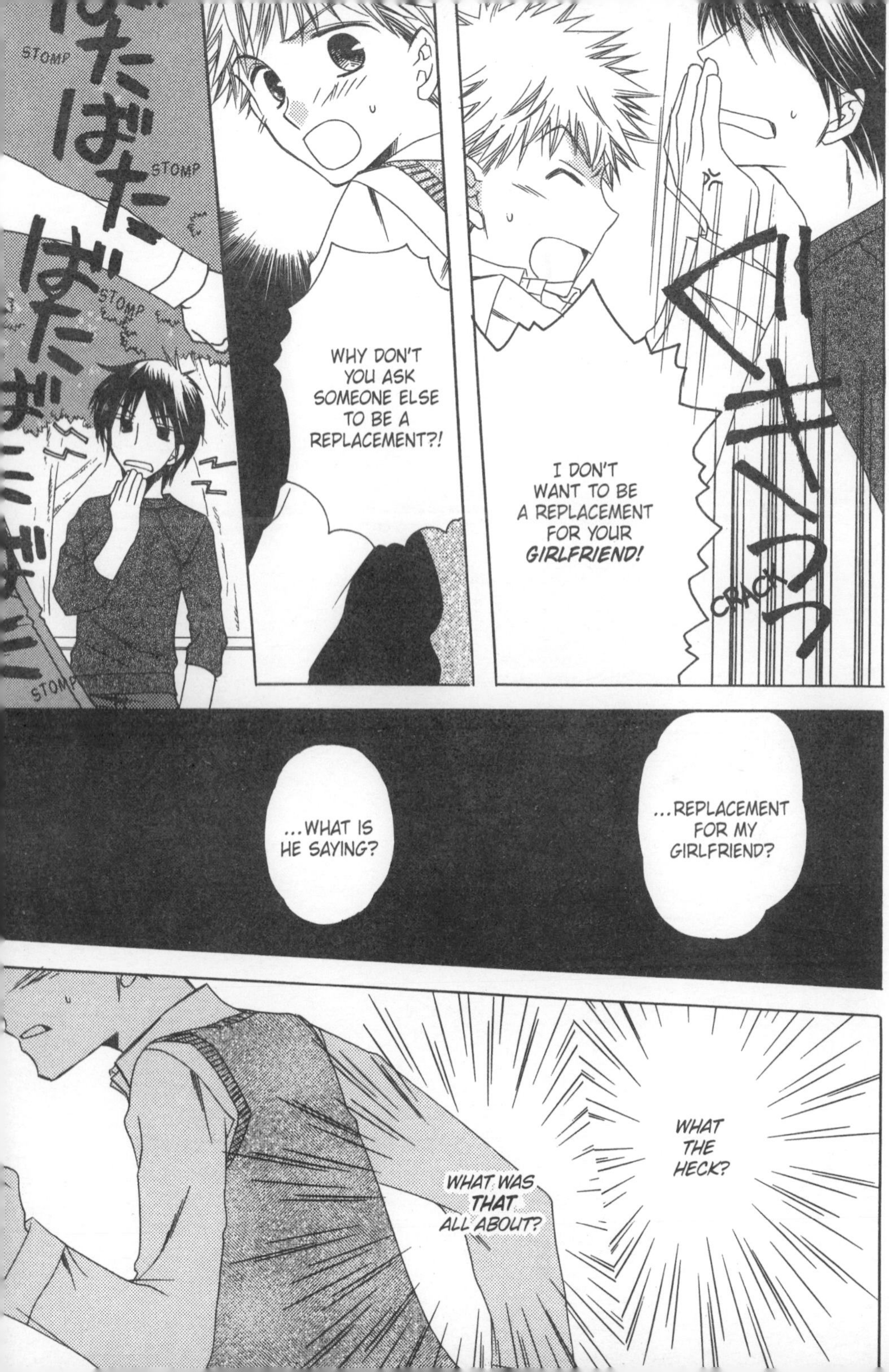
I DON'T WANT TO BE A REPLACEMENT FOR YOUR GIRLFRIEND!
CRACK
WHY DON'T YOU ASK SOMEONE ELSE TO BE A REPLACEMENT?!
STOMP
STOMP
STOMP
STOMP
...REPLACEMENT FOR MY GIRLFRIEND?
...WHAT IS HE SAYING?
WHAT THE HECK?
WHAT WAS THAT ALL ABOUT?

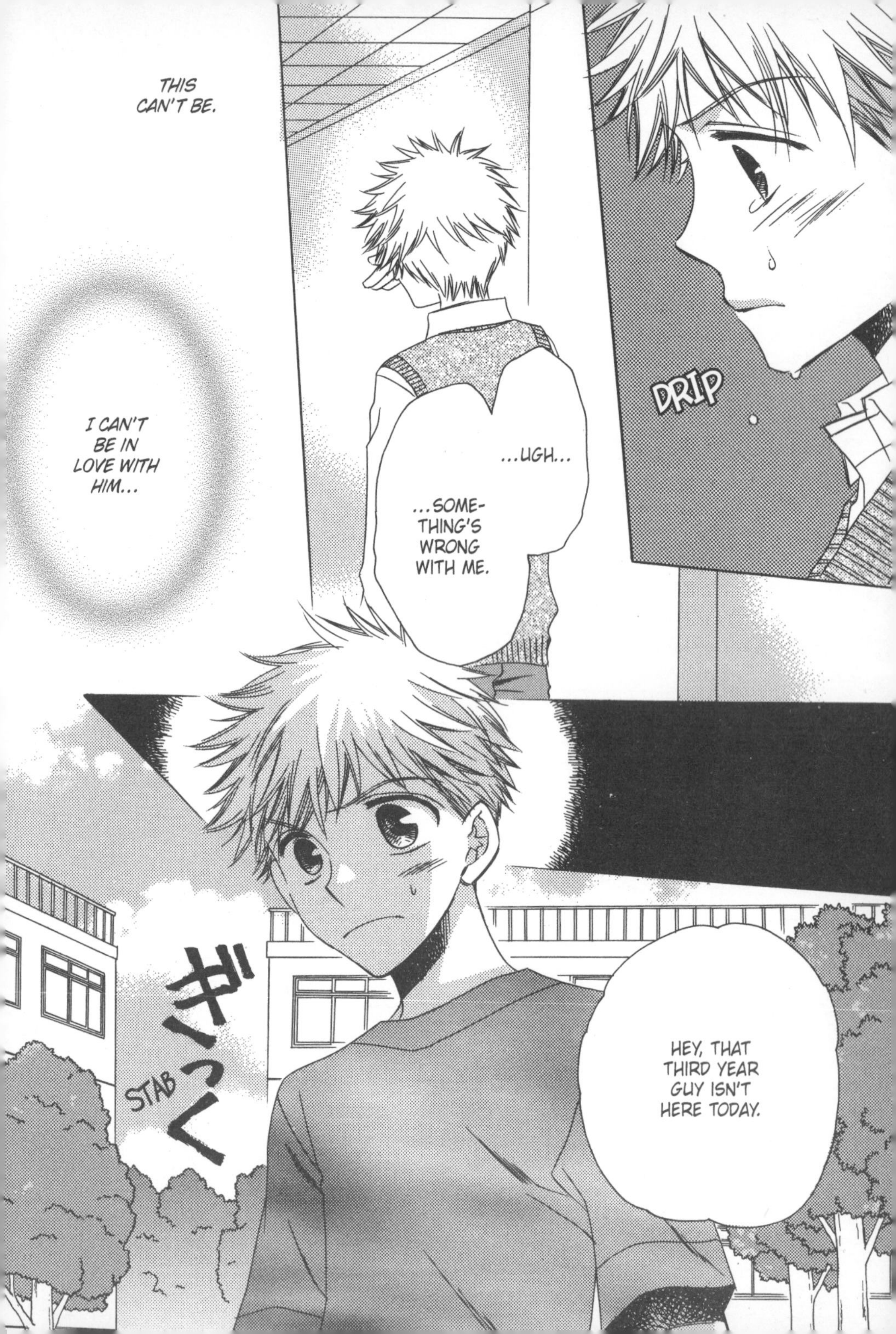
DRIP
...UGH...
...SOME-THING'S WRONG WITH ME.
THIS CAN'T BE.
I CAN'T BE IN LOVE WITH HIM...
HEY, THAT THIRD YEAR GUY ISN'T HERE TODAY.
ぎっく
STAB

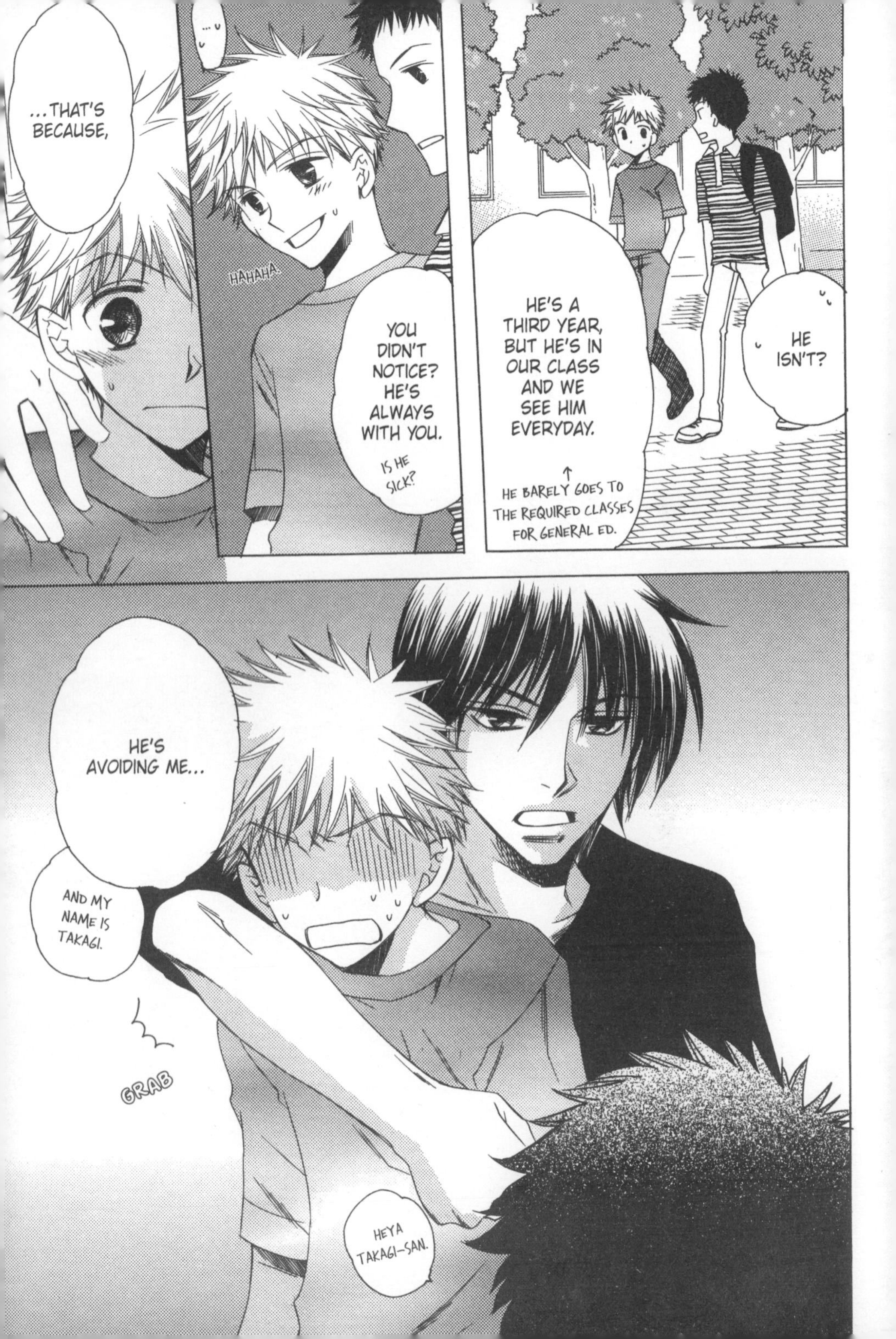
HE ISN'T?
HE'S A THIRD YEAR, BUT HE'S IN OUR CLASS AND WE SEE HIM EVERYDAY.
HE BARELY GOES TO THE REQUIRED CLASSES FOR GENERAL ED.
...
YOU DIDN'T NOTICE? HE'S ALWAYS WITH YOU.
IS HE SICK?
HAHAHA.
...THAT'S BECAUSE,
HE'S AVOIDING ME...
AND MY NAME IS TAKAGI.
GRAB
HEYA TAKAGI-SAN.

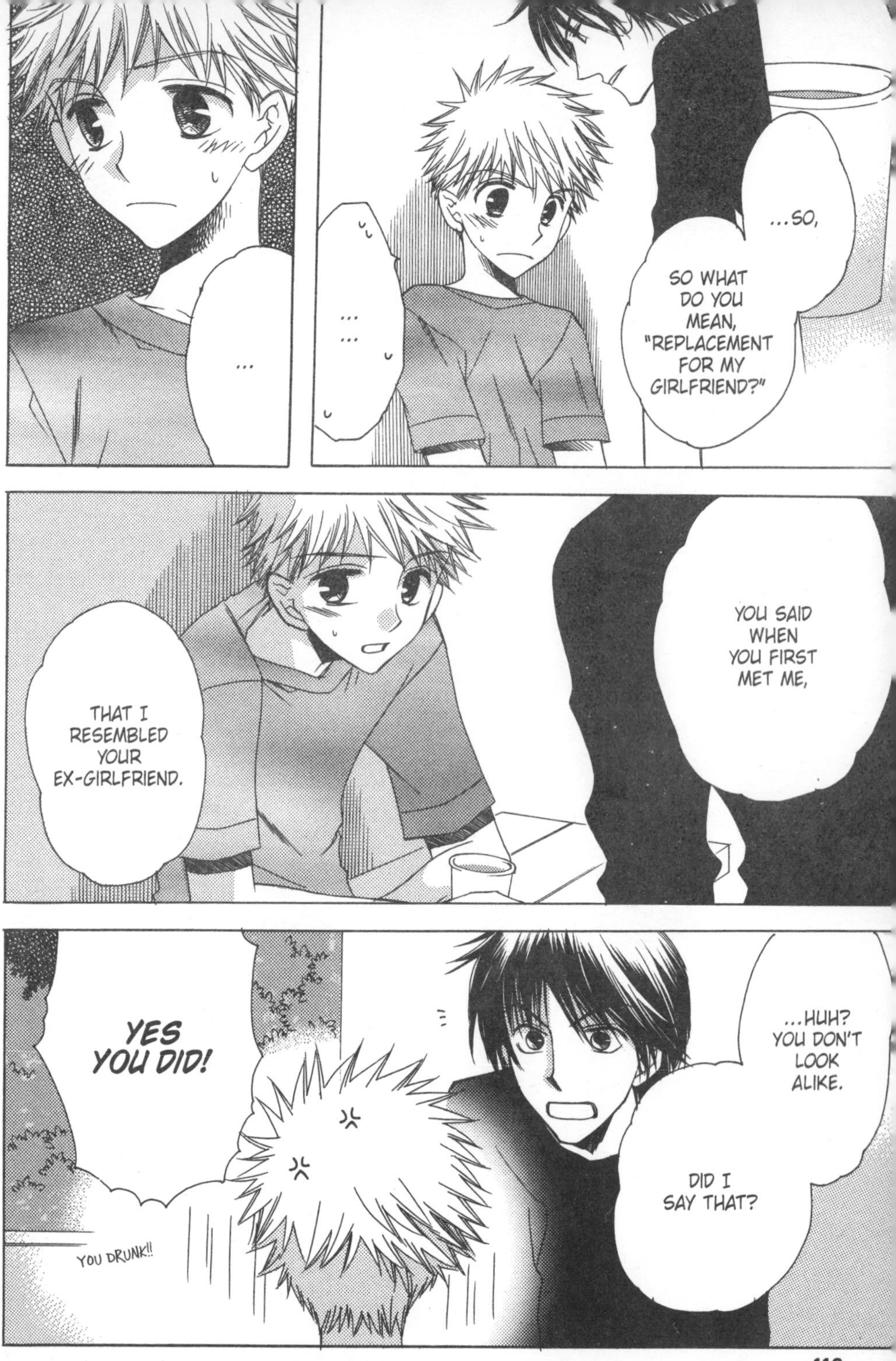
...SO,
SO WHAT DO YOU MEAN, "REPLACEMENT FOR MY GIRLFRIEND?"
... ...
...
YOU SAID WHEN YOU FIRST MET ME,
THAT I RESEMBLED YOUR EX-GIRLFRIEND.
...HUH? YOU DON'T LOOK ALIKE.
DID I SAY THAT?
YES YOU DID!
YOU DRUNK!!

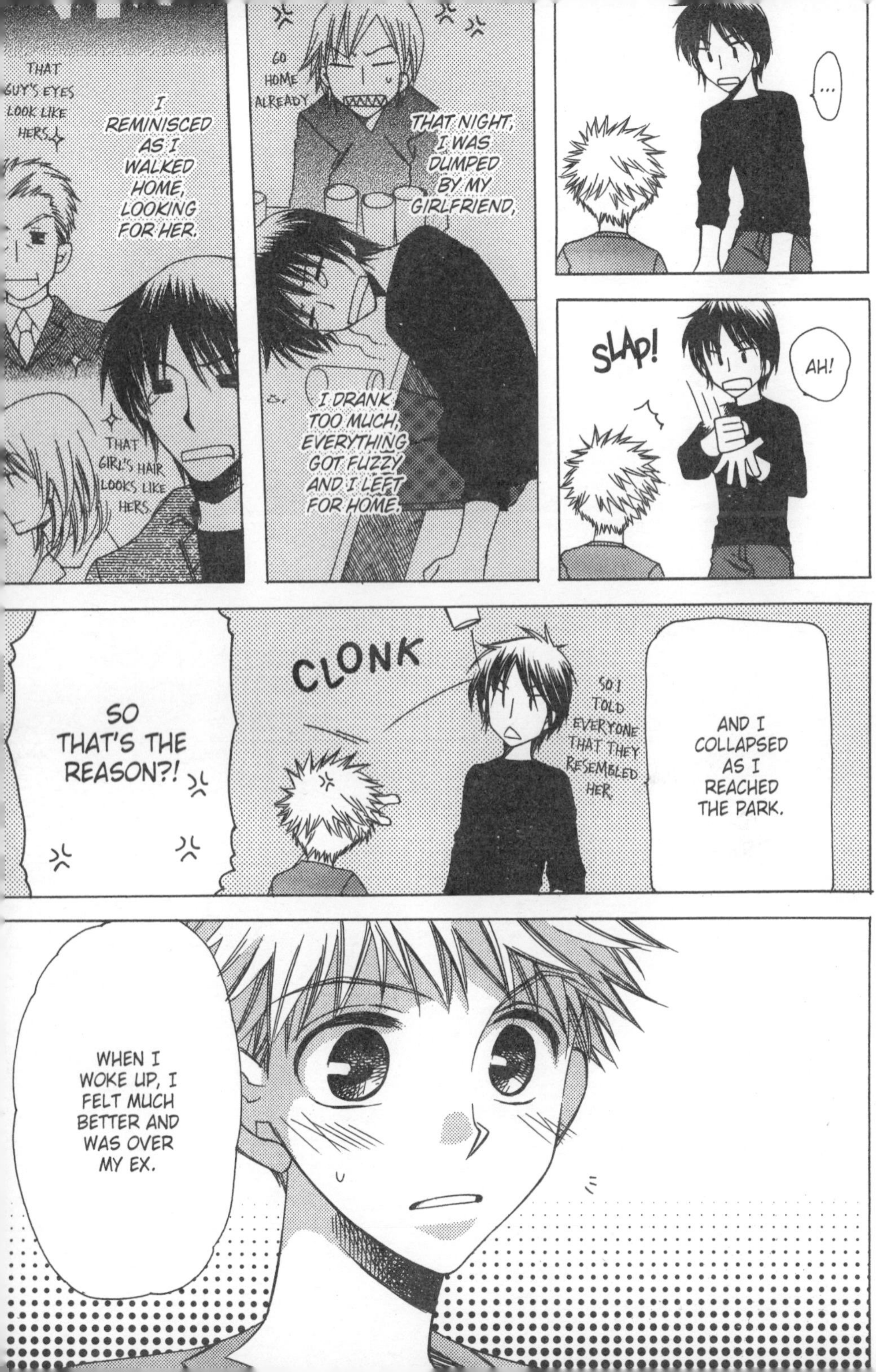
...
SLAP!
AH!
GO HOME ALREADY
THAT NIGHT, I WAS DUMPED BY MY GIRLFRIEND,
I DRANK TOO MUCH, EVERYTHING GOT FUZZY AND I LEFT FOR HOME.
I REMINISCED AS I WALKED HOME, LOOKING FOR HER.
THAT GUY'S EYES LOOK LIKE HERS.
THAT GIRL'S HAIR LOOKS LIKE HERS.
AND I COLLAPSED AS I REACHED THE PARK.
SO I TOLD EVERYONE THAT THEY RESEMBLED HER.
CLONK
SO THAT'S THE REASON?!
WHEN I WOKE UP, I FELT MUCH BETTER AND WAS OVER MY EX.

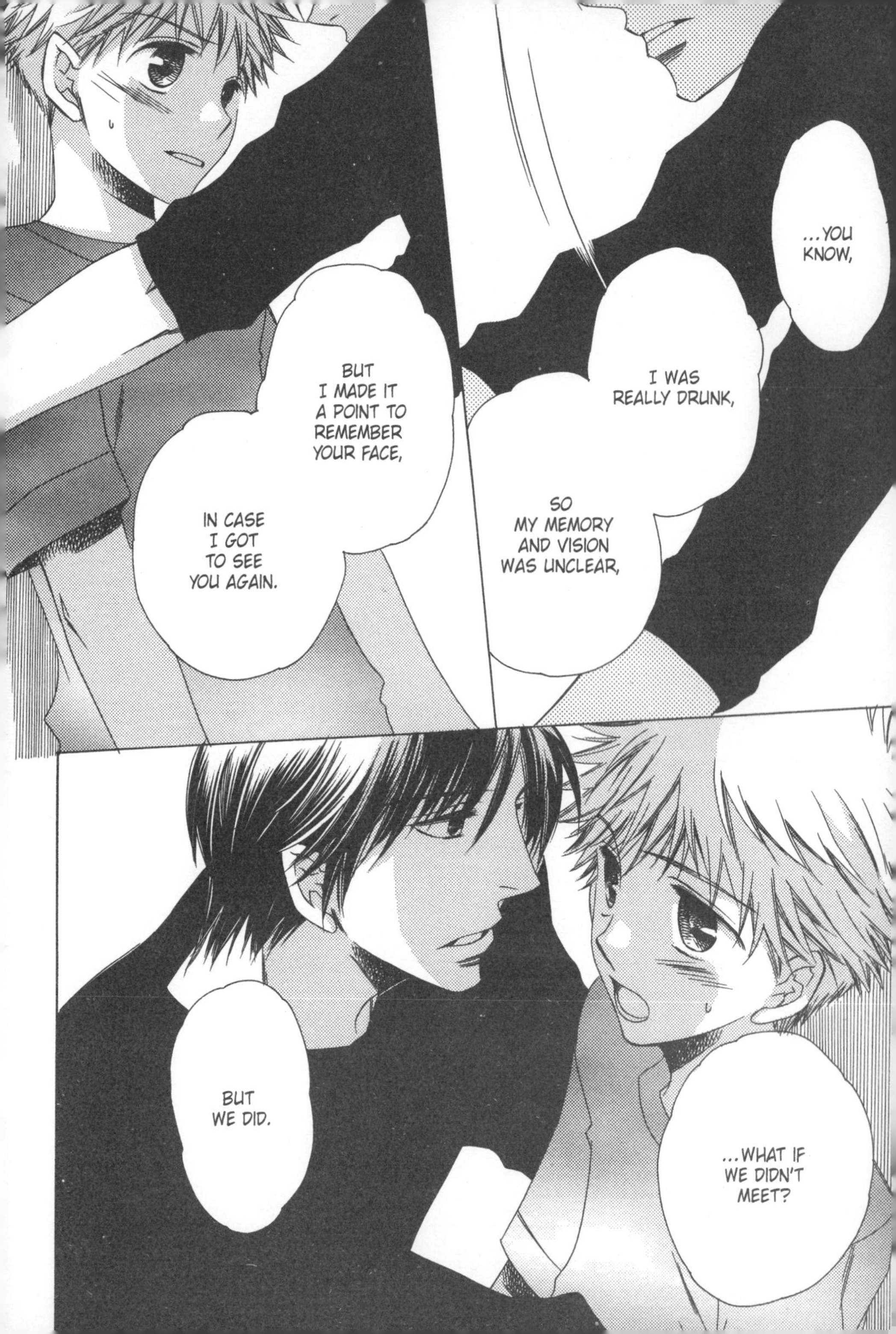
...YOU KNOW,
I WAS REALLY DRUNK,
SO MY MEMORY AND VISION WAS UNCLEAR,
BUT I MADE IT A POINT TO REMEMBER YOUR FACE,
IN CASE I GOT TO SEE YOU AGAIN.
...WHAT IF WE DIDN'T MEET?
BUT WE DID.

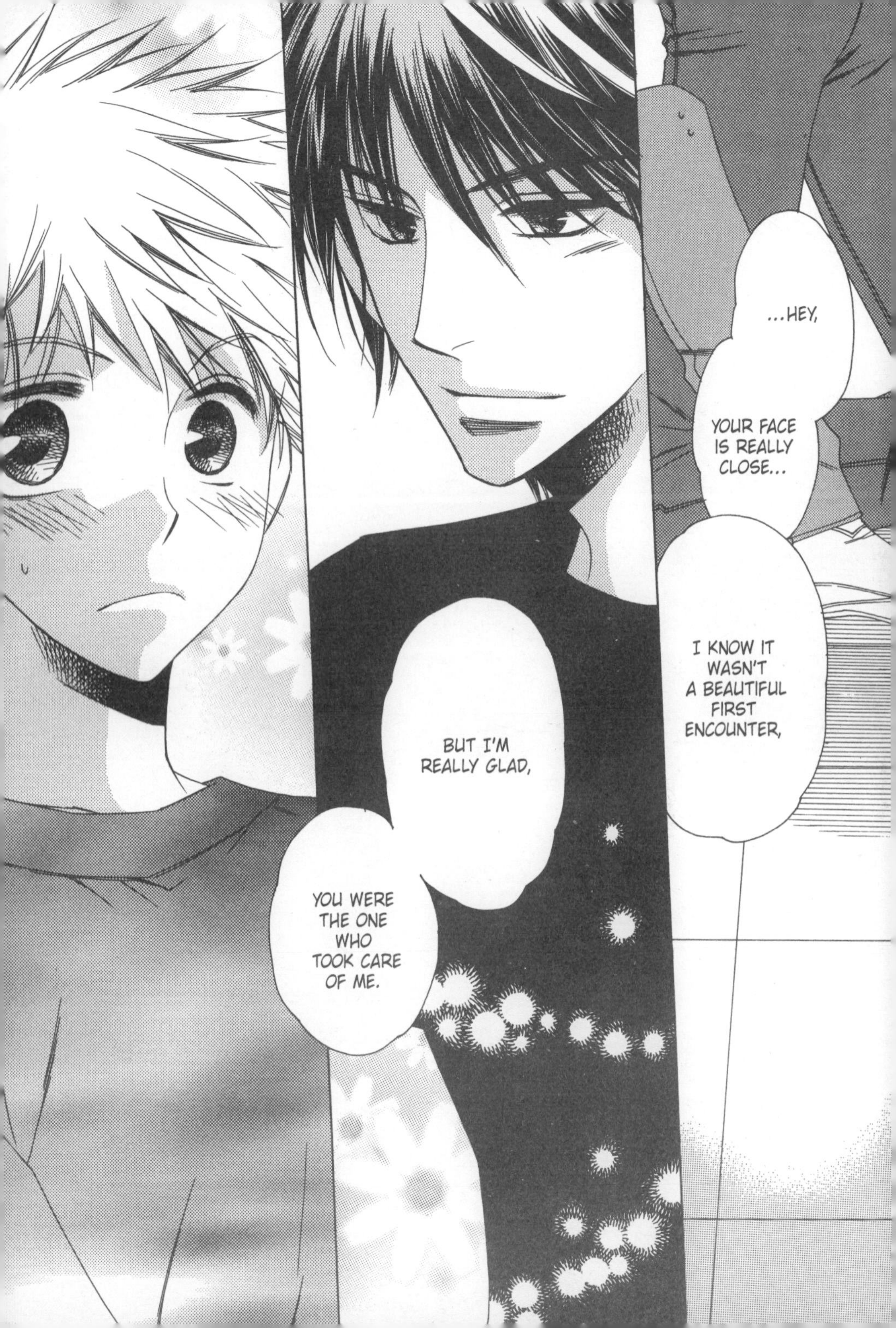
...HEY,
YOUR FACE IS REALLY CLOSE...
I KNOW IT WASN'T A BEAUTIFUL FIRST ENCOUNTER,
BUT I'M REALLY GLAD,
YOU WERE THE ONE WHO TOOK CARE OF ME.

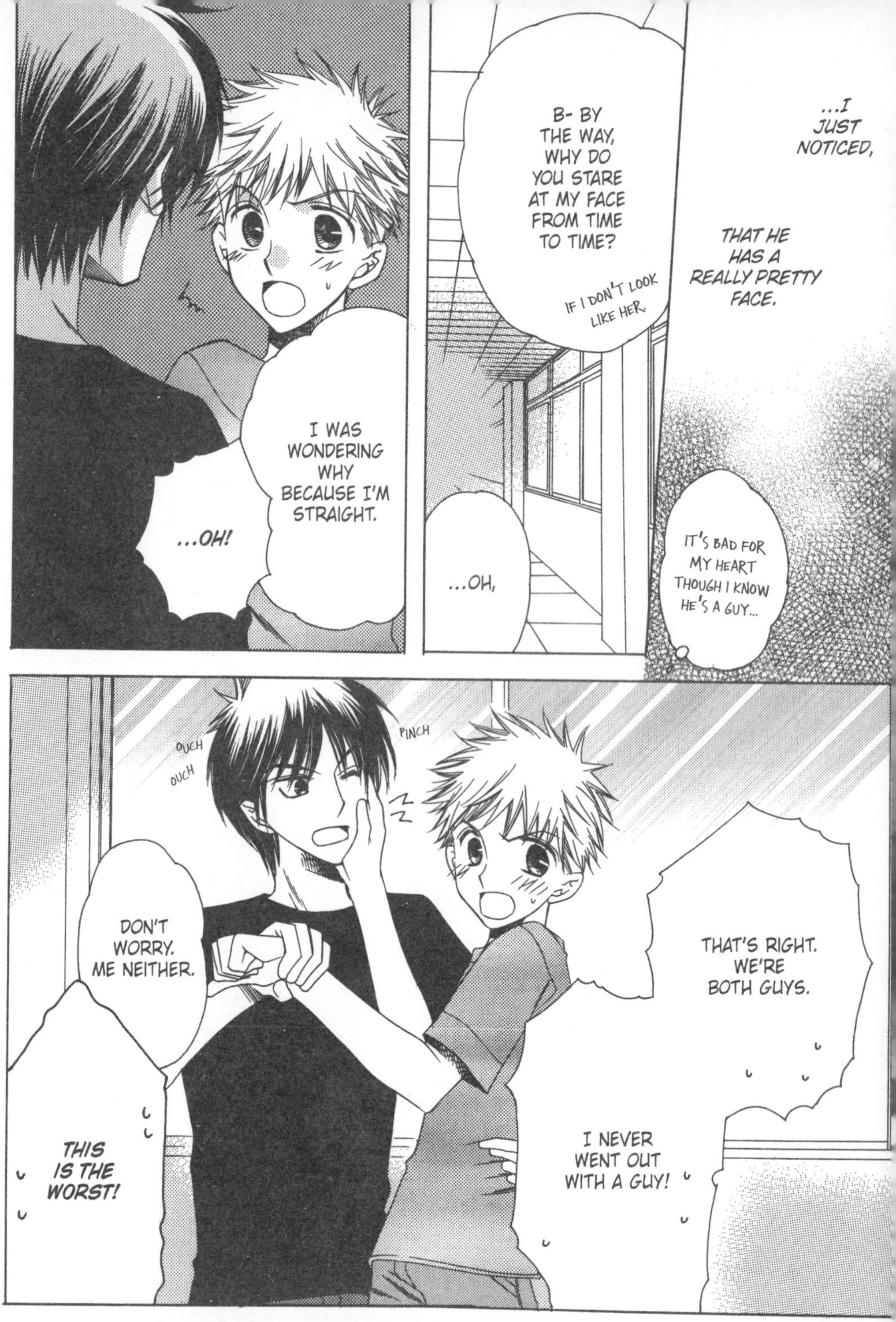
...I JUST NOTICED,
THAT HE HAS A REALLY PRETTY FACE.
IT'S BAD FOR MY HEART THOUGH I KNOW HE'S A GUY...
B- BY THE WAY, WHY DO YOU STARE AT MY FACE FROM TIME TO TIME?
IF I DON'T LOOK LIKE HER.
...OH,
I WAS WONDERING WHY BECAUSE I'M STRAIGHT.
...OH!
THAT'S RIGHT. WE'RE BOTH GUYS.
I NEVER WENT OUT WITH A GUY!
PINCH
OUCH
OUCH
DON'T WORRY. ME NEITHER.
THIS IS THE WORST!

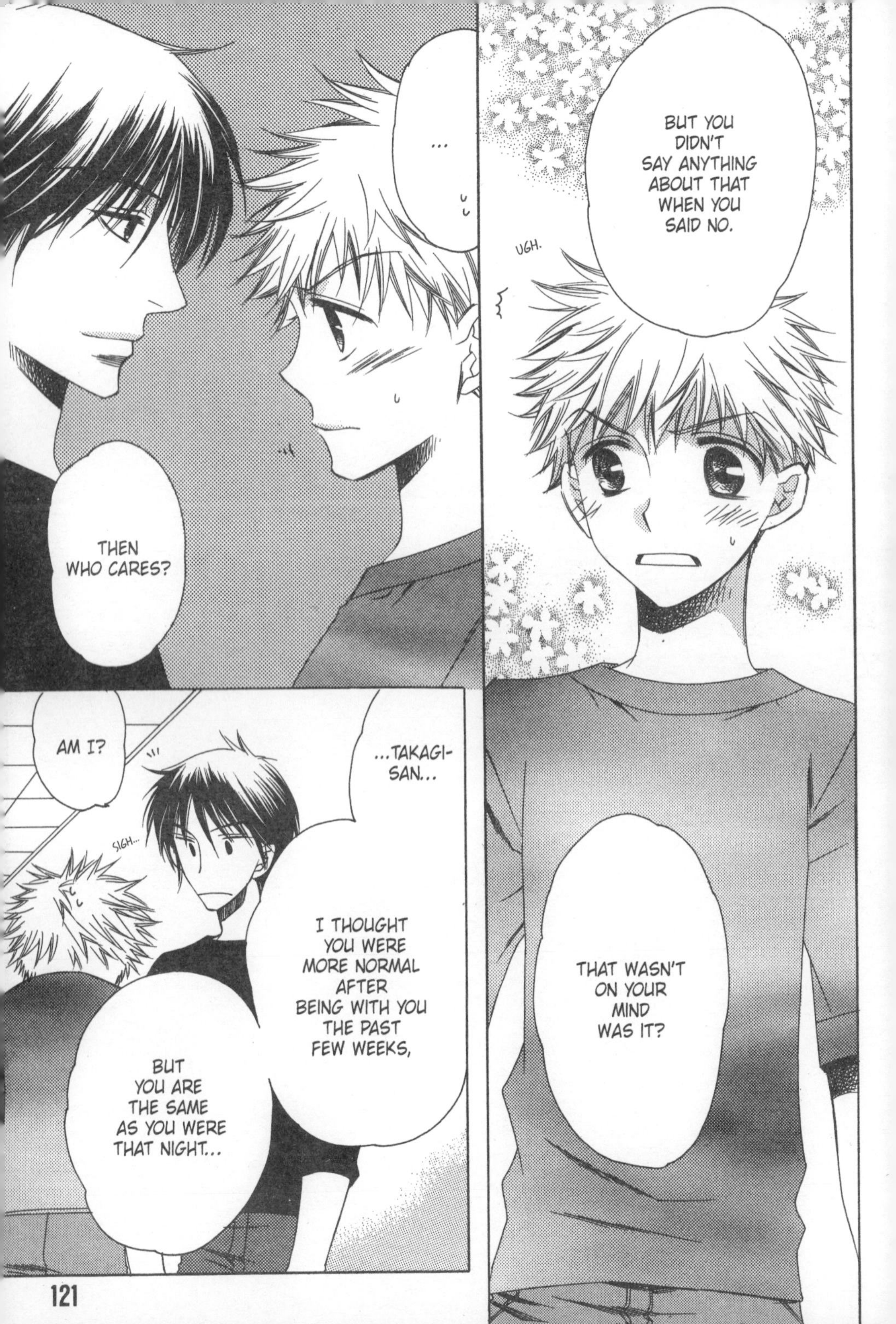
BUT YOU DIDN'T SAY ANYTHING ABOUT THAT WHEN YOU SAID NO.
UGH.
THAT WASN'T ON YOUR MIND WAS IT?
...
THEN WHO CARES?
...TAKAGI-SAN...
I THOUGHT YOU WERE MORE NORMAL AFTER BEING WITH YOU THE PAST FEW WEEKS,
BUT YOU ARE THE SAME AS YOU WERE THAT NIGHT...
AM I?
SIGH...

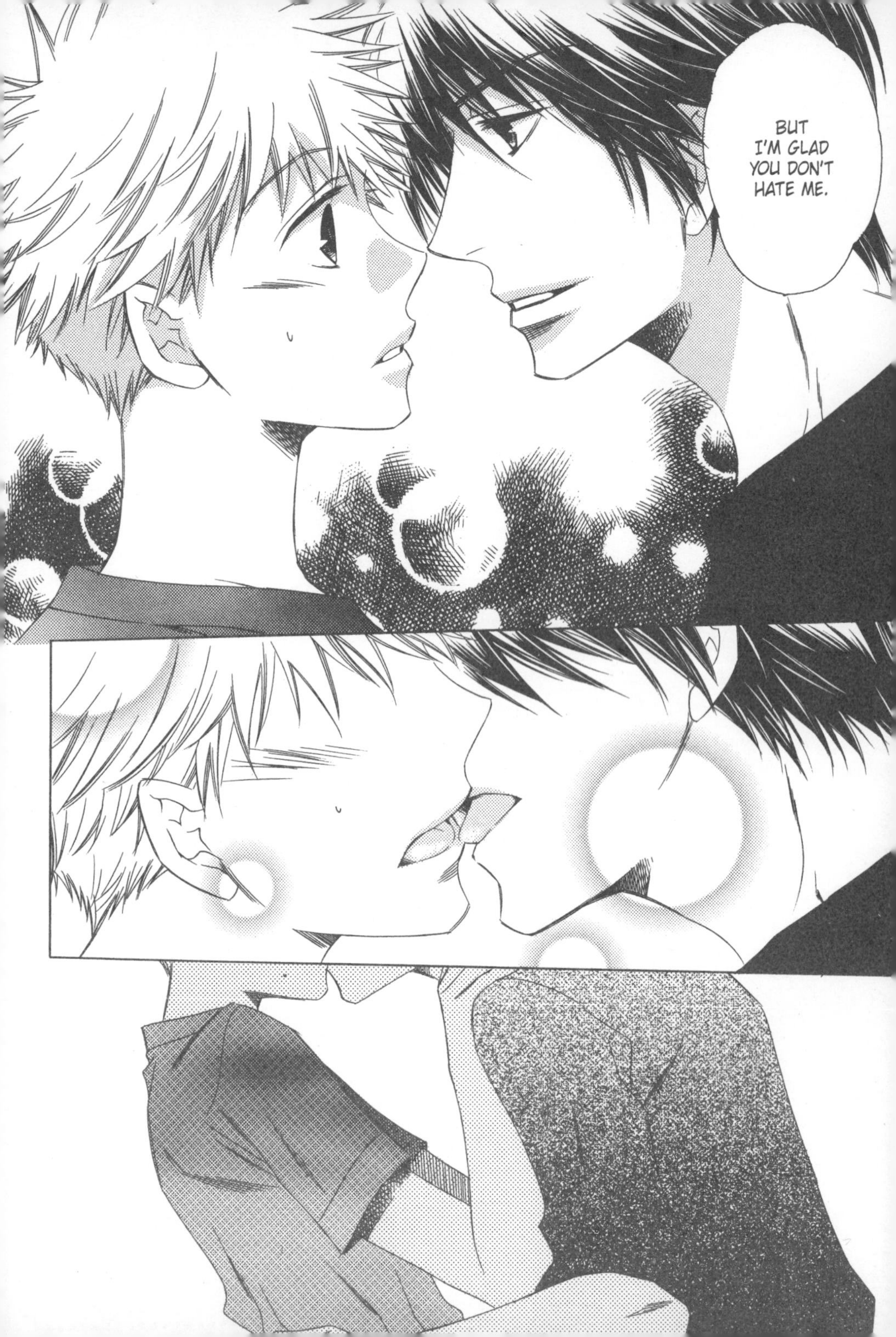
BUT I'M GLAD YOU DON'T HATE ME.

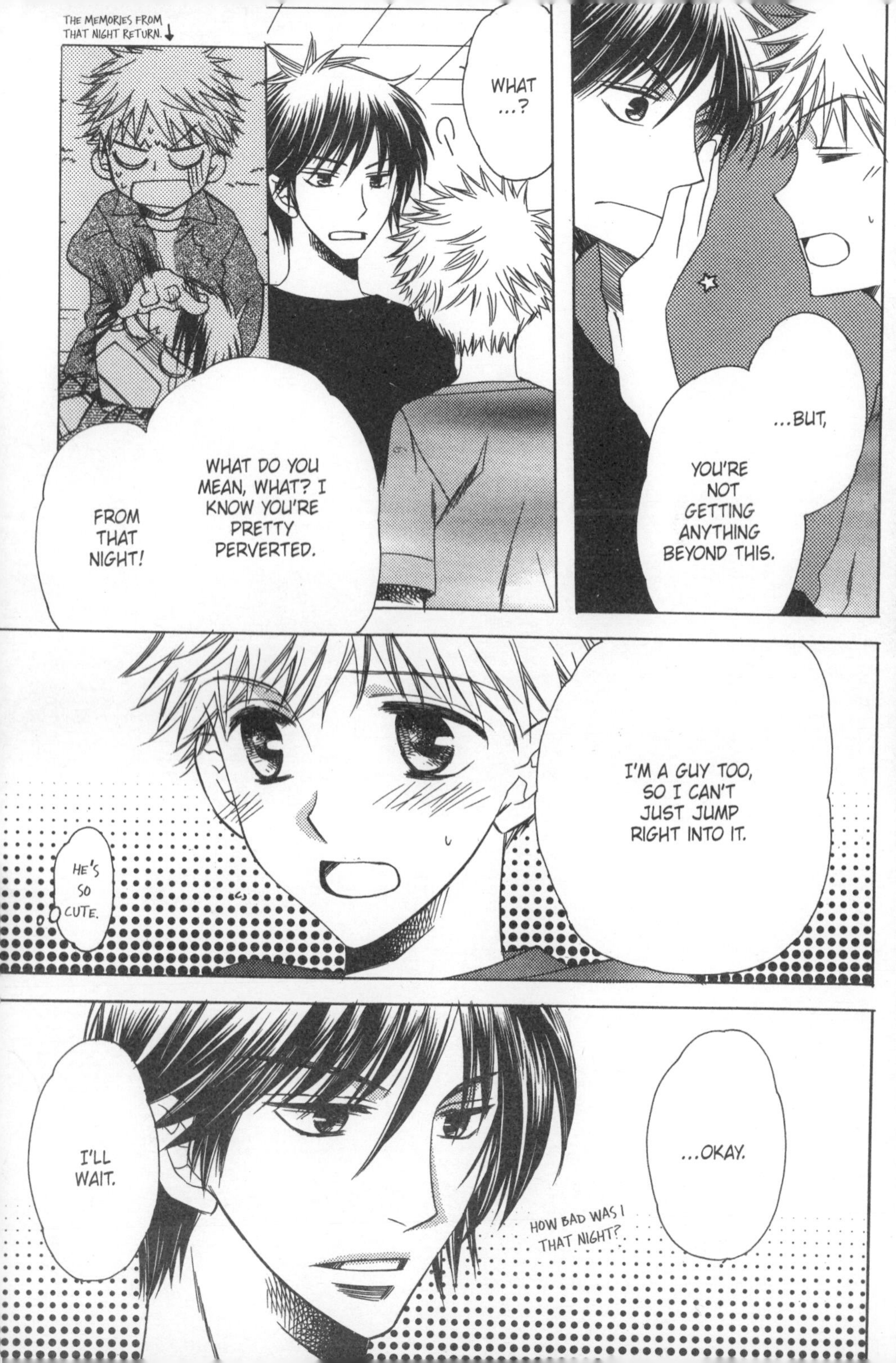
...BUT,
YOU'RE NOT GETTING ANYTHING BEYOND THIS.
WHAT ...?
WHAT DO YOU MEAN, WHAT? I KNOW YOU'RE PRETTY PERVERTED.
FROM THAT NIGHT!
THE MEMORIES FROM THAT NIGHT RETURN.
I'M A GUY TOO, SO I CAN'T JUST JUMP RIGHT INTO IT.
HE'S SO CUTE.
...OKAY.
HOW BAD WAS I THAT NIGHT?
I'LL WAIT.

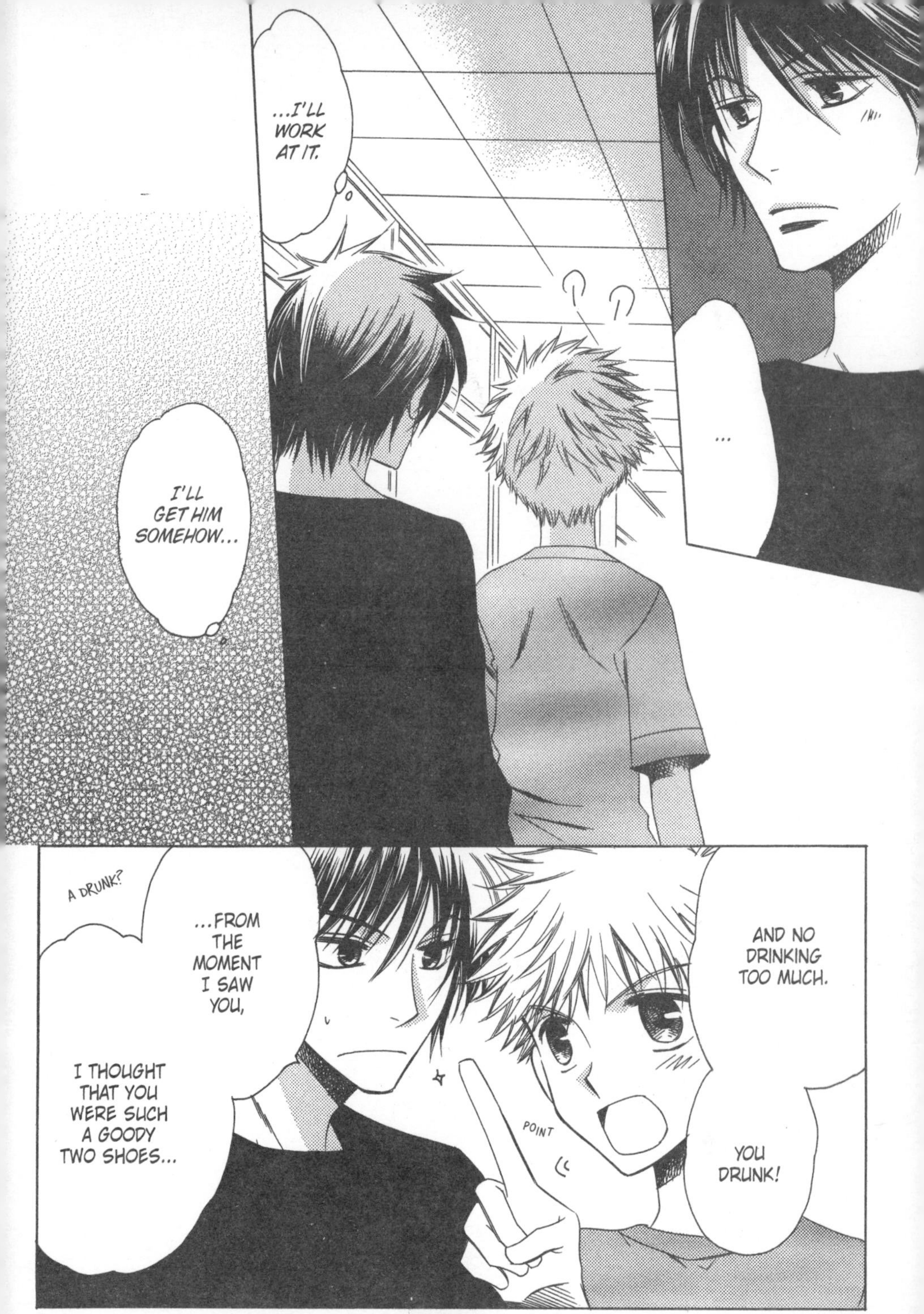
...
...I'LL WORK AT IT.
I'LL GET HIM SOMEHOW...
AND NO DRINKING TOO MUCH.
YOU DRUNK!
POINT
...FROM THE MOMENT I SAW YOU,
I THOUGHT THAT YOU WERE SUCH A GOODY TWO SHOES...
A DRUNK?

END

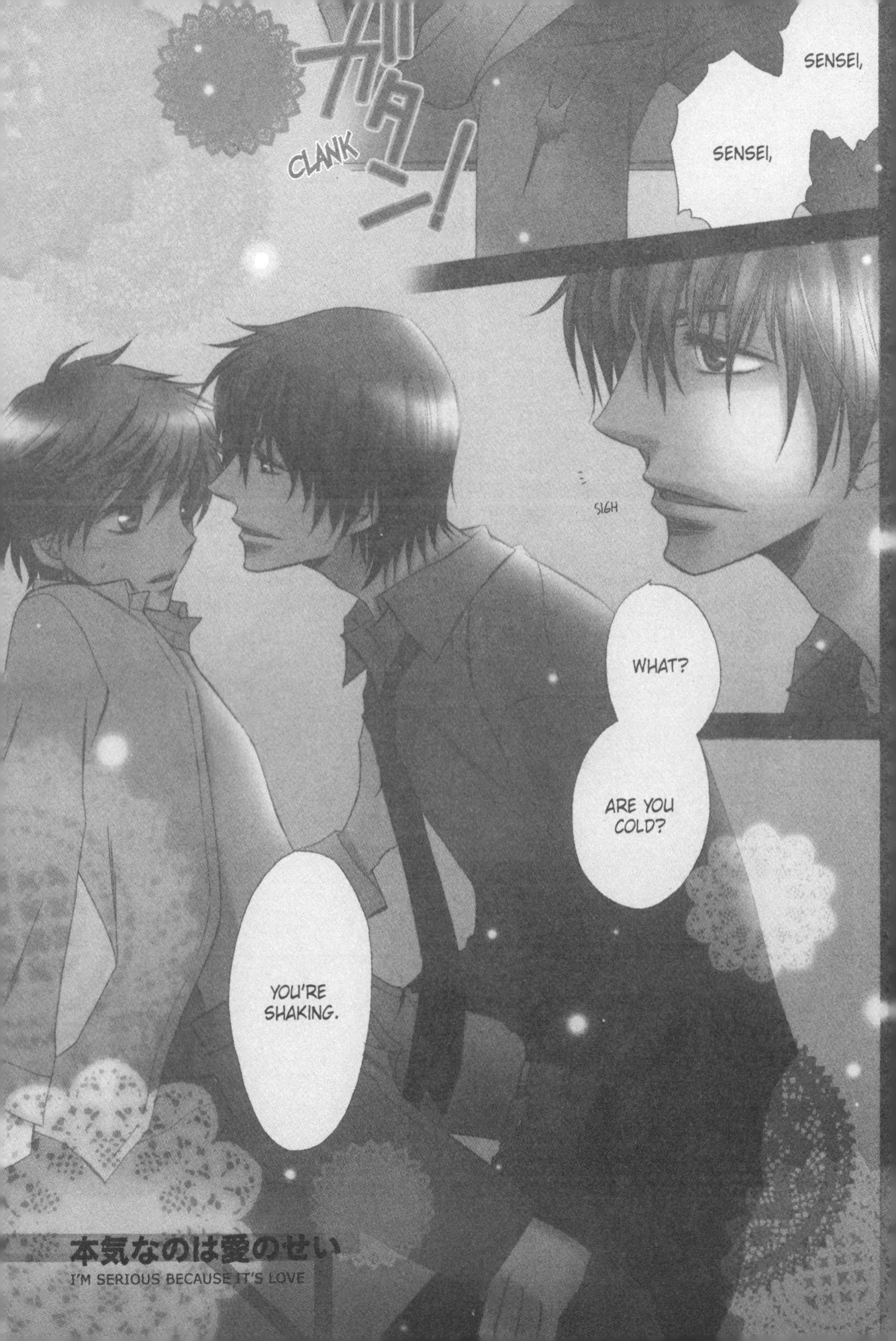
SENSEI,
SENSEI,
CLANK
SIGH
WHAT?
ARE YOU COLD?
YOU'RE SHAKING.
本気なのは愛のせい
I'M SERIOUS BECAUSE IT'S LOVE

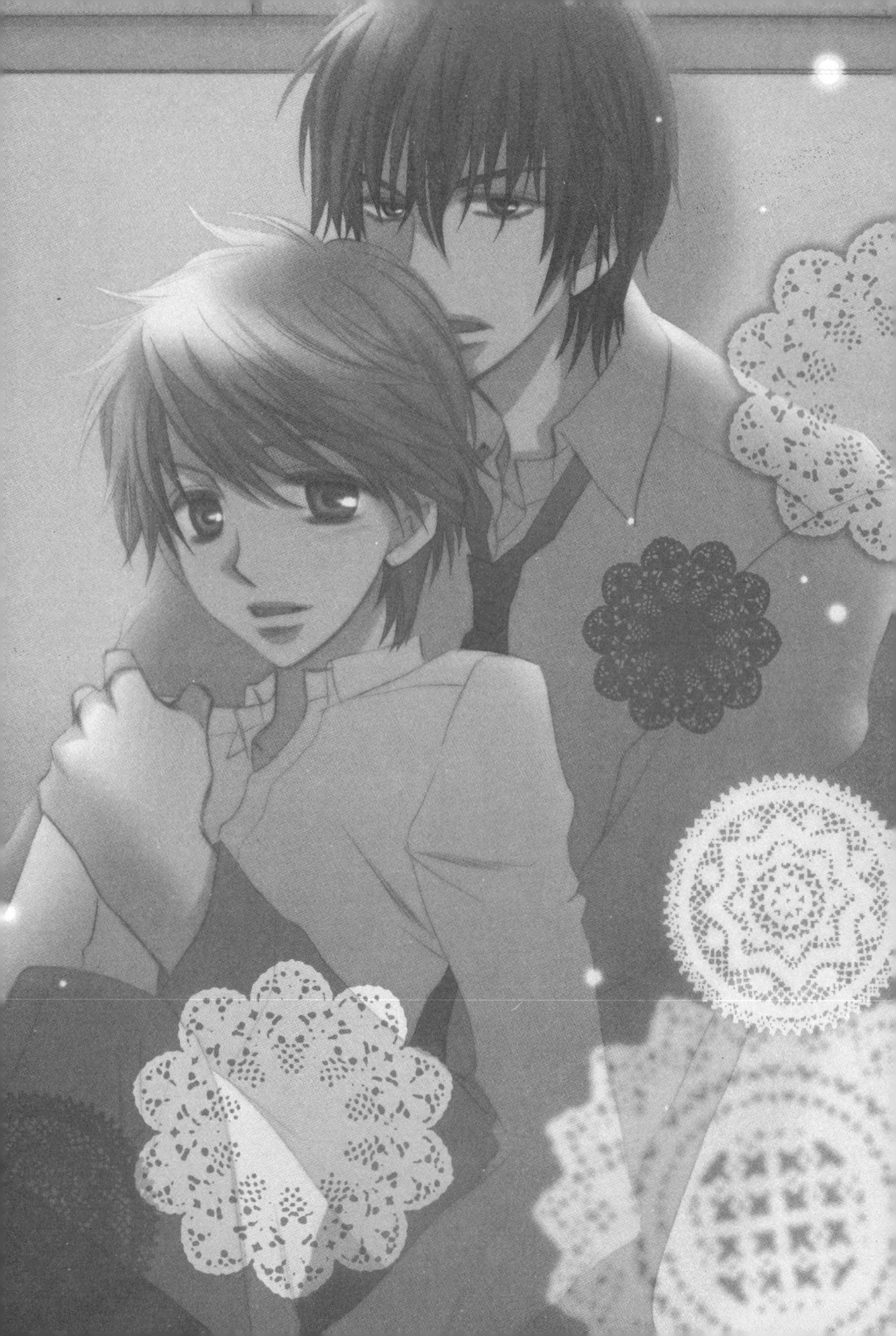

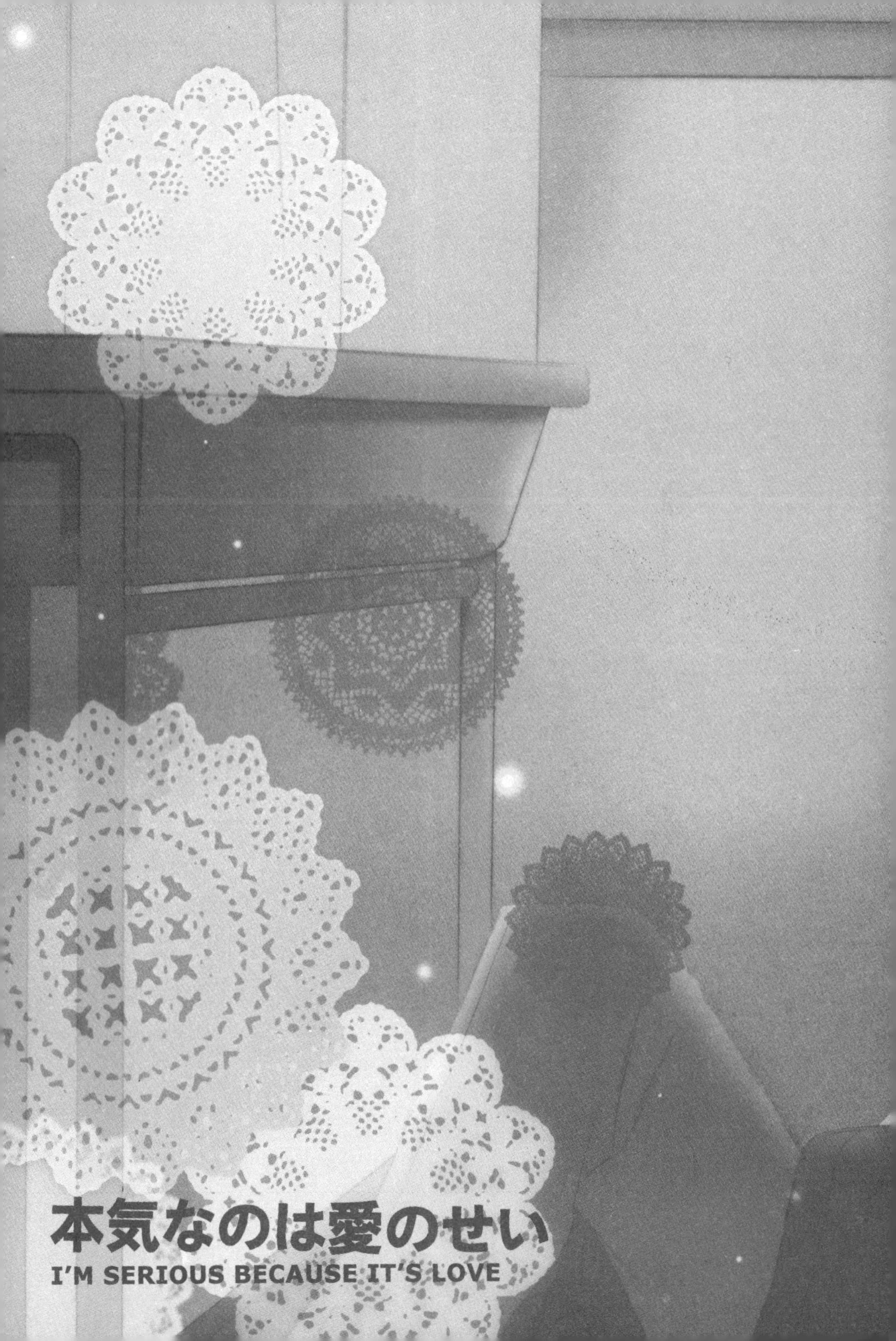

本気なのは愛のせい
I'M SERIOUS BECAUSE IT'S LOVE

AFTERTHOUGHTS

NICE TO MEET YOU AND HELLO! FIRST OF ALL, THANK YOU ALL FOR BUYING THIS COMIC! I WAS ABLE TO MAKE A COMIC BOOK WITH THE HELP OF HANATO COMICS. ONCE AGAIN, THANK YOU VERY MUCH. I WAS REALLY SURPRISED WHEN THIS WAS BROUGHT UP.

I STILL WONDER HOW I WAS ABLE TO GET THIS OPPORTUNITY. THERE ARE SOME STORIES THAT YOU MAY HAVE SEEN BEFORE ELSEWHERE BUT I THANK YOU ALL FOR READING THROUGH MY MANGA.

THANK YOU

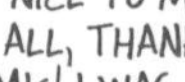 CHAN

EDITOR (K SAMA, T SAMA)
TO ALL THAT HELPED ME
AND TO ALL MY FANS THAT
READ MY WORK IN THE
MAGAZINES.

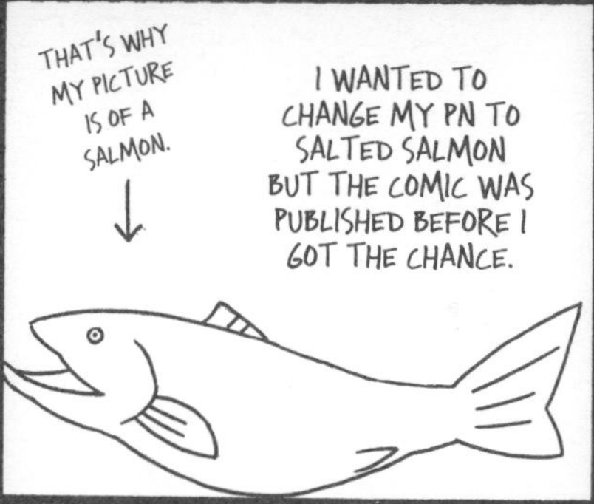
I WANTED TO CHANGE MY PN TO SALTED SALMON BUT THE COMIC WAS PUBLISHED BEFORE I GOT THE CHANCE.
THAT'S WHY MY PICTURE IS OF A SALMON.

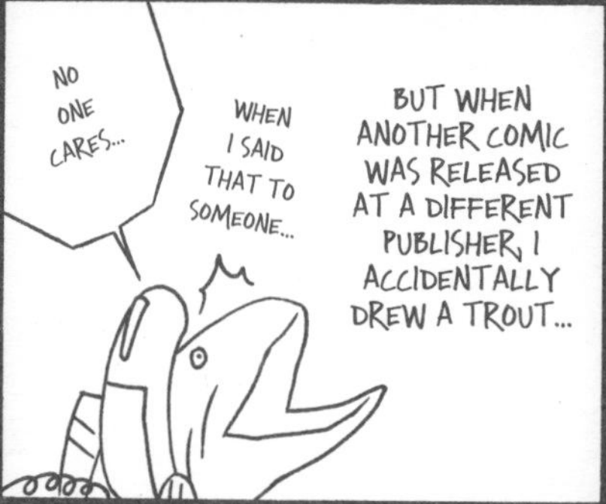
BUT WHEN ANOTHER COMIC WAS RELEASED AT A DIFFERENT PUBLISHER, I ACCIDENTALLY DREW A TROUT...
WHEN I SAID THAT TO SOMEONE...
NO ONE CARES...

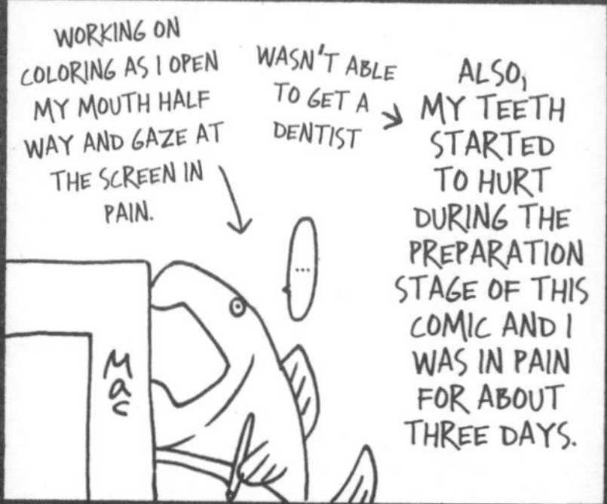
ALSO, MY TEETH STARTED TO HURT DURING THE PREPARATION STAGE OF THIS COMIC AND I WAS IN PAIN FOR ABOUT THREE DAYS.
WASN'T ABLE TO GET A DENTIST
WORKING ON COLORING AS I OPEN MY MOUTH HALF WAY AND GAZE AT THE SCREEN IN PAIN.
...
Mac

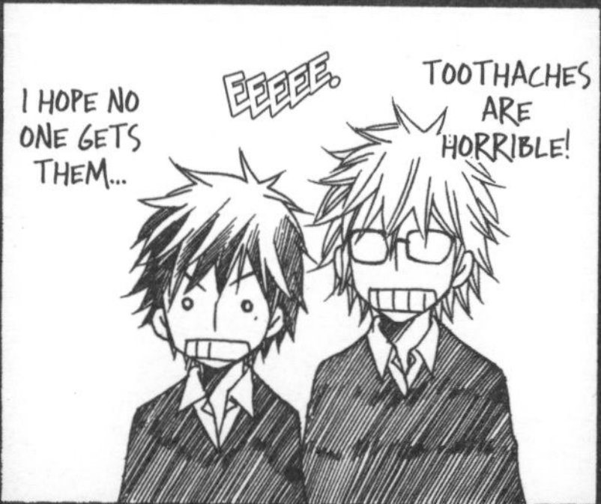
TOOTHACHES ARE HORRIBLE!
EEEEE.
I HOPE NO ONE GETS THEM...

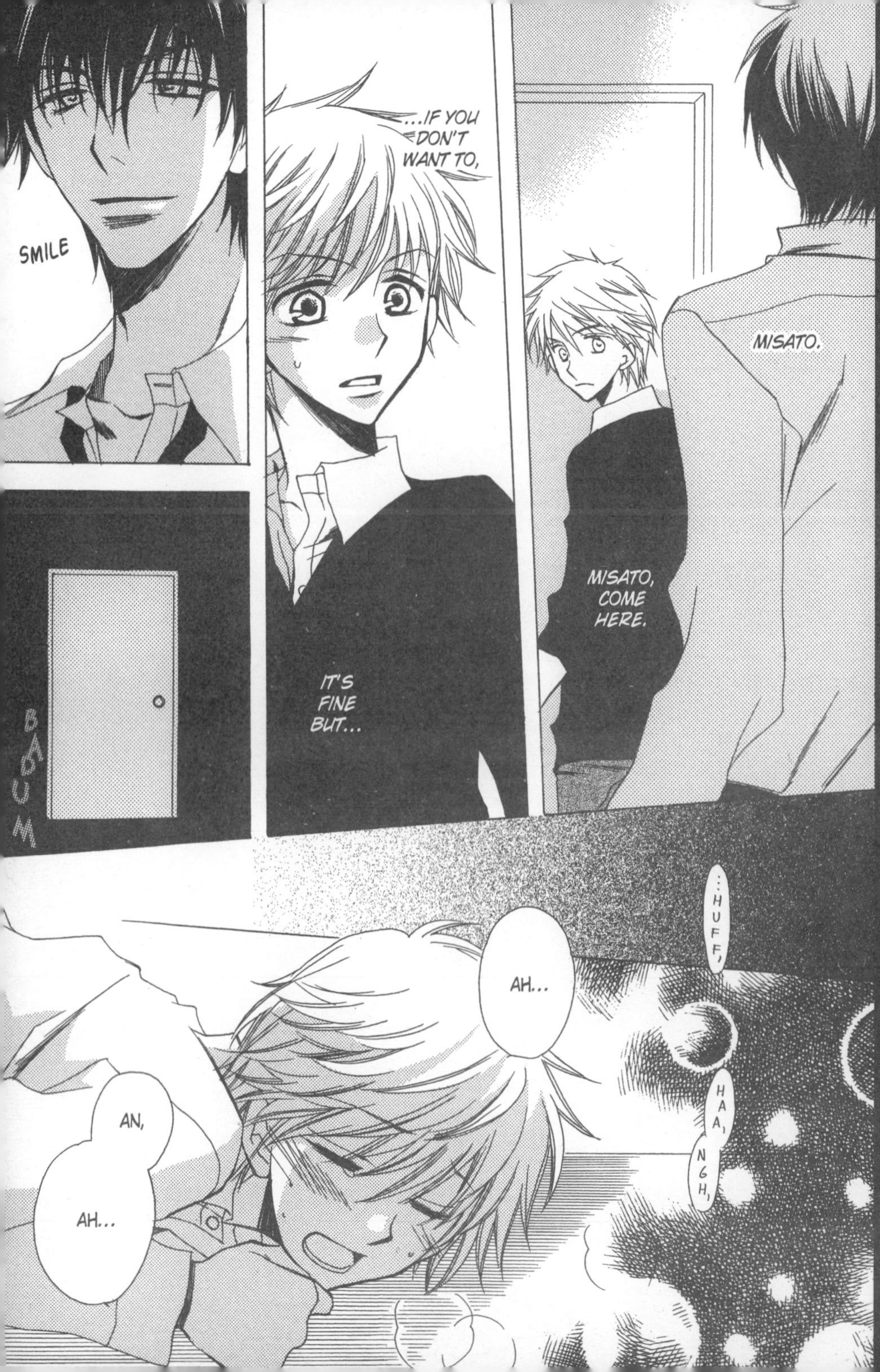
MISATO.
MISATO, COME HERE.
...IF YOU DON'T WANT TO,
IT'S FINE BUT...
SMILE
BADUM
...HUFF,
HAA,
NGH,
AH...
AN,
AH...

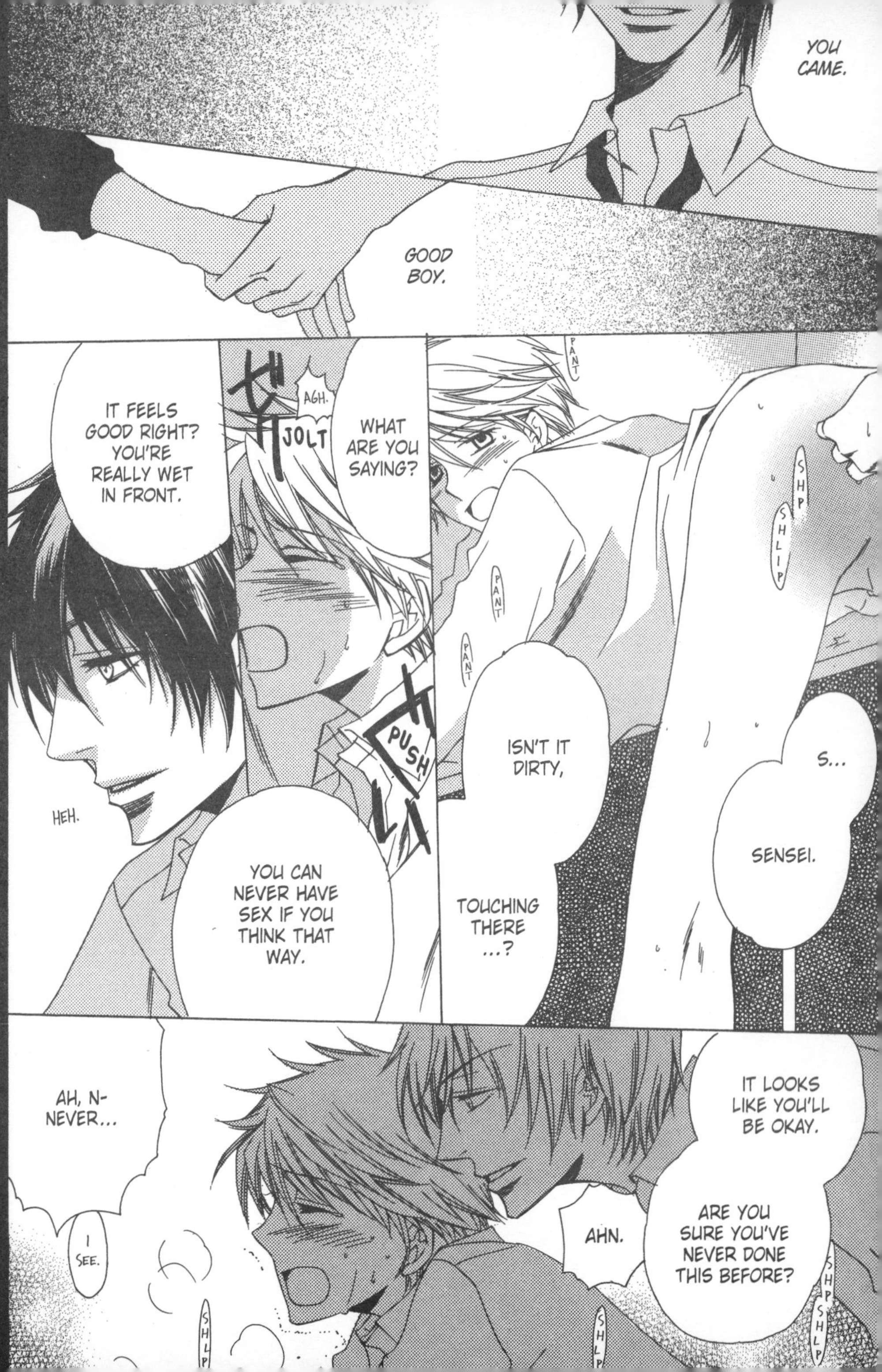
YOU CAME.
GOOD BOY.
PANT
SHP
SHLIP
PANT
PANT
S...
SENSEI.
ISN'T IT DIRTY,
TOUCHING THERE ...?
AGH.
JOLT
WHAT ARE YOU SAYING?
IT FEELS GOOD RIGHT? YOU'RE REALLY WET IN FRONT.
PUSH
HEH.
YOU CAN NEVER HAVE SEX IF YOU THINK THAT WAY.
IT LOOKS LIKE YOU'LL BE OKAY.
SHP SHLP
ARE YOU SURE YOU'VE NEVER DONE THIS BEFORE?
AHN.
SHLP
AH, N- NEVER...
I SEE.
SHLP

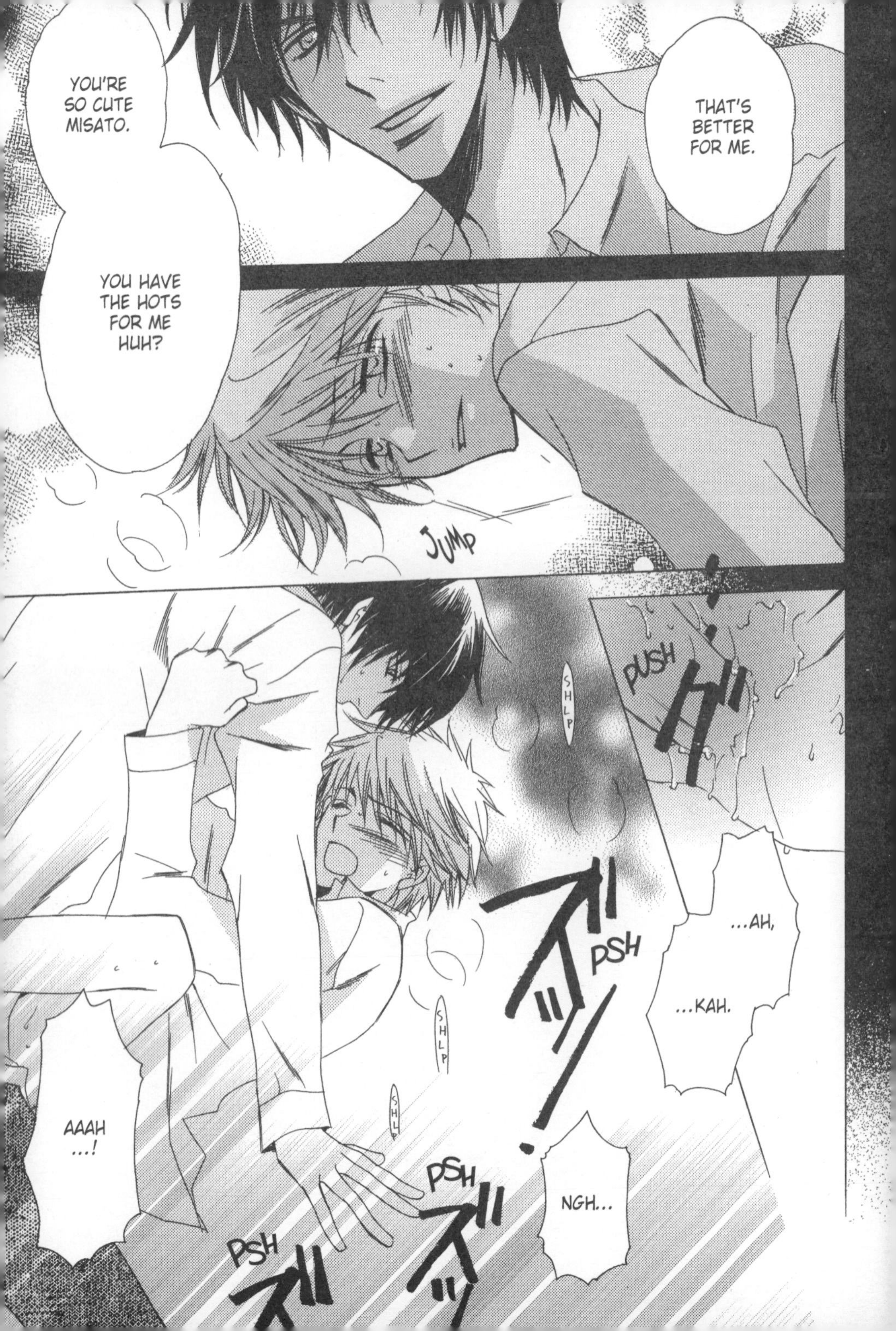
THAT'S BETTER FOR ME.
YOU'RE SO CUTE MISATO.
YOU HAVE THE HOTS FOR ME HUH?
JUMP
PUSH
SHLP
...AH,
...KAH.
PSH
SHLP
SHLP
NGH...
PSH
AAAH ...!
PSH

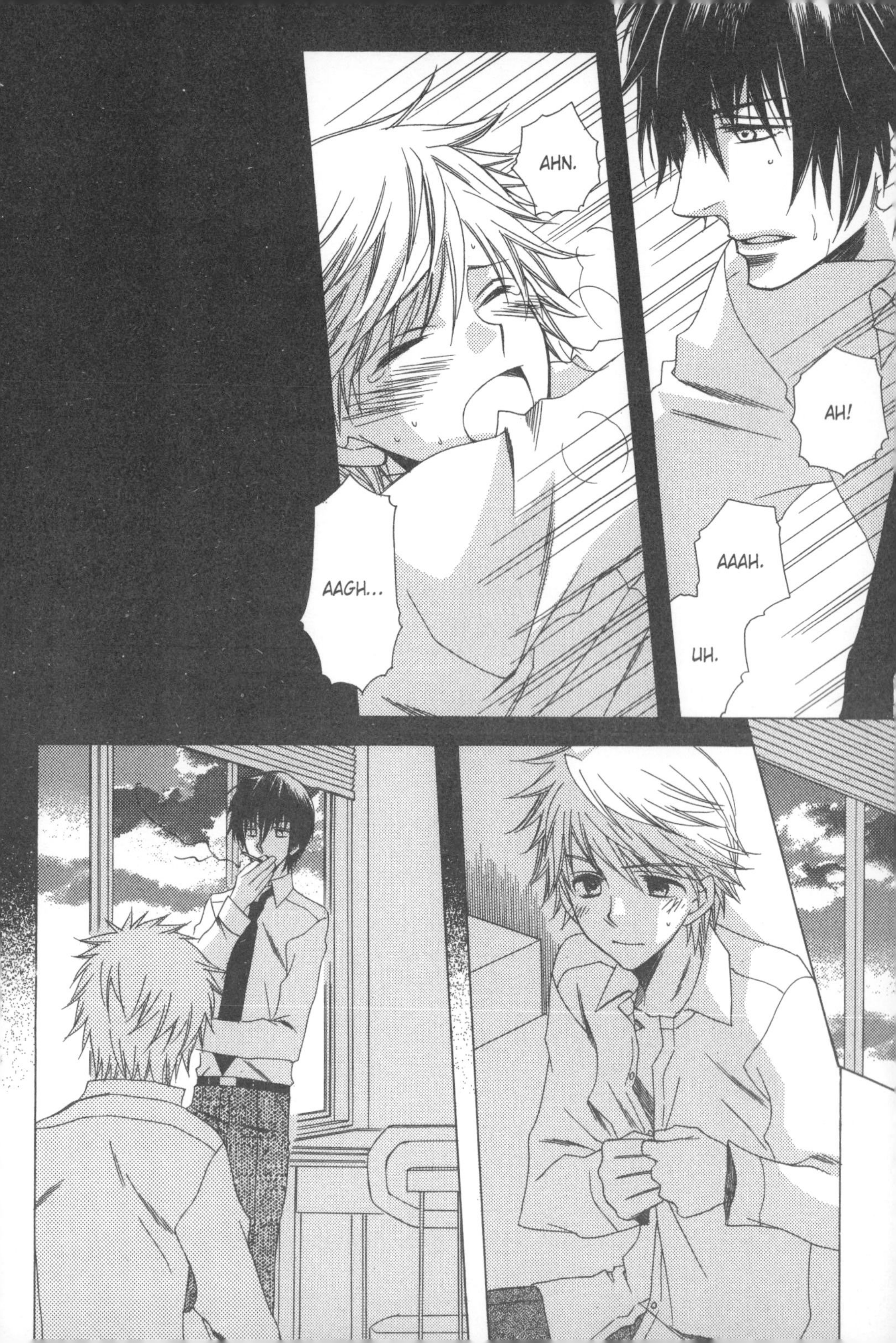
AH!
AAAH.
UH.
AHN.
AAGH...

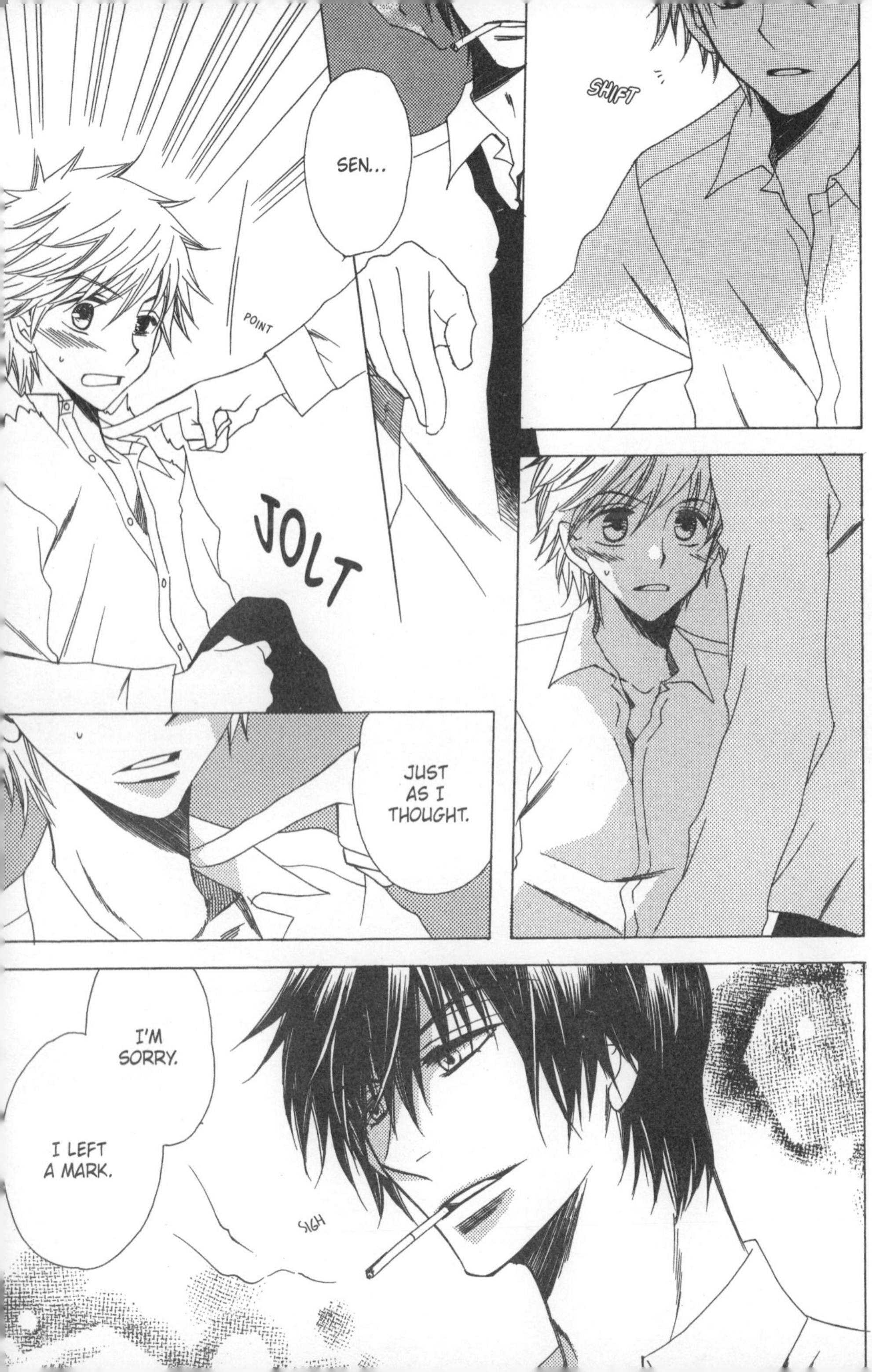
SHIFT
SEN...
POINT
JOLT
JUST AS I THOUGHT.
I'M SORRY.
I LEFT A MARK.
SIGH

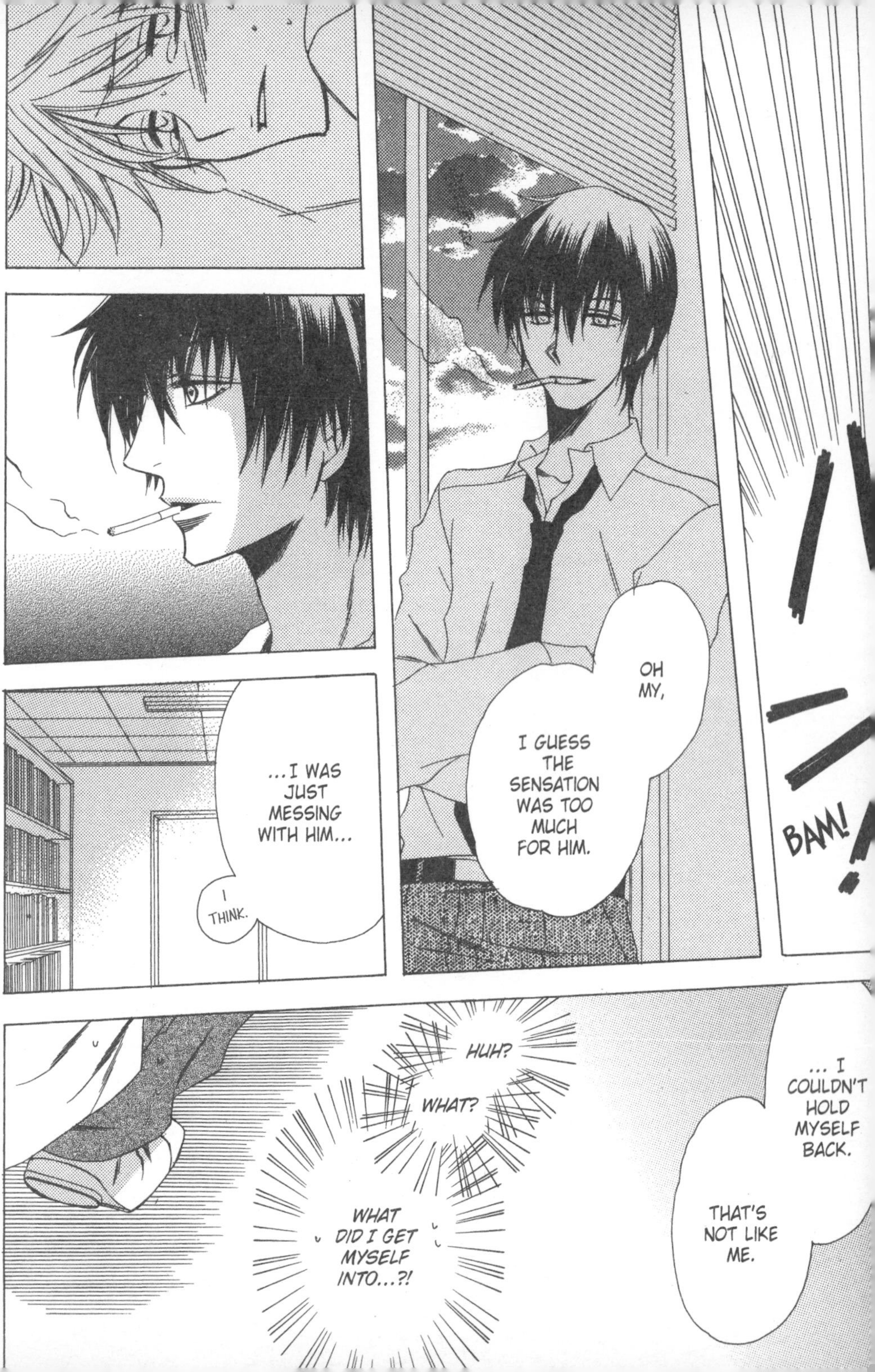
BAM!
OH MY,
I GUESS THE SENSATION WAS TOO MUCH FOR HIM.
...I WAS JUST MESSING WITH HIM...
I THINK.
... I COULDN'T HOLD MYSELF BACK.
THAT'S NOT LIKE ME.
HUH?
WHAT?
WHAT DID I GET MYSELF INTO...?!

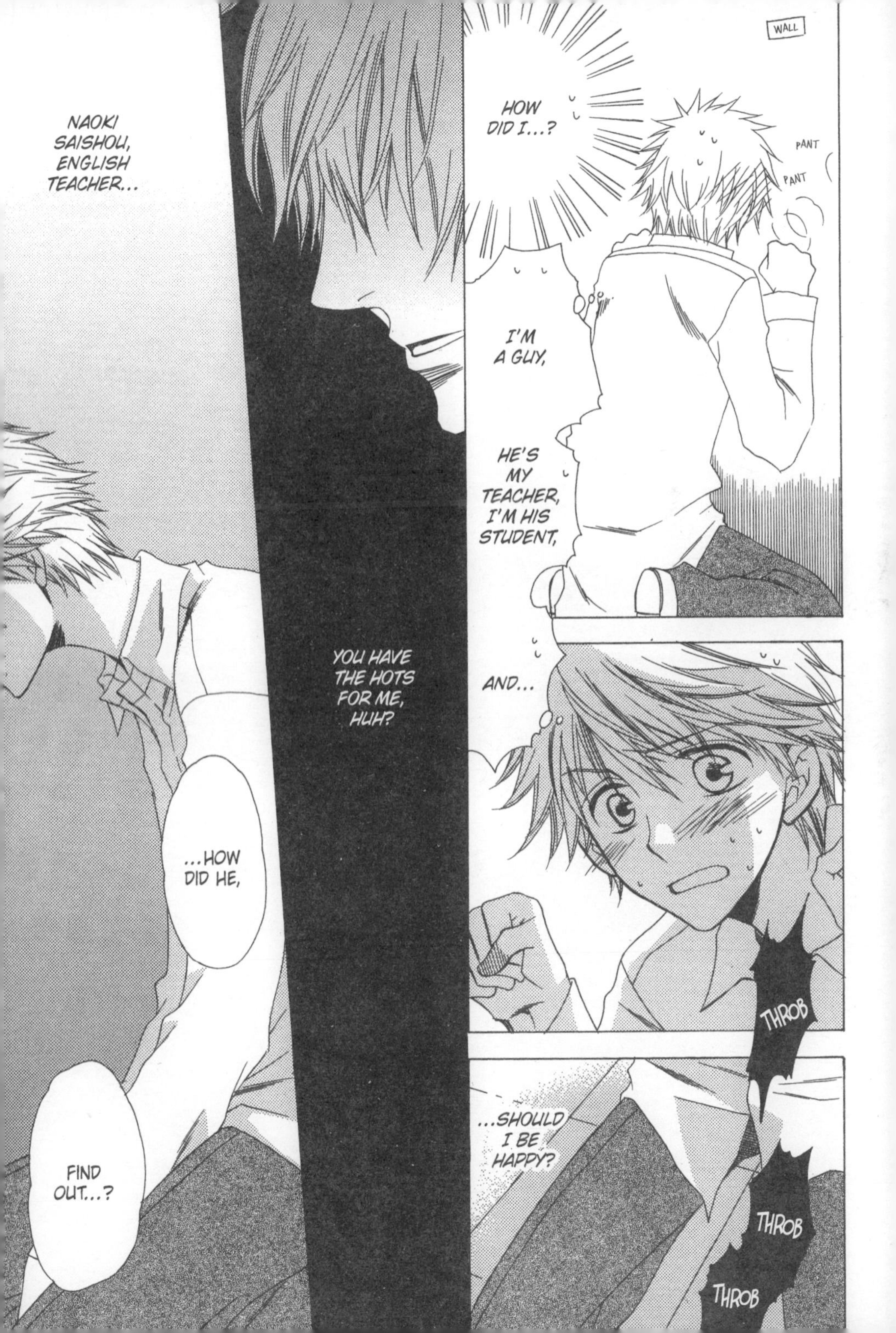
WALL
PANT
PANT
HOW DID I...?
I'M A GUY,
HE'S MY TEACHER, I'M HIS STUDENT,
AND...
THROB
...SHOULD I BE HAPPY?
THROB
THROB
YOU HAVE THE HOTS FOR ME, HUH?
NAOKI SAISHOU, ENGLISH TEACHER...
...HOW DID HE,
FIND OUT...?

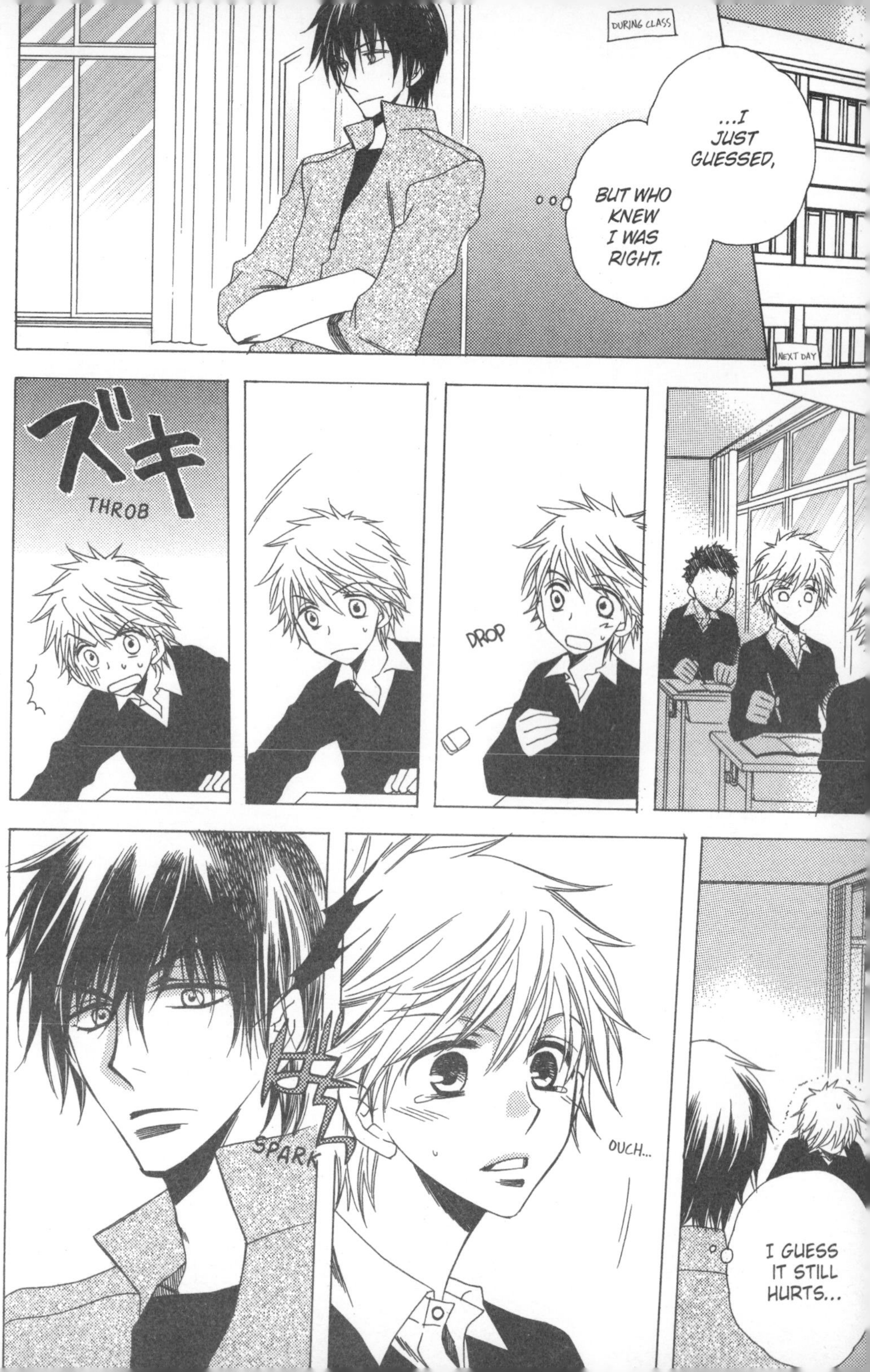
NEXT DAY
DURING CLASS
...I JUST GUESSED, BUT WHO KNEW I WAS RIGHT.
DROP
ズキ
THROB
I GUESS IT STILL HURTS...
OUCH...
SPARK

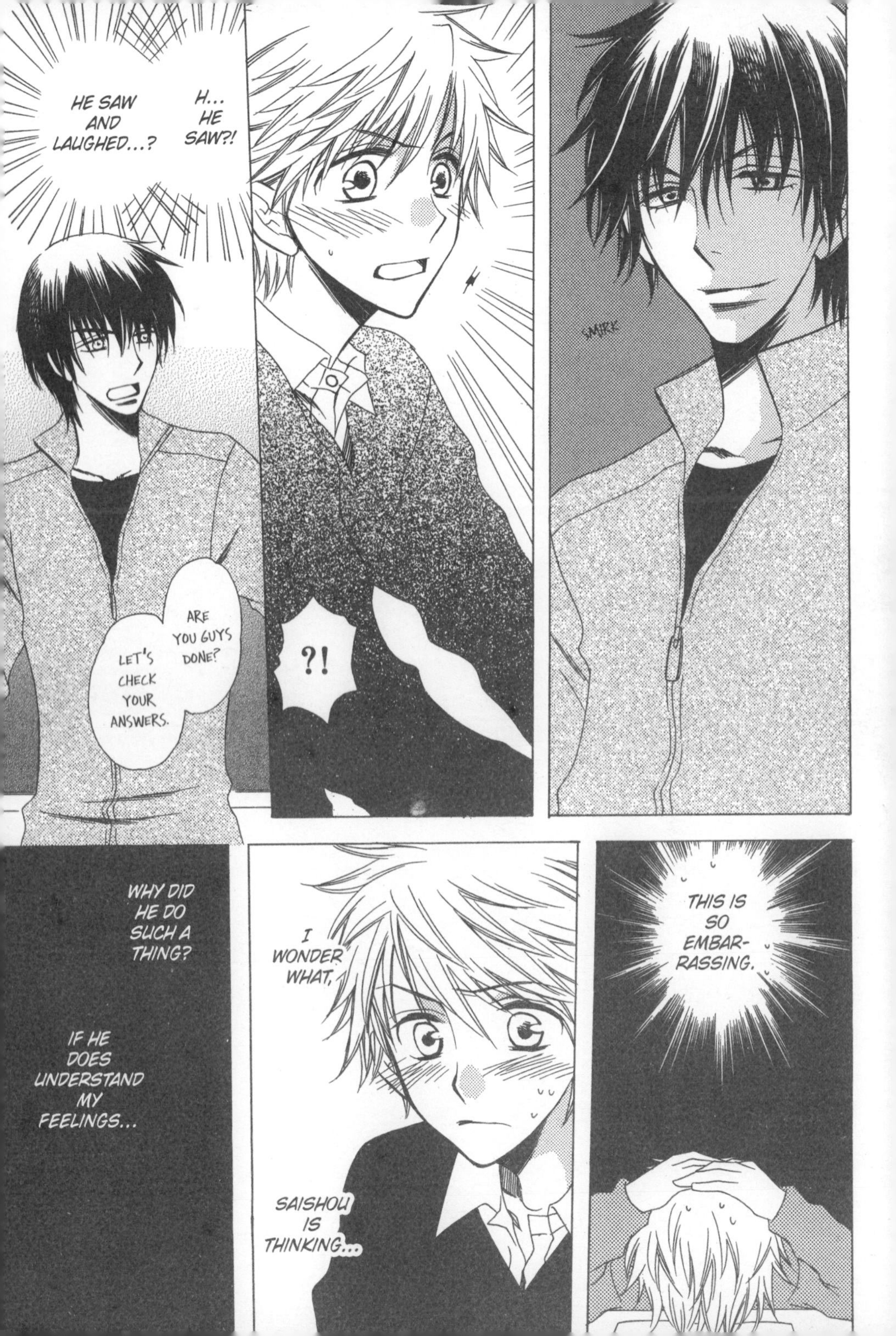
SMIRK
?!
H... HE SAW?!
HE SAW AND LAUGHED...?
ARE YOU GUYS DONE?
LET'S CHECK YOUR ANSWERS.
THIS IS SO EMBARRASSING.
I WONDER WHAT,
SAISHOU IS THINKING...
WHY DID HE DO SUCH A THING?
IF HE DOES UNDERSTAND MY FEELINGS...

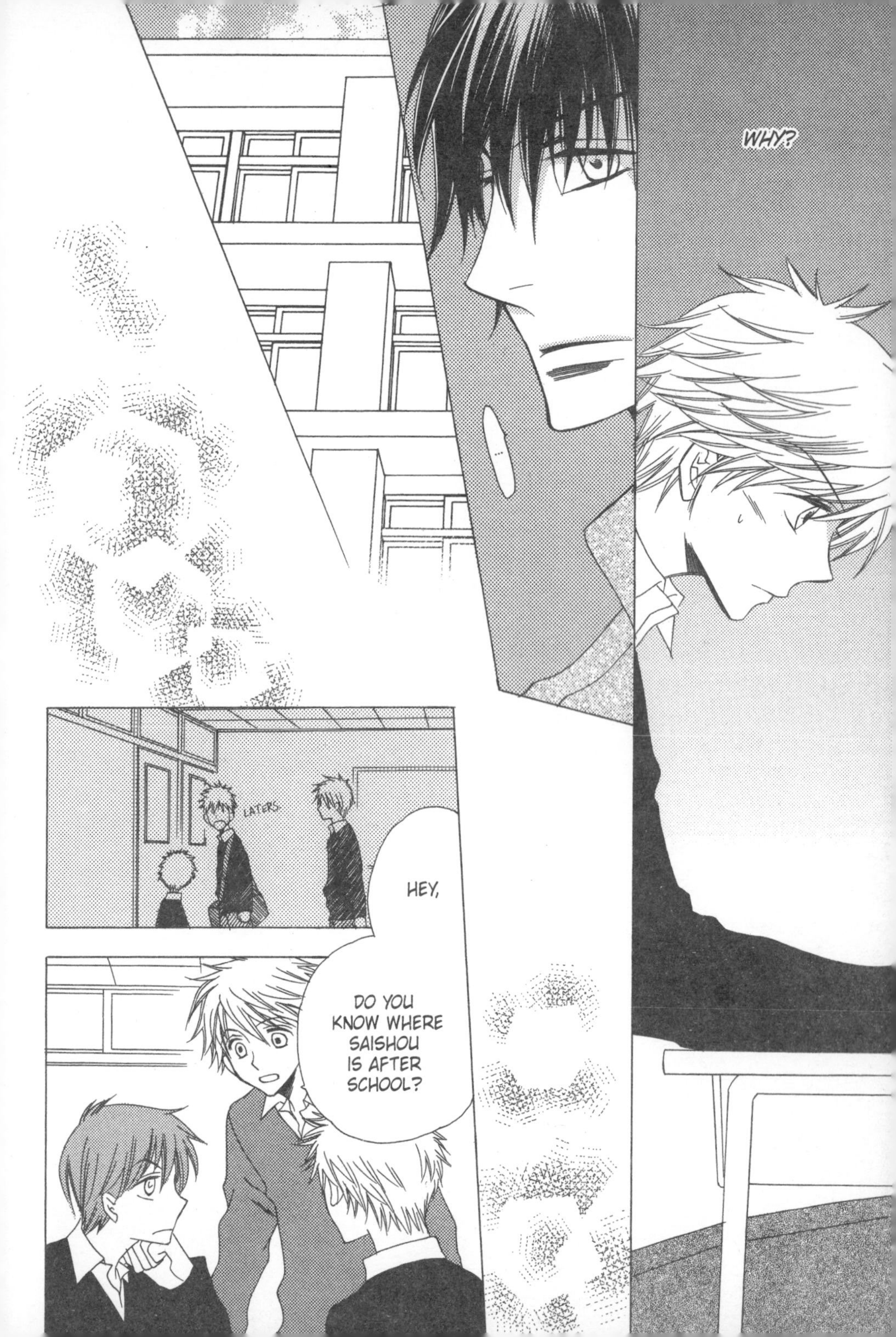
WHY?
...
LATERS.
HEY,
DO YOU KNOW WHERE SAISHOU IS AFTER SCHOOL?

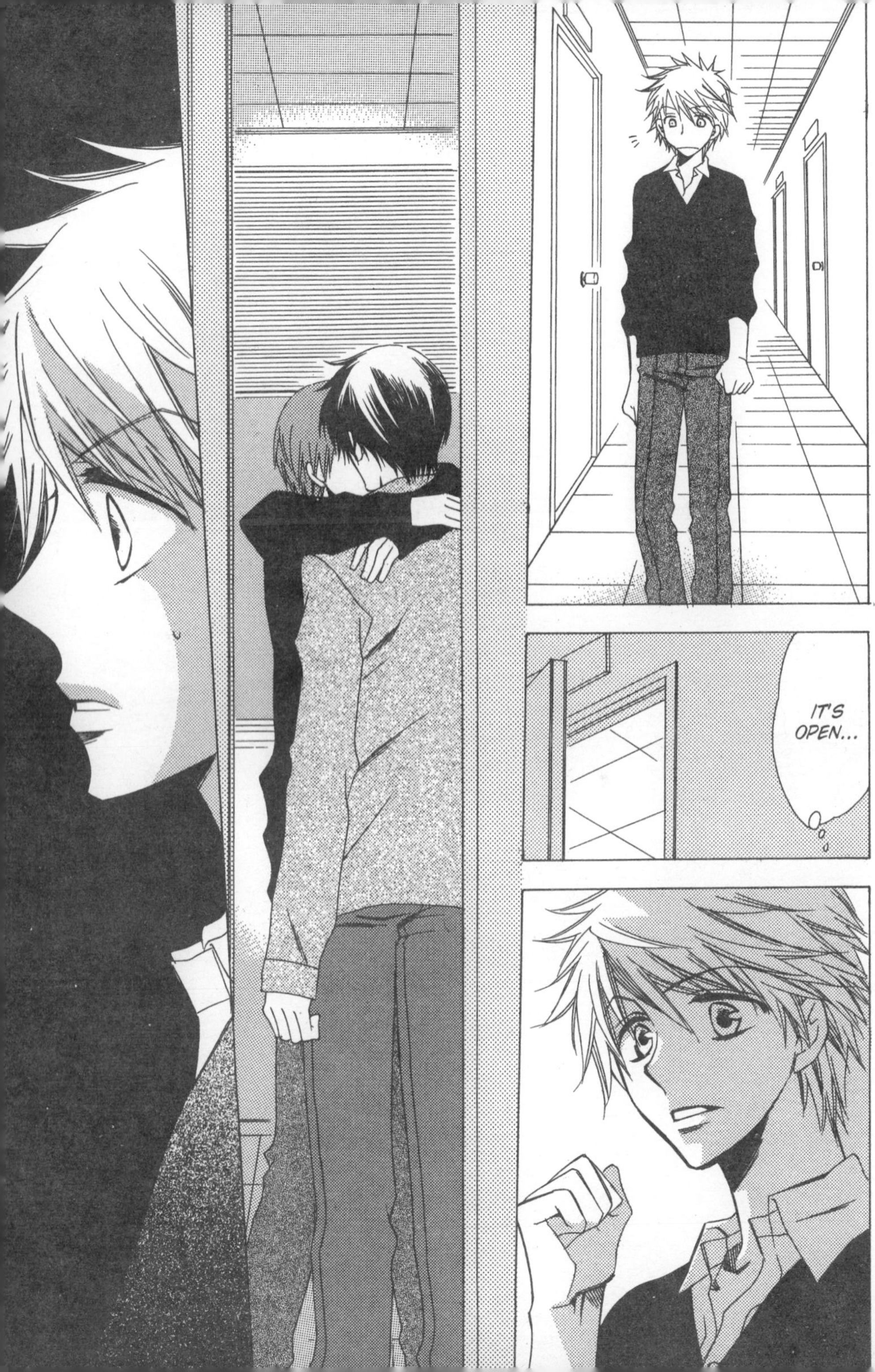
IT'S OPEN...

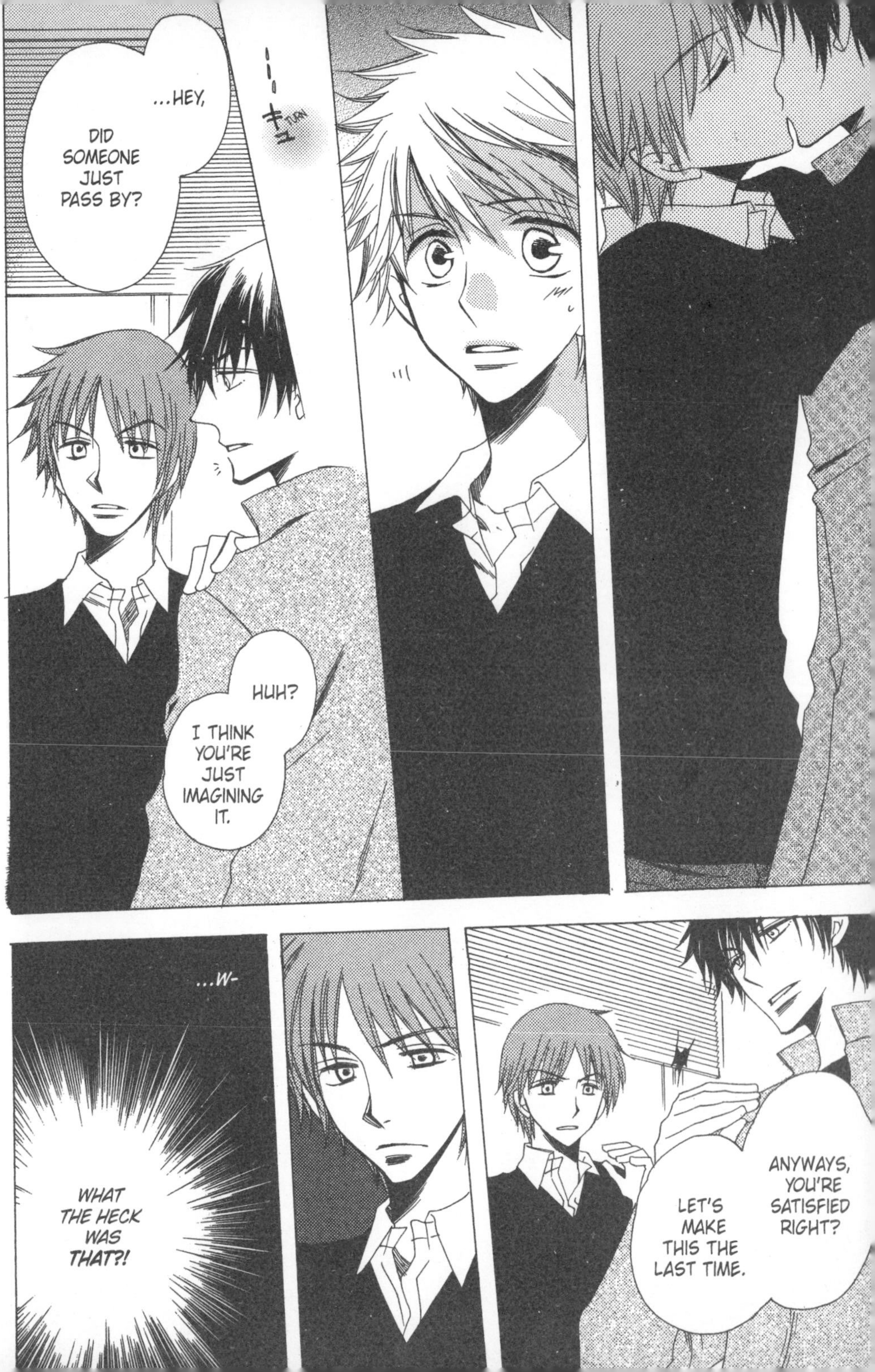
TURN
...HEY,
DID SOMEONE JUST PASS BY?
HUH?
I THINK YOU'RE JUST IMAGINING IT.
ANYWAYS, YOU'RE SATISFIED RIGHT?
LET'S MAKE THIS THE LAST TIME.
...W-
WHAT THE HECK WAS THAT?!

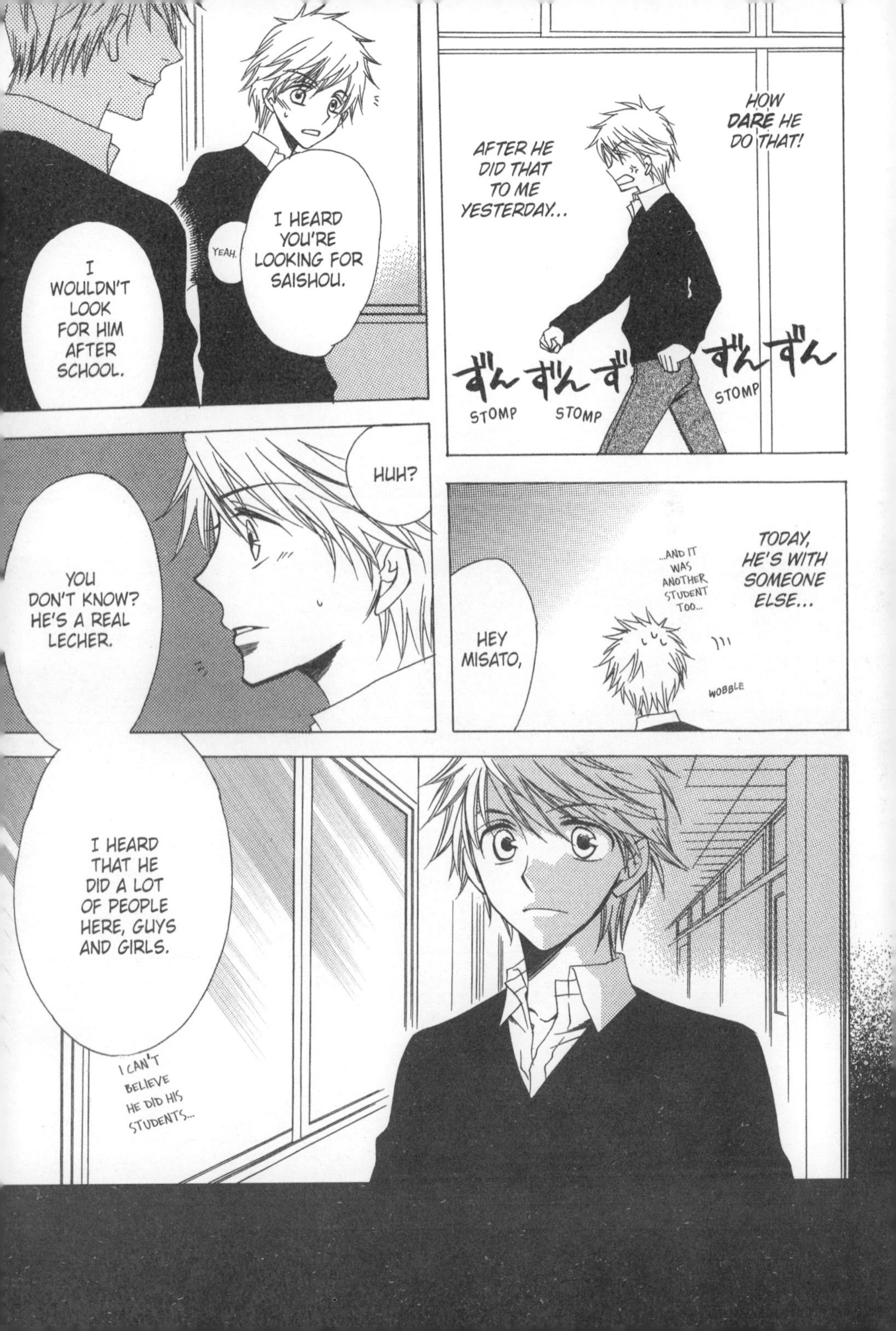
HOW DARE HE DO THAT!
AFTER HE DID THAT TO ME YESTERDAY...
ずんずん
STOMP
ずんずんず
STOMP
STOMP
I HEARD YOU'RE LOOKING FOR SAISHOU.
YEAH.
I WOULDN'T LOOK FOR HIM AFTER SCHOOL.
TODAY, HE'S WITH SOMEONE ELSE...
...AND IT WAS ANOTHER STUDENT TOO...
WOBBLE
HEY MISATO,
HUH?
YOU DON'T KNOW? HE'S A REAL LECHER.
I HEARD THAT HE DID A LOT OF PEOPLE HERE, GUYS AND GIRLS.
I CAN'T BELIEVE HE DID HIS STUDENTS...

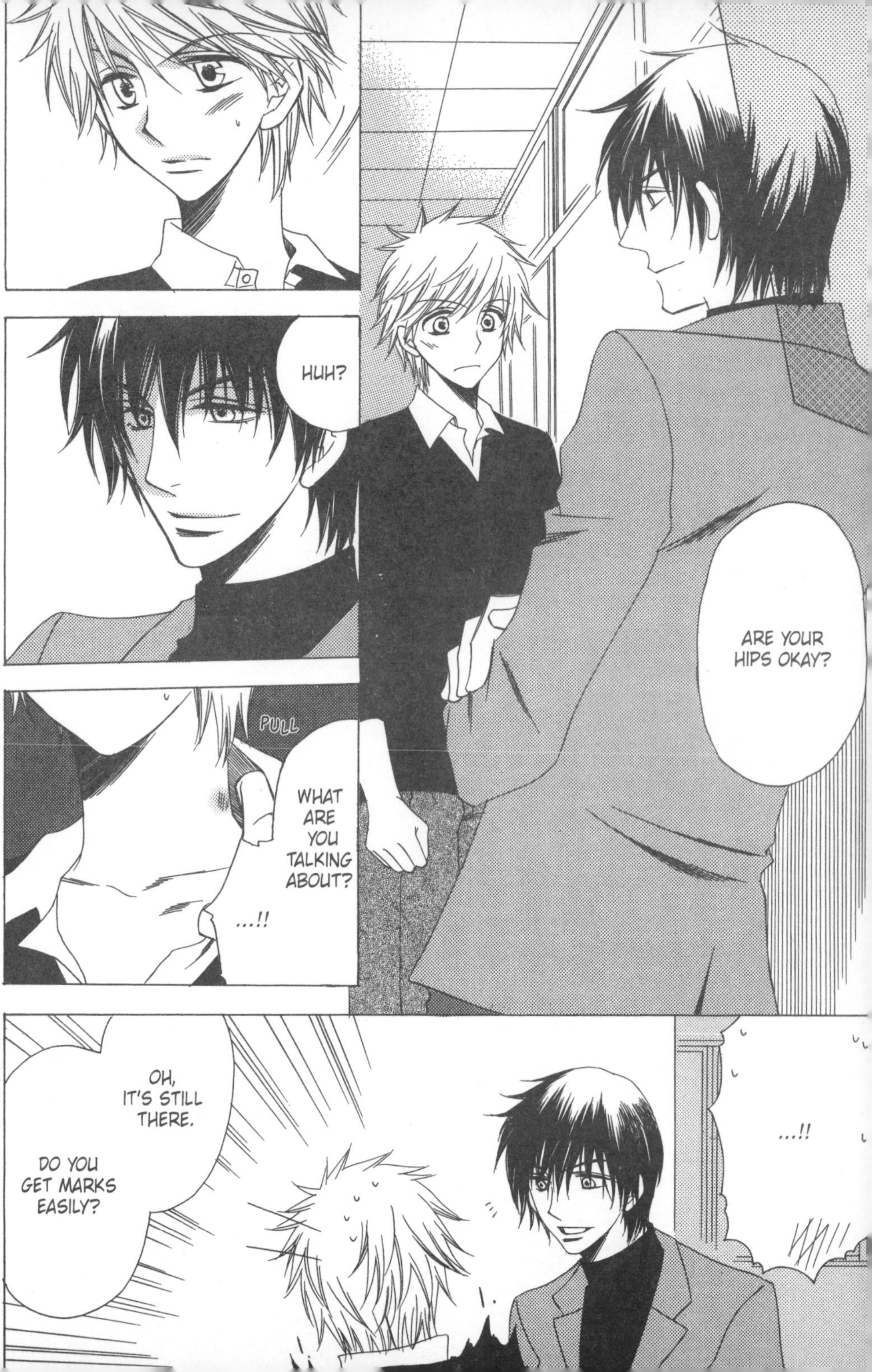
ARE YOUR HIPS OKAY?
HUH?
PULL
WHAT ARE YOU TALKING ABOUT?
...!!
...!!
OH, IT'S STILL THERE.
DO YOU GET MARKS EASILY?

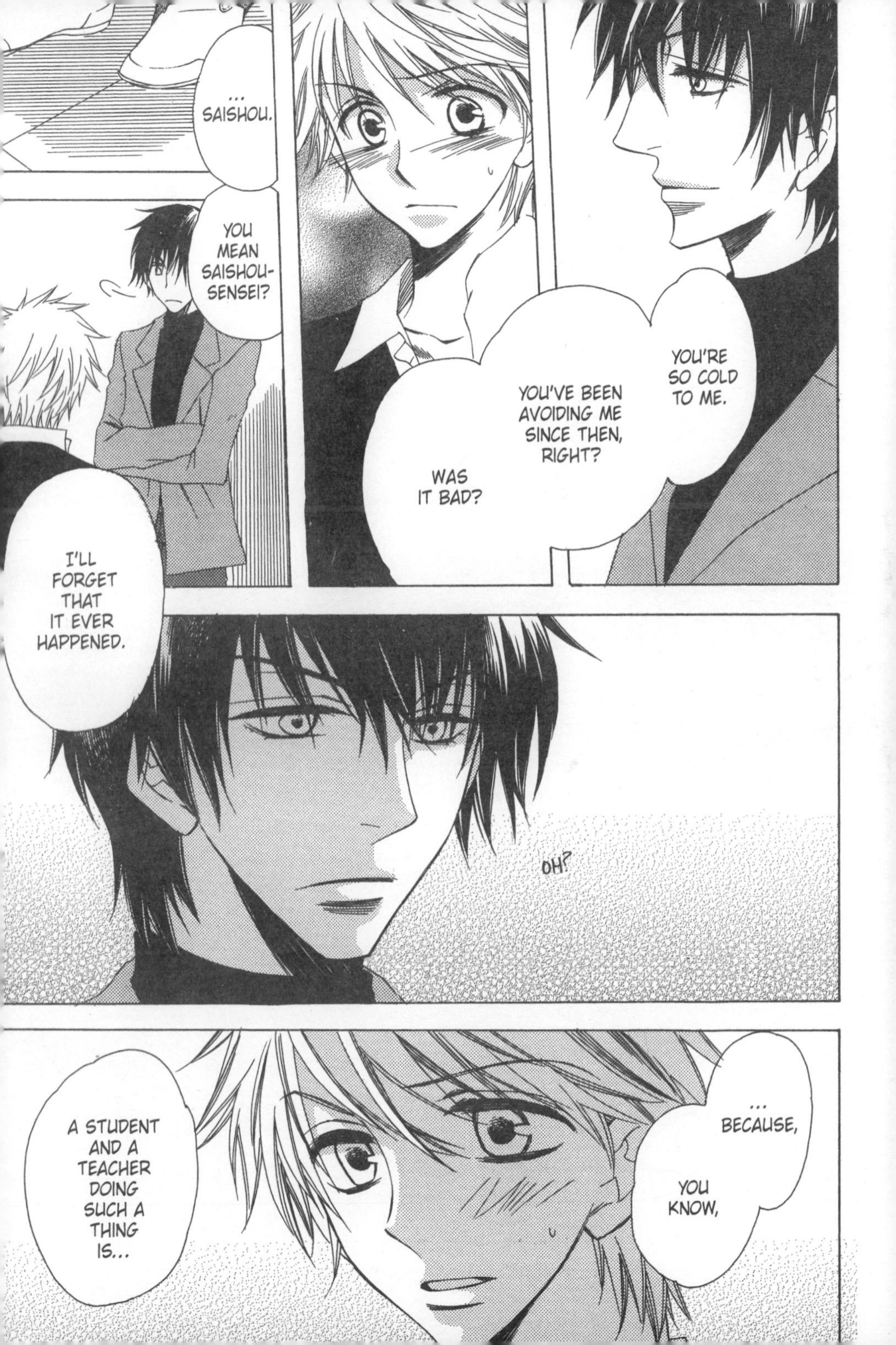
YOU'RE SO COLD TO ME.
YOU'VE BEEN AVOIDING ME SINCE THEN, RIGHT?
WAS IT BAD?
... SAISHOU.
YOU MEAN SAISHOU-SENSEI?
I'LL FORGET THAT IT EVER HAPPENED.
OH?
... BECAUSE,
YOU KNOW,
A STUDENT AND A TEACHER DOING SUCH A THING IS...

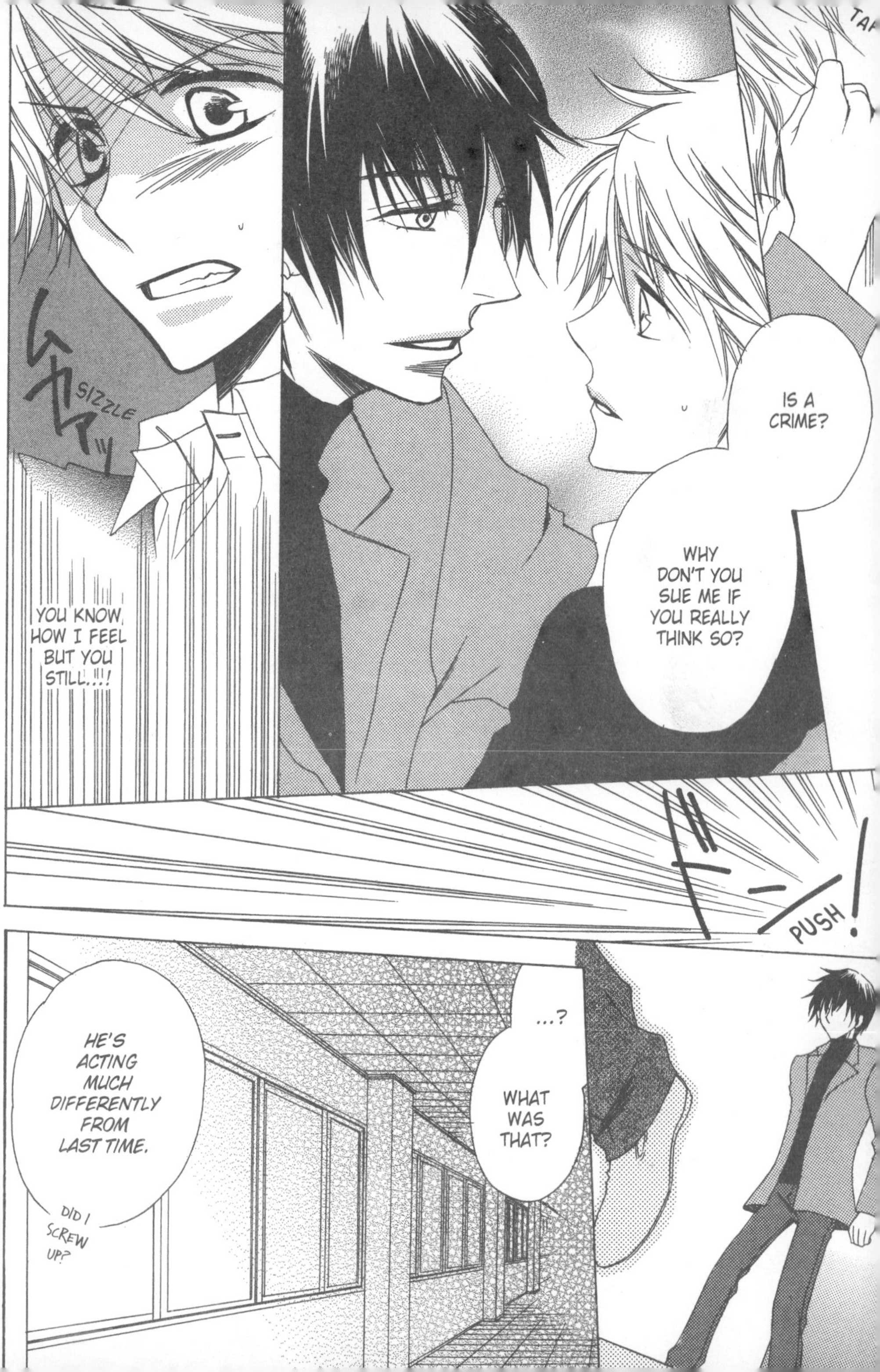
IS A CRIME?
WHY DON'T YOU SUE ME IF YOU REALLY THINK SO?
SIZZLE
YOU KNOW HOW I FEEL BUT YOU STILL...!!
PUSH!
...?
WHAT WAS THAT?
HE'S ACTING MUCH DIFFERENTLY FROM LAST TIME.
DID I SCREW UP?

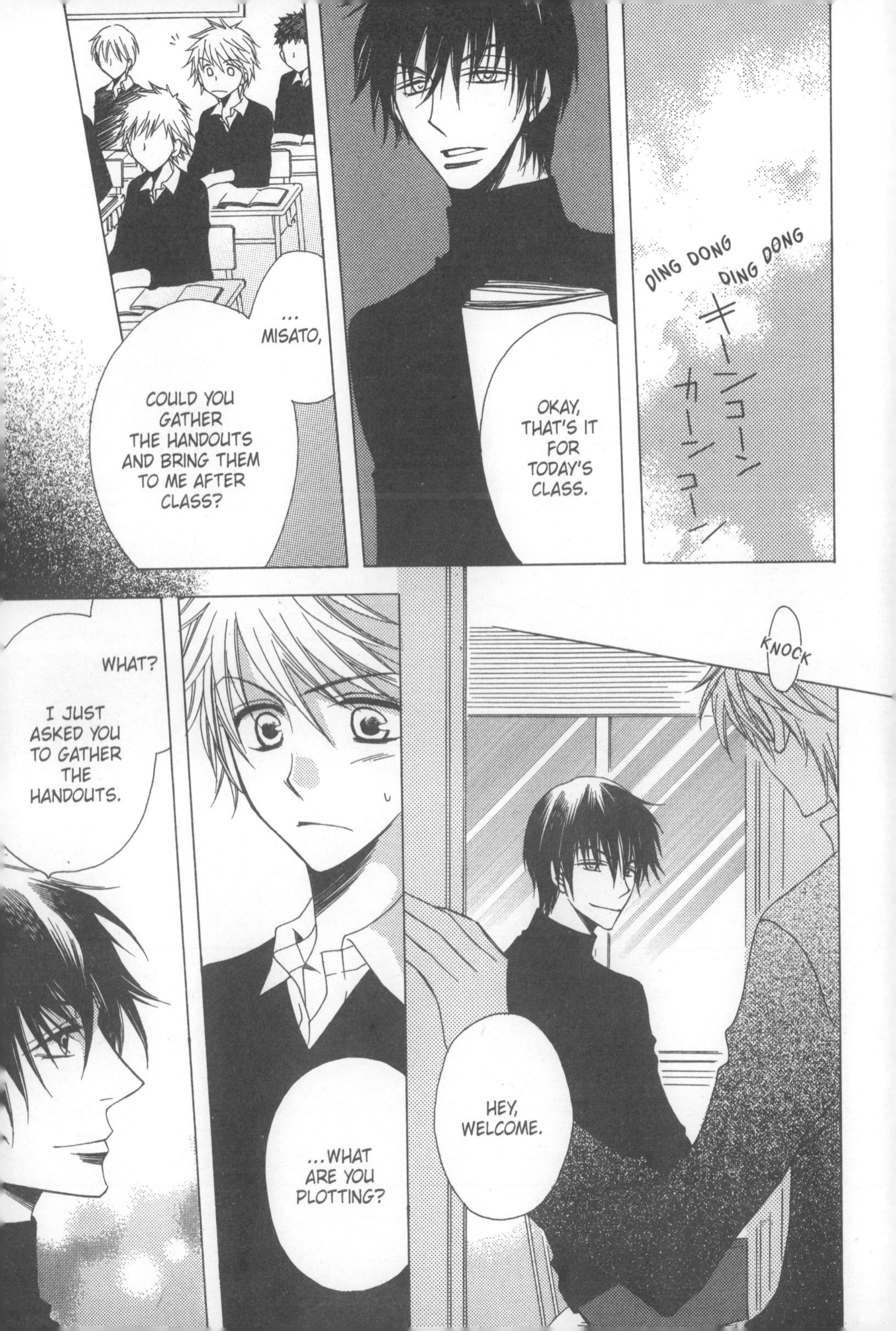
DING DONG
DING DONG
キーンコーン
カーンコーン
OKAY, THAT'S IT FOR TODAY'S CLASS.
...MISATO,
COULD YOU GATHER THE HANDOUTS AND BRING THEM TO ME AFTER CLASS?
KNOCK
HEY, WELCOME.
...WHAT ARE YOU PLOTTING?
WHAT?
I JUST ASKED YOU TO GATHER THE HANDOUTS.

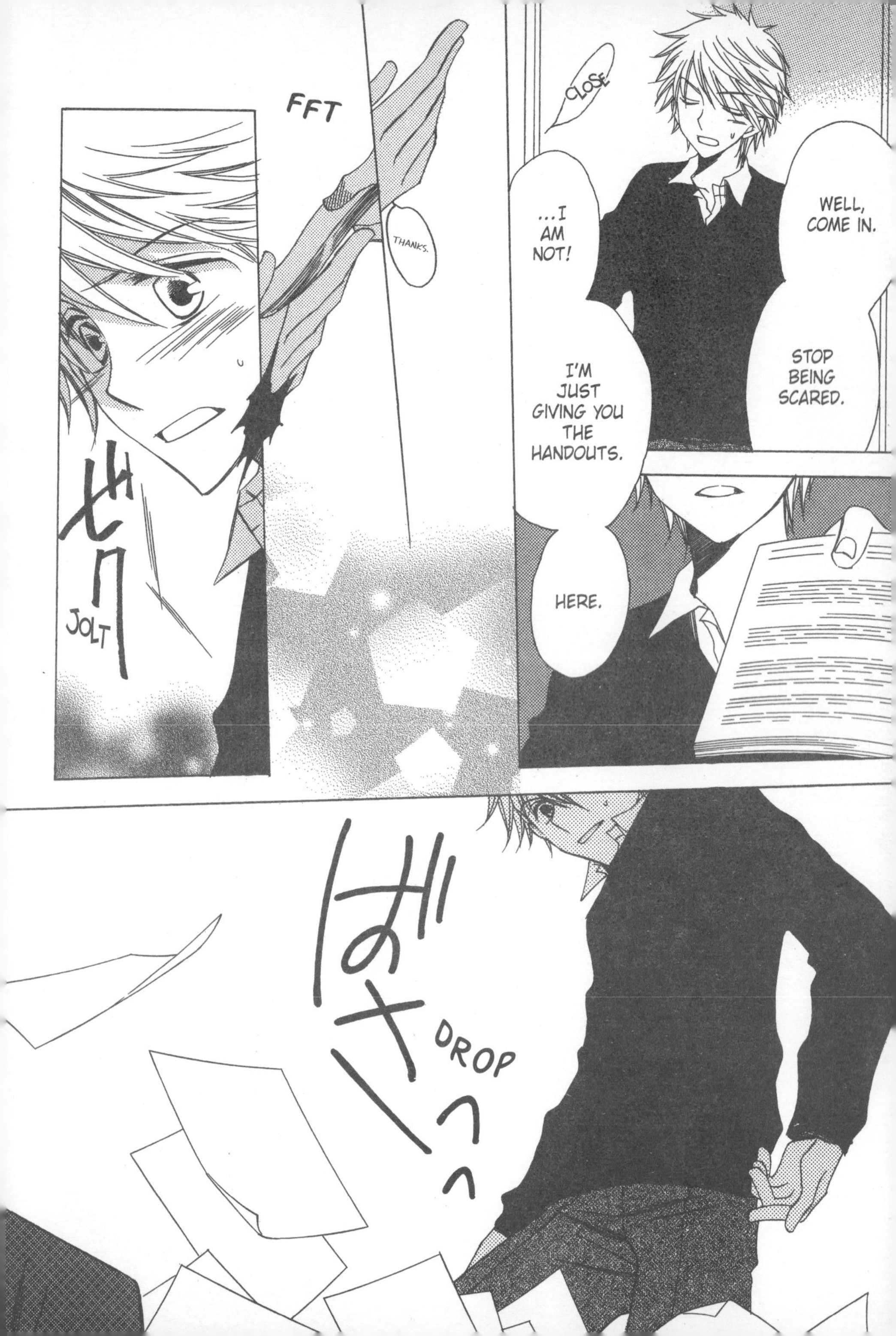
CLOSE
WELL, COME IN.
STOP BEING SCARED.
...I AM NOT!
I'M JUST GIVING YOU THE HANDOUTS.
HERE.
FFT
THANKS.
JOLT
DROP

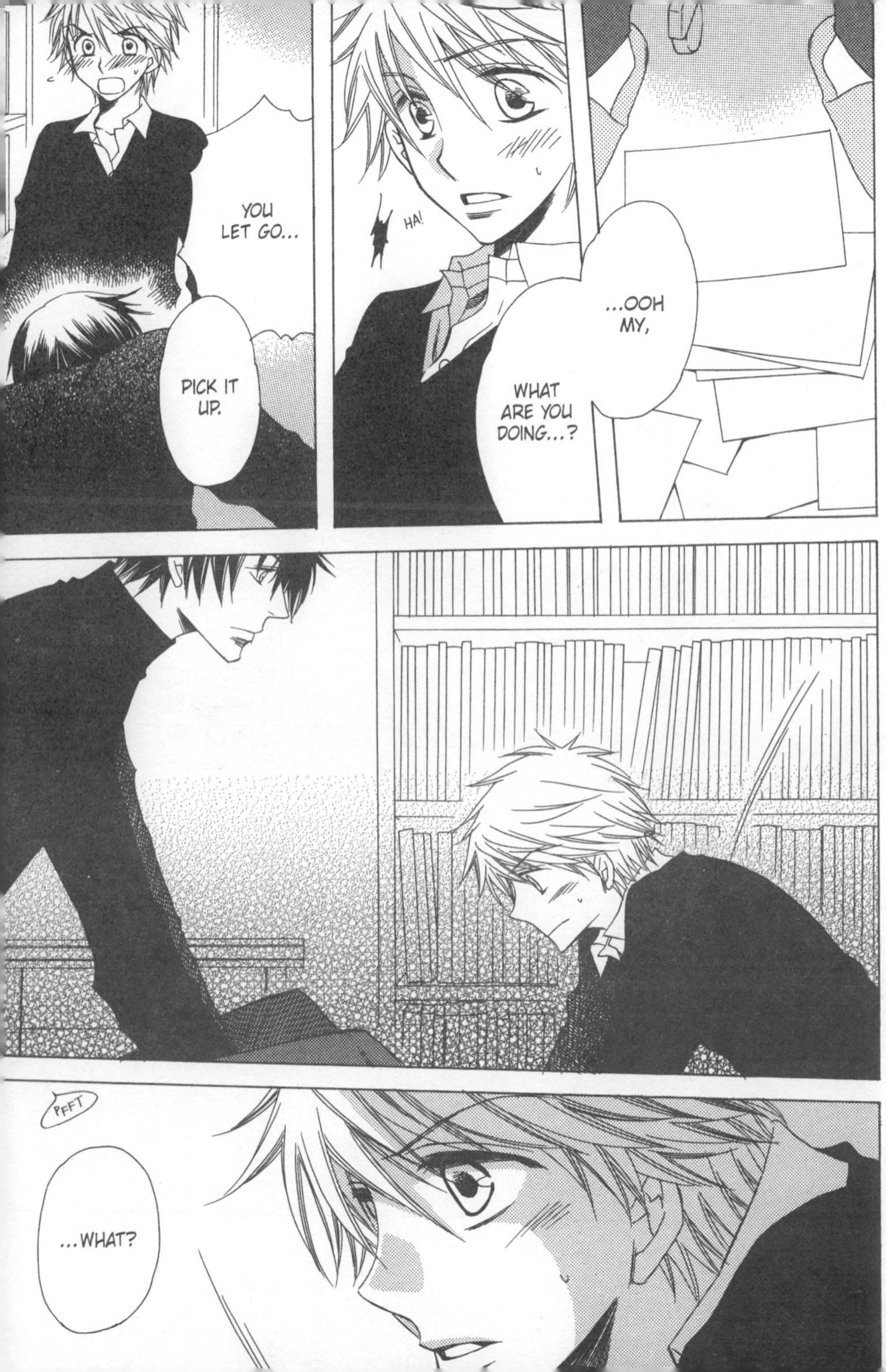
...OOH MY,
WHAT ARE YOU DOING...?
HA!
YOU LET GO...
PICK IT UP.
PFFT
...WHAT?

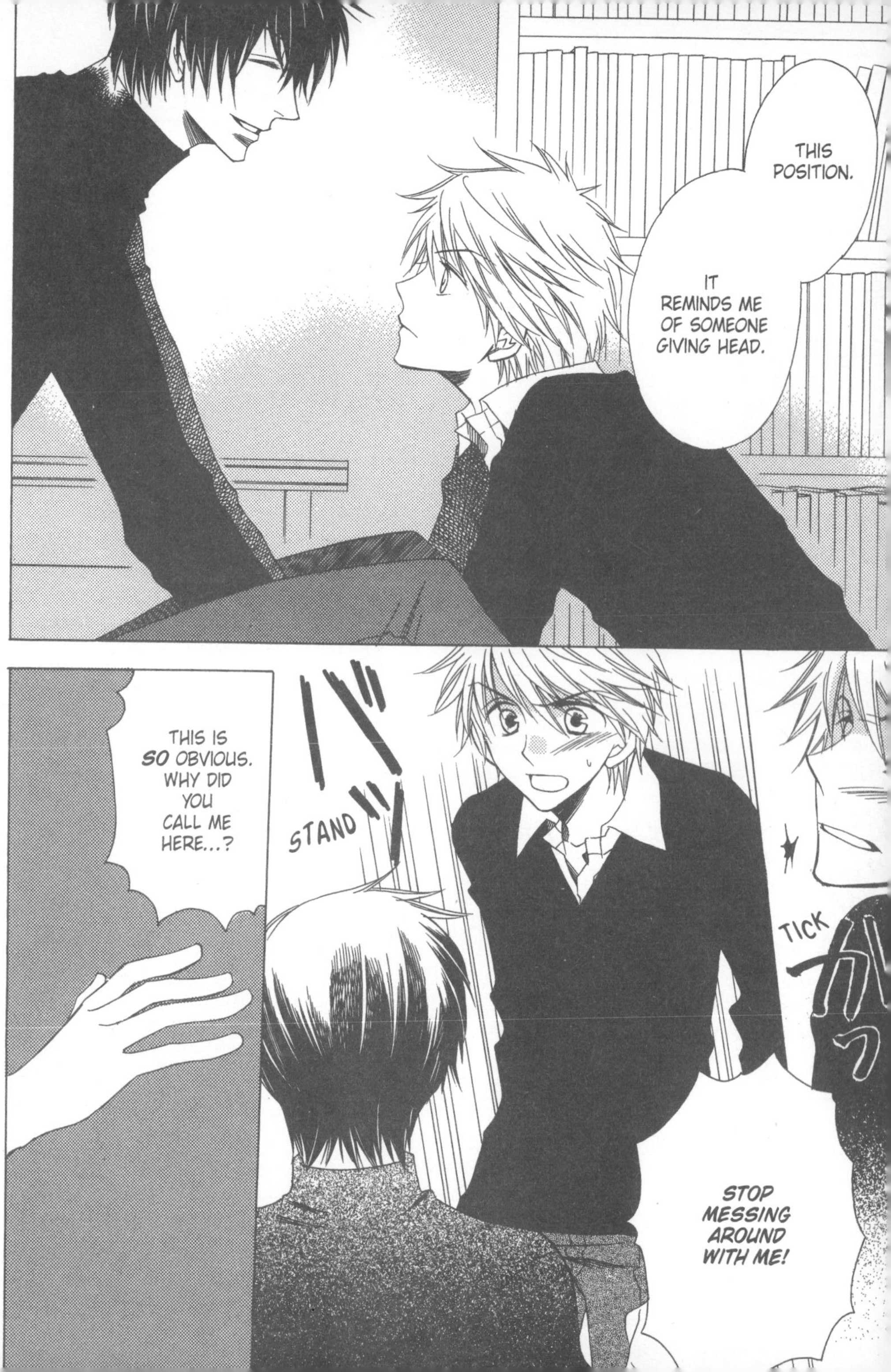
THIS POSITION.
IT REMINDS ME OF SOMEONE GIVING HEAD.
TICK
STAND
STOP MESSING AROUND WITH ME!
THIS IS SO OBVIOUS. WHY DID YOU CALL ME HERE...?

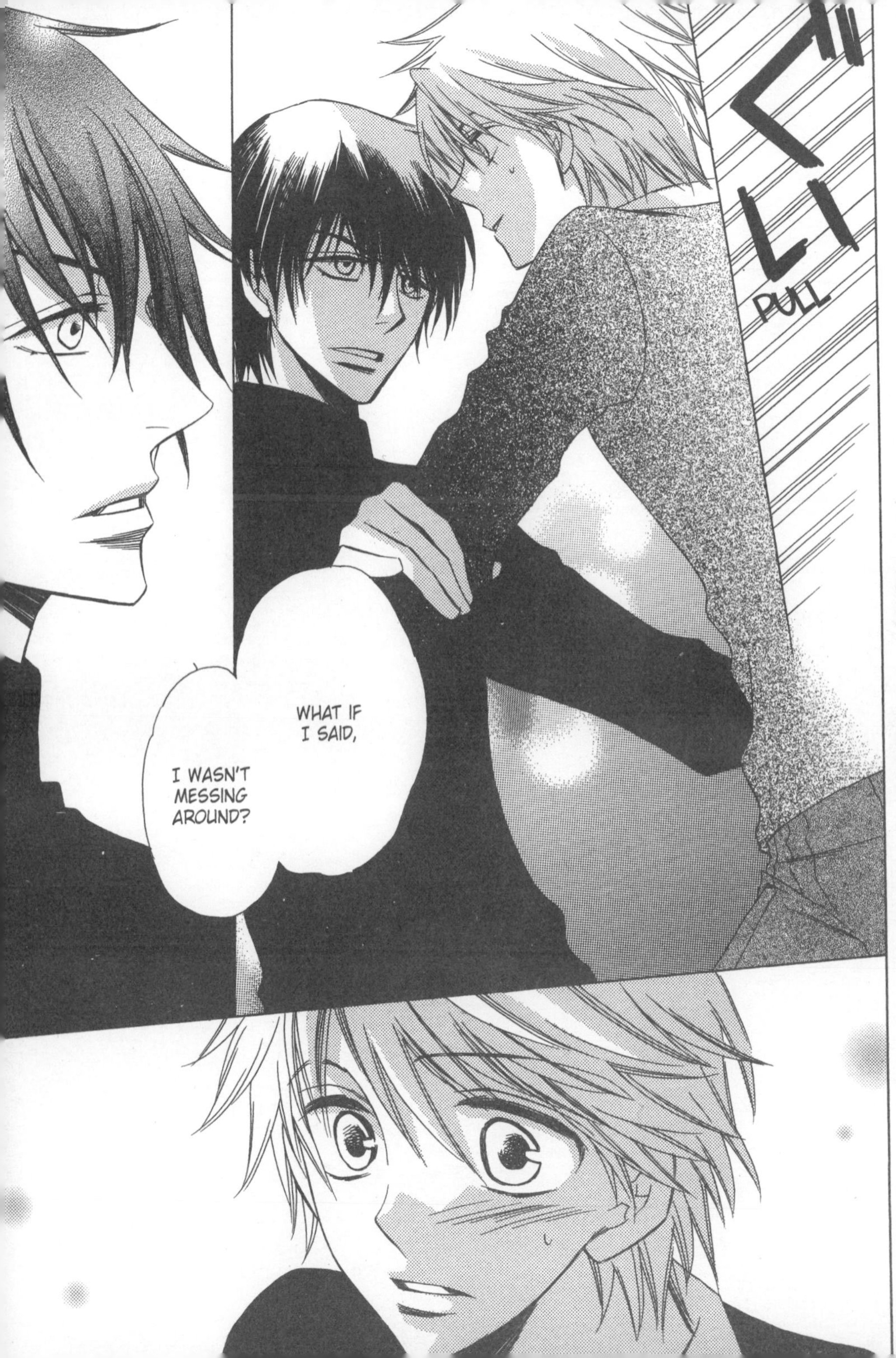
グイ
PULL
WHAT IF I SAID,
I WASN'T MESSING AROUND?

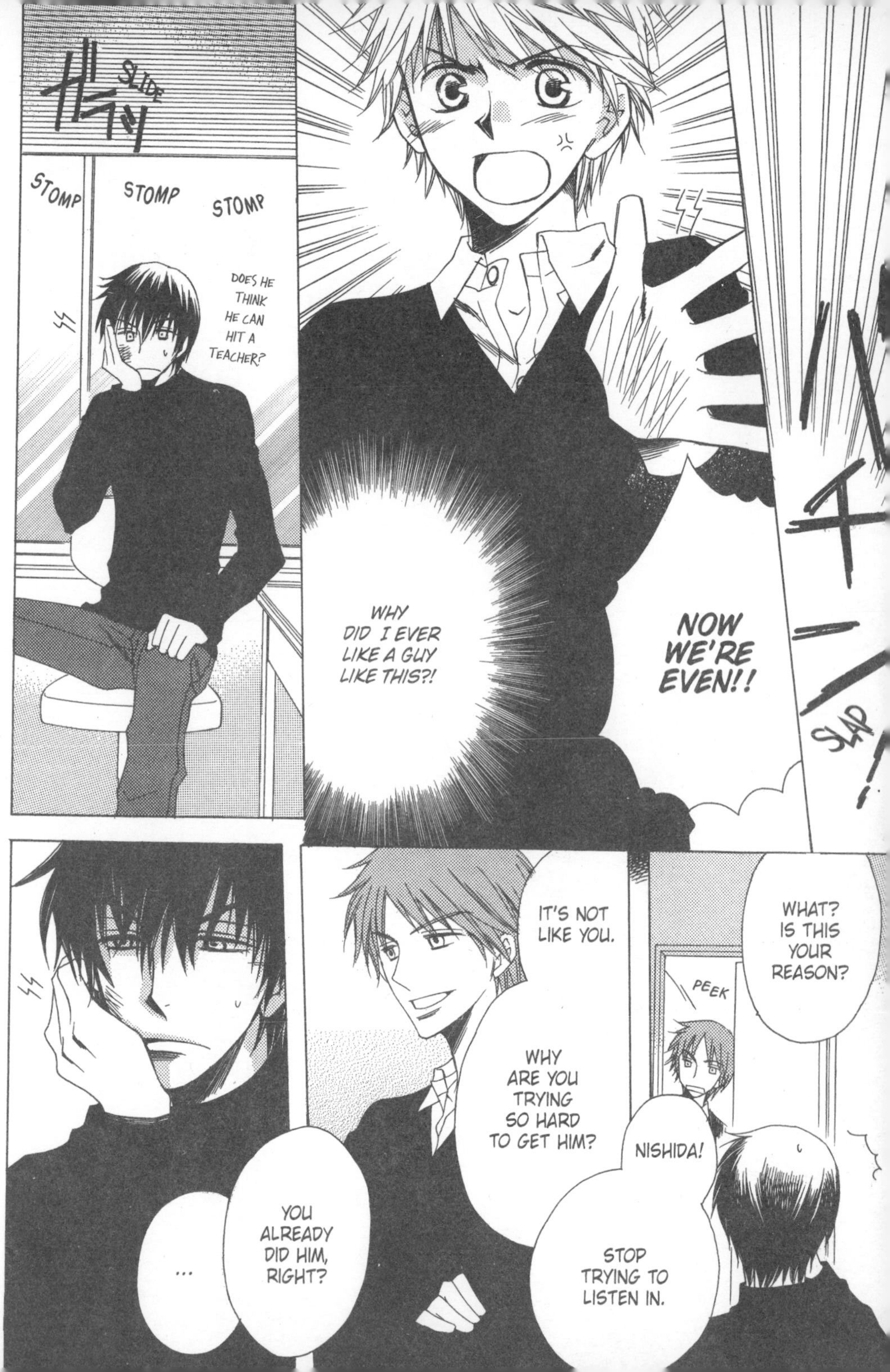
SLAP
NOW WE'RE EVEN!!
WHY DID I EVER LIKE A GUY LIKE THIS?!
SLIDE
STOMP
STOMP
STOMP
DOES HE THINK HE CAN HIT A TEACHER?
WHAT? IS THIS YOUR REASON?
PEEK
NISHIDA!
STOP TRYING TO LISTEN IN.
IT'S NOT LIKE YOU.
WHY ARE YOU TRYING SO HARD TO GET HIM?
YOU ALREADY DID HIM, RIGHT?
...

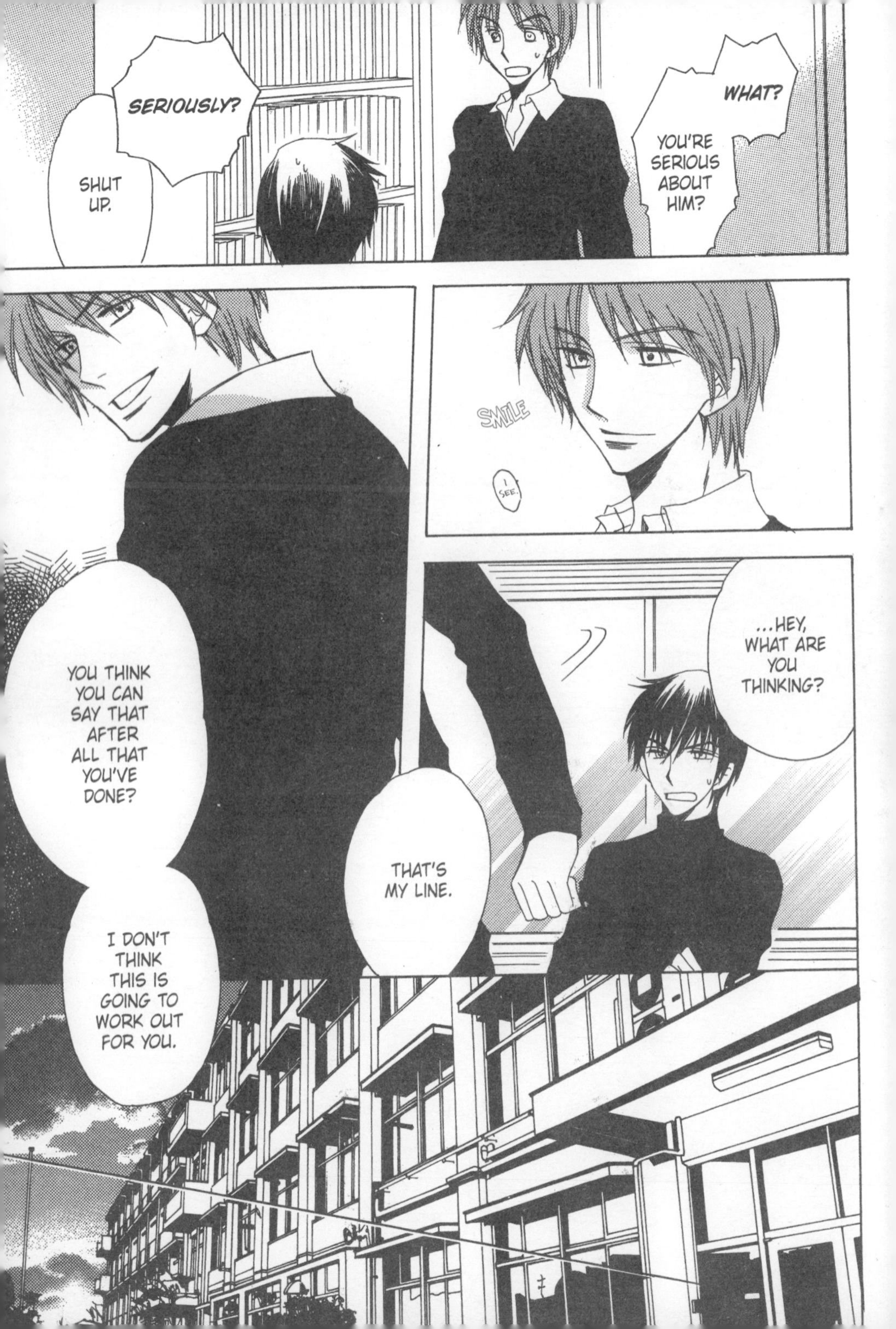
WHAT?
YOU'RE SERIOUS ABOUT HIM?
SERIOUSLY?
SHUT UP.
SMILE
I SEE.
...HEY, WHAT ARE YOU THINKING?
THAT'S MY LINE.
YOU THINK YOU CAN SAY THAT AFTER ALL THAT YOU'VE DONE?
I DON'T THINK THIS IS GOING TO WORK OUT FOR YOU.

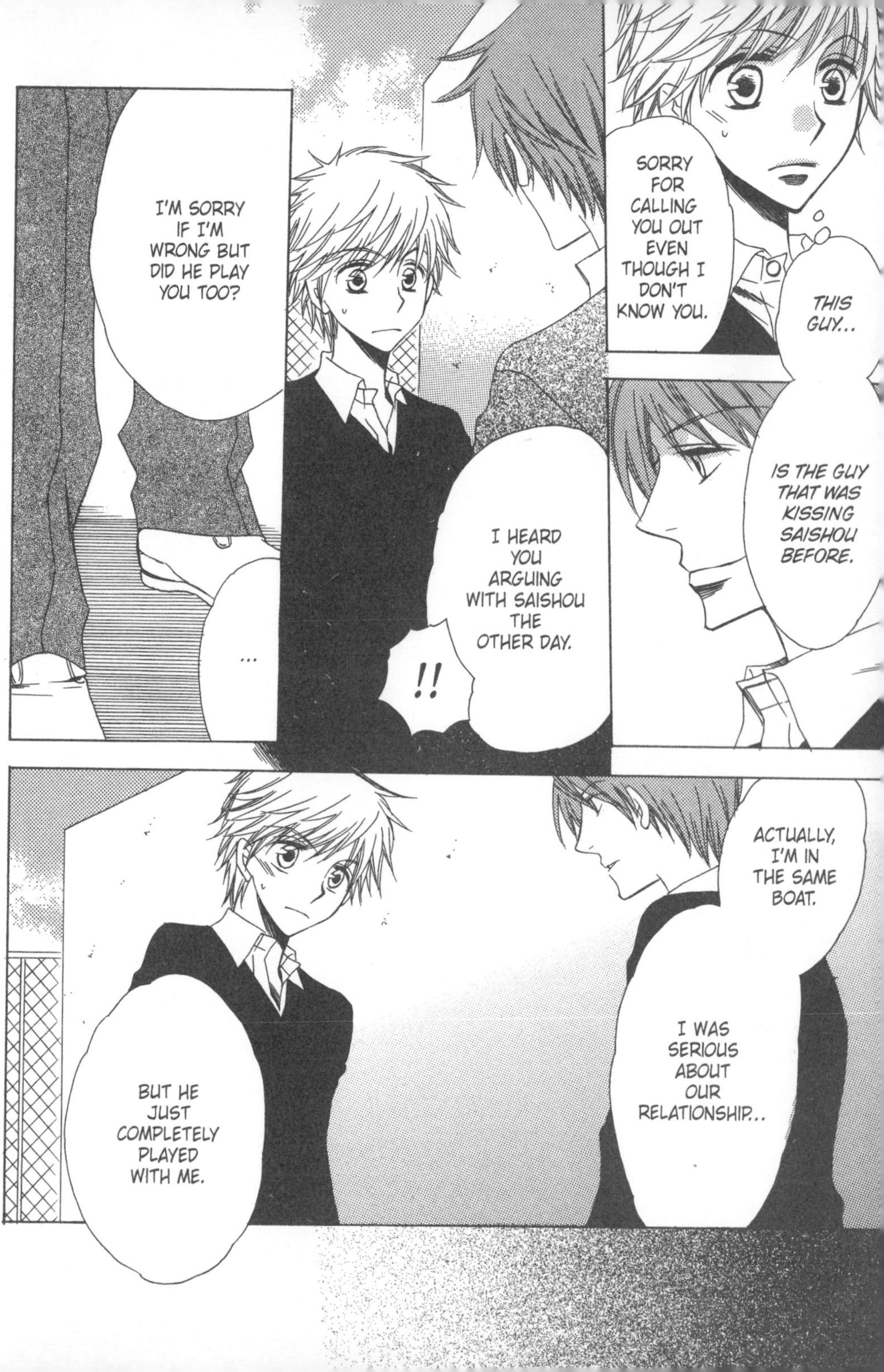
SORRY FOR CALLING YOU OUT EVEN THOUGH I DON'T KNOW YOU.
THIS GUY...
IS THE GUY THAT WAS KISSING SAISHOU BEFORE.
I HEARD YOU ARGUING WITH SAISHOU THE OTHER DAY.
!!
I'M SORRY IF I'M WRONG BUT DID HE PLAY YOU TOO?
...
ACTUALLY, I'M IN THE SAME BOAT.
I WAS SERIOUS ABOUT OUR RELATIONSHIP...
BUT HE JUST COMPLETELY PLAYED WITH ME.

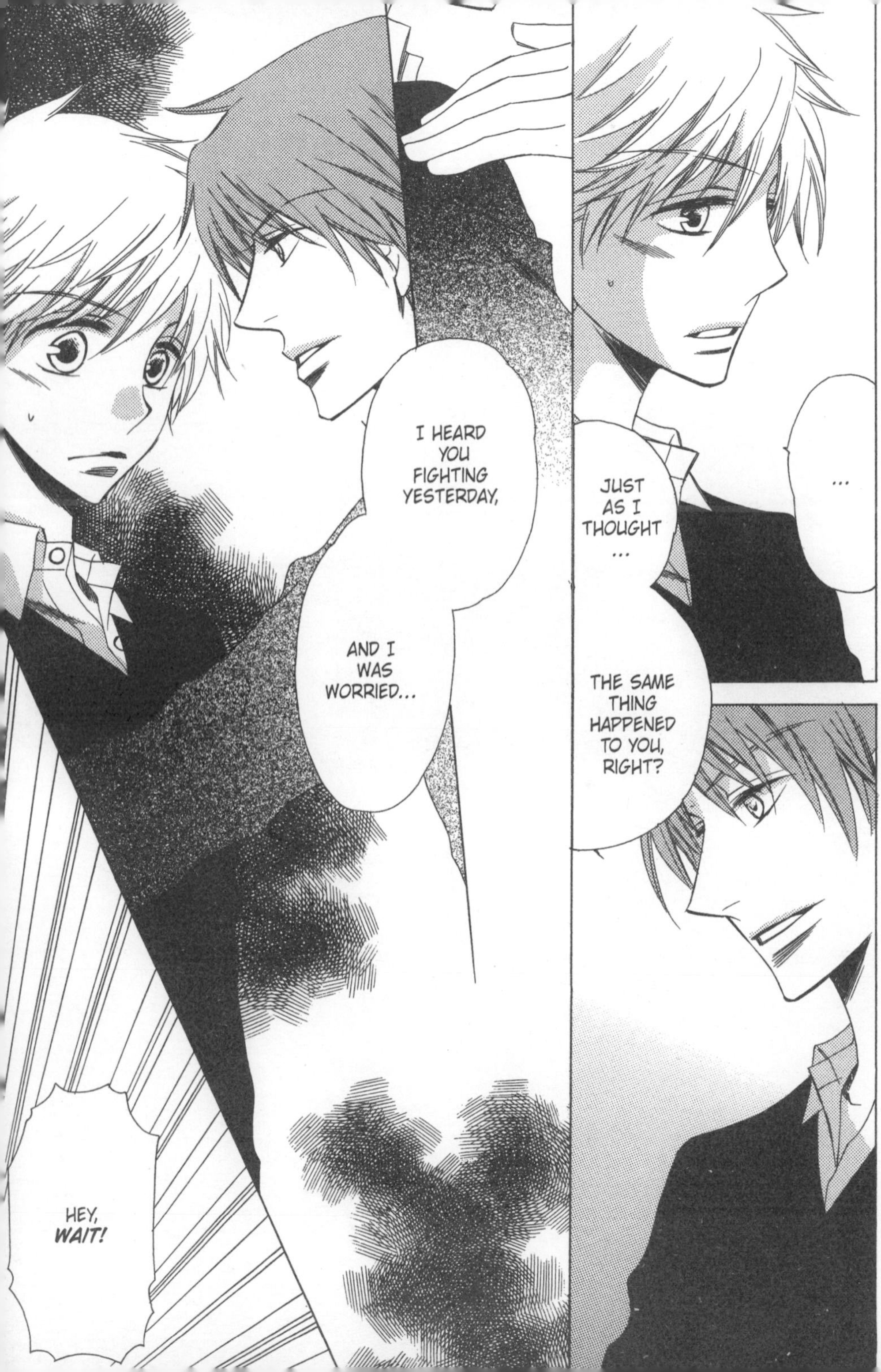
...
JUST AS I THOUGHT ...
THE SAME THING HAPPENED TO YOU, RIGHT?
I HEARD YOU FIGHTING YESTERDAY,
AND I WAS WORRIED...
HEY, WAIT!

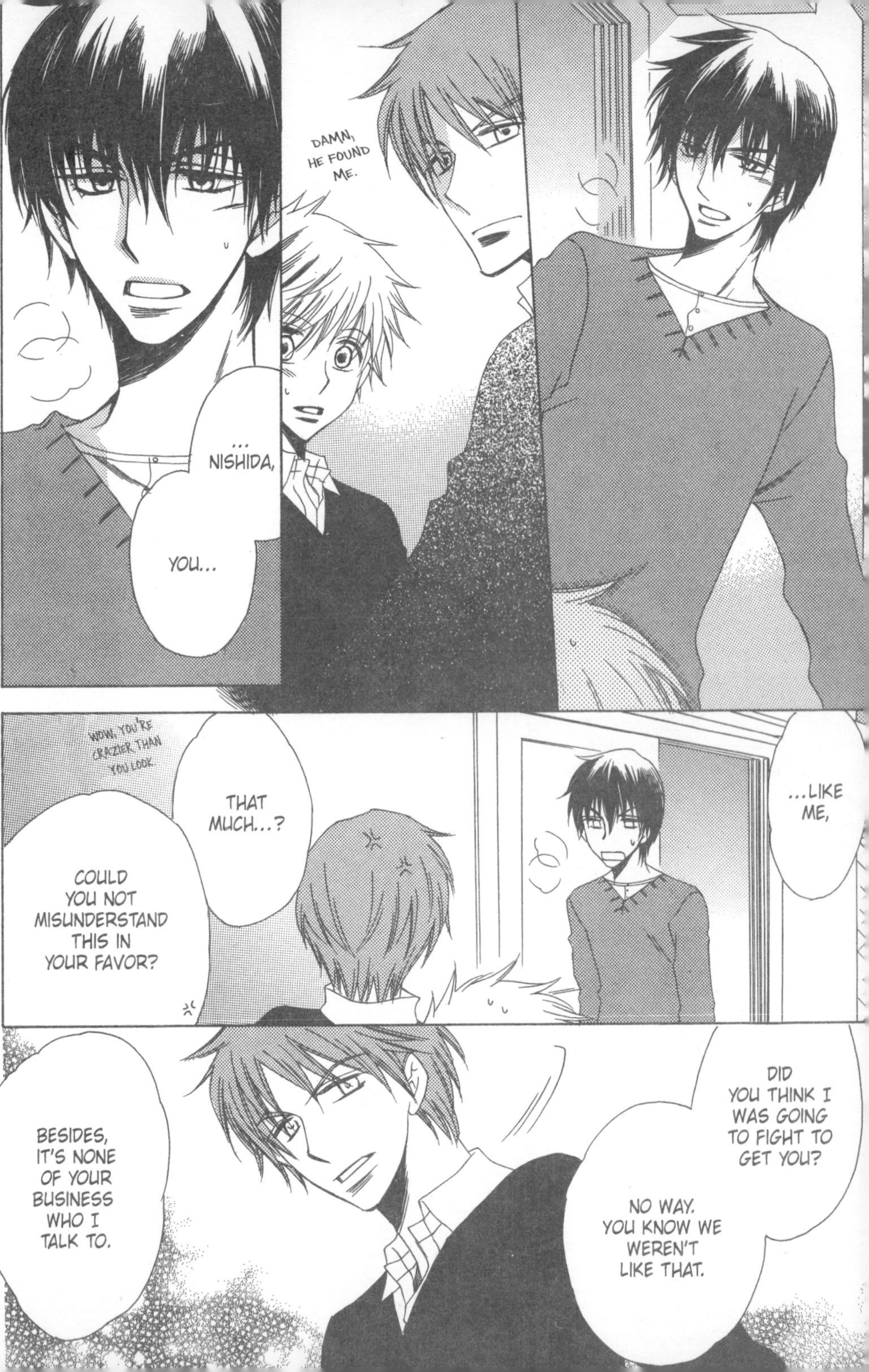
DAMN, HE FOUND ME.
...NISHIDA,
YOU...
...LIKE ME,
THAT MUCH...?
WOW, YOU'RE CRAZIER THAN YOU LOOK.
COULD YOU NOT MISUNDERSTAND THIS IN YOUR FAVOR?
DID YOU THINK I WAS GOING TO FIGHT TO GET YOU?
NO WAY. YOU KNOW WE WEREN'T LIKE THAT.
BESIDES, IT'S NONE OF YOUR BUSINESS WHO I TALK TO.

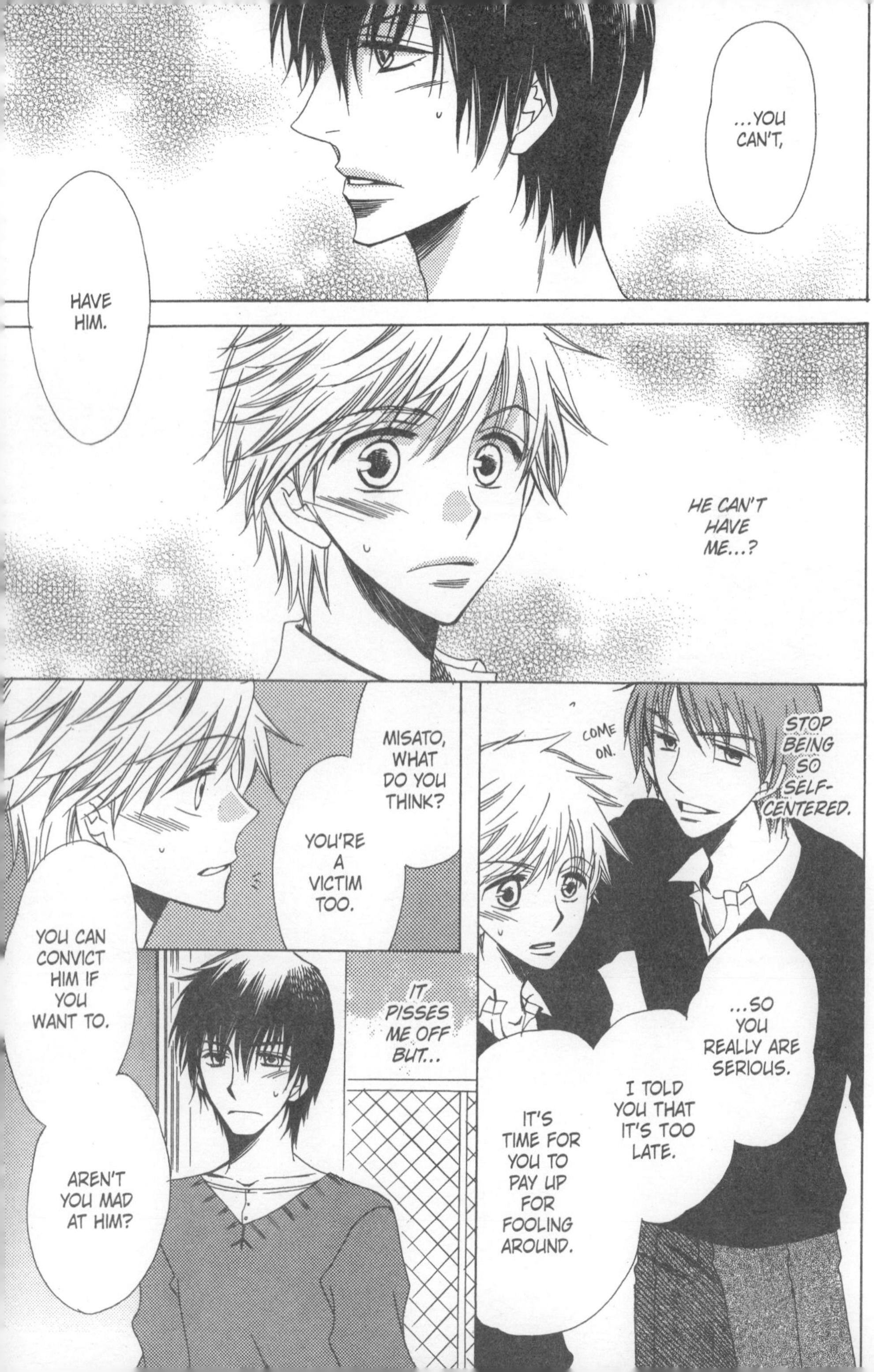
...YOU CAN'T,
HAVE HIM.
HE CAN'T HAVE ME...?
STOP BEING SO SELF-CENTERED.
COME ON.
...SO YOU REALLY ARE SERIOUS.
I TOLD YOU THAT IT'S TOO LATE.
IT'S TIME FOR YOU TO PAY UP FOR FOOLING AROUND.
MISATO, WHAT DO YOU THINK?
YOU'RE A VICTIM TOO.
YOU CAN CONVICT HIM IF YOU WANT TO.
IT PISSES ME OFF BUT...
AREN'T YOU MAD AT HIM?

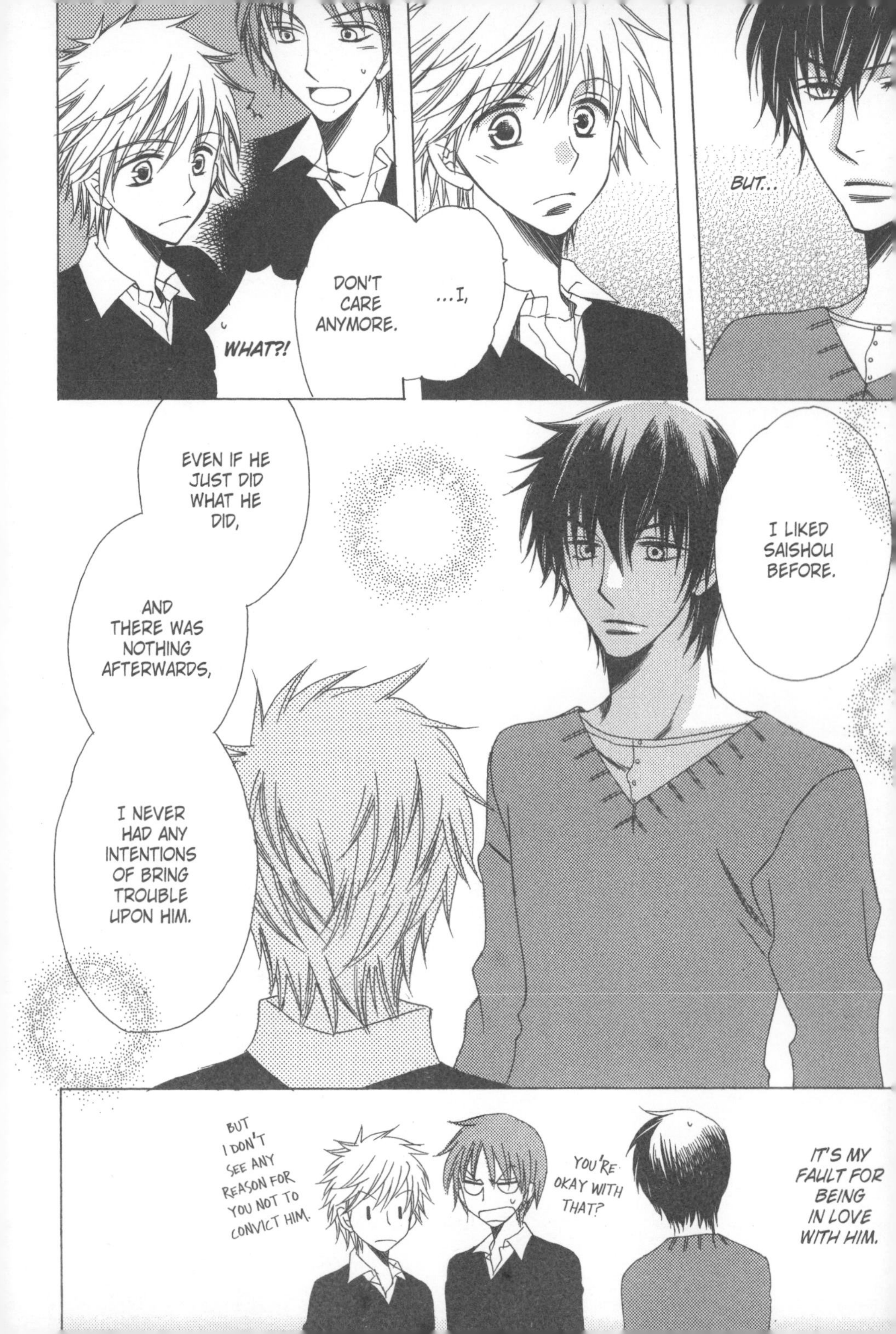
BUT...
...I,
DON'T CARE ANYMORE.
WHAT?!
I LIKED SAISHOU BEFORE.
EVEN IF HE JUST DID WHAT HE DID,
AND THERE WAS NOTHING AFTERWARDS,
I NEVER HAD ANY INTENTIONS OF BRING TROUBLE UPON HIM.
IT'S MY FAULT FOR BEING IN LOVE WITH HIM.
YOU'RE OKAY WITH THAT?
BUT I DON'T SEE ANY REASON FOR YOU NOT TO CONVICT HIM.

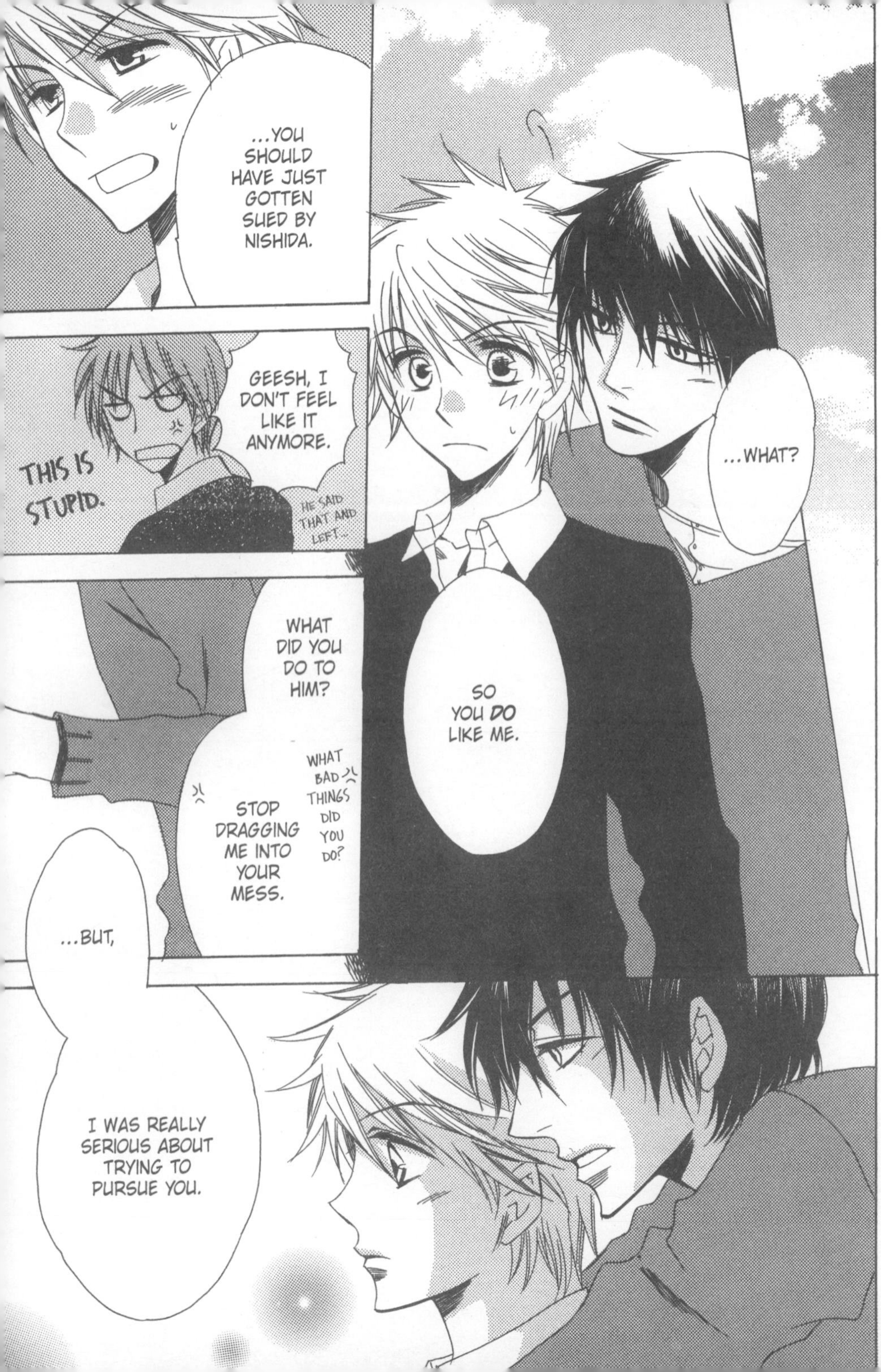
...WHAT?
SO YOU DO LIKE ME.
...YOU SHOULD HAVE JUST GOTTEN SUED BY NISHIDA.
GEESH, I DON'T FEEL LIKE IT ANYMORE.
THIS IS STUPID.
HE SAID THAT AND LEFT...
WHAT DID YOU DO TO HIM?
WHAT BAD THINGS DID YOU DO?
STOP DRAGGING ME INTO YOUR MESS.
...BUT,
I WAS REALLY SERIOUS ABOUT TRYING TO PURSUE YOU.

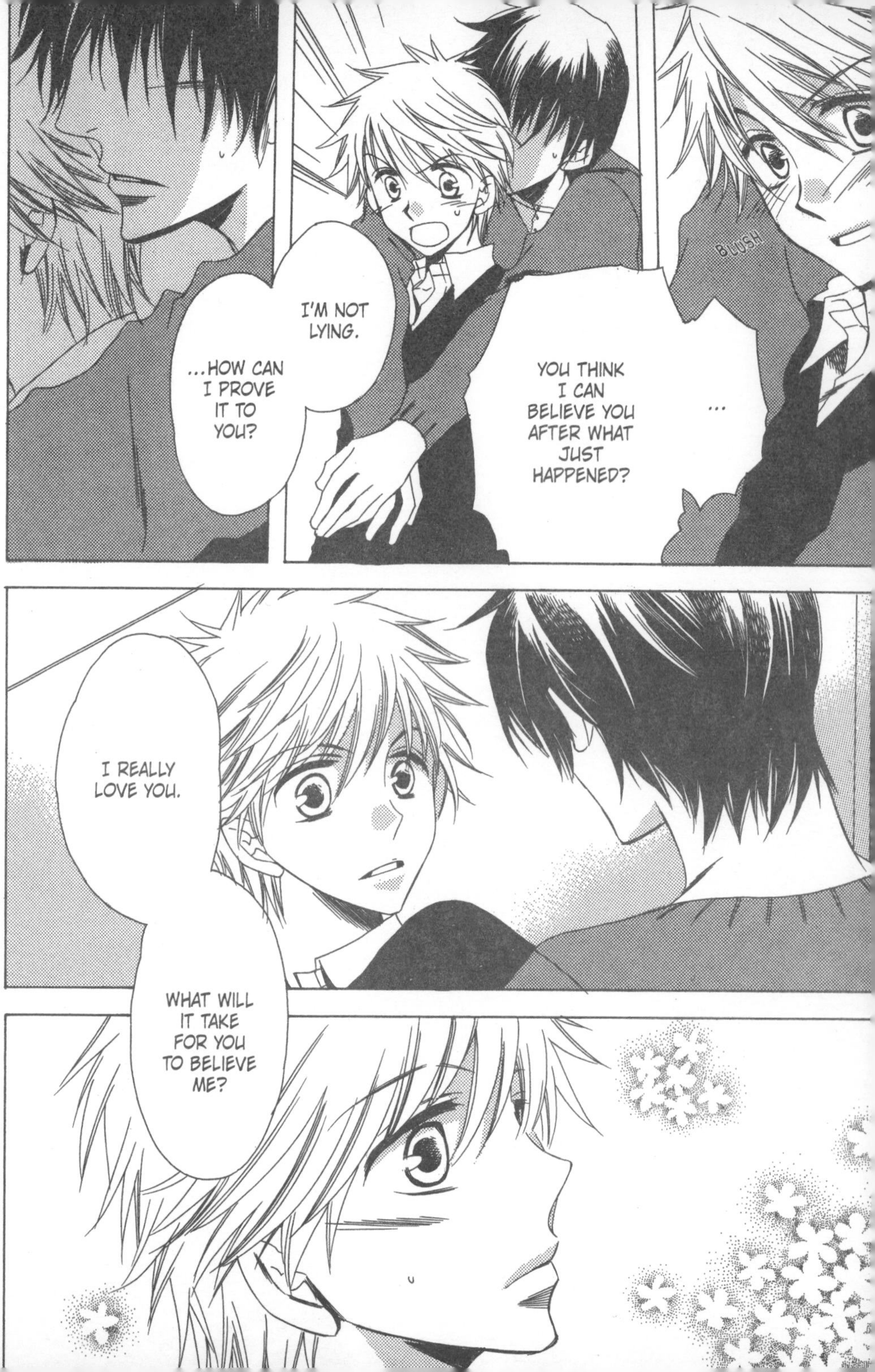
BLUSH
...
YOU THINK I CAN BELIEVE YOU AFTER WHAT JUST HAPPENED?
I'M NOT LYING.
...HOW CAN I PROVE IT TO YOU?
I REALLY LOVE YOU.
WHAT WILL IT TAKE FOR YOU TO BELIEVE ME?

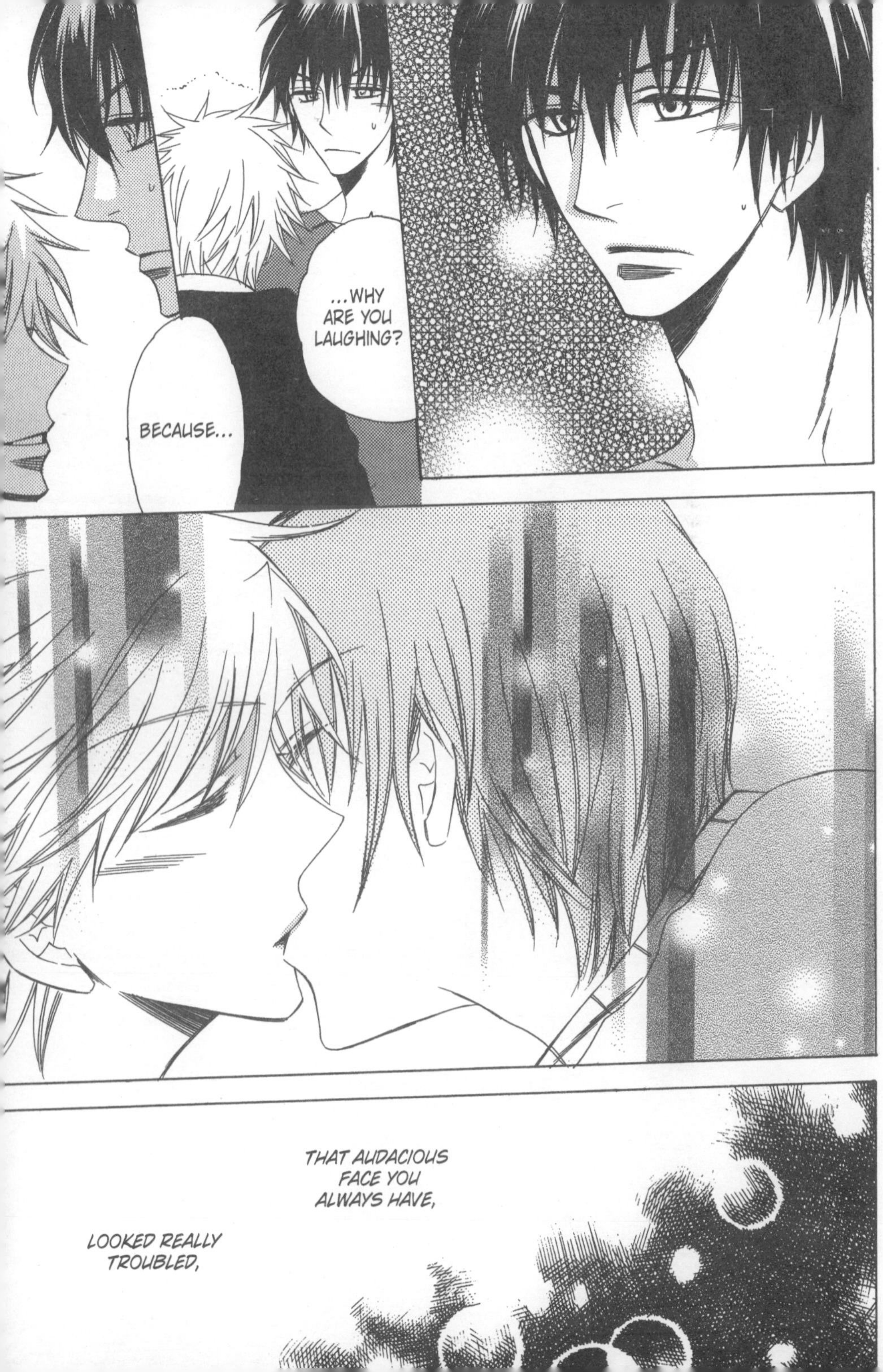
...WHY ARE YOU LAUGHING?
BECAUSE...
THAT AUDACIOUS FACE YOU ALWAYS HAVE,
LOOKED REALLY TROUBLED,

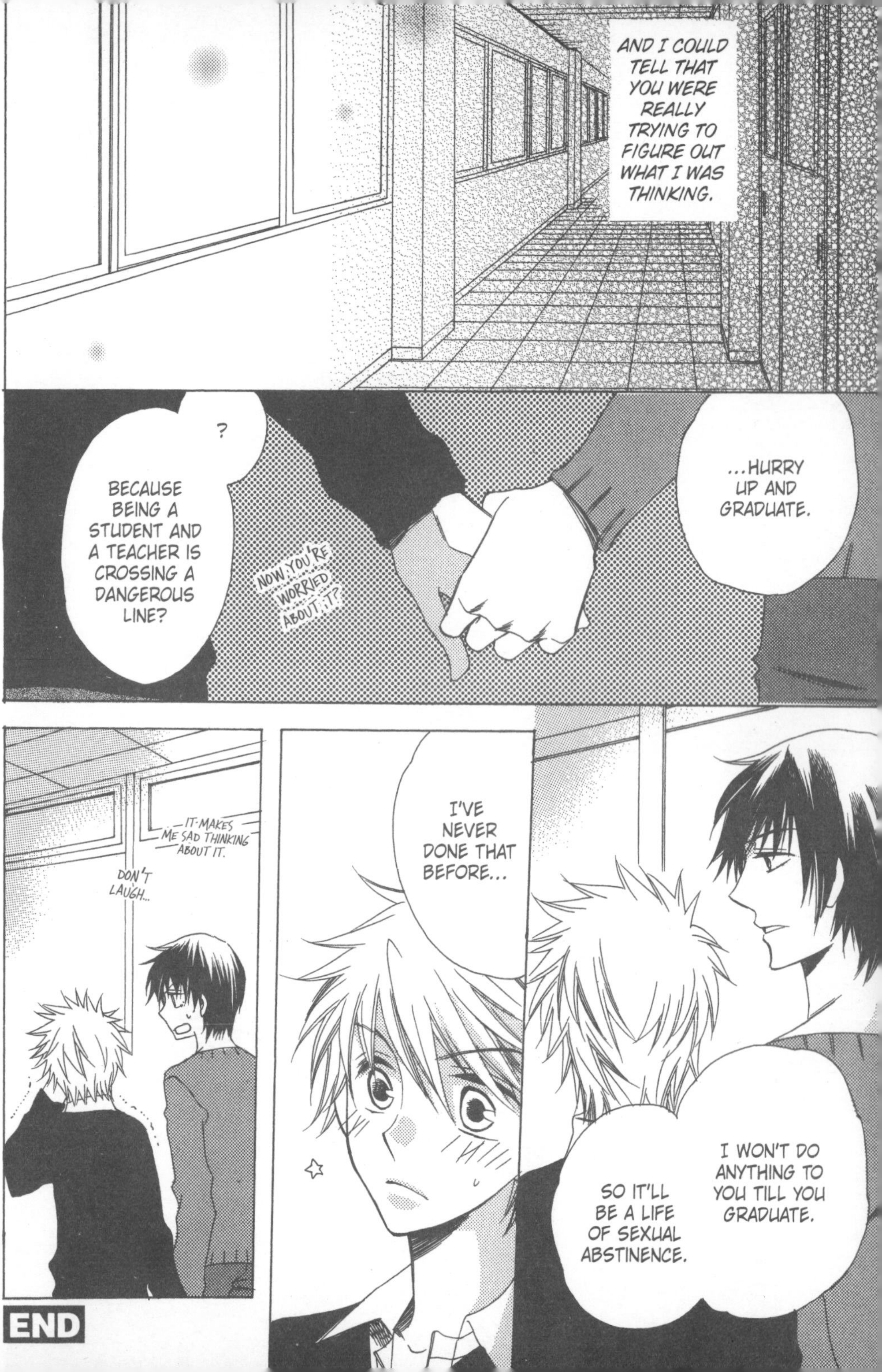
AND I COULD TELL THAT YOU WERE REALLY TRYING TO FIGURE OUT WHAT I WAS THINKING.
...HURRY UP AND GRADUATE.
?
BECAUSE BEING A STUDENT AND A TEACHER IS CROSSING A DANGEROUS LINE?
NOW YOU'RE WORRIED ABOUT IT?
I WON'T DO ANYTHING TO YOU TILL YOU GRADUATE.
SO IT'LL BE A LIFE OF SEXUAL ABSTINENCE.
I'VE NEVER DONE THAT BEFORE...
IT MAKES ME SAD THINKING ABOUT IT.
DON'T LAUGH...
END

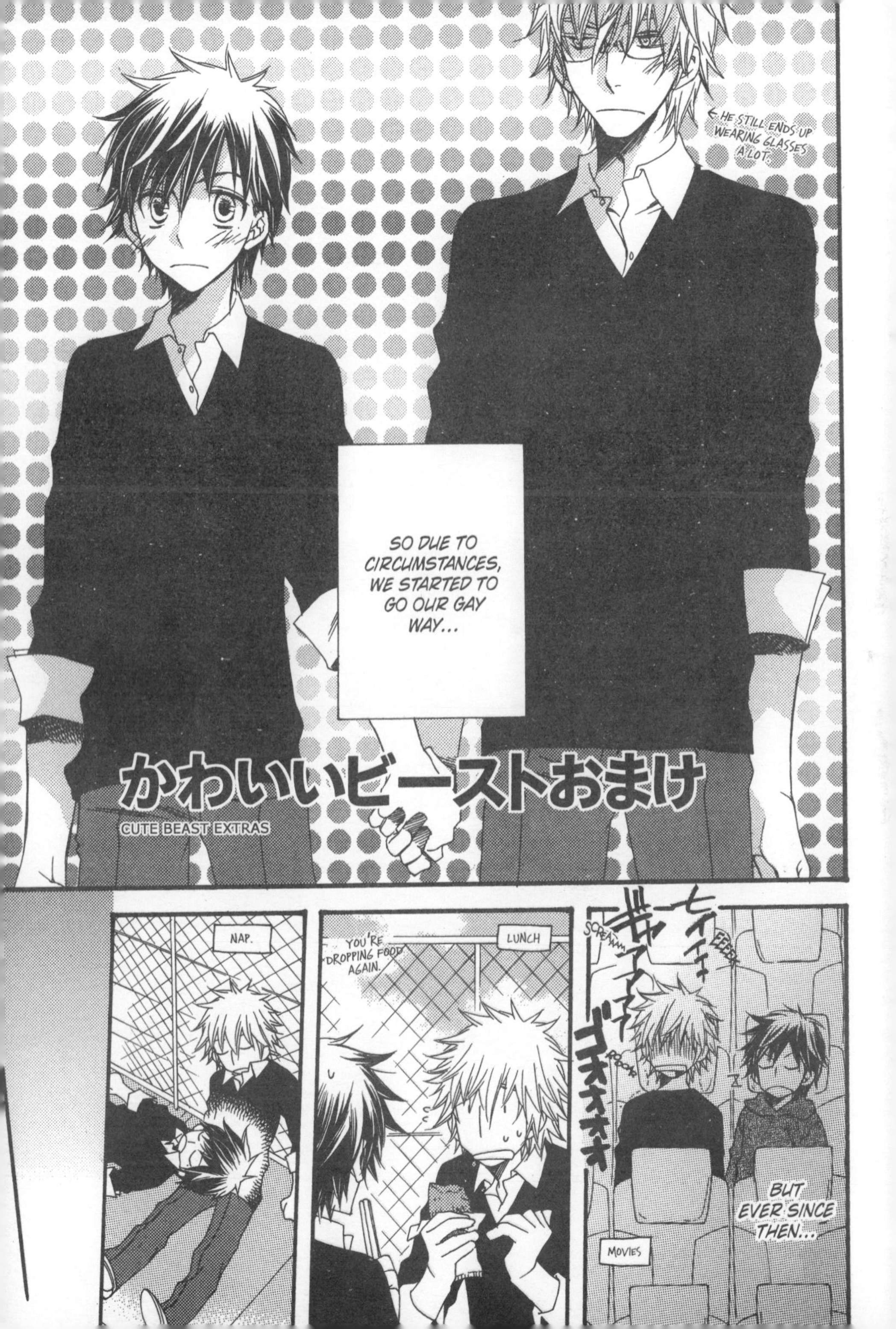
← HE STILL ENDS UP WEARING GLASSES A LOT.
SO DUE TO CIRCUMSTANCES, WE STARTED TO GO OUR GAY WAY...
かわいいビーストおまけ
CUTE BEAST EXTRAS
SCREAAAM
EEEEEK
ROOOAR
Z
BUT EVER SINCE THEN...
MOVIES
LUNCH
YOU'RE DROPPING FOOD AGAIN.
NAP.

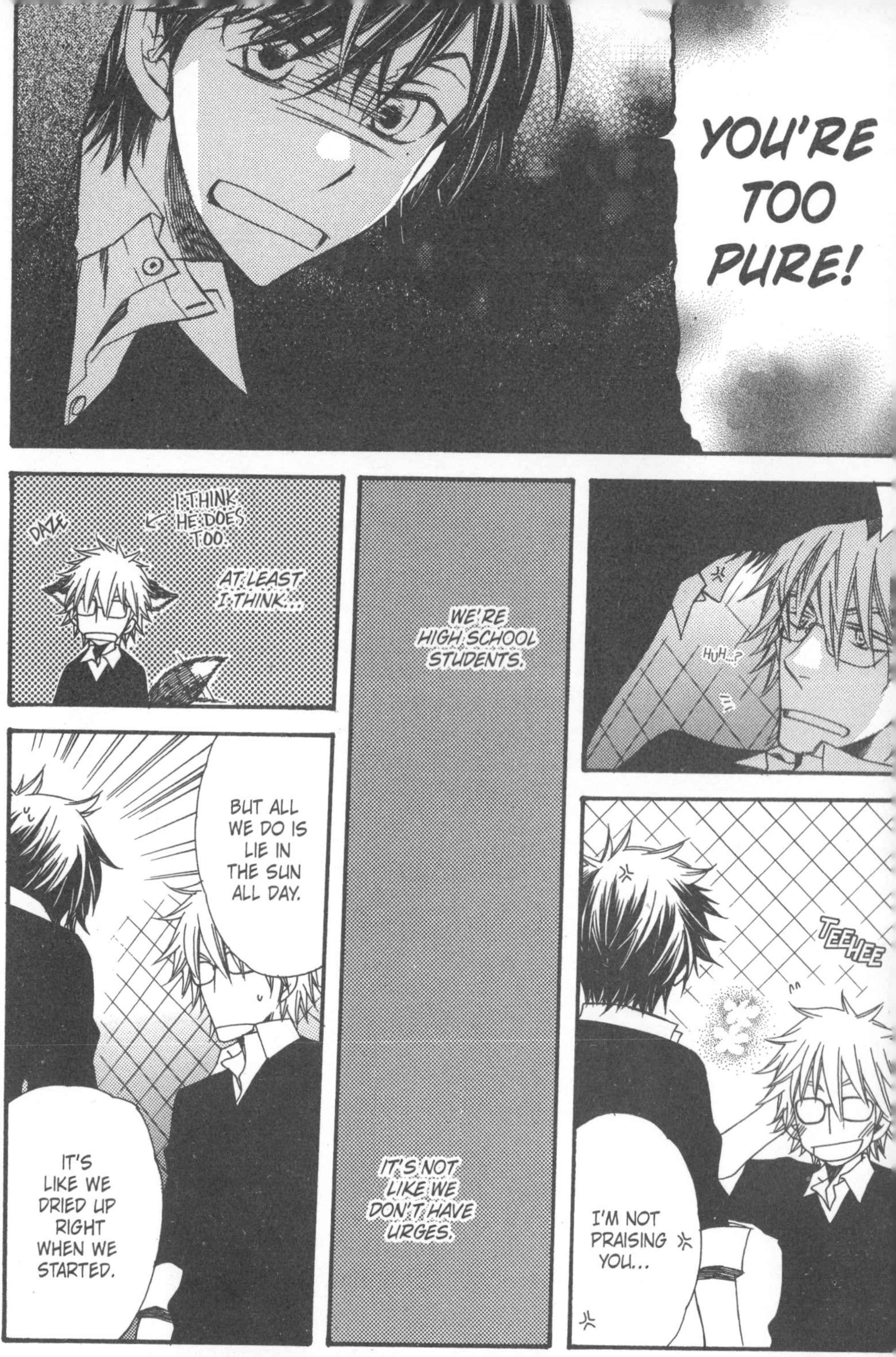
YOU'RE TOO PURE!
HUH...?
TEEHEE
I'M NOT PRAISING YOU...
WE'RE HIGH SCHOOL STUDENTS.
IT'S NOT LIKE WE DON'T HAVE URGES.
DAZE
I THINK HE DOES TOO.
AT LEAST I THINK...
BUT ALL WE DO IS LIE IN THE SUN ALL DAY.
IT'S LIKE WE DRIED UP RIGHT WHEN WE STARTED.

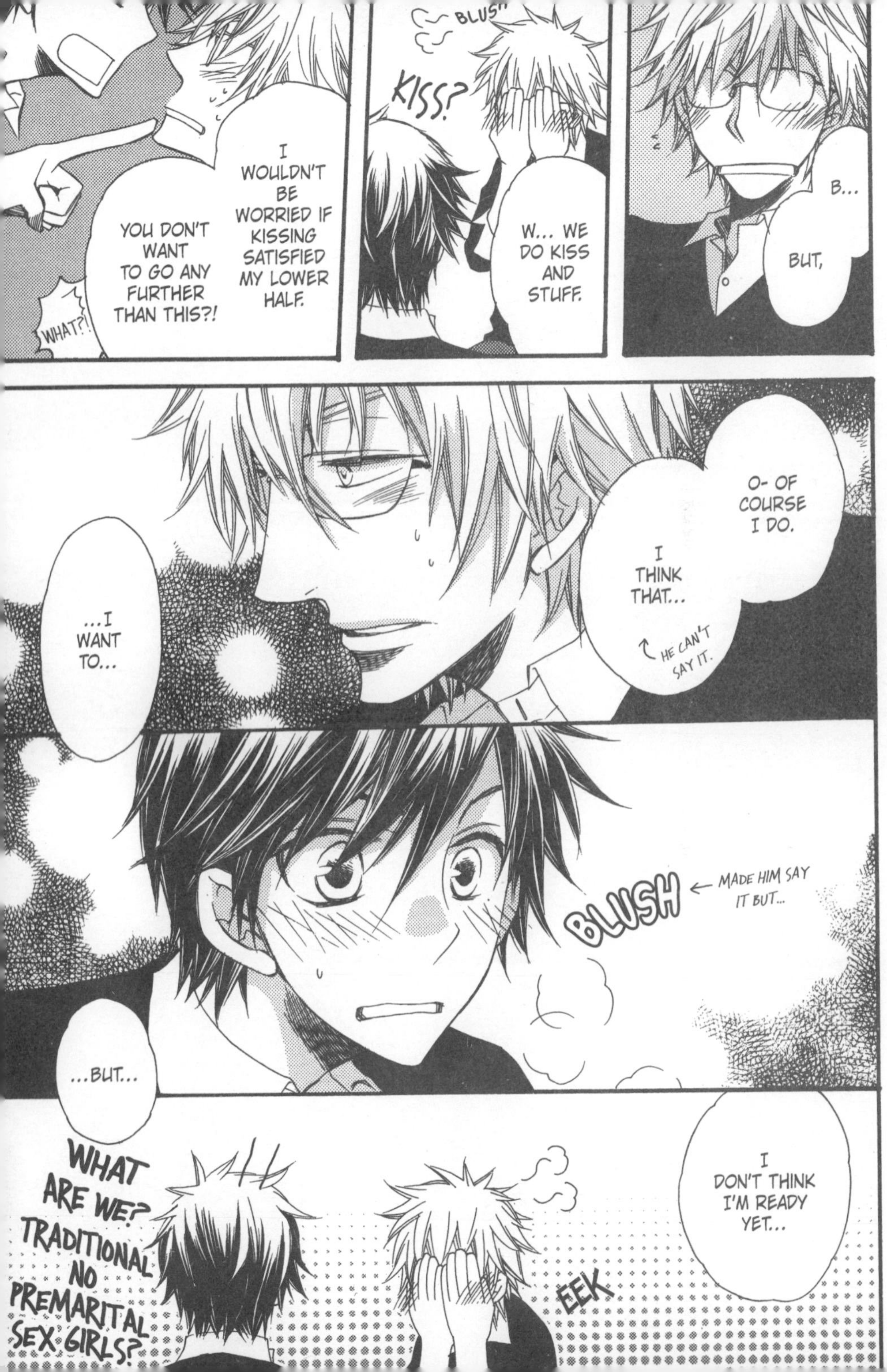
B...
BUT,
BLUS
KISS?
W... WE DO KISS AND STUFF.
I WOULDN'T BE WORRIED IF KISSING SATISFIED MY LOWER HALF.
YOU DON'T WANT TO GO ANY FURTHER THAN THIS?!
WHAT?!
O- OF COURSE I DO.
I THINK THAT...
HE CAN'T SAY IT.
...I WANT TO...
BLUSH
MADE HIM SAY IT BUT...
...BUT...
I DON'T THINK I'M READY YET...
EEK
WHAT ARE WE? TRADITIONAL NO PREMARITAL SEX GIRLS?

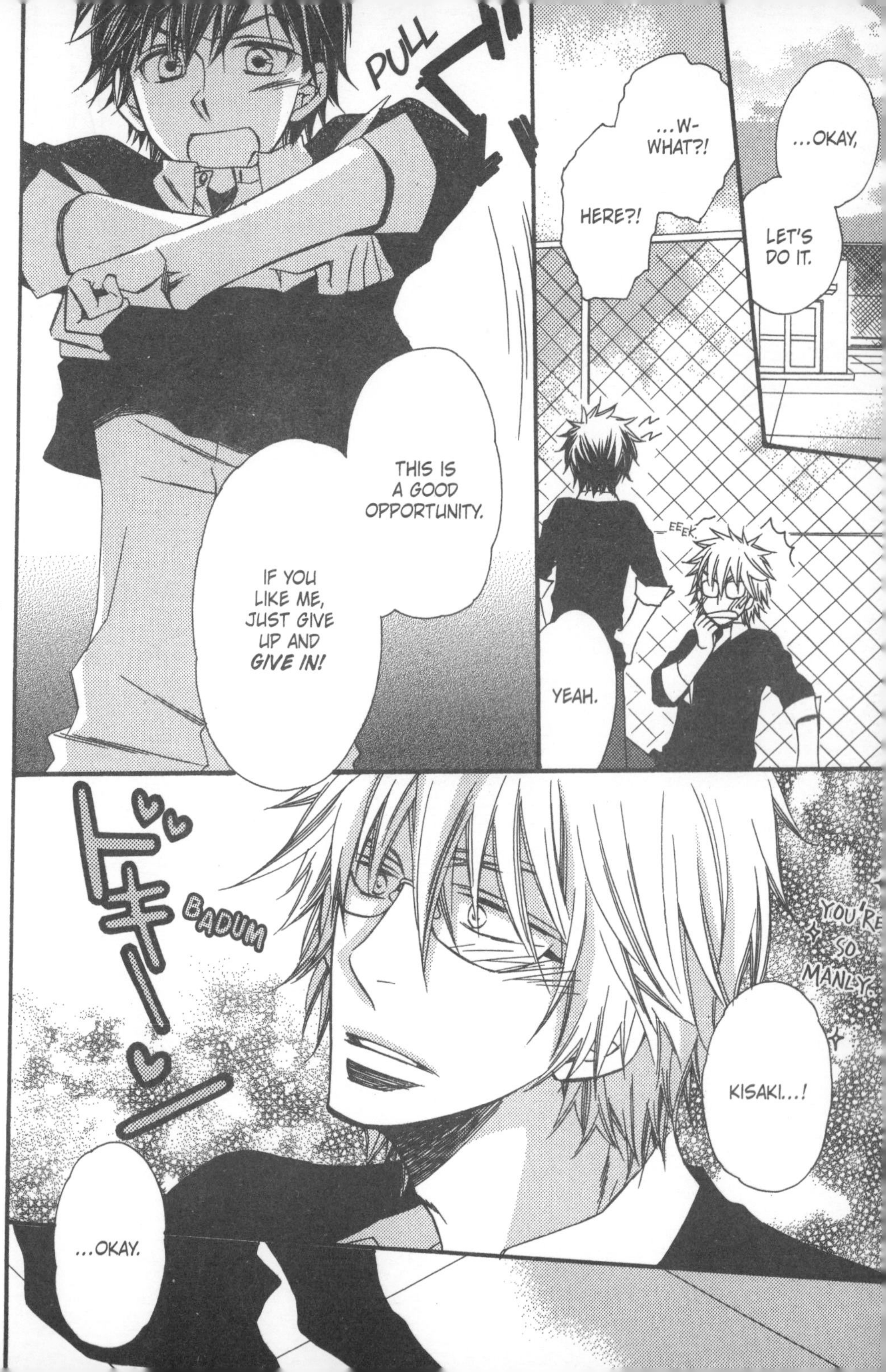
...OKAY,
LET'S DO IT.
...W-WHAT?!
HERE?!
EEEK
YEAH.
PULL
THIS IS A GOOD OPPORTUNITY.
IF YOU LIKE ME, JUST GIVE UP AND *GIVE IN!*
YOU'RE SO MANLY
KISAKI...!
BADUM
...OKAY.

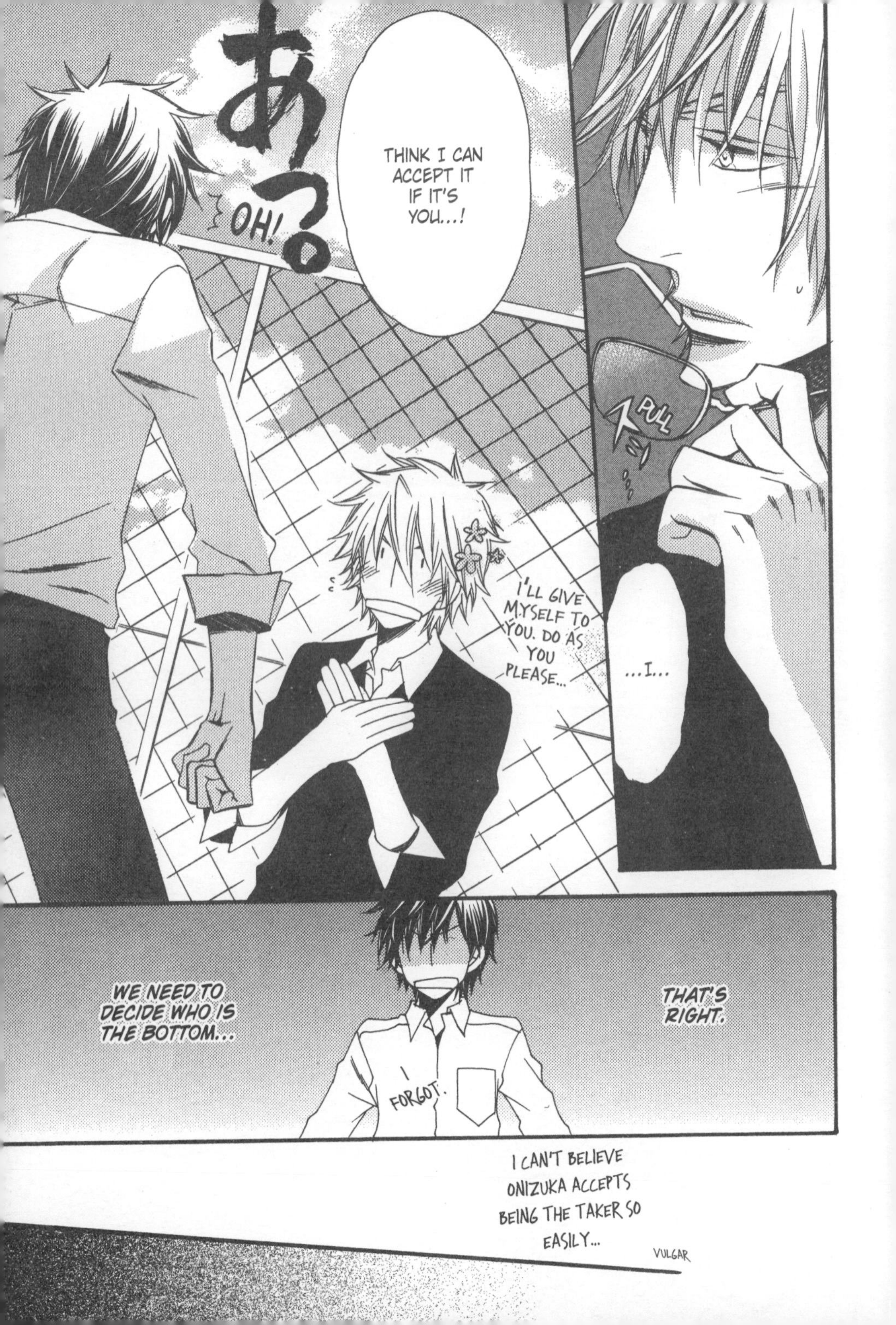
PULL
...I...
THINK I CAN ACCEPT IT IF IT'S YOU...!
I'LL GIVE MYSELF TO YOU. DO AS YOU PLEASE...
あっ
OH!
THAT'S RIGHT.
WE NEED TO DECIDE WHO IS THE BOTTOM...
I FORGOT.
I CAN'T BELIEVE ONIZUKA ACCEPTS BEING THE TAKER SO EASILY...
VULGAR

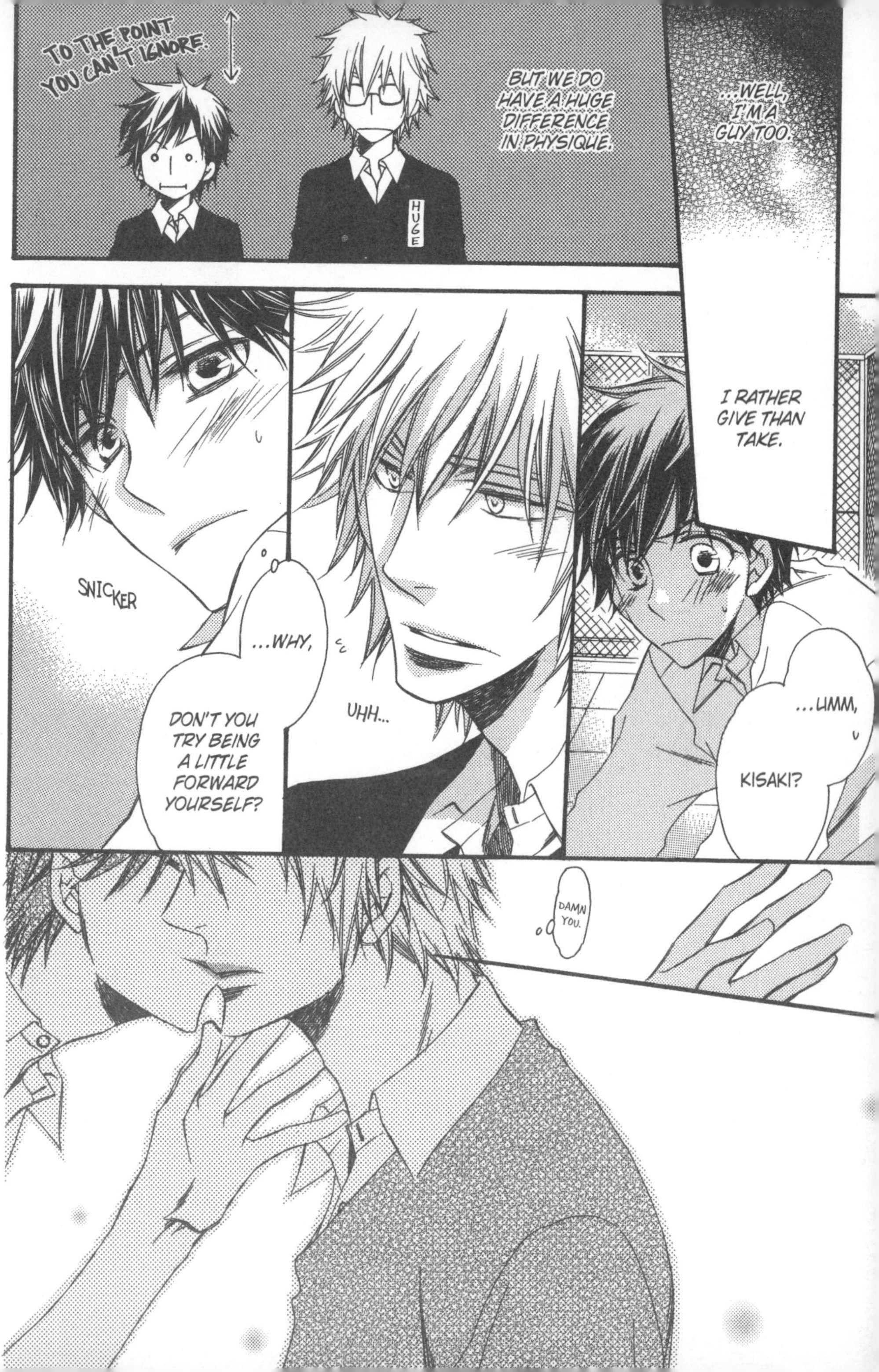
...WELL, I'M A GUY TOO.
BUT WE DO HAVE A HUGE DIFFERENCE IN PHYSIQUE.
TO THE POINT YOU CAN'T IGNORE.
HUGE
I RATHER GIVE THAN TAKE.
...UMM,
KISAKI?
UHH...
...WHY,
DON'T YOU TRY BEING A LITTLE FORWARD YOURSELF?
SNICKER
DAMN YOU.

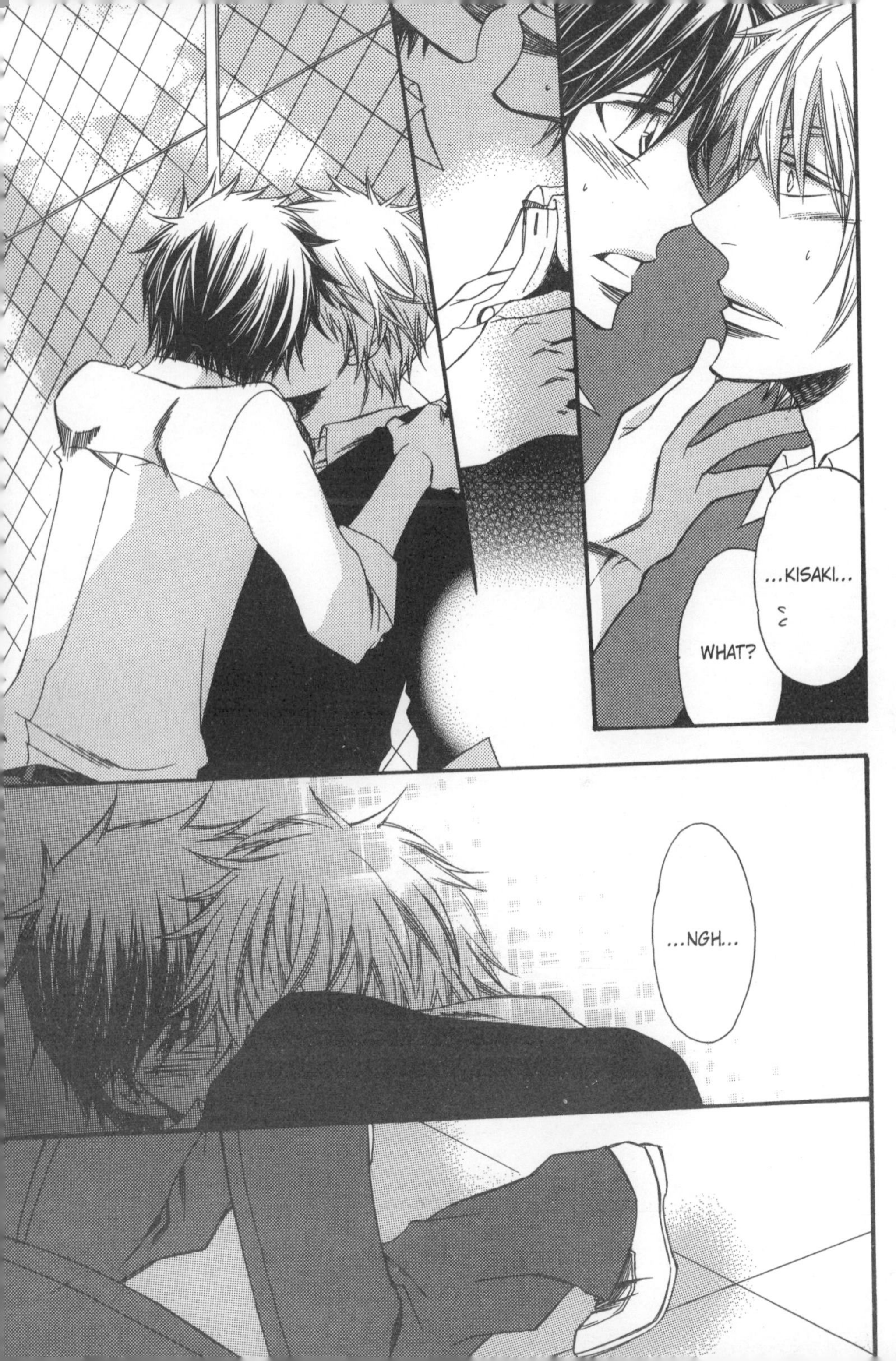
...KISAKI...
WHAT?
...NGH...

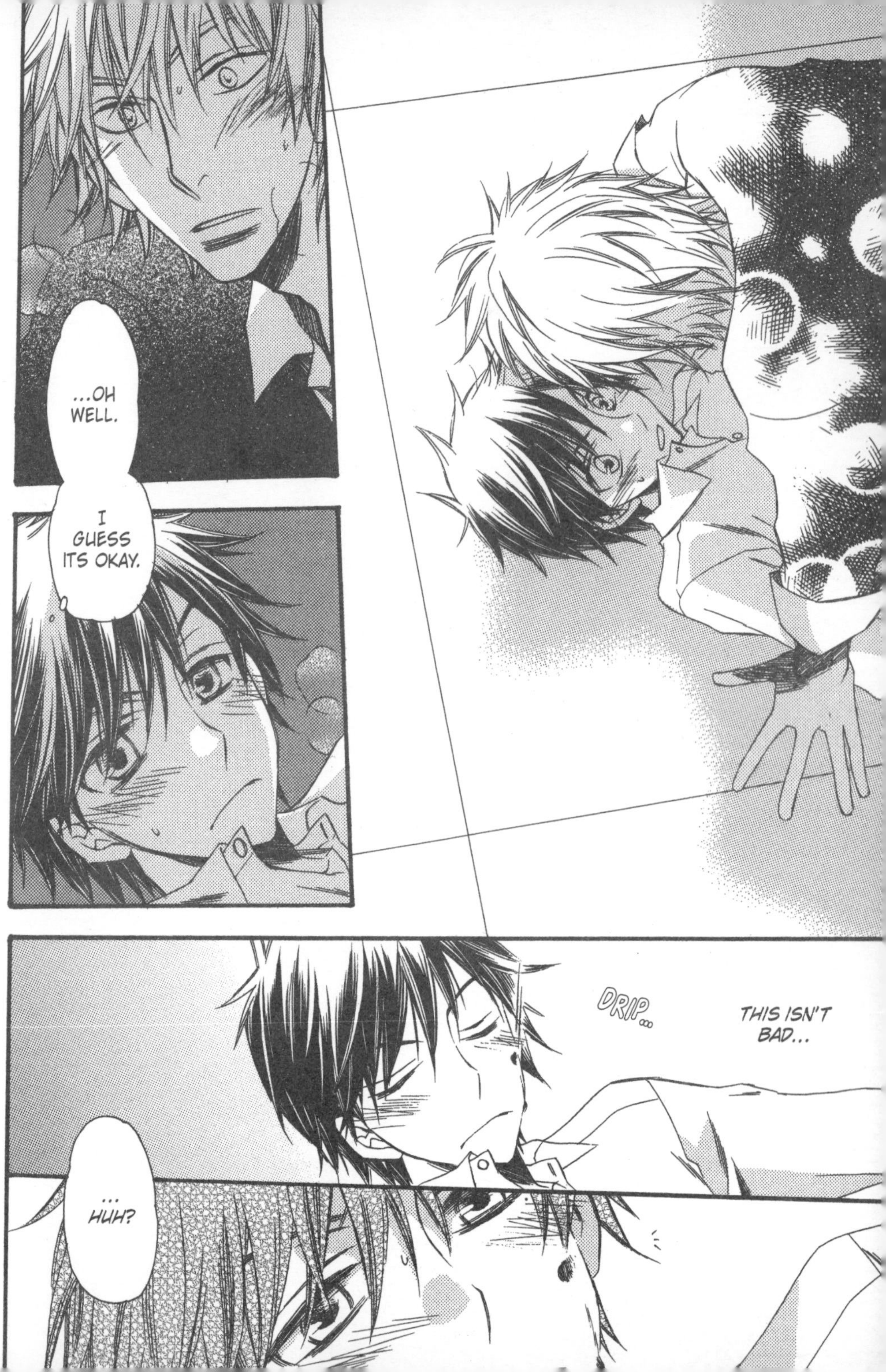
...OH WELL.
I GUESS ITS OKAY.
THIS ISN'T BAD...
DRIP...
... HUH?

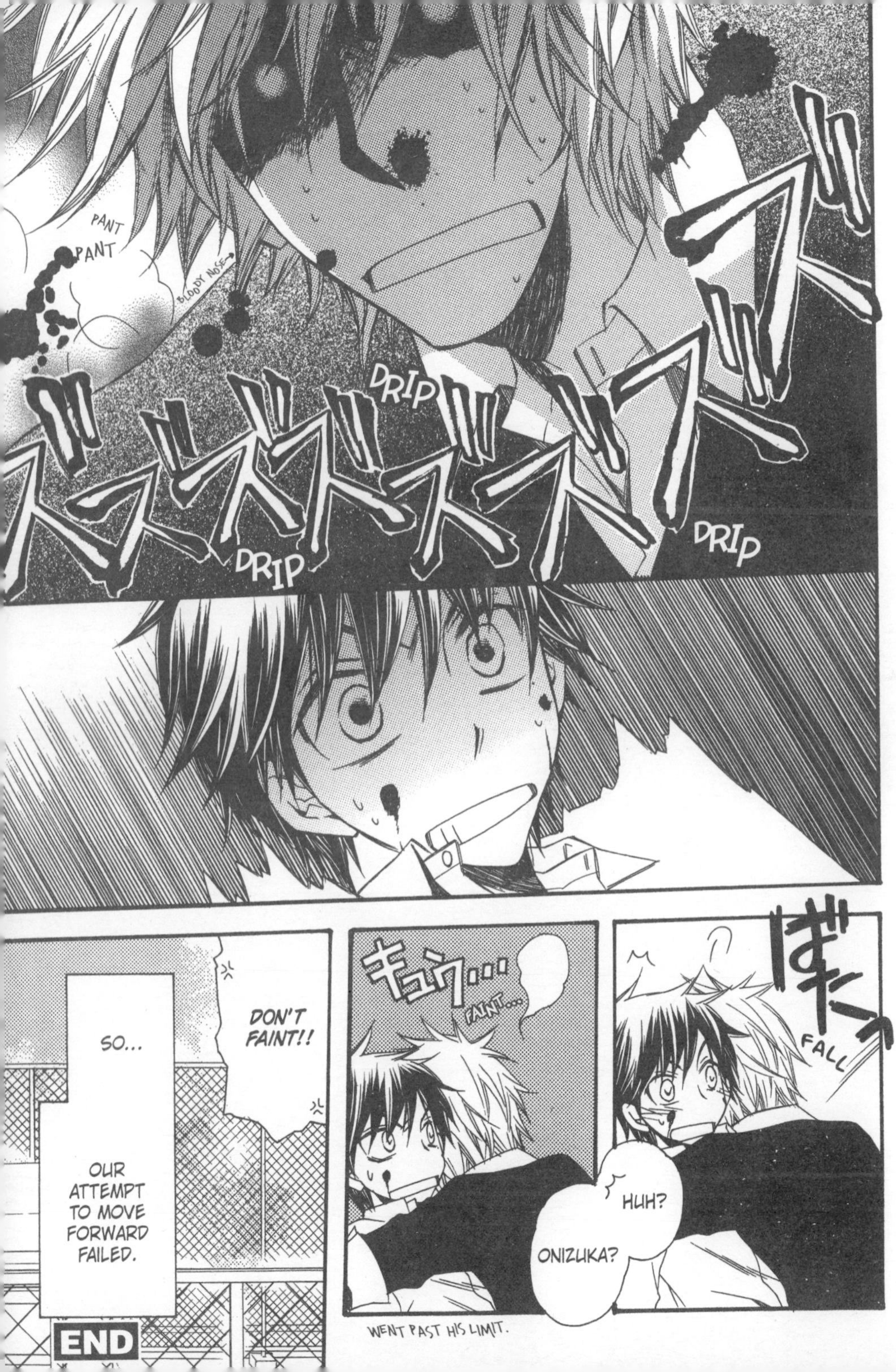
PANT
PANT
BLOODY NOSE
DRIP
DRIP
DRIP
FALL
HUH?
ONIZUKA?
FAINT...
DON'T FAINT!!
SO...
OUR ATTEMPT TO MOVE FORWARD FAILED.
END
WENT PAST HIS LIMIT.

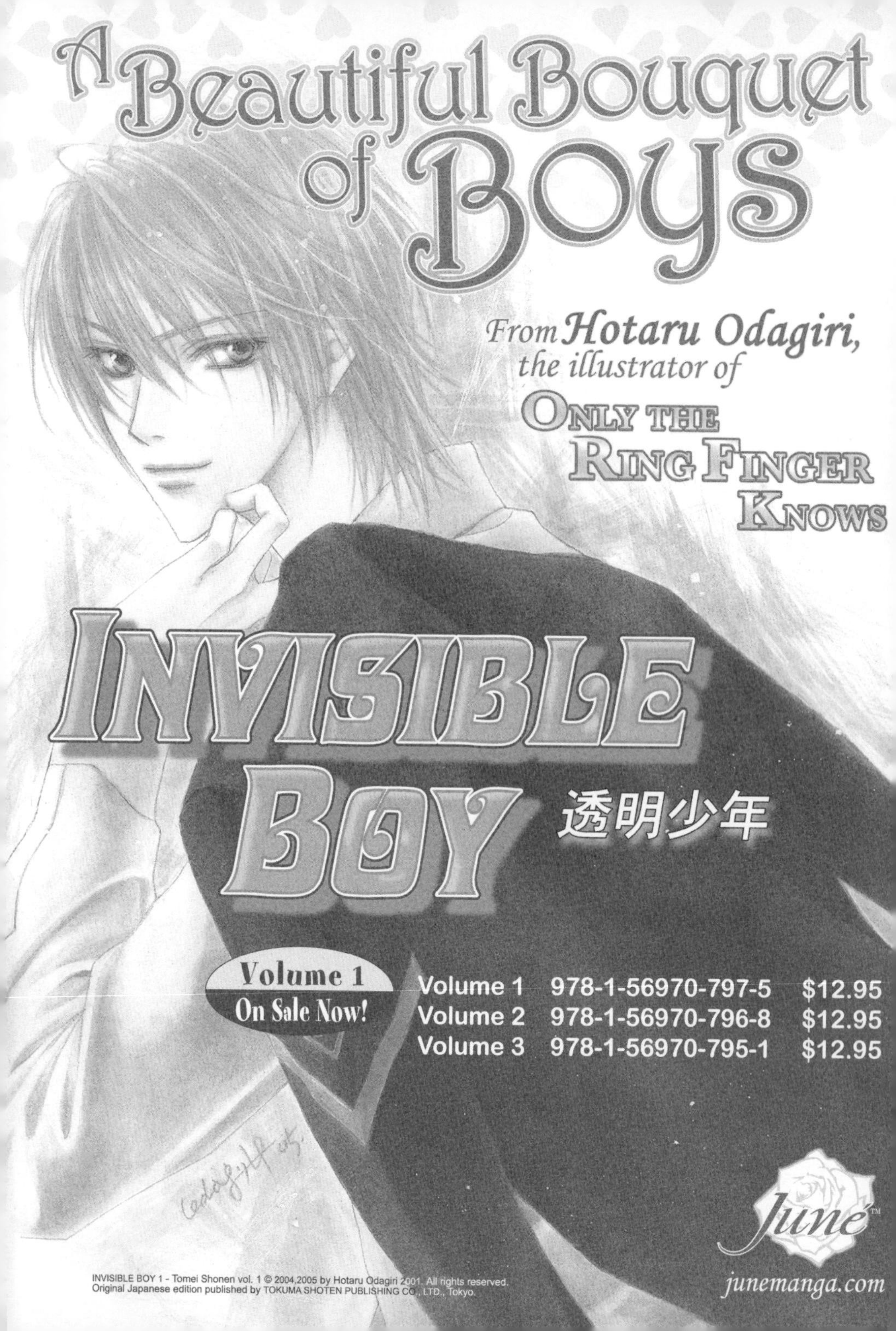
A Beautiful Bouquet of BOYS
From Hotaru Odagiri, the illustrator of
ONLY THE RING FINGER KNOWS
INVISIBLE BOY
透明少年
Volume 1
On Sale Now!
Volume 1 978-1-56970-797-5 $12.95
Volume 2 978-1-56970-796-8 $12.95
Volume 3 978-1-56970-795-1 $12.95
INVISIBLE BOY 1 - Tomei Shonen vol. 1 © 2004,2005 by Hotaru Odagiri 2001. All rights reserved.
Original Japanese edition published by TOKUMA SHOTEN PUBLISHING CO., LTD., Tokyo.
June™
junemanga.com

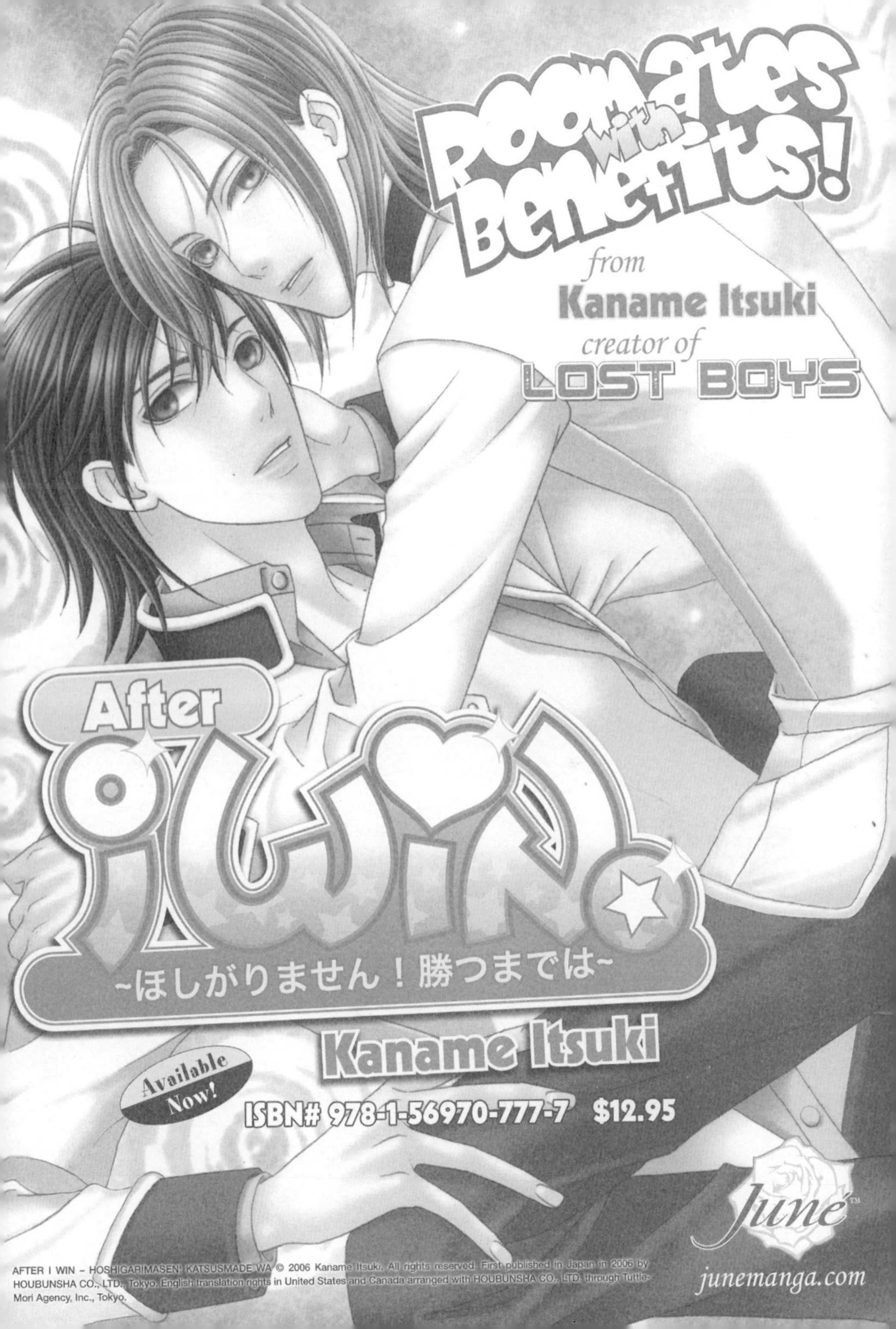
Roommates with Benefits!
from
Kaname Itsuki
creator of
LOST BOYS
After I Win
~ほしがりません！勝つまでは~
Kaname Itsuki
Available Now!
ISBN# 978-1-56970-777-7 $12.95
June
AFTER I WIN – HOSHIGARIMASEN! KATSUSMADE WA © 2006 Kaname Itsuki. All rights reserved. First published in Japan in 2006 by HOUBUNSHA CO., LTD., Tokyo. English translation rights in United States and Canada arranged with HOUBUNSHA CO., LTD. through Tuttle-Mori Agency, Inc., Tokyo.
junemanga.com

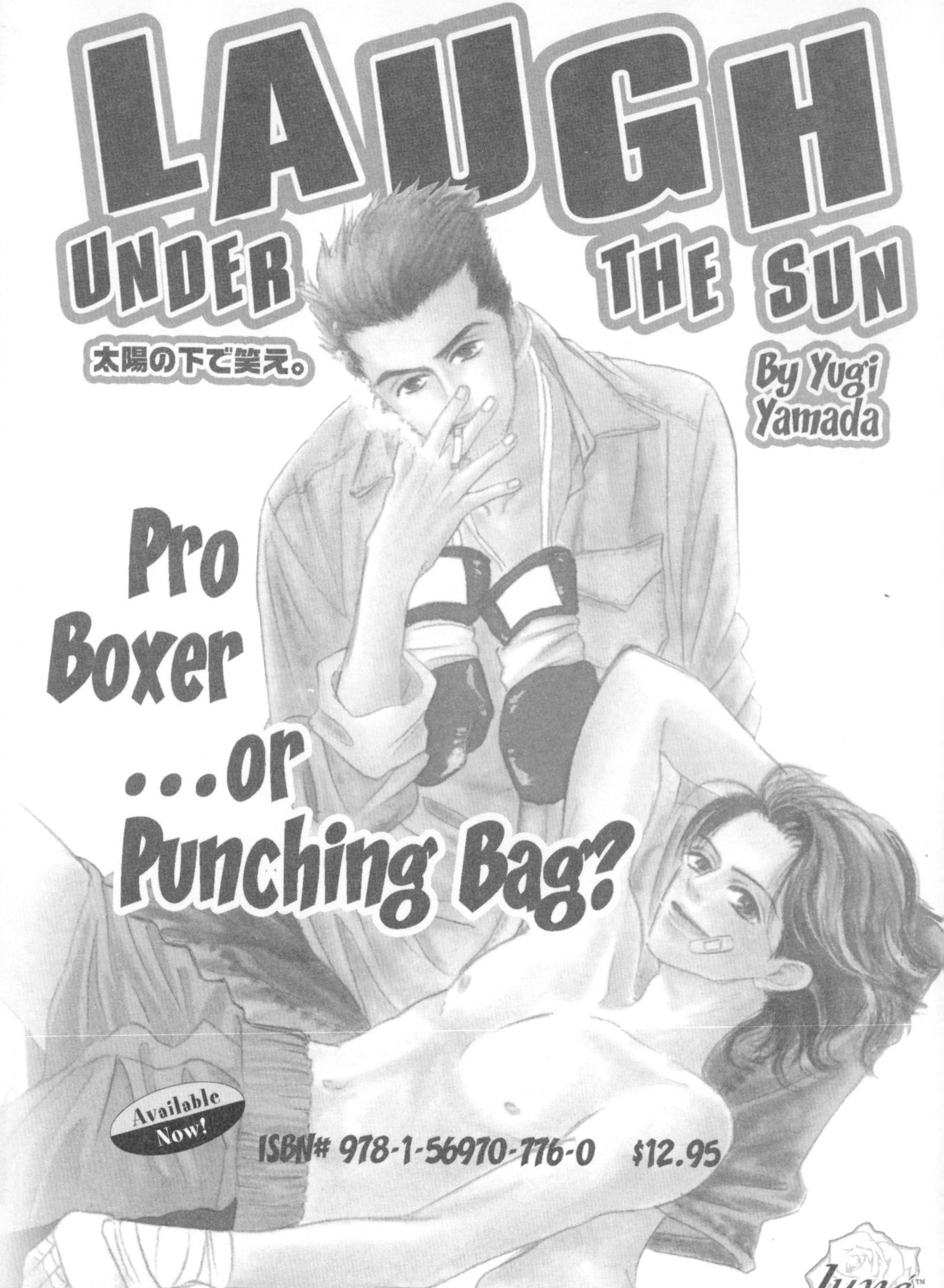
LAUGH
UNDER THE SUN
太陽の下で笑え。
By Yugi Yamada
Pro Boxer
...or
Punching Bag?
Available Now!
ISBN# 978-1-56970-776-0 $12.95
June™
junemanga.com

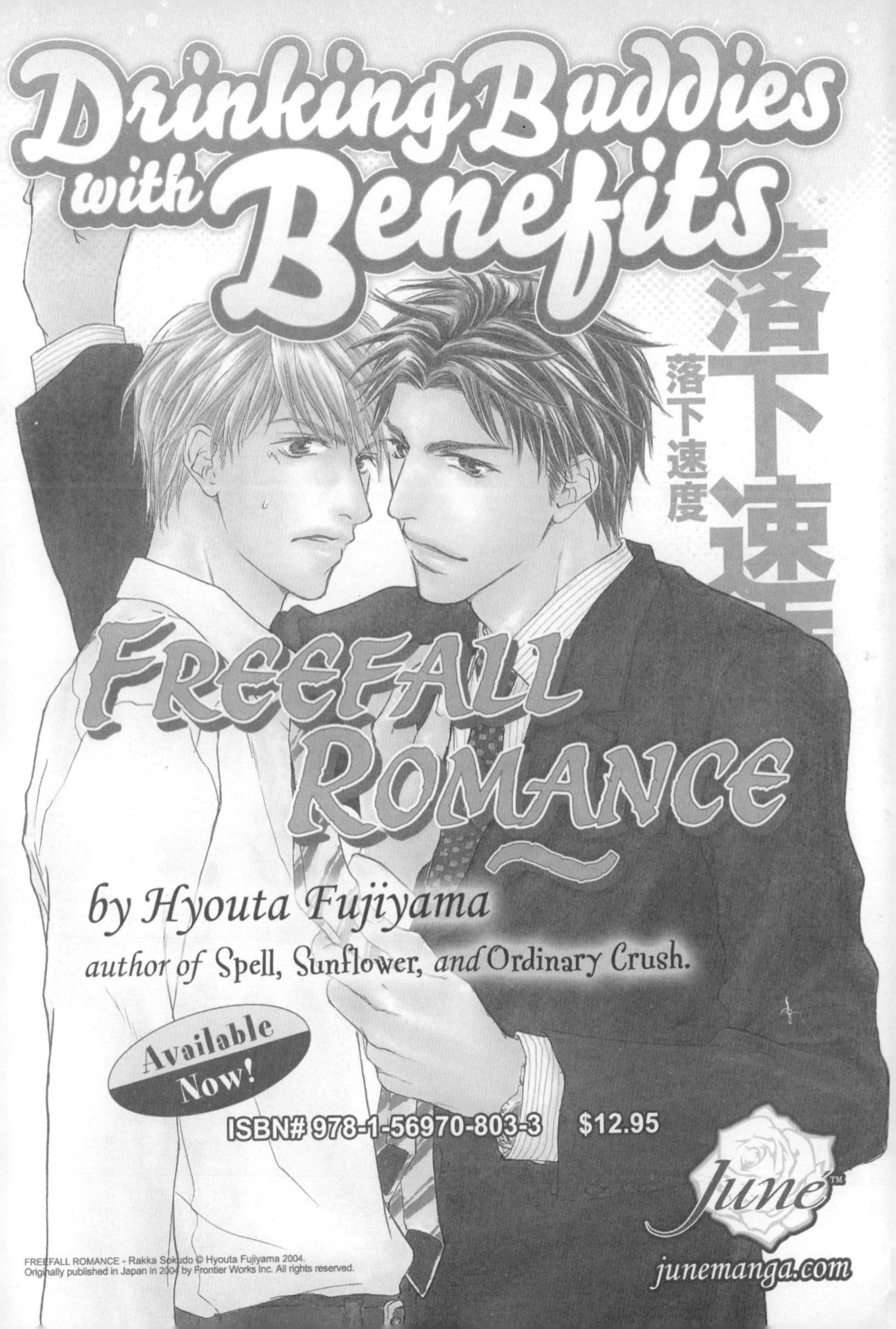
Drinking Buddies with Benefits
落下速度
落下速度
FREEFALL ROMANCE
by Hyouta Fujiyama
author of Spell, Sunflower, and Ordinary Crush.
Available Now!
ISBN# 978-1-56970-803-3 $12.95
June™
junemanga.com
FREEFALL ROMANCE - Rakka Sokudo © Hyouta Fujiyama 2004.
Originally published in Japan in 2004 by Frontier Works Inc. All rights reserved.

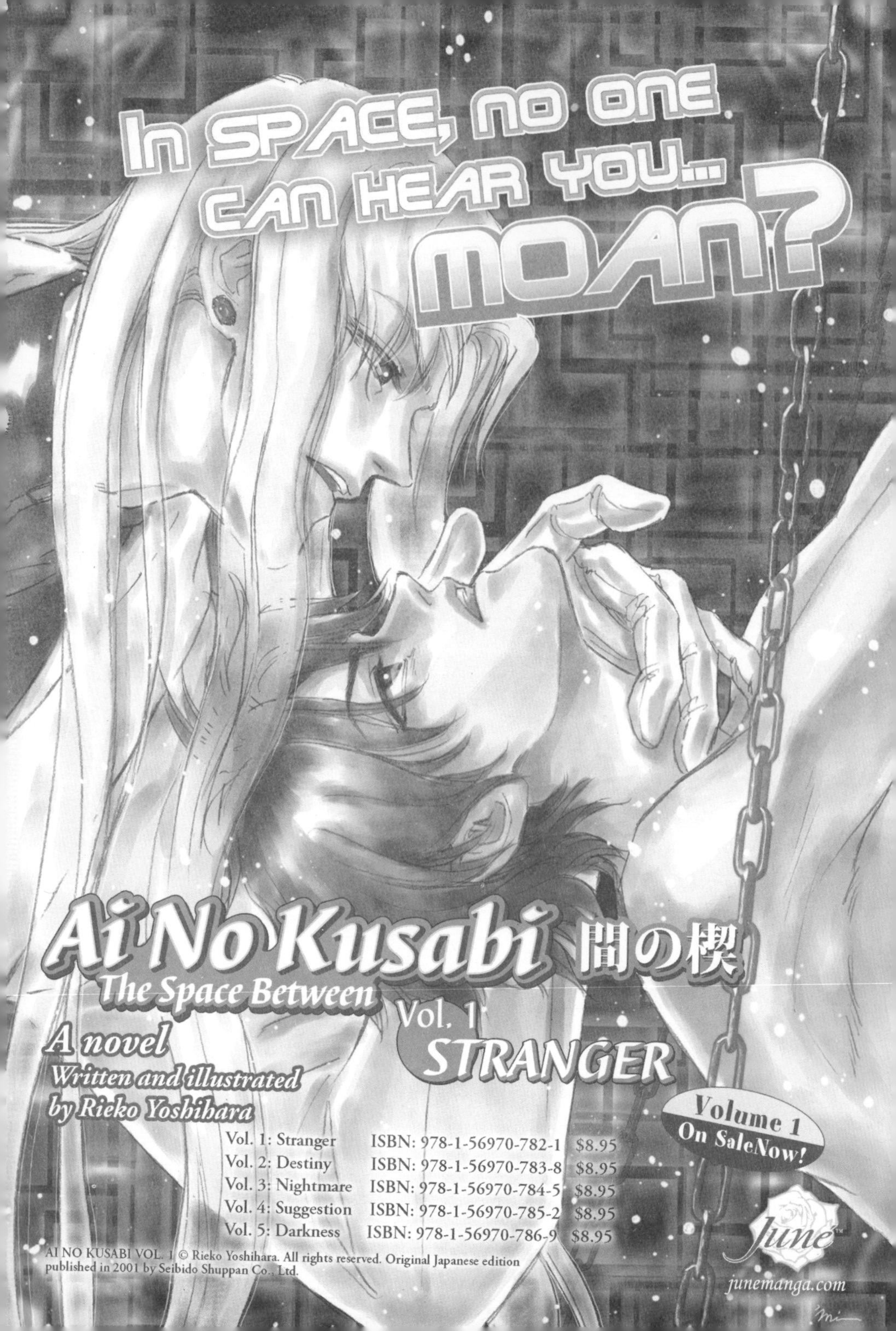
In SPACE, NO ONE
CAN HEAR YOU...
MOAN?
Ai No Kusabi 間の楔
The Space Between
Vol. 1
STRANGER
A novel
Written and illustrated
by Rieko Yoshihara
Volume 1
On SaleNow!
Vol. 1: Stranger ISBN: 978-1-56970-782-1 $8.95
Vol. 2: Destiny ISBN: 978-1-56970-783-8 $8.95
Vol. 3: Nightmare ISBN: 978-1-56970-784-5 $8.95
Vol. 4: Suggestion ISBN: 978-1-56970-785-2 $8.95
Vol. 5: Darkness ISBN: 978-1-56970-786-9 $8.95
June™
junemanga.com
AI NO KUSABI VOL. 1 © Rieko Yoshihara. All rights reserved. Original Japanese edition published in 2001 by Seibido Shuppan Co., Ltd.